Basic Cookery

Basic Cookery

Fundamental Recipes and Variations

Richard E. Martland

Senior Lecturer in Catering Studies,
North Warwickshire College of Technology and Art

Derek A. Welsby

Senior Lecturer in Hotel and Catering Studies,
Henley College, Coventry

Heinemann: London

William Heinemann Ltd
10 Upper Grosvenor Street, London W1X 9PA
LONDON MELBOURNE TORONTO
JOHANNESBURG AUCKLAND

First published 1980
Reprinted 1982, 1984
434 92232 3

All illustrations drawn by Christoper Ake

Filmset in 10/11pt Plantin by
Reproduction Drawings Ltd., Sutton, Surrey
Printed in Great Britain by
Redwood Burn Limited
Trowbridge

Preface

These studies are founded upon basic cookery principles and aim to explain the hows and whys of culinary operations. The authors have attempted to examine these principles in relation to a wide range of foods and to show how they can be extended to produce many culinary products. Chapters 3 and 4 focus attention on certain underlying scientific aspects, which may be encountered in everyday kitchen practice.

It is envisaged that this text will be primarily of benefit to students following craft, technician and supervisory courses, which relate to catering education, and to students studying for the following qualifications:

City and Guilds of London Institute 706/1/2/3, 705 craft courses;
H.C.I.M.A. Parts A and B;
O.N.D., H.N.D., T.E.C. and N.E.B.S.S. catering courses;
degree courses in hotel and catering management.

In addition the text will prove beneficial to professionals working within the hotel and catering industry and to the enterprising amateur.

R. E. Martland
D. A. Welsby

Contents

Preface   v
List of Recipes   x
Acknowledgements   xvii
Introduction   1

1   KITCHEN ATTIRE   8
    Equipment and Organization
    Protective clothing—Chefs' knives—Manual kitchen
    equipment—Cooking vessels in general use—Kitchen
    organization

2   MODERN DEVELOPMENTS IN KITCHEN EQUIPMENT   2
    Micro-wave and Convection ovens – High pressure
    steamers – Pressureless convection steamer – Liquidizer –
    Vertical cutter/mixer – Bratt pans – Régéthermic regenerating
    ovens – Computerized fryers

3   THE COOKING OF FOOD   49
    Heat and heat transfer – Cooking methods listed and
    discussed – Reasons for cooking food – Effects of cooking on
    foods (changes in texture, flavour, colour and odour)

4   THICKENING AND BINDING MECHANISMS   61
    Starch gelatinization – Protein coagulation and gelation –
    Emulsification

5   BASICS OF CULINARY PRACTICE   71
    Practical applications of thickening and binding agents –
    Basic flavourings – Stocks, essences and glazes – Sauces,
    foundation and miscellaneous – Garnishes and other basic
    preparations – Ancillary larder/pastry preparations

6   SOUPS   115
    Soup classification explained; purées, creams, veloutés,
    thickened brown, bisques, broths, consommés and
    unclassified soups

7   BASIC EGG COOKERY AND EXTENSIONS   139
    Introduction – Poached, boiled, en cocotte, sur le plat, fried,
    scrambled, omelets

8   FARINACEOUS COOKERY AND EXTENSIONS   153
    Introduction – rice, pasta, gnocchi preparations

9   THE PRINCIPLE AND PRACTICE OF BOILING   168
    Boiling explained – applied to: fish, butcher's meat, offal,
    poultry and vegetables – garnishes and accompaniments

10 THE PRINCIPLE AND PRACTICE OF POACHING   188
    Poaching explained – applied to: fish, poultry,
    offal – garnishes and accompaniments

11 THE PRINCIPLE AND PRACTICE OF STEAMING   200
    Steaming explained – applied to: fish, butcher's meat, offal,
    poultry, vegetables – garnishes and accompaniments

12 THE PRINCIPLE AND PRACTICE OF FRYING   204
    Deep frying explained – safety factors – organizational
    factors – fats and oils used – frying temperatures – protective
    coatings for food – applied: fish, poultry, butcher's meat,
    offal, vegetables – garnishes and accompaniments. Shallow
    frying explained – applied as above to include, game and
    application as a quick method of re-heating foods

13 THE PRINCIPLES AND PRACTICE OF STEWING
    AND BRAISING   246
    Stewing explained and applied: fish, butcher's meat, offal,
    poultry, game, vegetables, fruits for breakfast cookery –
    garnishes and accompaniments.
    Braising explained – applied as above to include comments
    on ancillary larder work

14 THE PRINCIPLE AND PRACTICE OF ROASTING   294
    Roasting explained – analysis chart – applied: butcher's meat,
    poultry, game, vegetables – carving – garnishes and
    accompaniments

15 THE PRINCIPLE AND PRACTICE OF POT-ROASTING   308
Pot-roasting explained – applied: butcher's meat, poultry,
game, offal – modes of service – garnishes and
accompaniments

16 THE PRINCIPLE AND PRACTICE OF BAKING   313
Baking explained and applied: fish, butcher's meat, poultry,
game, vegetables, garnishes and accompaniments,
miscellaneous preparations

17 THE PRINCIPLE AND PRACTICE OF GRILLING   329
Grilling explained – comments on ancillary larder
preparations – applied: fish, butcher's meat, offal, poultry,
vegetables, – garnishes and accompaniments

18 COMBINED METHODS OF COOKERY   347
Introduction and explanation – applied: fish, butcher's meat,
offal, poultry, game – garnishes and accompaniments

19 VEGETABLE EXTENSIONS INVOLVING A
COMBINATION OF PRINCIPLES   369
Introduction and explanation – applied: diverse vegetable and
potato preparations

20 SAVOURIES AND HOT HORS D'OEUVRES   376
Introduction applied: diverse preparations in common
use – garnishes and accompaniments

21 BREAKFAST COOKERY   383
Breakfast cookery explained – applied: English and
Continental preparations – entrées and relevés

GLOSSARY   387

INDEX   395

List of Recipes

Number	English	French	Page
1		Mirepoix	72
2		Duxelle	73
3		Tomates Concassées	74
4	STOCKS: BROWN WHITE	Fonds: brun, blanc	79
5		Estouffade	80
6	FISH STOCK	Fumet de poisson	81
7	BASIC WHITE SAUCE	Béchamel	87
8	BASIC BLOND SAUCE	Sauce Veloutée	88
9	BASIC BROWN SAUCE	Espagnole	92
10	HALF-GLAZE	Demi-Glace	93
11	HOLLANDAISE SAUCE	Sauce Hollandaise	98
12	BEARNAISE SAUCE	Sauce Béarnaise	99
13	MAYONNAISE SAUCE	Sauce Mayonnaise	101
14	THICKENED GRAVY	Jus Lié	102
15	CURRY SAUCE	Sauce Kari, Cari	103
16	TOMATO SAUCE	Sauce Tomate	103
17	PORTUGUESE SAUCE	Sauce Portugaise	104
18		Sauce Provençale	104
19	ORANGE SAUCE	Sauce Bigarade	105
20	SWEET AND SOUR SAUCE		105
21	LOBSTER SAUCE	Sauce Homard (Américaine)	106
22	SOUR CREAM SAUCE	Sauce Smitane	107
23	SAVOURY MEAT SAUCE	Sauce Bolognaise	107
24	APPLE SAUCE	Sauce Pommes	108
25	BREAD SAUCE	Sauce Pain	108
26	CRANBERRY SAUCE	Sauce Airelles Cousinettes	109
27	CUMBERLAND SAUCE		109
28	HARD BUTTER SAUCES	Beurre Composé	111

Number	*English*	*French*	*Page*
29	SHORT PASTRY	Pâte à Foncer	112
30	SUET PASTRY		113
31	PUFF PASTRY	Feuilletage	113
32	CHEESE STRAWS	Paillettes au Fromage	114
33	SAVOURY EGG CUSTARD	Royale	114
34	PUREE SOUP, PULSE	Potage Purée	116
35	PUREE SOUP, AQUEOUS	Potage Purée	117
36	CREAM SOUP	Crèmes	119
37	VELOUTE SOUPS	Veloutés	120
38	VEGETABLE VELOUTES	Veloutés des Legumes	122
39	THICKENED BROWN SOUPS	Potages Brun Lié	123
40	SHELLFISH SOUPS	Bisques	124
41	BROTHS	Bouillons, Potages	125
42	BROTHS	Bouillons, Potages	125
43	SHELLFISH BROTH	Chowder	127
44	CONSOMME	Consommé	129
45	FRENCH ONION SOUP	Soupe à l'oignon Française	131
46	MULLIGATAWNY		131
47	TOMATO SOUP	Potage de Tomates	132
48		Crème Solférino	132
49	FISH SOUP	Soupe de Poissons Moderne	133
50	RUSSIAN BORTSCH	Bortsch à la Russe	134
51		Potage Germiny	135
52	GREEN PEA SOUP	Crème St Germain	135
53		Gazpacho	136
54		Vichyssoise	137
55		Petite Marmite	137
56	SCRAMBLED EGGS	Oeufs Brouillés	147
57	BOILED RICE	Riz Nature	154
58	STEWED SAVOURY RICE	Risotto	155
59	BRAISED SAVOURY RICE	Pilaff, Pilaw, Pilau	155
60		Paella	157
61	CHOUX PASTRY	Pâte à Choux	158
62	ROMAN STYLE DUMPLINGS	Gnocchi Romaine	158
63	PARIS STYLE DUMPLINGS	Gnocchi Parisienne	159
64	POTATO DUMPLINGS	Gnocchi Piémontaise	159
65	CORN MEAL DUMPLINGS	Polenta	160
66	NOODLE DOUGH	Pâte à Nouilles	161
67	RAVIOLI PASTE	Pâte à Ravioli	162
68	SPINACH STUFFING	Farce à la Florentine	162
69	ITALIAN STUFFING	Farce Italienne	163
70		Ravioli, Canneloni	163
71		Lasagne	165
72	BOILING AND REHEATING PASTA		165
73		Spetzli, Spätzle	167
74	BOILED MEATS	Viandes Bouillies	170
75	CALF'S HEAD VINAIGRETTE SAUCE	Tête de Veau Vinaigrette	172

Number	English	French	Page
76	BOILED PIGS TROTTERS	Pieds de Porc Bouillis	173
77	BOILED CHICKEN	Poulet Bouilli/Poché	173
78		Court-bouillon (oily fish)	175
79		Court-bouillon (white fish)	176
80	BOILED FISH	Poisson Bouilli/Poché	176
81	BLUE TROUT	Truite au Bleu	177
82	BLANC	Blanc	179
83	BOILED POTATOES	Pommes de Terre Bouillies	185
84	POACHED CHICKEN BREAST	Suprême de Volaille Poché	190
85	POACHED CALVES'/LAMBS' BRAINS	Cervelles de Veau/d'Agneau Pochées	191
86	POACHED FISH	Poisson Poché	194
87	POACHED SHELLFISH		197
88	POACHED SMOKED FISH		198
89	HADDOCK MONTE CARLO		199
90	STEAMED BEEFSTEAK PUDDING		202
91	FRYING IN YEAST BATTER	Frit/Pâte à Frire	206
92	FRYING IN EGG BATTER	Frit/Pâte à Frire	207
93	CHOUX PASTRY FRITTERS	Beignets Soufflés	215
94	DEEP FRIED FRUITS	Beignets de Fruits	215
95	SHALLOW FRIED CHICKEN	Poulet Sauté	218
96	SHALLOW FRIED CHICKEN BREASTS	Suprêmes de Volaille Sautés	221
97	BEEF SAUTES	Sautés de Boeuf	224
98	LAMB SAUTES	Sautés d'Agneau	227
99	VEAL/PORK SAUTES	Sautés de Veau/Porc	230
100	VENISON SAUTEES	Sautées de Venaison	233
101	SHALLOW FRIED OFFAL	Sautés d'Abats	234
102	SHALLOW FRIED KIDNEYS	Rognons Sautés	234
103	SHALLOW FRIED CHICKEN LIVERS	Foie de Volaille Sauté	235
104	SHALLOW FRIED CALVES SWEETBREADS	Ris de Veau Sauté	235
105	FORCEMEAT FOR BITOKS	Bitoks	237
106	FORCEMEAT FOR POJARSKI	Côtelette de Veau/Volaille Pojarski	238
107	SHALLOW FRIED FISH	Poisson Meunière	240
108	SHALLOW FRIED SCAMPI/SCALLOP	Scampi/Coquille St Jacques Sauté	242
109	SCAMPI NEWBURG	Langoustine Newburg	242
110	SCAMPI THERMIDOR	Langoustine Thermidor	243
111	SHALLOW FRIED EGG PLANT/BABY MARROW	Aubergine/Courgette Sautée	243
112	SHALLOW FRIED MUSHROOMS	Champignons Sautés	244
113	SHALLOW FRIED POTATOES	Pommes de Terre Sautées	244
114	BROWN STEW	Ragoût Brun	249
115	WHITE STEW	Blanquette	252
116	WHITE STEW	Fricassée	253

Number	English	French	Page
117	MEAT CURRY	Kari de Viande	255
118	HUNGARIAN GOULASH	Goulache Hongroise	256
119	STEWED BEEF MEXICAN STYLE	Chili Con Carne	257
120	STEWED KNUCKLE OF VEAL	Osso-Bucco	258
121	CHICKEN IN RED WINE	Coq au Vin	258
122	FEATHERED GAME STEW	Salmis de Gibier	259
123	RED WINE MARINADE		260
124	FURRED GAME STEW	Civet de Lièvre/Venaison	261
125	LANCASHIRE HOT-POT		262
126		Chop d'Agneau Champvallon	263
127	IRISH STEW		263
128	STEWED TRIPE AND ONIONS		264
129	EEL STEW	Matelote d'Anguille	264
130	FRENCH FISH SOUP/STEW	Bouillabaisse	265
131	LOBSTER AMERICAN	Homard Américaine	266
132	LOBSTER NEWBURG	Homard Newburg	267
133	STEWED MUSSELS IN WHITE WINE	Moules Marinière	268
134	STEWED PEAS	Petits Pois Étuvés	269
135	MARROW/PUMPKIN PROVENCALE	Courge/Potiron Provençale	270
136		Ratatouille	270
137	STEWED FRUITS	Compote de Fruits	271
138	BROWN BRAISED MEATS/POULTRY	Viande/Volaille Braisée à Brun	273
139	BEEF BRAISED IN BEER	Carbonnade de Boeuf	274
140		Daube de Boeuf/Mouton	275
141	BRAISED OX TAIL	Queue de Boeuf Braisée	276
142	BRAISED LAMBS' HEARTS	Coeur d'Agneau Braisé	276
143	BRAISED LIVER AND ONIONS	Foie de Boeuf Braisé Lyonnaise	277
144	BRAISED LAMBS' TONGUES	Langues d'Agneau Braisées	278
145	BRAISED SWEETBREADS (BROWN)	Ris Braisés à Brun	278
146	BROWN BRAISED MEATS	Pièce de Viande Braisée à Brun	279
147	BRAISED DUCK WITH ORANGE	Caneton Braisé à l'Orange	281
148	BRAISED SWEETBREADS (WHITE)	Ris Braisés à Blanc	282
149	BRAISED VEAL (WHITE)	Piéce de Veau Braisé à Blanc	283
150	BRAISED FISH	Poisson Braisé	285
151	BRAISED VEGETABLE	Légumes Braisés	287
152	BRAISED CHESTNUTS	Marrons Braisés	288
153	BRAISED RED CABBAGE FLEMISH STYLE	Chou-Rouge Flamande	289
154	BRAISED SAUERKRAUT	Choucroute Braisée	289
155	SAUERKRAUT WITH GARNISH	Choucroute Garniture	290
156	POTATOES (BRAISED)	Pommes Berrichonne	290
157	POTATOES (BRAISED)	Pommes Boulangère	291

Number	English	French	Page
158	POTATOES (BRAISED)	Pommes Savoyarde	291
159	POTATOES (BRAISED)	Pommes Dauphinoise	292
160	POTATOES (BRAISED)	Pommes Delmonico	292
161	POTATOES (BRAISED)	Pommes Fondant	293
162	SAGE AND ONION STUFFING	Farce de Sauge et Oignon	298
163	LEMON PARSLEY AND THYME STUFFING	Farce de Persil et Thym au Citron	299
164	SAUSAGEMEAT STUFFING (FORCEMEAT)		300
165	CHESTNUT STUFFING	Farce de Marrons	300
166	YORKSHIRE PUDDING		301
167	ROAST VEGETABLES	Légumes Rôtis	307
168	POT-ROASTING	Poêle	310
169	BAKED PIES		314
170	POULTRY AND GAME PIES		316
171	HOT VEAL AND HAM PIE		317
172	FILLET OF BEEF IN PUFF PASTRY	Filet de Boeuf Wellington	317
173	CORNISH PASTIES		318
174	TOAD IN THE HOLE		318
175	BAKED FISH	Poisson au Four	319
176	BAKED POTATOES	Pommes au Four	321
177	ANNA POTATOES	Pommes Anna	323
178	PIZZA		324
179	BASIC PIZZA FILLING		325
180	BASIC PREPARATION OF QUICHES		326
181	CHEESE SOUFFLE	Soufflé au Fromage	327
182	BAKED SAVOURY SOUFFLES		328
183	GRILLING ON SKEWERS	En Brochette (Kebab)	341
184	CHICKEN PIE		347
185	SALPICON OF CHICKEN	Salpicon de Volaille	348
186	CHICKEN PANCAKES	Crêpes de Volaille	349
187	CHICKEN A LA KING	Émincé de Volaille à la King	350
188	CHICKEN IN CURRY SAUCE	Cari de Volaille	350
189	COOKED FILLING FOR STEAK PIES/PUDDINGS		351
190	BEEFSTEAK AND POTATO PIE		352
191	COTTAGE PIE		353
192	MIROTON OF BEEF	Miroton de Boeuf	353
193	CORNED BEEF HASH CAKES		354
194	MOUSSAKA		354
195	EPIGRAMMES OF LAMB'S BREAST	Poitrine d'Agneau en Epigrammes	355
196	SCOTCH EGGS		356
197	PIGS TROTTERS WITH DEVILLED SAUCE	Pieds de Porc Grillés Diable	356
198	BRAISED HAM WITH MADEIRA	Jambon Braisé au Madère	357
199	BASIC COOKED FORCEMEAT		358

Number	English	French	Page
200	DURHAM CUTLETS		360
201	RISSOLES		360
202	RUSSIAN FISH PIE	Coulibiac de Saumon à la Russe	361
203	FISH PIE		362
204	SALPICON OF FISH	Salpicon de Poisson	362
205	FISH IN SCALLOP SHELL	Coquilles de Poisson	363
206	SAVOURY PANCAKE BATTER	Appareil à Crêpe	364
207	FISH PANCAKES	Crêpes de Poisson	364
208	CURRIED PRAWNS	Cari de Crevettes Roses	365
209	FISH KEDGEREE		365
210	LOBSTER IN CHEESE SAUCE	Homard Mornay	366
211	LOBSTER NEWBURG	Homard Newburg	366
212	LOBSTER CARDINAL	Homard Cardinal	367
213	DEEP FRIED FISH CAKES	Medaillons de Poisson Frites	368
214	DUCHESS POTATO MIXTURE	Pommes Duchess	369
215	EXTENSIONS OF BOILED/STEAMED POTATOES		372
216	STUFFED ARTICHOKE BOTTOMS WITH CHEESE	Fonds d'artichauts Farcis au Gratin	374
217	STUFFED EGG PLANT	Aubergine Farcie au Gratin	374
218	SHALLOW-FRIED CORN CAKES	Galettes de Maïs Sautées	375
219	BUBBLE AND SQUEAK		375
220	PUFF PASTRY CASES WITH CURRIED SHRIMPS	Bouchées à l'Indienne	381
221	CHEESE AND HAM WITH BREAD	Croque-Monsieur	381

Acknowledgements

We wish to thank Michael Newton Clifford PhD, BSc, AIFST, Lecturer in Food Technology at Surrey University for his contribution to and advice on Chapters 3 and 4 and also Neville Winston Walton BA (Manc) for his guidance on French terminology.

For assistance with information concerning equipment we extend our thanks to the following companies:

Bartlett and Son Ltd
Benham and Sons Ltd
Electricity Council
Frialator International Ltd
Hobart Manufacturing Co Ltd
Litton Systems, Inc
Market Forge
Phillips Electrical Ltd
Régéthermic (UK) Ltd
Sharp Electronics (UK) Ltd
South Bend Corporation
Stotts of Oldham
Thorn Domestic Appliances (Electrical) Ltd

We wish, in particular to extend our thanks to Mick Cash (retired, Head of Catering Department) whose inspiration initiated this project.

R.E.M
D.A.W

Introduction

Culinary work is broadly classified into three basic activities:

Larder
Kitchen / Stove }   Operations
Pastry

Each of these activities is further sub-divided in accordance with the size, type, class, and work load of the catering unit. This book is composed of a series of studies related to that aspect of culinary work known as kitchen/stove operations.

Modern trends in food production and service are moving away from the labour intensive systems towards more rationalized types of operation, incorporating the use of purpose designed systems, new machinery and an ever increasing range of convenience foods. However, whether a system be traditional or futuristic the classification of culinary work remains unchanged. The areas studied in this book are as follows:

Stocks
Sauces
Soups
Egg preparations
Farinaceous preparations
Fish preparations
Entrées
Relevés
Roasts
Grills
Vegetable preparations including potatoes
Savouries and hot hors d'oeuvres
Breakfast cookery.

1

How to Use This Book

About the Recipe Formulations

The Concise Oxford Dictionary defines the word recipe as 'a statement of ingredients and procedures for preparing a dish', and the word formulae as 'illustrating rules and principles.' The recipe formulations used in the following studies embrace both meanings.

By using this system students and caterers become involved with the formulation of standard recipes designed to meet portion control requirements to suit particular catering operations. Furthermore the compilation of recipes from set formulae enables the student to appreciate the basic composition of many different dishes. The difference is often found to be a slight variation on a basic principle, i.e. the main ingredient used and the seasonings and flavourings change. For example:

(a) Ragoût de boeuf — brown beef stew
(b) Boeuf bourguignonne — brown beef stew in red wine
(c) Navarin d'agneau — brown lamb stew
(d) Goulash de veau — paprika flavoured veal stew.

The above dishes are prepared using the same basic recipe formulations and mode of cookery, the variations being the main ingredient and flavourings used.
Advantages of using basic recipe formulations:

1. Ease of conversion into either metric or Imperial measurements.
2. Simple conversion into any given quantity.
3. Ratios are more easily understood and remembered compared with complex recipes.
4. The recipe formulations teach students to appreciate recipe balance.
5. Formulae may be changed to meet the specific cost and quality requirements of different types of catering establishments. They also help to simplify purchasing, costing and the control of commodities.

Metrication

No attempt has been made to change imperial weights and measurements into their metric equivalents. It must be noted that the amounts given relate to the ratio formulae used and are not in relation to each other. It is believed that this approach is more advantageous in the interests of accurate formulae balances and yields. Therefore it may be observed that 1 oz may equate with 25 or 30 g depending upon the product in question.

How to Use the Recipe Formulations

The recipe formulations are designed to be worked out in relation to the first and largest ingredient in each case. It is important that all ingredients in any one formula are based on the same unit of measurement e.g. lb, oz, kilogram, or gram. Where, therefore, the formula includes a combination of solids and liquids it is necessary to convert the liquid measurements into weights.

e.g. 1 pt of liquid   = 20 fluid oz
     1 l of liquid   = 1,000 g

Example 1

Basic white sauce: Béchamel

Unit	Ingredient	Metric	Imperial
1	Milk	1 l = 1,000 g	1 pt = 20 oz
$^1/_{10}$	Butter/margarine	100 g	2 oz
$^1/_{10}$	Flour	100 g	2 oz
	Onion clouté		

Example 2

Cream soups (vegetable based): Les Potages—Crèmes

Unit	Ingredient	Metric	Imperial
1	White stock	5 l = 5 kg	1 gal = 10 lb
$^2/_5$	Main vegetable (aqueous)	$^2/_5$ × 5 = 2 kg	$^2/_5$ × 10 = 4 lb
$^1/_5$	Vegetable adjunct or mirepoix	$^1/_5$ × 5 = 1 kg	$^1/_5$ × 10 = 2 lb
$^1/_5$	Béchamel	$^1/_5$ × 5 = 1 kg	$^1/_5$ × 10 = 2 lb
$^1/_{20}$	Butter or margarine	$^1/_{20}$ × 5 = $^1/_4$ kg (250 g)	$^1/_{20}$ × 10 = $^1/_2$ lb
$^1/_{20}$	Cream (optional)	$^1/_{20}$ × 5 = $^1/_4$ kg (250 g)	$^1/_{20}$ × 10 = $^1/_2$ lb
	Seasoning		
	Bouquet garni		

Example 3

Shows how the recipes are set out in the studies.

7
Basic White Sauce Béchamel

Yield: 1 l (1 qt)
Cooking time: 30 min

Unit	Ingredient	Metric	Imperial
1	Milk (heated)	1 l	2 pt
$^1/_{10}$	Butter/margarine	100 g	4 oz
$^1/_{10}$	Flour	100 g	4 oz
	Onion clouté		

Method

Form a white roux using butter and . . . etc.

Examples of Sauces Derived from Béchamel: Added ingredients in relation to 1 unit i.e. ½ l/1 pt basic sauce

English term	Unit	Ingredient	Metric	Imperial	French term
Cream sauce	⅕	Fresh cream. Add to basic sauce, correct seasoning	100 ml	4 fl oz	Sauce Crème
Egg sauce	⅕	Chopped hard-boiled egg. Add ingredients to basic sauce and correct seasoning	100 g	4 oz	Sauce aux Oeufs

Notes for Guidance

All ingredients, including garnishes outlined in these studies are listed at prepared weights unless otherwise stated. For example:

  (a) vegetables are washed and peeled,
  (b) meat is trimmed in readiness for use.

Consequently the methods generally omit these preparatory instructions. We recommend the use of the following pastry and larder books in conjunction with this text:

  (a) *Patisserie* by L. J. Hannemann (Heinemann: 1971)
  (b) *The Larder Chef* by M. J. Leto and W. K. H. Bode (Heinemann: 1969).

Metric and Imperial (British) units of Weights and Measures Commonly used in Professional Cookery and in this Text

Identification and explanation of *metric* weights and capacities.

Weights

	Name	Abbreviation used
	gram	g
	kilogram	kg
1,000 g is equal to	1 kg/1.0 kg	
500 g is equal to	½ kg/0.5 kg	
250 g is equal to	¼ kg/0.25 kg	

Capacities

	Name	Abbreviation used
	millilitre	ml
	decilitre	dl
	litre	l

1,000 ml	is equal to	1 l/1.0 l
500 ml	is equal to	$\frac{1}{2}$ l/0.5 l
250 ml	is equal to	$\frac{1}{4}$ l/0.25 l
100 ml	is equal to	1 dl
10 dl	is equal to	1 l

Identification and explanation of *Imperial* weights and capacities.

Weights

	Name	Abbreviation used
	ounce	oz
	pound	lb

16 oz	is equal to	1 lb
8 oz	is equal to	$\frac{1}{2}$ lb
4 oz	is equal to	$\frac{1}{4}$ lb

The ounce may be further divided into; $\frac{3}{4}$ oz, $\frac{1}{2}$ oz, $\frac{1}{4}$ oz.

Capacities

	Name	Abbreviation used
	fluid ounce	fl oz
	gill	gill
	pint	pt
	quart	qt
	gallon	gal

1 gal	is equal to	8 pt or 4 qt or 160 fl oz	$\frac{3}{4}$ pt	is equal to	15 fl oz or 3 gill
$\frac{1}{2}$ gal	is equal to	4 pt or 2 qt or 80 fl oz	$\frac{1}{2}$ pt	is equal to	10 fl oz or 2 gill
1 qt	is equal to	2 pt or 40 fl oz	$\frac{1}{4}$ pt	is equal to	5 fl oz or 1 gill
1 pt	is equal to	20 fl oz			

N.B. It should be noted that the authors have purposely avoided the comparison and conversion of Imperial and metric weights and capacities. We advise students to think about and become familiar with each system independently as this approach will be more beneficial and practical.

In most cases the thin liquids used in cookery processes consist of; water, stock, wine, milk, or vinegar. When it is required to express these liquids as weights the following guides may be used:

	Metric		*Imperial*	
1 l weighs	1,000 g or 1 kg		1 gal weighs	10 lb
$\frac{1}{2}$ l weighs	500 g or $\frac{1}{2}$ kg		$\frac{1}{2}$ gal weighs	5 lb
$\frac{1}{4}$ l weighs	250 g or $\frac{1}{4}$ kg		1 qt weighs	$2\frac{1}{2}$ lb
			1 pt weighs	$1\frac{1}{4}$ lb
			$\frac{1}{2}$ pt weighs	10 oz
			1 gill weighs	5 oz

Convenience Products

These foods may be described as preparations from which varying degrees of labour have been removed making them more convenient and easy to use in the practical situation. The recipes in this text have not specifically included the utilization of convenience products as such foods vary in content, quality, and mode of use. Furthermore we consider that before comparisons are made regarding fresh and convenience foods it is essential that students of cookery are first able to recognize and appreciate the quality and cost of freshly produced items. Once students have developed their skills in, and understanding of professional cookery it is anticipated that they will be able to utilize convenience foods by means of culinary innovation or as major components in their own right. For example, utilizing soup powders in conjunction with freshly prepared raw materials. This may allow a reduction in raw material costs yet provide a high quality product.

Egg Sizes and their Weights

Imperial	Metric
	Size 1
Large	70 g
2 $^3/_{16}$ oz	Size 2
	65 g
	Size 3
Standard	60 g
	Size 4
1$^7/_8$ oz	55 g
Medium	Size 5
1$^5/_8$ oz	50 g
Small	Size 6
1$^1/_2$ oz	45 g
Extra small	Size 7

The chart illustrates the weight bands in which eggs are categorized. For example, size 1 eggs are 70 g or over; size 2 eggs weigh between 65 − 70 g; etc.

Normal Oven Temperature Guide (approximations)

Description	°C − Celsius	°F − Fahrenheit	Regulo 1 − 9
Very hot	230—260°	450—500°	8—9
Hot	205—230°	400—450°	6—7
Moderately hot	175—205°	350—400°	5
Moderate	150—175°	300—350°	3—4
Cool	120—150°	250—300°	1—2
Very cool	120° and below	250° and below	$^1/_2$ and below

N.B. In order to attain selected oven temperatures a pre-heating period is required which will vary according to the type of oven in use.

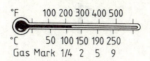

Steaming Pressures

The following information may be useful when converting pressures expressed in Imperial units (lb/sq in or psi) to their metric equivalents or kg/cm^2.

	1 lb	= 454 g	= 0.454 kg
	1 in	= 2.54 cm	
therefore	1 sq in	= (2.54 sq cm)	= 6.45 sq cm
therefore	1 lb/sq in	= 0.454 kg/sq in	= 0.454 kg

$$= \frac{0.454 \text{ kg}}{6.45 \text{ sq cm}}$$

$$= 0.0704 \text{ kg/sq cm (conversion factor)}$$

Example 1. The metric equivalent of 5 lb/sq in is calculated as follows:

$$5 \text{ lb/sq in} = 5 \times 0.0704 \text{ kg/sq cm}$$
$$= 0.352 \text{ kg/sq cm}$$

Example 2. The metric equivalent of 10 lb/sq in is calculated as follows:

$$10 \text{ lb/sq in} = 10 \times 0.0704 \text{ kg/sq cm}$$
$$= 0.704 \text{ kg/sq cm}$$

Example 3. The metric equivalent of 15 lb/sq in is calculated as follows.

$$15 \text{ lb/sq in} = 15 \times 0.0704 \text{ kg/sq cm}$$
$$= 1.056 \text{ kg/sq cm}$$

Note

In scientific usage kg/sq cm are expressed in kilopascals (kPa). To convert lb/sq in to kilopascals multiply by 6.9.

1

Kitchen Attire, Equipment, and Organization

Protective Clothing

The chef's or cook's uniform has varied according to current fashion and needs. Whatever the fashion the criteria for the design and type of modern kitchen dress may be summarized as follows:

(a) to meet general and personal hygiene requirements;
(b) to act as safe and protective clothing to the wearer;
(c) to provide a uniform suitable for use in the working environment, which is comfortable, durable, and economically viable;
(d) to encourage a sense of pride, confidence, and responsibility in catering staff regarding their culinary vocation.

The kitchen uniforms illustrated show both male and female attire, pin-pointing the salient safety, hygiene and comfort factors.

General Points

Kitchen clothes of necessity are subject to frequent and thorough laundering including the starching of some items. It is expedient therefore, that caterers purchase or are provided with a plentiful supply of kitchen clothes, so that high standards of hygiene, safety, and comfort are maintained.

The following lists are a general guide to weekly requirements giving consideration to laundering and possible overtime duties.

Male

4 chef's hats, 6 chef's double breasted jackets, 6 neckerchiefs, 8 white aprons, 4 pairs of check trousers, 8 kitchen cloths (rubbers).

Female

4 overalls, 8 bib-aprons, 4 hats (net covering), 8 kitchen cloths.

Male Uniform

Chef's hat covers hair, height allows circulation of air

Neckerchief absorbs perspiration

Double breasted jacket to give protection from heat

Long sleeves protect arms from heat and spillages

Long apron protects legs from spillages

Check trousers

Stout shoes give comfort and protection to feet

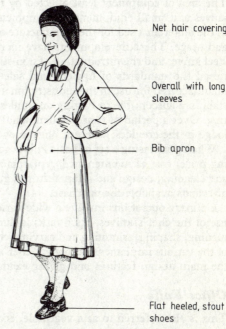

Net hair covering

Female Uniform

Overall with long sleeves

Bib apron

Flat heeled, stout shoes

N.B. The white garments reflect the heat, and act to reduce discomfort experienced when working in hot conditions. From the hygiene aspect they show stains and dirt which indicates to the wearer the need to change. Correctly dressed catering staff demonstrate a sense of professionalism that gives confidence to customers.

Footwear

Kitchen footwear should bring comfort and safety to the wearer and ease to the feet during long periods of walking and standing, as experienced by catering staff. For both sexes footwear worn in the kitchen should be essentially stout, durable, kept in good repair and be styled to protect completely the feet. Elevated heels are not suitable as they may cause instability and subsequent accidents. Likewise split shoes or worn heels are serious hazards to safety and in some industrial kitchens 'safety shoes' with reinforced toe-caps are recommended.

Fabrics and Materials used for Kitchen Uniform

Kitchen uniforms are available in pre-shrunk cotton drill or polyester/cotton and terylene/cotton mixtures. Cotton drill is best starched as part of the laundering process. The fabrics which are comprised of a mixture of man-made and natural fibres are easily laundered, do not require starching and may be drip-dried with a minimum of ironing. Recent developments include the use of disposable materials e.g. paper based chefs' hats and jackets. The hat is of the normal height and can be adjusted to fit various head sizes. Special features may include crown ventilation and a cloth head band to absorb perspiration. Such items are available for bulk purchase from suppliers.

Chef's Knives

The area of equipment least affected by technological change is that of the chef's basic knives and small equipment. Developments that have taken place have brought changes in the materials used for the manufacture of this equipment, rather than changes in design and usage. These developments have included the manufacture of high quality stainless steel knives and the introduction of non-slip, moulded plastic handles. Such changes have raised the standards of hygiene and safety. Steel knives with wooden handles are still manufactured for use in the industry but are considered less hygienic as the blades readily stain, are susceptible to rusting and unless constantly maintained suffer from metal pitting. Over a period of time wooden handles may become loose allowing food particles to lodge in the crevices, where if not removed they become a hygiene hazard.

When purchasing a set of basic knives consideration should be given to; initial purchasing price; cost of maintenance; replacement costs; discount rates; durability; ease of use and cleaning; design and safety features; guarantees; knife wallets or cases; and the variety of brands available for purchase.

Culinary operations involve a wide variety of manual skills most of which employ the use of the chef's knives. Such tasks include, chopping, slicing, dicing, boning, filleting, turning, shaping, trimming and carving, etc. These tasks have dictated the size and design of the various implements known as chef's knives. An illustrated list is provided showing the main design features and giving examples of uses for each knife.

Office Knife

This is also referred to as a vegetable, economy or paring knife.

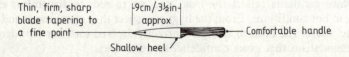

Thin, firm, sharp
blade tapering to
a fine point

9cm/3½in
approx

Shallow heel

Comfortable handle

Its uses are: peeling onions; turning vegetables; turning mushrooms; segmenting fruit; eyeing tomatoes; etc.

Filleting Knife

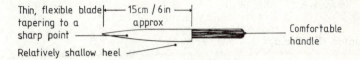

Its uses are: filleting flat and round fish; segmenting fruit. The flexible blade facilitates ease of movement, which enables the operator to remove fish fillets clear from the bone with the minimum of waste.

French Cook's Knives

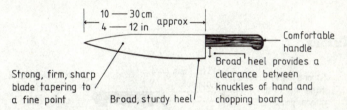

These knives could be considered as general purpose knives, as they are used for a variety of tasks, which include: the slicing, chopping, shaping, and dicing of foods. The broad heel and sharp pointed blade facilitates ease of use.

Chopping Knives (large and extra heavy)

Resembles the French cook's knife in shape and design.

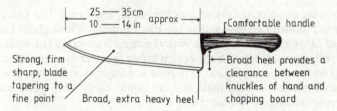

Its uses are: as for French cook's knife but the extra heavy heel makes this knife ideal for use when chopping through light bone structures, e.g. chicken frame, light chine bones.

Carving Knives

These consist of two main shapes

(1) French carving knife (tranchelard), which resembles a long version of a filleting knife.

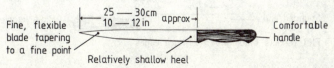

(2a) Carving knife

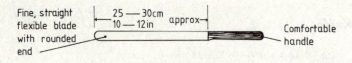

Fine, straight flexible blade with rounded end   25 — 30cm / 10 — 12in approx   Comfortable handle

(2b) Granton (Sheffield)

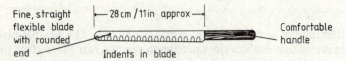

Fine, straight flexible blade with rounded end   28 cm / 11in approx   Indents in blade   Comfortable handle

Its uses are: carving of butcher's meat, poultry and game, etc. The flexible long blade facilitates ease of movement, enabling the operator to carve evenly and economically.

Boning Knives

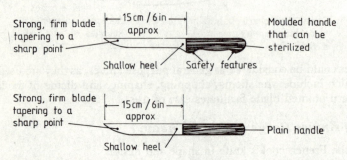

Strong, firm blade tapering to a sharp point   15 cm / 6 in approx   Shallow heel   Safety features   Moulded handle that can be sterilized

Strong, firm blade tapering to a sharp point   15 cm / 6 in approx   Shallow heel   Plain handle

Its uses are: boning out butcher's meat, poultry, offal, and game. The firm, sharp pointed blade is designed to facilitate ease and safety when boning. Throughout boning the knife should be held 'dagger' fashion, that is with the thumb covering the rounded end of the handle. This technique, along with the design safety features prevents the operator's hand from slipping on to the sharp blade. There is a danger that the hand, which becomes moist and greasy when handling meat and fat, could easily slide down on to the blade, unless the correct technique is adopted.

Palette Knives

There are two main shapes in use.

(a) Straight handled palette knife

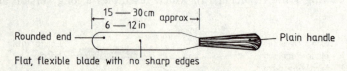

Rounded end   15 — 30cm / 6 — 12 in approx   Plain handle

Flat, flexible blade with no sharp edges

(b) Cranked handled palette knife

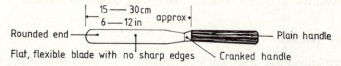

The width of blades may also vary. Its uses are: spreading and smoothing soft mixtures, e.g. purée of vegetables; shaping foods, e.g. potato galettes; lifting and turning foods during cooking, e.g. Vienna steaks, fish fillets, etc.

Small Equipment

In addition to the range of chef's basic knives, certain other small implements are commonly used. The main items are illustrated below.

Cook's Forks

Many designs exist as illustrated below. Each fork has two sharp prongs, which vary in length between 15 cm − 20 cm/6 − 8 in approximately.

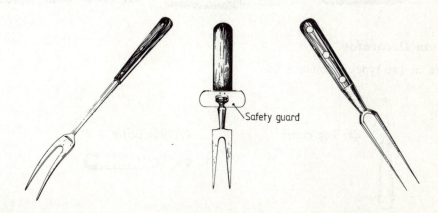

Its uses are: holding hot and cold meats in position for carving, and for placing carved portions on to service dish. It is not advisable to pierce the meat with the fork during or after cooking, as meat juices escape resulting in a loss of flavour and moisture, try to hold the meat firm with the fat or bone structure whenever possible. The fork may be of assistance when turning roast meats, etc. during cooking. In this instance the fork pierces the light bone structure, fat, or engages the trussing string to turn the meats.

Cook's Steel

This is produced from magnetized steel. The magnetism draws the knife on to the steel. The design and length of 'steel' vary, but as a guide the length may range from 25 − 30 cm (10 − 12 in) approximately.

Its use is: to maintain a sharp edge on the chef's knives. For safe practice and to avoid damage to knives, the technique of knife sharpening should be learned.

Knife Box or Wallet

In order to keep knives and other small equipment safe and in good order, some type of container is required. When a limited collection of knives is involved, the knife wallet is adequate as it is designed to hold each knife separately and safely in position. This prevents metal contact which could blunt the knive's edges. As the collection of knives and small equipment increases it is necessary to obtain a specially designed box or case.

Potato Peeler/Apple Corer

These are used for peeling and eyeing potatoes, certain vegetables and fruit. Some models have a removeable plastic handle, which once removed, enables the frame to be used for apple coring. The apple corer is used for removing core from apples particularly when apples are being cooked whole or cut into whole round slices, e.g. for apple fritters.

Lemon Decorator

There are two types in common use.

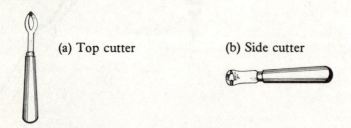

(a) Top cutter   (b) Side cutter

Both are used to decorate whole lemons by removing strips of rind from the outside skin. They may also be used to decorate vegetables in a similar manner, e.g. carrots.

Lemon Zester

This is used to remove fine zest from skin of citrus fruit, e.g. oranges and lemons.

Vegetable Scoops

These are used for cutting out rounds or oval shapes from fruits and vegetables.

(a) Round scoops (often referred to as Parisienne cutters)

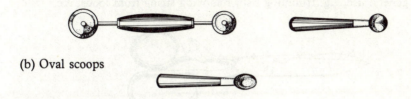

(b) Oval scoops

Vegetable scoops are available in various sizes.

Oyster Knife

This is used for opening fresh oysters safely.

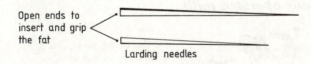

Safety guard

Larding Needles/Pin

These are mainly used to insert strips of fat into very lean joints or cuts of meat, poultry or game.
N.B. All needles are available in various sizes

(a) French larding pin

Cavity designed to accept strips of fat

French larding pin

(b) Larding needles

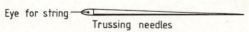

Open ends to insert and grip the fat

Larding needles

(c) Trussing needles

Eye for string

Trussing needles

Poultry Secateurs

These are used for jointing and trimming raw and cooked poultry.

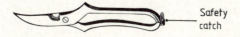

Safety catch

Kitchen Scissors

These are for general use, e.g. trimming fish, removing string from foods, etc.

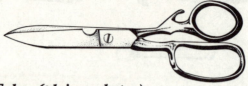

Savoy Bag and Tubes (plain and star)

These are used for piping potato dishes, gnocchi Parisienne, etc. They are available in various shapes and sizes, too numerous to outline and the bags can be made from terylene or nylon, which can be disposable. The tubes can be made from tin or nylon.

Pastry Cutting Wheel (with plain or fluted edge)

This is used for cutting ravioli paste. The wheel can be made of brass or wood.

Moulin (manually operated mill)

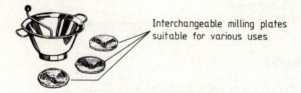

Interchangeable milling plates suitable for various uses

The moulin is used for the preparation of fruit and vegetable purées and soups and is available in various sizes. Interchangeable milling plates suitable for various uses are shown.

Slicing Utensils

  (a) Mar-For/French slicer
  (b) Mandolin slicer
  (c) Universal slicer

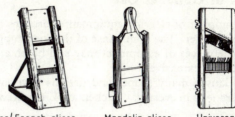

Mar-For/French slicer   Mandolin slicer   Universal slicer

All slicing utensils are designed with adjustable blades, either plain or corrugated made of steel and wood or stainless steel. They are used for slicing potatoes, and vegetables and their approximate size is 38 cm (15 in).

Conical Strainer (Chinois)

These are available in fine, medium, and coarse mesh and in various sizes. They are made of tinned steel, aluminium or stainless steel and are used for straining sauces and soups, etc.

Cook's Sieves

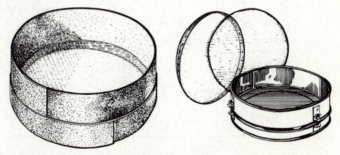

These are available with interchangeable fine, medium and coarse meshes (in wire or nylon) and in various sizes, e.g. 30 cm (12 in) diameter. The frames are usually made of wood or steel.

Grilling Tongs

These are used to move or turn foods being grilled. Their approximate size is 50 cm (20 in) and they are usually made of heavy steel or light stainless steel.

Cooking Vessels in General Use

A visit to any major supplier of catering equipment illustrates the vast range of cooking vessels available to the caterer. The dominance of tin-lined copper vessels has long gone and, although such fine pieces of equipment may still be obtained, the range manufactured from other metals is extensive.

As with the chefs' knives many shapes and designs have evolved as a result of the manifold culinary operations in every-day kitchen work, e.g. stew pans, frying pans, sauce pans, baking trays etc.

Metals Employed

The selection of metals used in the production of cooking vessels is of prime importance and the main criteria which influence choice are as follows:

(a) degree of conductivity;
(b) toxicity—whether non-toxic when in contact with food;
(c) durability—whether the metal can withstand continual usage in an industrial kitchen;
(d) viability—able to be manufactured economically in relation to purchase price, replacement and maintenance costs, etc.;
(e) heat resistance—ability to withstand high temperatures without undue damage or danger;
(f) rust resistant whenever possible.

The metals chosen include copper, aluminium, tin, iron/steel, and the alloy stainless steel. Silver in conjunction with copper is used in the manufacture of chafing pans (pans used for cooking in the restaurant) but is too expensive for general use.

Thermal conductivities and melting points of metals used for cooking vessels

Metal/alloy	Melting point ° C approx	Coefficient of thermal conductivity $W/m^{-1}/K^{-1}$
Silver	960	418
Copper	1,083	385
Aluminium	660	238
Iron/steel	1,539	80
Tin	231	64
Stainless steel	1,425	24

This table illustrates the coefficient of thermal conductivity of the metals with silver, copper, and aluminium identified as the better conductors of heat.

Special Factors Concerning Copper Vessels

As shown above copper is a good conductor of heat and as such is ideally suited to the manufacture of cooking vessels. However, when used in general cooking operations, copper is poisonous. Furthermore when in contact with the atmosphere a toxic substance known as *verdigris* appears as a thin green film on the metal surface. By regular maintenance and cleaning this film can be removed. In order to counteract these problems manufacturers line the interior of copper cooking vessels with a coating of tin, which resists corrosion from water and the atmosphere, and which is non-toxic when in contact with food. Eventually the tin lining begins to wear thin and the copper interior becomes exposed. Re-tinning is then necessary and these requirements along with purchasing and cleaning costs make copper vessels relatively expensive.

N.B. Copper sugar boilers are excepted from the tinning process because the high temperatures encountered cause the tin to soften and wear thin as the melting point of tin is relatively low.

Special Factors Concerning Aluminium Vessels

Aluminium is a soft metal and various gauges are used in the manufacture of cooking vessels, e.g. light, medium, and heavy gauges. However, owing to the softness of the metal, the resilience of the vessels to 'pitting' and general damage is lessened. Light gauge equipment in particular is subject to denting. After a period of time aluminium cooking vessels, when in contact with hot or boiling tap water or with certain foodstuffs, take on a dulled appearance. This is a result of a darkening effect of the natural oxide film which is always present on aluminium but which is normally colourless. The discoloration is an optical effect only and is quite harmless when in contact with food. Although this microscopic oxide film does not contaminate food it may cause discoloration, particularly when a white appearance is required, e.g. white sauces. Therefore when cooking such products in aluminium vessels care must be taken not to remove this oxide film from the sides of the saucepan. The use of a wooden spatula rather than a metal implement reduces this risk.

Certain foods exist which are unsuitable for cooking in aluminium vessels as these foods react with the metal and become discoloured, e.g. artichoke bottoms and red cabbage take on an unwanted dark appearance. In these instances other types of cooking vessels are used.

Because of its 'softness' aluminium tends to absorb and hold grease, consequently thorough cleaning, washing, and rinsing is required if greasiness is to be kept to the minimum.

Special Factors Concerning Iron/Steel Vessels

Pure iron is soft, of silver white colour and scarcely known. The metal commonly referred to as iron has an added mixture of some other substance usually carbon and varies in colour from tin white to dark grey. In general terms iron when used for the manufacture of cooking vessels takes the form of:

(a) cast iron;
(b) wrought iron;
(c) steel.

These vary marginally in carbon content and also in their properties. Iron when in contact with moisture is susceptible to rusting and consequently iron/steel cooking vessels are best employed in cooking processes that involve fat or oil rather than water. As a general rule iron/steel cooking vessels should not be washed but cleaned out with a dry clean cloth or absorbent kitchen paper. This maintains a film of grease that protects from moisture (rust) and prevents food from sticking to the vessel. For the special preparation of wrought iron omelet pans *see* p. 149.

Vitrified Cast Ironware

Recent trends include the development of cast iron vessels with coating of vitreous enamel. The enamel is fused on to the iron, protects from rust and provides a smooth cooking surface. As a result of this process these particular cast iron vessels are used for a wide variety of cooking methods that include contact with moisture, e.g. sauces and soups.

Special Factors Concerning Stainless Steel Vessels

Stainless steel is an alloy of iron, chromium, nickel and is used in the manufacture of various cooking vessels. Unlike copper (verdigris), iron (rust), or aluminium (oxide film), stainless steel does not easily tarnish or discolour as its name suggests. It is also durable and easy to clean.

These factors as well as the others previously outlined make stainless steel suitable for use in the manufacture of cooking equipment. However, stainless steel has a relatively low thermal conductivity and in order to overcome this deficiency certain vessels feature a copper or aluminium base. Vessels made entirely of stainless steel are also readily available to the caterer.

Cooking Vessels in Common Use

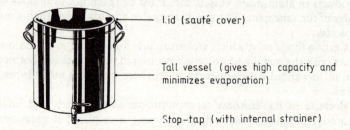

Lid (sauté cover)

Tall vessel (gives high capacity and minimizes evaporation)

Stockpot

Stop-tap (with internal strainer)

The stockpot is usually made from tin-lined copper, aluminium or stainless steel. Its capacity is usually from 30 l (17 pt) upwards.

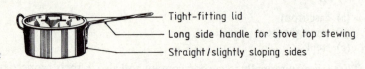

Tight-fitting lid

Long side handle for stove top stewing

Shallow Stew-pan

Straight/slightly sloping sides

N.B. Also available with short side handles for oven stewing. The stew-pan may be made from tin lined copper or aluminium.

(a) capacity: 1.6 l (2¾ pt) upwards
(b) diameter: 18 cm (7 in) upwards
(c) depth: 7 cm (2¾ in) upwards.

General Purpose Stew-pans/Saucepans

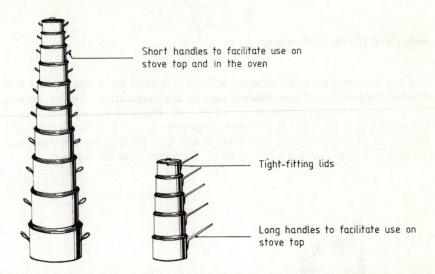

Short handles to facilitate use on stove top and in the oven

Tight-fitting lids

Long handles to facilitate use on stove top

These pans may be made from tin-lined copper, aluminium, stainless steel or vitrified iron. Their capacity is from 0.5 l (1 pt) upwards.

Tight-fitting lid

Side handles

Oval Braising Vessel

This can be made from tin-lined copper or aluminium and its capacity is from 14 l (25 pt) upwards

Bain-Marie Vessels

These are tall, slender vessels, made from tin-lined copper or aluminium with long or short side handles and tight fitting lids. They are designed to ensure maximum use of storage space in bain-marie and minimum evaporation and are available in a wide variety of sizes (capacities).

Sauteuse (French design)

This is a shallow, long handled vessel with sloping sides and a wide surface area, made of tin-lined copper. It is predominantly used in the preparation of sauces in which reductions or rapid reducing (evaporation) is required. The wide surface area ensures a speedy evaporation. It is also used for reheating vegetables in butter as the sloping sides facilitate 'tossing' of vegetables during this process and may be used for stove top stewing. It is available in various sizes, e.g. 20 cm (8 in) diameter, 7 cm (2¾ in) deep.

Plat à Sauter/Sauté Pan

This is a shallow, long handled vessel, made of tin-lined copper or aluminium with straight sides and a wide surface area. It is ideal for use when preparing meat sautés where the food's juices are incorporated as an integral part of the finished product. It is available in various sizes, e.g. 15 cm (6 in) diameter, upwards.

Frying Pan

Frying pans are solid based pans, made of iron, steel, aluminium, vitrified iron or stainless steel, with shallow sloping sides and a wide surface area to ensure even heat for frying foods. They are available in various sizes with long or side handles, e.g. 15 cm (6 in) base diameter, upwards.

Omelet Pan

Firm, long handle
Rounded, inner edge
Shallow sloping sides
Heavy, flat base

Omelet pans are made of heavy black wrought steel, aluminium or tin-lined copper and are available in various sizes, e.g. 15 cm (6 in) base diameter, upwards.

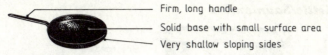

Firm, long handle
Solid base with small surface area
Very shallow sloping sides

Pancake Pan (Crêpe Pan)

Pancake pans are made of heavy, black wrought steel and are available in various sizes.

Roasting Tray (Plaque à Rôtir)

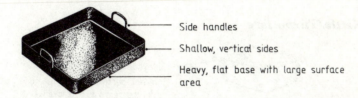

Side handles

Shallow, vertical sides

Heavy, flat base with large surface area

Roasting trays are made of heavy, black wrought steel, aluminium or tin-lined copper and are available in various sizes, e.g. 30 cm × 20 cm × 5 cm (12 in × 8 in × 2 in) approximately.

Baking Sheet (Open Ended)

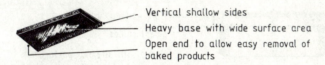

Vertical shallow sides
Heavy base with wide surface area
Open end to allow easy removal of baked products

Baking sheets are made of heavy, black wrought steel and are available in various sizes.

Baking Sheet/Grilling Tray

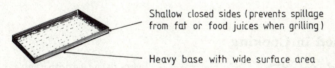

Shallow closed sides (prevents spillage from fat or food juices when grilling)

Heavy base with wide surface area

These are made of heavy, black wrought steel, aluminium or tin-lined copper and are available in various sizes, e.g. 30 cm × 25 cm (12 in × 10 in) approximately.

Deep Frying Vessel/Friture

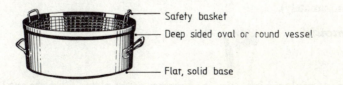

Safety basket
Deep sided oval or round vessel

Flat, solid base

These are made of heavy, black wrought steel or aluminium and are available in various sizes, e.g. approximate capacity 13 l (24 pt).

Salmon Kettle/Saumonière

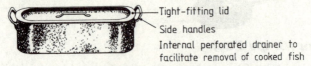

Tight-fitting lid

Side handles

Internal perforated drainer to facilitate removal of cooked fish

This is designed specifically for cooking large, whole, round fish and is made of aluminium or tin-lined copper. It is available in various sizes, e.g. 60 cm × 20 cm × 15 cm (24 in × 8 in × 6 in) approximately.

Turbot Kettle/Turbotière

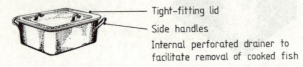

Tight-fitting lid

Side handles

Internal perforated drainer to facilitate removal of cooked fish

This is designed specifically for cooking whole turbot and is made of aluminium or tin-lined copper. It is available in various sizes, e.g. 50 cm × 35 cm × 15 cm (19 in × 14 in × 6 in) approximately.

Trout Kettle

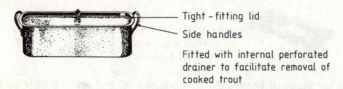

Tight-fitting lid

Side handles

Fitted with internal perforated drainer to facilitate removal of cooked trout

These kettles are tin-lined and used for both cooking and service in the restaurant. They are available in two sizes, e.g. 30 cm × 12 cm × 8 cm (12 in × 4¼ in × 3¼ in) approximately.

Moulds Used in Cooking

Anna mould

Tight-fitting lid with centre handle

Straight-sided mould designed for the cooking of anna potatoes

This is usually made of tin-lined copper. It is 15 cm (6 in) diameter and 7.5 cm (3 in) in depth (approximately).

Dariole mould

These are made of aluminium, tin-lined copper or tin plate. They are available in various sizes e.g. 5 cm depth × 5 cm diameter (2 in × 2 in) and used for a variety of purposes including sweet preparations. Other uses, e.g. baking savoury egg custard, moulding rice pilaff.

Other Cooking Vessels/Dishes

Sur le Plat

This is a white eared fireproof china egg dish used in the preparation of Oeuf sur le Plat. They are available in various sizes e.g. 10 cm (4 in) base diameter.

Cocotte

This is a fireproof china egg dish for Oeuf en Cocotte and is available in various sizes, e.g. 9.5 c.m. ($3\frac{3}{4}$ in) diameter.

Oval Sole Dish

This dish made of French fireproof china is used for cooking and service of poached fish. It is available in various sizes, e.g. 24 cm × 13 cm ($9\frac{1}{2}$ in × $5\frac{1}{4}$ in) approximately.

Oval/Round Gratin Dish

This dish, made of tin-lined copper or vitrified iron is available in various sizes, e.g. 15 cm (6 in) diameter, 20 cm (8 in) oval approximately.

Oval/Round/Casseroles

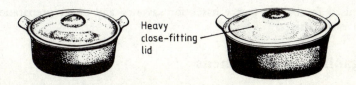

These casseroles are made of vitrified iron or ovenproof stoneware and are available in various sizes, e.g. 2.3 l (4 pt) approximately.

Soufflé Dish/Case

These are made of French fireproof china or ovenproof stoneware and are used for the preparation of hot and cold soufflés. They are available in various sizes, e.g. 20 cm (8 in) diameter approximately and have straight sides.

Pie Dish

Pie dishes can be made in aluminium, stainless steel or ovenproof stoneware. They are available in various sizes, e.g. 15 cm × 11 cm × 3 cm (6 in × 4½ in × 1¼ in) approximately.

Pudding Sleeve

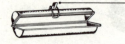

Tight-fitting locking device

This is used for cooking savoury and sweet puddings, e.g. steak and kidney pudding. Its standard length is 38 cm (15 in).

Pastry Tins

(a) *Tartlet*   (b) *Barquette* (boat shaped)   (c) *Patty tin*

These are used for baking pastry cases for savoury and sweet preparations, and are available in various sizes.

The Organization of Kitchens

In order that a trade kitchen is operated efficiently, it is necessary to have a planned, controlled and co-ordinated system. The organization will vary from one establishment to another according to particular requirements, e.g. volume of trade, style of service, range and type of menus, etc. However, where traditional systems exist culinary activities are departmentalized with each section having clearly defined areas of work. The purpose of creating specialized departments is to make efficient use of labour and equipment by ensuring that the work load is evenly spread. In addition members of staff may become highly skilled by working in a specialist department.

This system of organization is generally referred to as the 'Partie system' with each partie denoting a section of kitchen work. The following plan illustrates the diverse activities, which are encountered in certain large establishments.

The Kitchen Brigade   La Brigade de Cuisine

Head Chef/Chef de Cuisine
Second or Deputy Head Chef/Sous Chef
Partie Chefs/Chefs de Partie
    Chefs responsible for each department and its work detailed as follows:

Pastry Chef/Chef Pâtissier
Baker/Boulanger   } Pastry operations
Larder Chef/Chef Garde-Manger   Larder operations
Sauce Chef/Chef Saucier
Fish Chef/Chef Poissonnier
Roast Chef/Chef Rôtisseur
Grill Chef/Chef Grillardin   } Kitchen/stove operations
Vegetable Chef/Chef Entremettier
Soup Chef/Chef Potager
Relief Chef/Chef Tournant
Assistant Chefs/Commis Chefs
Apprentice/Apprenti

Other personnel employed dependent upon size and nature of the establishment include:

Breakfast Chef/Chef du Petit Déjeuner
Night Chef or Duty Chef/Chef de Nuit ou Chef de Garde
Butcher/Boucher
Staff Chef/Chef Communard
Fishmonger/Poissonnier
Hors d'Oeuvre Chef/Hors d'Oeuvrier

Ancillary personnel:

Kitchen announcer (barker)/Aboyeur
    Person responsible for shouting out the customers' orders to the kitchen staff
Sculleryman (pot washer)/Plongeur
Kitchen porters
    Responsible for the general cleaning of the kitchen area
Stillroom staff
    Responsible for the preparation of certain beverages and accompaniments, e.g. tea, coffee, melba toast, breakfast toast. Afternoon teas are sometimes served from this department.
Storeman, etc.

Duties and Responsibilities of Main Kitchen Staff

Chef de Cuisine

In large traditional establishments the head chef is a member of the management team and his work is of an administrative nature. Examples include: menu planning; organization of staff and rotas; purchasing of raw materials and equipment; control of resources to achieve profit margins; etc. The exact description of a head chef's job will vary according to the size and type of establishment in which he/she is employed. In smaller units the term 'working head chef' may be used to describe the administrative and active culinary duties carried out by the head chef.

Sous Chef

The second chef deputizes for the head chef in his or her absence. In large traditional catering establishments a number of sous chefs are employed, each having clearly defined areas of authority, e.g. banquet production, speciality restaurant, floor service catering. In general, sous chefs are responsible for the daily supervision of kitchen operations.

Chefs de Partie (kitchen/stove operations)

Partie chefs may be described as technical section supervisors. They directly supervise staff, equipment and the processing of raw materials in specialized areas of food production, e.g. soups are prepared under the direction of the Potager. In addition to supervisory skills, the chef de partie must have acquired a high level of expertise in culinary skills and knowledge. This is essential as he or she is actively involved in the preparation of food for the table and the practical training of staff.

Chef Saucier

The sauce chef actively supervises the cooking and presentation for service of the following culinary products:

(a)   entrées and relevés (see p. 385) with accompanying garnishes and sauces;
(b)   certain sauces for use by other departments in the kitchen, e.g. tomato sauce to accompany egg or farinaceous dishes.

It must be noted, however that the saucier *does not* prepare:

(a)   sweet sauces for pastry products;
(b)   fish sauces;
(c)   sauces to accompany roasts;
(d)   cold sauces and dressings;

as these are prepared by the respective sections involved.

Chef Poissonnier

The fish chef cooks and presents for service the majority of hot fish products except those that are deep-fried or grilled. He/she is responsible for sauces and garnishes to accompany the dishes they produce.

Chef Rôtisseur/Chef Grillardin

Roast and grill chefs, cook and present for service the following:

(a) roast butcher's meat, poultry, offal and game;
(b) grilled butcher's meat, poultry, offal, game, fish and vegetables; and some fruits used as a garnish;
(c) deep fried meats, poultry, game, offal, fish, vegetables and fruits for garnish;
(d) preparations to be served as a savoury course at the end of a meal.

Most but not all accompanying garnishes and sauces of these products are prepared by this section.

Chef Entremettier

This chef is mainly responsible for the preparation, cooking, and presentation for service of vegetable products, except those that are deep fried or grilled. In addition this section may be responsible for farinaceous dishes, cheese and vegetable soufflés, etc.

Chef Potager

The soup chef is chiefly responsible for the preparation, cooking and presentation of hot soups and their garnishes. Cold soups are often prepared by the soup chef but are served from the larder section. In addition this section is responsible for many hot egg courses.

Chef Tournant

The relief chefs deputize for various chefs de partie on days off and during holiday periods.

Commis Chefs

Commis chefs assist the various chefs de partie with food production. They are usually graded according to their position and experience, e.g. first commis, second in command of a section.

Apprenti

Apprentices/trainee chefs are involved with learning the technical aspects of kitchen operations. They obtain knowledge from all sections of the kitchen through a controlled training scheme.

Chef de Partie (Larder operations)

Garde-Manger

The larder chef actively supervises the preparation of butcher's meat, poultry, offal, game, fish, and shell fish for use by the other sections of the kitchen, e.g. joints for roasting, fish for poaching, small cuts and large joints for entrées and relevés. In addition to such basic preparation the larder department is responsible for the provision of cold buffet, cold hors d'oeuvres and canapés, cold pies and pâtés, cooked meats and salads, cold sauces and dressings, sandwiches and many made-up preparations, e.g. cooked and raw forcemeats, etc. The following chefs, including commis and apprentices are under the direct supervision of the Chef Garde-Manger:

(a) butcher/boucher
(b) fishmonger/poissonnier
(c) hors d'oeuvre chef/hors d'oeuvrier
(d) buffet chef/chef du froid.

Chef de Partie (Pastry operations)

Chef Pâtissier

The pastry chef actively supervises the preparation, cooking and presentation of all hot and cold sweets and accompanying sauces, confectionery items and various breads. In addition this section provides the kitchen with pastry items required for savoury products, e.g. cheese straws, vol-au-vents, pastry cases, etc. According to the nature and size of the kitchen brigade the following chefs including commis and apprentices are under the direction supervision of the Chef Pâtissier:

(a) Baker/Boulanger
(b) Ice-cream Chef/Glacier

Modified Kitchen Organizations

The traditional 'Partie System' is by nature labour intensive and expensive to operate in its entirety. It is generally used where large-scale forms of traditional luxury catering exist.

Other sections of the hotel and catering industry, e.g. institutional, industrial, popular and fast food operations, etc., may employ a modified version of the partie system or operate a purpose-designed labour system to suit their own particular requirements. Terminology referring to specialist jobs may differ according to the establishment's requirements or be related to the traditional partie system. Different levels of skill will be demanded to meet the needs of various styles of catering operations, examples of which are given below.

Hospital Catering

Kitchen organization will vary in numbers and grades of staff according to the requirements of the Whitley Councils for the Health Services. The list below outlines a sample range of kitchen organization within the hospital sector indicating the nature of their respective duties.

Kitchen Superintendent or Head Cook

Both grades are mainly concerned with the general supervision of one or more kitchens. Their duties may include the following:

1. organization of the kitchen;
2. allocation of work;
3. supervision, direction and control of preparation and cooking;
4. ensuring proper standards of cleanliness;
5. ensuring the observance of safety regulations and procedures;
6. ensuring the correct and economical use of materials and equipment;
7. checking of meals issued for quantity, quality, and appearance;
8. arrangement of duty rotas;
9. discipline, training and welfare of staff;
10. requisitioning of small kitchen equipment and maintenance of inventories;
11. reporting mechanical defects and repairs;
12. control of kitchen linen and laundry;
13. indenting for kitchen supplies;

Assistant Head Cook

The nature of this post is that of a 'working' supervisor responsible to a Head Cook or Kitchen Superintendent for the direct supervision of cooks, assistant cooks and other kitchen staff dealing with the preparation, cooking, and serving of food. Other duties include assisting Head Cook or Kitchen Superintendent and deputizing for them during their 'off duty' periods.

Cook

Main duties include preparation, cooking, and despatch of all types of meals and instruction of lower grades of kitchen staff.

Assistant Cook

Assists the cook in the preparation, cooking, and service of food.

Catering Assistants

General duties in kitchens, dining rooms and associated areas; including the service of food, cleaning of premises and equipment, certain aspects of food preparation; taking cash or meal tickets; replenishing vending machines; keeping related records.

N.B.   A Senior Catering Assistant's duties relate to supervisory aspects of the Catering Assistant's work.

Kitchen Porter

Duties include: light portering and messenger tasks; operation of mechanical scrubbing machines and simple preparation of vegetables and fish, etc.

Industrial and Welfare Catering

According to size and nature of the establishment, these operations are organized similarly to Hospital catering as outlined above with different terminology used for certain jobs, e.g. Head Chef/Head Cook, Second Chef, Pastry Cook, Vegetable Cook, etc.

Popular/Fast Food Catering

These establishments require personnel with a limited range of skills. For example a popular style 'Grill Room' operation may employ a specialized Grill Chef capable of producing a limited range of grills and a proportion of convenience preparations, e.g. starters, vegetables and sweets. Similarly 'Fast Food Operations' may utilize semi-skilled staff to produce a standard range of products for the consumer.

2

Modern Developments in Kitchen Equipment

Microwave Oven

The microwave oven which is a relatively modern cooking appliance, can be described as an electronic cooking device in which food is heated by means of high frequency radio waves, known as microwaves. The microwaves are produced by a power source identified as a magnetron. This form of cooking was developed in the U.S.A. as a peaceful application of the principles used in radar during World War II.

The conventional methods of cookery employ the use of conducted, convected and radiated heat, which are briefly explained on p. 50. As can be seen these methods provide heat which penetrates food gradually from the exterior to the centre. Microwaves on the other hand do not give such heat to food, nor do they create heat within the oven cavity as experienced with conventional methods. Instead the oven is designed to beam high-frequency energy from the magnetron at the food so that the molecules of water in food are violently disturbed creating molecular friction. The friction generates heat, which converts the food's moisture into steam, heating the food throughout. Furthermore microwaves have the capacity to penetrate through certain foods instantly and produce heat wherever moisture is present. However the sealing and colouring effects associated with conventional methods are not noticeably achieved. The depth of wave penetration will depend, amongst other factors, upon the food's density but generally waves extend into food from between 2 and 3 in and beyond this depth the passage of heat relies on conduction only.

Characteristics of Microwaves

Microwaves like light rays have the following important characteristics:

(a) penetration;
(b) reflection;
(c) absorption.

Penetration

The waves are able to pass through certain substances without being absorbed. For example, glass, plastics, chinaware, scarcely absorb microwaves and allow them to pass through. Therefore food containers made from such materials do not become hot from the microwaves but they may conduct heat from the food being cooked in the oven cavity.

Reflection

Microwaves are reflected from such substances as metals, i.e. good conductors of electricity. This characteristic is used to advantage within the oven in that waves are reflected from the metallic surfaces. Consequently foods placed in the oven absorb the waves from all directions, the cooking period is fast and the need to turn foods for even cooking is eliminated. However, as a result of this reflecting characteristic, metal or metal-banded *containers* are generally unsuitable for use in microwave ovens, as waves are reflected from the container surfaces and not absorbed by the food.

Absorption

Cooking is achieved by the molecular disturbance created when the radio wave energy is absorbed by the food. As previously noted substances containing a high proportion of water easily absorb microwaves and this is true not only of food but of paper or cloth soaked with water.

Construction

A microwave oven consists of the following main components:

1. Power transformer – supplies power to the magnetron;
2. Magnetron – produces high frequency electro-magnetic waves (microwaves);
3. Waveguide – guides the microwaves from the magnetron into the oven cavity;
4. Oven cavity – a metal box in which food is placed for cooking by microwaves which enter from above;
5. Finder/window – a window in the oven door containing *very fine* perforations dimensioned to prevent any loss of microwave energy and to enable viewing of food without opening the oven door;
6. Stirrer fan/agitator – used to distribute the microwaves coming into the oven from the waveguide and to diffuse reflected energy to achieve more even cooking;
7. Stirrer motor – drives the stirrer fan;
8. Oven shelf – shelf upon which containers and food are placed for cooking.

Ovens are fitted with a built-in ventilation system to effect cooling of the magnetron and other vital components. The air may be drawn through a special dust filter that keeps the electrical and mechanical parts dust-free. Other refinements include timer controls for defrosting, cooking and reheating with automatic signalling devices. The controls may also incorporate a 'repeating feature', which enables the operator to cook a number of similar items one after the other, without having to re-set the timer. All ovens feature automatic safety devices that inactivate microwave power when the oven door is opened.

Various designs and sizes of oven are manufactured. Size is measured by output power, e.g. 1 kW, 2 kW, etc., and not by the size of the oven cavity. Oven dimensions are chosen on the basis of the frequency used and the optimum exploitation of generated energy.

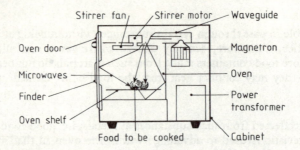

Technologists are continually improving equipment and microwave ovens are no exception. Three problems commonly associated with microwave cookery are as follows:

(a) uneven cooking or heating due to 'cold spots' (uneven wave distribution and absorption) in the oven;
(b) inability of microwave energy to achieve significant colour changes (browning) of food compared with conventional cooking methods;
(c) relatively small oven capacity, which places a limit on its utility in some catering situations, e.g. volume catering.

To counteract these problems certain innovations and technological advances have been implemented.

Counteracting Cold Spots

(a) *Dual magnetrons*—in order to overcome 'cold spots' manufacturers have fitted some ovens with *two* magnetrons, which produce more microwave energy for distribution within the oven.
(b) *Turntable*—other manufacturers have incorporated a revolving oven shelf (turntable) to ensure that foods do not experience 'cold spots' throughout the length of the cooking period.

Colouring Foods (browning)

(a) Techniques to effect browning of food include the development of combined units that incorporate a microwave oven with a separate infra-red grill, where the grill is used to colour the food prior to or following the period of cooking by microwaves.
(b) *Micro-browners*—another patented development is the use of micro-browners, which comprise specially designed ceramic containers that are able to absorb microwave energy. The containers are pre-heated in the microwave oven and their surface becomes sufficiently heated to give colour to foods placed on them, as would be expected by cooking on a griddle or in a shallow frying vessel. The use of these ceramic containers involves the turning of foods when colouring of both sides is required.

Micro-Aire Ovens

Micro-Aire ovens may be described as being different from but related to the conventional microwave oven. They differ in the following ways:

(a) they combine forced-air convection and microwave energy in a single unit;

(b) they offer increased oven capacity and can be used to carry out most of the culinary operations associated with conventional and microwave cookery;
(c) they effect the browning of foods generally associated with conventional cooking methods;
(d) the oven cavity becomes heated during the cooking period;
(e) when combined systems are operated the cooking times are longer than with microwaves but are shorter when compared with conventional cooking times;
(f) both cooking methods can be used simultaneously or independently as required;
(g) traditional containers can be successfully used in the oven including those made from metals.

Combined Methods

The combined cooking is effected by the use of 'pulsed' microwaves (i.e. microwave energy is emitted intermittently at 7 second intervals throughout cooking), along with forced-air convected heat. Manufacturers claim that the oven will carry out most of the culinary operations associated with conventional and microwave units. The oven is most versatile in that it combines the speed of microwaves with the fast heat transfer of forced-air convection to cook with traditional colour, texture and flavour associated with high quality foods.

Oven Capacity

With a large potential capacity and throughput the use of the micro-aire oven is extended over a wide range of catering operations. For example, when used as the combined system it is able to cope with a 1 × 1 Gastronorm tray or six to eight separate items at the same time. Alternatively when used independently as a convection oven the insertion of a three tier rack allows for the cooking of greater numbers of portions e.g. multiportion packs (50 to 80 portions) reheated at the same time.

Examples of Cooking Times

Recent examples quoted by manufacturers include:

(a) 12 kg turkey in 55 minutes;
(b) 7 kg leg of pork in 48 minutes.

General Factors on Microwave Cooking

The speed at which food is electronically heated is determined by a number of variables and the following general observations may be of value.

Chemical Structure

Food scientists state that in general the more complex the chemical structure of food the more quickly the product will attain a high temperature. For example, 1 l of milk will reach boiling point before 1 l of water.

Shape and Form

Thinner pieces of food cook more quickly than larger and thicker portions as it is more difficult for microwaves to penetrate to the core of large, thick pieces. So cutting and slicing food into smaller/thinner portions enables the microwaves to penetrate more quickly and often instantaneously throughout the product, speeding up the heating process.

Arranging Foods

For even cooking or heating food should be distributed evenly in containers. Piling foods on to a tray in an *ad hoc* fashion may result in uneven cooking or heating.

Loss of Moisture

Food tends to release water when heated by microwaves. In order to minimize loss of moisture foods may be placed in a covered container or wrapped in plastic film.

Quantities of Food

When cooking a small quantity of food any microwave energy not absorbed by that item is wasted. This wasted energy could have been used to cook a larger quantity over a similar cooking period. In general an increase in the volume of food requires a further increase in cooking time. However if full use is made of available energy cooking times remain short and do not necessarily increase proportionately with the volume of food.

Initial Temperature of Foods

The lower the initial temperature of food before cooking or heating commences the longer the time required to complete the operation. When heating frozen items either to thaw or cook the speed of wave penetration is retarded because ice-crystals act as wave reflectors and the rise in temperature is slowed down.

State of the Food

Microwaves are able to deal with food in a raw, partly cooked or completely cooked state. The heating times will vary accordingly.

Food Containers

The materials chosen for use as containers are those that absorb little of the high frequency energy. They must be capable of withstanding high temperatures which are reached within the food during cooking, e.g. 100°C plus. The materials used must not reflect the microwaves (as is the case with metals) but allow them to pass through as light rays through a window. Cling-film wrap and roast-a-bags may be used as containers.

Summary and Safety

For recommended cooking/heating times and further detailed information consult recognized manufacturers.

It is believed that defective doors are the main source of radiation leakage from microwave ovens. Therefore, units are fitted with safety features to prevent leakage during cooking and also ensure that when the door seal is interrupted the oven will not function. However microwave ovens should be carefully checked against leakage or the possibility of exposure which could lead to microwave injury.

Forced-Air Convection Ovens

A wide range of forced-air convection ovens are manufactured, designed to meet the specific needs of a variety of catering operations. These ovens may differ in their design specifications, energy source, output potential, and utility in a similar way to conventional ovens. The principal difference between a convection oven and an ordinary (conventional) oven is the accelerated air movement within the oven cavity and the varying heat inputs applied.

According to a leading designer in this area, forced-air convection ovens may, for the sake of simplicity, be categorized as follows:

Hard Units

These are ovens that have the highest air movement speed, generally combined with the highest heat input. These units are most suitable for the reheating of bulk and individual frozen foods, but are not suitable for prime cooking or baking.

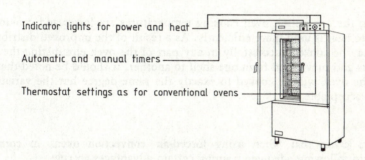

Indicator lights for power and heat

Automatic and manual timers

Thermostat settings as for conventional ovens

Medium Units

These are ovens that have a lower air movement speed, generally combined with a lower heat input. These ovens are suitable for prime cooking, some baking and if required reheating frozen foods.

Soft Units

These are ovens that have the lowest air movement speed and heat input. These ovens are suitable for some prime cooking and for baking but unsatisfactory for reheating frozen food because the time taken to reheat may constitute a health hazard.

Therefore when purchasing forced-air convection ovens, prospective buyers should consult recognized specialists who can advise on the best selection to suit the buyer's specific requirements. Some special design features which illustrate this point are listed below:

(a) bakery convection oven with steam injection facility;
(b) water injection facility, which may be used for steaming foods;
(c) counter top models for snack bar operations;
(d) roll in—roll out models where racks of food are wheeled on trolleys, direct from refrigeration or cold store, into the oven for cooking, then rolled out for service;
(e) multi-purpose units that combine a convection oven with some of the following: eye level grill; bain-marie; boiling top; griddle; or plate warmer;
(f) safety features may include; doors opening to 180°; flame failure protection devices; shelf runners to prevent food tipping on withdrawal; separate mains, control and timer switches; etc.

The Principle of Forced-Air Convection

On heating, air rises and when trapped within an oven cavity forms a convection current, which circulates within the oven. In ordinary ovens the current of heated air circulates slowly, which affects the time taken to reach the required cooking temperature. In addition variations of temperature, within the oven, occur particularly following the introduction of cooler air once the oven doors are opened.

In contrast, when employing a forced-air convection oven the circulating current of hot air is forced speedily around the oven chamber by a motorized fan or blower. This technique creates a more even and constant temperature throughout the oven because of improved heat distribution, and also shortens the time taken to pre-heat the oven. Furthermore the current of continuous moving air strips away the thin layer of moisture and cool air from the surface of foods placed into the oven, allowing heat to penetrate and cook more quickly.

When using the convection oven cooking temperatures are lower and cooking times shorter because heat is used more efficiently. As a result of the improved distribution of heat, foods may be cooked successfully in any part of the oven eliminating the need to open the doors and move food from one shelf to another. It should be noted that not all the food in the oven will be cooked to exactly the same degree but the variations experienced are acceptable.

Advantages

Manufacturers claim that when using forced-air convection ovens in correct circumstances and following adequate training certain advantages accrue:

(a) time saving—cooking and labour time;
(b) energy saving—reduction in cooking temperatures, cooking times and pre-heating times;
(c) space utilization—ovens are designed to make maximum use of production space and at the same time increase volume output;·
(d) product quality and yield—foods cook more evenly giving a high quality finish with less shrinkage and therefore a higher portion yield. This is due to the shorter cooking time at lower temperatures.

Examples taken from a convection oven cooking guide

Food	Mark	Min	Shelves (Oven capacity)
Sirloin of beef 3 kg (6 lb) joints	5	115	4
Pork joints 1 kg (2½ lb)	6	55	4
Baked potatoes	7	45 – 60	6
Vol-au-vents	8	10	6
Rice pudding	1	60	6

Pressure Steamers

General Features

Modern pressure steamers vary in design, size, versatility, efficiency and volume output potential. Consequently models are designed to meet the needs of different types of catering operation. These models range from small back bar units designed to effect fast cooking and reheating of foods, to larger models designed to cope quickly and effectively with volume catering. Certain models feature more than one cooking compartment, providing the caterer with operational versatility so that large and small amounts of food can be steamed independently or simultaneously as demanded by the customer.

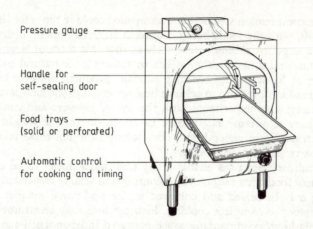

Pressure gauge

Handle for
self-sealing door

Food trays
(solid or perforated)

Automatic control
for cooking and timing

Steamer trays/pans are identified as solid/plain or perforated with either one being selected for use as required by the culinary operation in hand. As a general guide solid/plain trays are used where an amount of liquid is needed within the tray to assist cooking, or where the juice of the food being steamed is to be retained for culinary purposes, e.g. chicken essence for a sauce. Perforated trays, however, are employed when no liquid is required to assist in the cooking process, and also when foods are to be well drained. Manufacturers provide detailed charts concerning the steaming of various foods but the experienced chef will soon recognize the culinary potential of the modern pressure steamers.

Steam Supply and Pressure

All pressure steamers cook foods by using the concentrated heat of steam at varying pressures. The pressures used generally range from $0.35 - 1.05$ kg/cm^2 ($5 - 15$ psi) and are often described as:

(a) low pressure $- 0.35$ kg/cm^2 (5 psi);
(b) medium pressure $- 0.70$ kg/cm^2 (10 psi);
(c) high pressure (high compression) $- 1.05$ kg/cm^2 (15 psi).

Steam may be supplied directly from a central steam supply, from an external steam generator or from a heated water-well within the steamer compartment. Other modifications to date may include such refinements as: an automatic pressure sensitive defrost cycle, which prevents the commencement of cooking until the product has reached a given temperature (ideal when cooking from a frozen or semi-frozen state); the utilization of fine needle jets within the steamer compartment, which act to project the steam directly on to foods speeding up heat penetration and cooking time. A further development is the use of superheated dry steam created when purified water is fed through tubes cn to a casting which is heated to approximately 315°C (600°F). At impact the water turns to steam, rises into the compartment providing the cooking medium of heated dry steam.

Foods and Cooking Times

A wide variety of raw or pre-cooked foods may be steamed to effect cooking or reheating. Steamers according to manufacturers' specifications are able to cope effectively with many foods from a thawed or frozen condition. Cooking times commence once the correct steam pressure is reached and most models make use of automatic timers to control the selected cooking period.

When using high compression steamers recommended cooking times for listed products are remarkably swift, with the foods being cooked in an environment of dry steam from which air has been expelled. Manufacturers claim that this form of steaming prevents oxidation of vitamins and mineral salts, assists in retaining the natural colour, flavour, aroma and texture of foods during cooking. Certain products however are preferably steamed at low to medium pressure to achieve best results, e.g. steamed savoury or sweet puddings, and caterers may experiment with the use of pressure and cooking times to identify their culinary requirements. It must be stated that as the weight/load of food being steamed increases so in general does the cooking time but these increases do not appear to be extensive (*see* the table below).

Innovations in culinary practices enable many traditional dishes to be cooked in the steamer. For example foods that require the colouring and sealing associated with shallow frying or braising may be sealed and coloured in the traditional manner before being placed into the steamer to complete cooking. Fish portions may be steamed rather than poached and the masking/accompanying sauce prepared independently (an ideal technique for large scale banqueting).

Safety Factors

When using high compression steamers the door cannot be opened until all the pressure within the compartment has been released. When the steam is released from a conventional steamer it is wise to use the steamer door as a protective shield to safeguard oneself from hot steam that may remain within the compartment following initial steam release.

Summary

The information provided is in broad, general terms. Detailed technical information is available from manufacturers who specialize in the production and marketing of such equipment. The purchaser therefore is well advised to make full use of the advice concerning the many options now available.

Examples of recommended cooking times (approx) using a high compression steamer at 1.05 kg/cm² (15 psi)

Product	Load in kg (lb)	Timer setting (min)
Brussel sprouts (fresh)	2 (5)	4–6
Brussel sprouts (frozen)	6 (15)	11–13
Fish steaks (thawed)	1 (2)	3–6
Lobster, 1 kg (2½ lb) each (thawed)	6 (15)	11–12
Whole chickens, 1.5 kg (3 lb) each (thawed)	9 (18)	30

Pressureless Convection Steamer

Manufacturers of this most recent development in steaming equipment have designed a pressureless steaming unit, which equates with the efficiency and culinary utility of the modern high compression steamers previously described. It is argued that ideally food is best cooked at the lowest effective cooking temperature in order to avoid cellular damage, excess nutritional loss, over shrinkage and product discoloration. Furthermore cooking by steam in a constantly venting compartment (pressureless compartment) eliminates gases, volatiles and other undesirable by-products, which can have unfavourable effects upon the colour and flavour of foods. Therefore efficient cooking is ideal when using low temperature, constantly venting steam, but two major obstacles may remain:

(a) air;
(b) condensate.

Manufacturers state that the presence of only 0.5% of air in a steam environment can reduce the heat transfer coefficient by as much as 50%. Furthermore as air is an effective insulator its presence around food acts as a barrier to efficient heat transfer. A cooking compartment containing steam and air can only supply the temperature of the partial pressure of the steam and not of the total chamber pressure. It must however be stated that manufacturers of a high compression steamer claim to expel all air from the cooking atmosphere, therefore overcoming these problems. However physicists endorse that more heat is available for cooking in 1 lb of steam at atmospheric (zero pressure) than is available at 1 lb of steam at 15 lb of pressure. The pressureless convection steamer is designed to use the potential energy of steam at atmospheric pressure in an effective and efficient manner.

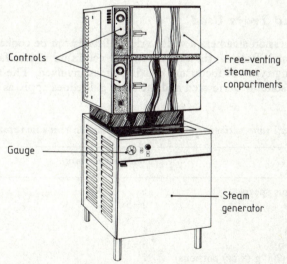

Condensate, it is claimed, is an additional barrier to efficient heat transfer because it forms around the food and insulates it against the heat energy of steam. By employing modern technology, manufacturers of the pressureless convection steamer are able to utilize the lowest practical temperature of steam i.e. 100°C (212°F) at atmospheric (zero) pressure to cook foods efficiently and retain a high level of quality control. The purified steam is generated in a boiler under pressure before being introduced into the cooking compartment directly over the food within. Because the compartment is on a constantly free-venting system no pressure build up occurs (pressureless steaming). The steam is made to act like a piston forcing out the air. Turbulent, controlled forced convection steam strips away the layer of insulative condensate from foods and cooling steam and condensate from foods is continually replaced by a fresh supply of steam from the generator.

Cooking therefore is achieved with low-temperature constantly-venting steam in a pressureless air-free environment of controlled convection, aptly described as cooking in a pressureless convection steamer. Certain models are dual purpose and may also be used as pressure steamers. Other refinements may include automatic timers with each compartment independently controlled for versatility of use. Steamer or compartment doors seal automatically when closed and may be opened safely at any time because there is no pressure within.

Forced convection steam—a turbulent high energy atmosphere—swirling in, around and through the food preserving moisture, nutriments and flavour.

Convection pressureless steam cooking

Conventional pressurized steam cooking

Food Cooked and Trays Used

As with high compression steamers a wide variety of foods can be cooked/reheated from raw/cooked states and from a thawed or frozen condition. Manufacturers provide guidelines concerning types of foods and cooking times involved. The types of steamer tray used are plain, solid or perforated and the same guidelines apply as for compression steamers.

Examples of approximate time settings recommended for pressureless convection steamer

Product	Timer setting (min)
Frozen jumbo asparagus spears	6
Frozen broccoli spears	2 – 3
Fresh cabbage	2 – 4
Fresh corn on the cob	6
Frozen corn on the cob	8 – 10
Frozen salmon steaks (200 g (8 oz) portions)	7
Frozen cod fillets	3
Fresh beef brisket (400 g (1 lb))	18 – 20

Summary

The information provided is of a general nature and interested caterers are advised to seek further and more detailed technical data from recognized sources.

Liquidizer

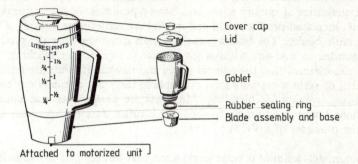

The liquidizer is a piece of kitchen machinery which uses a high speed motor to drive specially designed stainless steel blades to chop, purée, or blend foods very quickly and efficiently. Although it is not a large-scale piece of kitchen machinery its versatility and value are worth mentioning. This small machine operates at various speeds to suit the job in hand. It is particularly useful to the small volume caterer whose type of operation may not warrant investment in large-scale equipment to carry out similar work. Often the liquidizer reduces labour intensity and time taken to complete certain tasks by eliminating traditional methods, which are often laborious. In addition it may improve the overall quality of a finished product, e.g. consistency and flavour of soups, sauces, fruit juices, fruit and vegetable purées and pâtés, etc.

Examples of Culinary Uses

According to manufacturers' recommendations, this machine may be used as follows:

(a) to purée or blend, soups, sauces, fruit juices and dressings;
(b) to purée various pâtés and fruit preparations;
(c) to crush ice cubes or nuts;
(d) to mix batters, etc.

Vertical Cutter/Mixer (VCM)

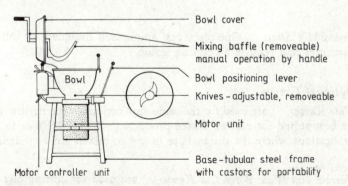

The VCM is a relatively large piece of versatile kitchen machinery which is able to cut and mix ingredients simultaneously. The machine could be described as a type of large-scale liquidizer. The high speed motor drives any one of a variety of purpose designed, interchangeable stainless steel blades that are positioned inside the bowl according to the job in hand. This machine is ideally employed in situations that require a speedy preparation of large quantities of quality foods and bakery products. Manufacturers claim that speed, volume, increased product yield and quality are achieved as a result of the cutting action of the knife blades. The blades move at a high speed and slice the products whilst they are suspended in mid-air, without giving rise to bruising or mashing. Where applicable it is also claimed that the natural juices and flavour of foods are retained. A full range of models of various capacities are available to carry out virtually any tasks that incorporate cutting, mixing, or blending. Machines are designed to suit both large and small operations but it is advisable to consult manufacturers for specialist information concerning the purchase of a VCM.

N.B.   Certain models without tubular steel frame, may be clamped on to a suitable bench or table.

Examples of Culinary Uses

According to manufacturers' recommendations these machines may be used as follows:

(a) prepare quantities of raw forcemeats, e.g. 12 kg (27 lb) hamburger mix in 40 sec;
(b) blend large volumes of soups and sauces in seconds, e.g. mayonnaise in 120 sec, soups in 30 sec;
(c) mix quantities of pastry and bread dough quickly, e.g. 11 kg (25 lb) bread dough in 90 sec, 11 kg (25 lb) pie pastry in 20 sec;
(d) cut/slice quantities of vegetables speedily, e.g. vegetables for coleslaw in 12 sec.

Knife Blades

Standard Accessories

Shaft with Narrow Knives   is used for all cutting operations, such as sausage or hamburger mix, wieners, bologna and other meat products, vegetables for salads and coleslaw, pastry products, cake batters, cheese spreads, and making certain types of salad dressings and processing yeast doughs where a fine texture is desired.

Knead/Mix Shaft   One-piece cast aluminium designed for mixing small quantities that require no cutting action.

Optional Extras

Wide Knives   are used for the same applications as the narrow knives but are best suited for cutting frozen products ($-2°C$ (28°F)) or in industrial applications where the products to be cut or mixed are very dense.

Narrow and Wide Wave Cut Knives   are used for cutting oily products; nuts, corn masa for Spanish foods, and some vegetables. Again, the wide knives are used for harder products.

Grating Shaft   is used for grating hard raw vegetables and for the mixing of dry ingredients.

 Mixing Shaft   is used for blending and mixing large quantities of ingredients where no cutting action is required.

Cleaning

The machine may be cleaned using a 10 sec run with warm detergent water which is poured away and followed by hand wiping.

Bratt Pan

This piece of equipment derives its name from the German word 'Braten' which translated refers to a number of cooking methods. Bratt pans are relatively new to the U.K. but have been widely and successfully used on the continent for many years. Gas and electric models are manufactured and the cooking pan is mainly constructed of stainless steel or cast iron. Models vary in design, shape, potential utility with special features offered. The models are produced to meet various catering requirements. At present the models available are designed to meet the requirements of large volume catering but manufacturers hope to engineer a model to meet the needs of the smaller catering operation.

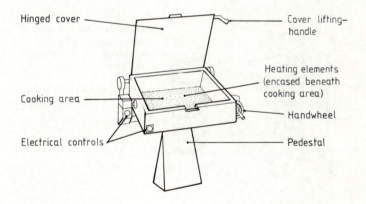

Special features may include:

(a) tilting pan with pouring lip designed to ensure safe movement of pan and also to facilitate transfer of hot foods to other receptacles;
(b) stainless steel lids (covers) hinged to open sideways and provide a working surface;
(c) operational controls sited conveniently for ease and safety of use;
(d) flame failure and thermostatic cut-out devices;
(e) automatic safety devices: to cut off heat when pan is tilted, to cut off heat if thermostat fails,
(f) non-tilt and portable models are available.

Culinary Uses

The bratt pan may be described as a multi-purpose piece of cooking equipment. Manufacturers claim that such equipment may be successfully used for: boiling; poaching; stewing; braising; shallow frying (sauté); deep frying; griddling; innovatory pot roasting; innovatory steaming; and also as a bain-marie. To have such versatility in one piece of equipment presents obvious major advantages to the catering industry. However when purchasing such equipment prospective buyers are well advised to consult recognized specialists and take advantage of the advisory services available, to ensure that the best possible model is obtained to meet the caterers own particular requirements.

Régéthermic Regenerating Oven (Cabinet)

Régéthermic ovens form part of a cook–chill food production system which was developed in France over 10 years ago. The system operates in France as well as many other countries including the U.K. The ovens are specifically designed to regenerate rather than cook foods. They vary in design and capacity according to operational requirements and are fitted with automatic timers and simple controls to facilitate ease of use. All foods are prepared and cooked in advance by employing traditional culinary techniques. Cooked food is placed into specially designed individual or bulk containers and speedily chilled in a blast chiller. It may then be stored for up to 3 days in a refrigerator at 3°C (37°F). The aim of the system is to allow cooked food to be reconstituted at the point of consumption in such a way as to prevent it drying up or changing in appearance. The food should look and taste the same as when freshly cooked and retain as much nutritional value as possible.

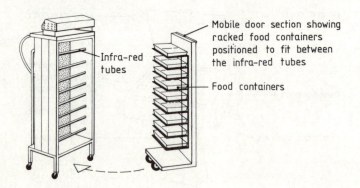

Infra-red tubes

Mobile door section showing racked food containers positioned to fit between the infra-red tubes

Food containers

Example model of régéthermic oven (cabinet)

The Principle of Régéthermic Regeneration

The method is based on two basic concepts:

1. The use of diffused infra-red rays operating on a predetermined wave length to achieve heat penetration requirements and characteristics. The exact degree of heat for regeneration within the oven is supplied by proportionally spaced infra-

red elements, see below. The ovens are fitted with groups of infra-red tubes, which have differing heating capacities. The less powerful elements are placed near the top of the oven allowing for the heating effect of convected hot air (heat rises). This ensures a uniform distribution of heat throughout the cabinet.

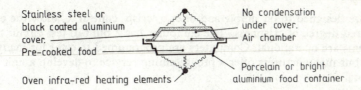

Sectional drawing of food container

2. The simultaneous reheating of special containers and their covers. In these containers food is kept under cover in a semi-sealed atmosphere. The container is subjected to infra-red radiation, which produces gentle, continuous and uniform heat. The container then stores heat like a thermal battery and the stainless steel cover is always hotter than the food. This acts to prevent condensation, keeping the food's flavour and aroma sealed within the container. The régéthermic regenerating method uses radiated, conducted, and convected heat (*see* p. 50) in varying proportions. The air chamber containing food is heated to serving temperature (60° – 65°C (140° – 149°F)).

Oven Utility

As previously stated régéthermic ovens are primarily designed to reconstitute pre-cooked, chilled foods, with an average regenerating time of 12 – 20 min. It is possible however to operate with freshly cooked foods and pre-cooked frozen foods. In the latter case regeneration time is increased.

Computerized Fryers

A recent development in deep frying equipment is the computerized fryer. Expertise, knowledge and certain manual operations normally associated with deep frying are built-in to the computerized models.

The 'fryer with a brain' may be programmed to control the following automatically:

(a) cooking times of a pre-selected range of products, to achieve the correct degree of cooking;

(b) the cooking temperatures, therefore eliminating the need for thermostats and calibration;

(c) high temperatures to ensure that the frying medium does not become too hot or reach flash point;

(d) low temperatures indicating by means of a signalling device when the oil/fat temperature drops excessively below 'set point';

(e) a shut-down effect if the fryer is not used over a pre-set period;
(f) a melt cycle to ensure safe melting of fat before the fryer automatically switches over to operating cycle;
(g) basket lifts, which operate automatically and independently to remove the products from the fryer once cooking is completed;
(h) holding timer, denoting that the holding period of the cooked product is over.

Controls are designed to be simple and offer a 'crisp' control to allow the operator to select preferred degree of crispness. The computer has a built-in test circuit to indicate that all systems are operational. Computers are programmed to cater for many standard menu items but manufacturers offer a programming service to develop a unit to suit individual needs.

Operational Information

Information is fed into the computer from a super-sensitive probe, which is immersed in the frying medium. The probe passes information about temperature and rates of temperature change created by one or more of the following variables:

(a) initial oil/fat temperature;
(b) volume of food being fried;
(c) fryer efficiency and capacity;
(d) fryer recovery rate;
(e) quantity and condition of oil/fat;
(f) product temperature and water content.

By using this information the fryer is able to compute the exact cooking times required with the end of the cooking period being indicated by an automatic signalling device. When the computer needs servicing it is easily replaced by plugging in another computer control.

General Factors

In addition to the special features outlined above, models maintain the general standards and refinements of modern fryers:

(a) compactly designed modular units;
(b) built-in filter to ensure removal of contaminants, moisture and fatty acids, therefore extending the life of the frying medium;
(c) *cool zone* that acts to keep solid particles from the heat source thus extending the life of the oil/fat and reducing the possibility of taste transfers;
(d) drain valve and oil receptacle to ensure safe and swift draining of the frying oil/fat.

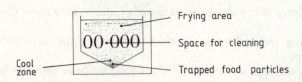

A wide range of single or multi-product models are manufactured, designed for use with gas or electric services. Potential buyers should obtain first-hand advice from manufacturers to ensure that their particular catering requirements are identified.

3

The Cooking of Food

Generally food is cooked when heat is transferred from a heat source, (e.g. stove) through to the exterior of foodstuffs by one or more of the following mechanisms:

(a) conduction
(b) convection
(c) radiation.

These processes function on the basis that where temperature differences exist heat will be transferred and directed towards areas of decreasing temperature. In order to understand how the heat transfer processes function it is helpful to know something of:

(a) the effects of heat upon food,
(b) the means by which heat is transferred through food to effect cooking.

Heat and Heat Transfer (general principles)

All foods and all bodies of matter, e.g. pots and pans consist of atoms/molecules, which are constantly in motion. When heat is applied to foods or cooking vessels this motion is greatly accelerated and friction within the foods and cooking vessels greatly increased. The friction creates heat which passes through these materials by conduction. It should be noted that in most cases heat transfer *within* foods is primarily via the conduction process, however this is *not* the case where food is mainly or exclusively liquid. In these instances heat transfer is chiefly convective and rapid when the liquid is free to move; as is the case with stock, unthickened soups and gravies, etc. Where however foods that are initially liquid become thickened and semi-solid on heating, e.g. certain starch-thickened products, then convected heat is only important at the initial cooking stage. Once the food is thickened and the movement of liquid restricted the process of heat transfer by conduction within the food increases.

Cooking with Conducted Heat

The shallow frying of fish is a good example of how the conduction process transfers heat from a hot stove to a frying pan, through to the cooking oil and on to the outer surface of the fish. Cooking is continued as heat is transferred from the exterior through to the centre of the fish by conduction. At all stages of this operation the principles associated with heat and heat transfer described in the previous section apply. These stages include the heating of the cooking vessel, the oil and fish with the latter being changed from a raw to a cooked condition by the passage of conducted heat within the fish.

Cooking with Convected Heat

Convection occurs in gases and liquids, as opposed to solids because they can move more freely. As the gas (e.g. air) or liquids (e.g. water, stock, oil) are heated their structure expands and becomes less dense. In this condition the heated areas of the gas or liquid rise to be replaced by the cooler and denser gas or liquid present. This movement forms a convection current within the air or liquid. The warmed and less dense air/liquid gradually cools by giving up heat to the foods that are being cooked. On cooling this air/liquid becomes more dense and sinks again to complete the cycle.

The *baking of pies* illustrates the use of convected hot air as a heat transfer medium. The cold air within the oven is heated becomes less dense and rises. This is replaced by cooler denser air and the convection current of hot air is set in motion. The heated air gives up heat energy to the pies where it is absorbed passing through the pies by means of conduction to effect the well-known changes associated with baked products.

Similarly convection currents occur in liquids where they are used as heat transfer mediums during such methods as boiling, poaching, stewing, braising, steaming, and deep frying. In these instances water, moisture, stock or oil are used as the convection medium, but it should be noted that the temperature of these mediums is raised by heat conducted through the cooking vessel or steam generator.

Cooking with Radiant Heat

The grilling of food is an apt illustration of how emitted heat (energy) waves are transferred rapidly through the air and directed on to the exterior surface of foods. The heat energy is absorbed at the surfaces of food where it acts to generate friction. This in turn creates heat. Cooking continues from the exterior surface of the food through to its centre as heat energy travels by means of conduction. When cooking by radiant heat the energy waves heat the foods exterior surfaces only (as their ability to penetrate further is limited) and beyond this depth cooking is accomplished by conduction.

Summary

From these notes it is evident that in most cooking operations more than one mode of heat transfer is acting simultaneously. Also where foods are cooked by these conventional methods of heat transfer, heat penetration is seen to be relatively slow, commencing at the exterior of food and gradually travelling inwards by conduction.

N.B.   For cooking with microwave energy *see* pp. 32–6.

Cooking Methods in Common Use

English term	French term	Heat transfer processes
To poach	Pocher	Conduction/convection
To boil/simmer	Bouillir/mijoter	Conduction/convection
To steam	Vapeuriser	Convection/conduction
To stew	Etuver	Conduction/convection
To braise	Braiser	Conduction/convection
To pot-roast	Poêler	Conduction/convection
To deep-fry	Frire	Conduction/convection
To shallow fry	Sauter	Conduction
To grill	Griller	Radiation/conduction
To roast (oven)	Rôtir	Convection/conduction
To roast (open-spit)		Radiation/conduction
To bake	Cuire	Convection/conduction

The Effects of Cooking on Foods

As previously stated, cooking methods involve the use of heat. These methods may differ in:

(a) how much heat or other radiant energy is applied to the food;
(b) the rate at which it is applied;
(c) the medium used for heat transfer, e.g. metal, water, fat, air;
(d) whether precautions are taken to prevent the loss of moisture or whether moisture is allowed to escape into the atmosphere.

The prime objective of cooking is to produce palatable, safe and attractive foods. However a particular food cannot necessarily be cooked by all the methods outlined in this section.

The effects described in the following sections occur during most cooking operations. The extent to which these changes occur depends upon the amount of heat energy transferred to the foods. Obviously the higher the temperature to which the food is heated and the longer the period of time for which the temperature is maintained, the greater the effects will be. As will be observed these effects will be modified by the medium employed for heat transfer, typically air (e.g. grilling, baking), water or steam (e.g. poaching, boiling, stewing) or fat (frying).

Cooking in fat creates an essentially dry environment that precludes reactions requiring water. When air is used it may be nearly dry or distinctly wet depending upon whether water is deliberately introduced (wet ovens) or derived only from the food being cooked. Cooking in water maximizes those reactions requiring the presence of water, e.g. gelling of starches and conversion of collagen in flesh foods to gelatin.

In the conventional methods of cooking there will be differences in temperature from the heat source to the centre of each item of food. The temperature differences are influenced by the nature and temperature of the heat source, the heat-conducting properties of any materials between the heat source and the food (e.g. air, cooking vessel, pastry layer, sauce, stock, oil, etc.) and their thickness. It follows that different results will be obtained when using containers of different *thermal conductivity*. For example, for best results daubes (types of stew) are generally cooked in an earthenware pot (daubière) to ensure steady even slow cooking, and certain copper-cooking vessels are often used for high speed cooking. Equally the extent of cooking-induced changes is always greater on the surface of a piece of food than at the centre; the greater the thickness of food, the greater the difference.

There are occasions when it is desirable to emphasize these differences e.g. production of a crisp brown skin on roast potatoes or French fries, the crackling on joints of pork, the semi-solid yolk and firm white of fried and soft boiled eggs. Equally there are occasions where such differences must be controlled, perhaps kept to a minimum. In principle temperature *differences* within a container can be kept to a minimum by agitation of the contents but in practice this might be undesirable where delicate foods could be broken up.

A common method to prevent differences in temperature is to use thin pieces or small portions of food which cook more quickly and more uniformly. For example, using sliced rather than whole potatoes, slicing joints of meat into steaks for grilling, frying or braising. It is possible to fry or grill entrecôte steak so that the centre is cooked and the outside browned but acceptable. It would be quite impossible to fry or grill a whole contrefilet so that the centre was cooked sufficiently without severely overcooking the outside. This problem is overcome by using a lower external temperature and a longer cooking period as used in roasting instead of frying or grilling. The same is true of sliced and whole potatoes, which may be fried, roasted or boiled.

With certain cooking methods there will be a moisture content gradient as well as a temperature gradient caused by the evaporation of moisture from an exposed surface e.g. baking and roasting, which lead to different chemical reactions at the surface compared with the centre. Water lost from the surface may be partially replaced by water moving from the interior towards the surface. This water will carry with it soluble components, particularly sugars and amino-acids, and these will be deposited at the surface as the water evaporates. Such substances are very susceptible to degrade and interact when heated, giving rise to yellow-brown or dark brown colours seen for example on the skin of roast potatoes, the crust of bread or the surface of roasted meats.

Poaching is often very brief and as it is a low temperature process its effects are mild. Frying and grilling are also brief operations that occur at much higher temperatures and are much more severe than poaching and boiling. Stewing is a long operation that permits certain changes to occur to a greater extent than during frying or grilling, and some to a lesser extent. For example, the extensive breakdown of some of the gristle is a very important feature of stewing that does not occur during frying or grilling. In contrast the fat breakdown is rather less. This marked difference occurs because stewing is a wet method, the presence of water facilitating (hydrolytic) reactions such as collagen breakdown. In contrast baking and grilling are relatively dry methods, although steam may be present during baking and foods that are grilled naturally contain water that has been at least partially sealed in the food at the beginning of the process. Cooking by immersing food in fat and oils (deep frying) is also a relatively dry process because a substantial part of the water originally present is boiled away during the frying operation.

It is important to appreciate that, from a scientific point of view, the *total time* of the cooking operation begins with the first application of heat and ends with the consumption of the food. Therefore any period of holding food in a hot condition (e.g. hot plate) prior to service or any reheating process increases the extent to which changes occur. It is quite possible that the effects of holding hot may be greater than the effects of cooking and the total effect could be an undesirable overcooking. Accordingly it can be less harmful to cook or part-cook, cool, and reheat immediately prior to service. If food is held for any length of time it is essential that a temperature is used that will prevent the growth of micro-organisms (e.g. bacteria and fungi).

The precise effects of cooking also depend upon the material being cooked. Fruits and vegetables for example differ considerably from flesh foods in structure and properties. Some of these differences are summarized in the table.

Differences in properties of foods from plant or animal origin

Foods of plant origin	Foods of animal origin
Usually *living* at the time of preparation in the kitchen	Tissues not living at this stage
Tissues have rigid cell walls	Tissues do not have distinct cell walls
Depend largely on turgor pressure* for raw texture – often served raw	Do not depend on turgor pressure for raw texture – rarely served raw
Protein content often low	Protein content often high
Starch content may be high	Starch content essentially low
Fat content usually low	Fat content variable, but usually higher

*Turgor pressure – gives raw foods of plant origin their firm and/or crisp texture before cell walls are damaged and water content is lost by preparation and cooking procedures.

The chemical and physical changes that occur during cooking operations are very complex and beyond the scope of this text but may be viewed as:

(a) physical changes in texture;
(b) chemical changes in flavour and odour;
(c) chemical changes in colour;
(d) chemical changes in nutritive value.

Since this text is not primarily concerned with nutritional aspects, the changes in nutritive value will not be discussed in detail. However everyone relies upon foods to supply the essential nutrients and it is desirable that nutrient losses should be minimized. In general the higher the temperature the longer the time of exposure to a particular temperature, the greater will be the loss. Holding cooked food hot and reheating food are particularly destructive and should only be used when unavoidable. Flavour, odour, texture and colour may also be adversely affected by these practices.

N.B. Students interested in more detailed in-depth information concerned with the above changes should consult a comprehensive food science text (e.g. *An Introduction to Science for Catering and Homecraft Students* by O. F. G. Kilgour, Heinemann: London) however the following notes are included to highlight some of the changes which can be seen during the preparation and cooking of foods.

Why Do We Cook Food?

There are certain dishes where some or all of the ingredients are eaten uncooked. However the majority of foods are cooked or re-heated from a cooked condition prior to service. Important reasons for cooking food are to destroy:

(a) many of the food spoilage micro-organisms;
(b) disease-producing pathogenic micro-organisms;
(c) parasites that were naturally/originally present.

Foods so treated are less susceptible to spoilage provided that there is no contamination after cooking. Accepting that the destruction of dangerous organisms is one reason for the cooking of food, the question as to how raw salads and products, such as steak tartare, can be safe, needs to be answered. Fresh fruits and vegetables are relatively unlikely to contain dangerous micro-organisms or dangerous parasites, and provided they are thoroughly washed during preparation there is little risk. Intact fruit and vegetables are living tissues and relatively resistant to attack by spoilage organisms, but the risk of spoilage rises rapidly once they are bruised or cut.

The muscles of healthy animals are normally free from dangerous micro-organisms but raw meat is more susceptible to contamination with pathogenic and spoilage organisms than raw fruits and vegetables. Accordingly raw meat for products such as steak tartare must be very fresh and handled in conditions of strict hygiene. In the absence of a cooking stage such meat would have to be visually examined for the possible presence of parasites.

A second reason for cooking food is to soften it and make it easy to chew and digest. The gelatinization of starch, the breakdown of proteins and foods' structure are significant in this respect.

A third reason for cooking food is the creation of attractive and interesting ways used to obtain the nutrients required for a healthy life.

Examples of the Effects of Cooking upon Foods

Texture Changes

When protein foods are subjected to cooking, changes in texture may occur which are referred to as setting, gelling and coagulating. Some of these changes can be observed as they occur during the cooking of meat, fish, poultry or eggs, etc. During the poaching of eggs the effect of protein breakdown (denaturation) and coagulation can be clearly seen. These effects may be speeded up by the addition of an acid (vinegar) or salt to the poaching water. The effects of denaturation and coagulation on flesh foods cause shrinkage so that the water and juices are squeezed out. These juices often form the basis of gravies and sauces which accompany the foods. Gently cooked meat on the bone will shrink less than severely cooked meat, or meat off the bone, as the extent of shrinkage depends upon the severity of the heat process, and the time length of exposure. The fact that bone does not shrink during cooking prevents the attached meat from shrinking freely.

Shrinkage of *muscle proteins** occurs at about 65°C. Meat, which is well cooked, will generally reach an internal temperature of about 80°C which is well above the shrinkage point. On the other hand meat which is cooked rare, e.g. beef will only reach an internal temperature of about 65°C and shrinkage will be less.

---

*Scientifically referred to as actin and myosin.

The setting/firming that occurs when cooked joints of meat are allowed to cool is associated with the cooling and setting of the fat that has dispersed throughout the meat during the cooking process.

Connective tissue proteins found in *flesh foods* as opposed to muscle proteins described above, behave differently during cooking. These proteins are commonly known as gristle (scientifically collagen, elastin and reticulin) Collagen when heated in liquid, e.g. stewed, breaks down to form water soluble gelatin. Any meat that is high in connective tissue, e.g. shin (20%) is best cooked by a slow, moist method to make it tender. Alternatively frying steak (3% connective tissue) can be cooked by a faster, dryer method and be tender. Tough stringy meat is due to a larger proportion of elastin and reticulin which do not breakdown during cooking but which can be removed from meat by careful butchery or broken up mechanically by mincing. The collagen found in *fish* is broken down much more easily than that found in meat and consequently many species of fish can be fried or grilled. It is for this reason that fish muscle easily separates (flakes) during cooking because the connective tissue, collagen has denatured to form gelatin. Fish is suited to quick methods of cookery because it contains little connective tissue.

Cooking damages the structure of *fruits* and *vegetables* and causes a rapid loss of turgor pressure (*see* p. 53). Water and water-soluble substances that were originally contained within the food structure are released and pass into air spaces between the cells. When there are extensive air spaces within the foodstuff loss of turgor pressure and replacement of air with water causes very marked changes in appearance and texture. This particular situation is illustrated by comparing cooked cabbage with raw cabbage, which when raw contains some 75% air by volume. Fruit such as apples contain some 25% air by volume but root vegetables such as carrots contain very little and accordingly there is less change in appearance and texture from this cause. The texture of vegetables and fruit is influenced by their composition as well as by cooking. Apples, pears and potatoes show marked differences in texture after cooking, reflecting their different content of several carbohydrates.

Tenderizing Methods

These apply to the preparation and cooking of flesh foods.

Before commenting on tenderizing methods applied in the preparation and cooking of flesh foods it is worth noting that the texture after cooking may vary depending on:

(a) type of animal – mammal, bird, fish, shellfish;
(b) age of animal – older muscles are tougher;
(c) location of muscle – muscles constantly in use tend to be tougher;
(d) fat content – generally the higher the fat content the juicier the texture;
(e) post-slaughter handling – incorrect handling can lead to tough flesh;
(f) cooking procedure – unsuitable cooking methods in relation to the type of flesh will lead to a tough product.

The Modification of Texture

(a) The Slaughter and Hanging of Meat

The slaughter and immediate post-slaughter handling and chilling or freezing of meat influences its quality to a considerable extent. However the caterer has no direct control during this period and must rely upon his supplier. Many caterers purchase sides of meat that are a few days old and these improve in quality if hung at chill temperatures for a period of time, e.g. lamb 3 – 5 days and beef 10 – 17 days. Game is also hung for a substantial period of time.

During this period of hanging, enzymes that are natural components of the flesh cause moderate breakdown of the tissues and produce meat of a more acceptable texture. Prolonged hanging also leads to flavour changes, particularly in game. It is most important that steps are taken during hanging to minimise microbial growth since this could lead to flavour taints or food poisoning, hence the use of chill temperatures, extreme cleanliness and sometimes ultra-violet lights in the store. Traditionally sides are hung from the Achilles tendon (in the ankle) but it is claimed that hanging from the aitch bone (in the thigh) gives more rapid tenderizing since the weight of the carcass pulls the muscle fibres apart. However, this method has less effect upon connective tissues than the traditionally enzymic method.

(b) Tenderizing Meat by Adding Enzymes

Softening (tenderization) occurs when enzymes are added to certain cuts/joints of meat for a period of time before cooking. Traditionally such enzymes are derived by introducing certain fresh fruits into the culinary product and the cooking process. Examples include meat cooked with fresh pineapple, figs, and papaya. Nowadays it is possible to purchase enzyme extracts, which can be sprinkled directly on to the meat's surface, thus avoiding the need for fresh tropical fruit and their flavouring effects.

It is important to appreciate that these added enzymes attack the meat from the outside and penetrate slowly. Further these enzymes are still active during the early stages of cooking and it is the outer layers that receive most heat and thus greater enzyme activity. Under such circumstances there is a very real risk of excessive softening (mushiness) on the outside and toughness at the centre.

An alternative approach is to inject the enzyme (typically papain derived from papaya) into the veins of the animal 30 minutes prior to slaughter. The heart and blood vessels then distribute the enzyme to all tissues of the animal (including the centre of large muscles that are to become large joints) prior to slaughter. After slaughter these enzymes operate in addition to those that were naturally present. If for some reason the animal is not slaughtered within approximately one hour of injection the enzyme is destroyed by the animals defence mechanisms and the animal suffers no harm. Carcases that have been so tenderized are available commercially. It is claimed that enzyme treatment before slaughter yields from a regular side of beef 70% of cuts suited to dry heat processing whereas without treatment only 30% of such cuts would be obtained.

Disadvantages of the treatment are over-tenderization of kidneys and tongue. It is said that the treated kidneys are well suited to uses where flavour rather than texture are required, and the tongue can be used provided the cooking process is more gentle than normal.

It is claimed that this enzyme treatment not only reduces inherent toughness but also reduces toughness induced by incorrect slaughter and post-slaughter cooling operations.

(c) Mincing

This breaks up the muscle of the connective tissue by mechanical means thus making chewing easier.

(d) Marinading

Marinades are essentially a mixture of oil and acid, which may be further flavoured by the addition of vegetables, herbs, seasoning, wine and/or spirit. Meats and fish can be marinaded in such mixtures for predetermined lengths of time to enhance flavour, in some instances effect colour changes, and generally tenderize the product. Any tenderizing effects are probably a result of alterations in acidity to a value that permits the protein to bind more water and dissolve some collagen into gelatin before cooking. These changes favour the continued conversion of collagen into gelatin during the subsequent cooking period.

(e) Pounding

Pounding is a milder form of mincing, which separates some of the fibres.

Flavour and Odour Changes

The chemistry of the flavour and odour of both raw and cooked foods is complex. Thousands of chemical compounds are known to possess specific odour and flavours and usually the smell or taste complex of any raw or cooked food contains at least 50 and possibly more than 500 such compounds, which are present in minute quantities. Changes of smell and taste that occur during cooking reflect the destruction of raw food compounds and the formation of new compounds in the cooked product. The majority of odour and flavour compounds are concentrated in the fatty components of food.

For example the fat content of meat plays an important role in contributing to juiciness after the cooking stage. During cooking the fat melts and passes through the tissues, with some passing into the drippings, also fat that is spread on the surface of meat melts and diffuses through the tissues making it more succulent. In such operations the surface temperature is sufficiently high for some fat breakdown to occur which leads to the production of characteristic odour and flavour.

Following standard recipes and procedures helps to prevent unwanted reactions since the most likely causes of unpleasant odour and flavour are:

(a) incorrect recipe balance and procedure;
(b) using inferior quality ingredients;

Incorrect cooking, e.g. overheating, localized heating due to lack of agitation or movement, can lead to overcooked, burnt, tough and bitter tasting products due to a greater than normal destruction of the ingredients present.

Starch has the ability to bind flavour and odour compounds and reduce their intensity. The harshness of overspiced products can often be corrected by adding a small quantity of starch or starch-rich ingredient.

Colour Changes

Changes in the colour of certain vegetables and fruit occur before cooking takes place and are a result of enzymic browning.

Enzymic Browning

Certain vegetables and fruits turn brown or even darker in colour when cut or damaged and exposed to air (enzymic browning). This can be minimized as follows:

(a) Adding an acid (citric acid or lemon juice)—to adjust the pH value to a level that inhibits enzymic browning.
(b) Heating—this action may however cause undesirable changes in texture and flavour.

(c) Immersion in water or coating cut surfaces with a thin film of melted butter/oil—these procedures minimize browning because they exclude oxygen from the surfaces.

Common examples of products susceptible to enzymic browning are peeled apples, potatoes, bananas, and pears. In the case of fried mushrooms enzymic browning contributes beneficially to their colour.

The Effects of Preparation and Cooking upon Foods – Colour and Colour Changes

The colour of food influences customer acceptability. Abnormal colours (discoloration) will rarely occur unless tainted ingredients and/or incorrect procedures are used.

Plant Foods

The colouring pigment of green vegetables is chlorophyll. Unless it is partially degraded, chlorophyll is not soluble in water. Loss in colour through normal cooking methods is therefore low and usually unimportant. However on contact with acid (which may come from the vegetable itself) chlorophyll is converted to a brownish pigment which results in vegetable discoloration. Such discoloration can be prevented as follows.

Adding an Alkali to the Cooking Water   Sodium bicarbonate – N.B. excessive additions will result in the destruction of vitamin C and thiamine and soften the vegetable's texture excessively.

Cooking in an Open Vessel   As most of the acids are volatile they are removed with the steam. In these cases it is wise to renew the cooking water for each batch of cooking. This method avoids the need to use sodium bicarbonate.

Traditionally the discoloration was avoided by adding copper in the form of a coin. This is not to be recommended since copper is poisonous.

Pale Coloured Fruits and Vegetables (e.g. potato, parsnip, onion)

These contain substances, which when cooked in alkaline water, take on a yellow/cream colour. This colour change is not severe and therefore presents no problem in catering operations. If desirable the addition of a few drops of acid (lemon juice) to the cooking water avoids this colour change.

Strongly Coloured Fruits and Vegetables (e.g. carrot, tomato, red pepper, pineapple, citrus fruits and radish)

These contain carotenoid pigments, which remain fairly stable on cooking. The result is a slight reduction in the colour intensity of such products.

The Soft and Stone Fruits (e.g. strawberries, raspberries, cherries, etc.)

These contain red or purple pigments, which are water soluble. Such foods loose pigment if they are damaged then placed in cold water and also by cooking. If these pigments are treated with alkaline water they change from purple/red to blue/green, a reaction which is reversed by the addition of an acid (lemon juice). Normally the fruits themselves are sufficiently acidic and resist this change in the first instance.

Some of these fruits react with iron and other metals, e.g. tin, aluminium to produce bluish tints. Accordingly they should not be cooked in, or handled in utensils made of these metals.

A few vegetables contain red or purple pigments and should be treated similarly, the most common of these being red cabbage.

Beetroot

This contains unique pigments, which are water soluble and which show a slight colour change in alkaline water of no consequence to the caterer.

Foods of Animal Origins

The main pigments of meat and poultry are haemoglobin in the blood and myoglobin in the muscle. Meat normally contains far more myoglobin than haemoglobin since most of the blood is removed at slaughter. However, the chemical properties of haemoglobin are essentially identical to those of myoglobin and thus when blood is present or added e.g. to some stews) the changes that occur will be as described here for myoglobin.

The content of myoglobin varies, being higher in the dark muscles of meat, fish and poultry than in the pale muscles. This variation is clearly illustrated in crab, mackerel, pork and chicken. Whatever the hue, fresh meat (i.e. not frozen) should have a relatively bright surface and duller interior. If this is not so then the meat should be rejected since it has been poorly handled. However, it must be noted that protein denaturation caused by freezing leads to a duller surface colour without necessarily indicating lower quality.

The colour produced after cooking depends upon the amounts of pigment present in the raw meat and the severity of the cooking process. Mild heating converts myoglobin to *haemochrome* which is pink and typical of lightly-cooked steak. Further heating converts *haemochrome* to a grey-brown *haemichrome* which is typical of a well-cooked steak.

Green colours should never be encountered but if they are they indicate gross microbial contamination and such meat is unfit for human consumption.

Meat, fish and particularly shellfish also contain carotenoid pigments. When found in meat they impart a yellow colour to the fat. This is most frequently encountered with beef and implies that the meat is from an old animal and that it may therefore be tough. Carotenoids in fish are usually red or pink and examples include redfish, salmon, and tuna. Similar colours may also be encountered in crustacean shellfish, but this type of fish may also contain blue caroteno-protein complexes. Cooking causes the complex to break and give rise to the more typical orange-red carotenoid colour, e.g. lobster shell turns from bluey black to red/orange on cooking.

Milk, dairy products and egg yolks are coloured mainly by carotenoids and the colour intensity mainly reflects the carotenoid content of the feed the animal received. High pigmentation is not necessarily a sign of high quality.

Discoloration that may be encountered in fish and shellfish includes a rusty colour on the cut surface of white fish fillets and a black colour (black spot) on prawns and shrimps. The former is caused by incorrect bleeding of the fish after capture and the latter by incorrect handling of the prawns which permits an enzymic browning type of reaction to occur. There is little the caterer can do except reject the material and, if necessary, change supplier.

Prepared Foods

Many foods take on a yellow or brown colour as a result of cooking. Typically the reactions responsible are known as non-enzymic browning and are chemically complex. The colour-producing ingredients are typically sugars and amino acids or protein, but may be modified by other ingredients particularly acids. Often colours of this type are considered desirable, e.g. caramel, toast, roasted coffee but on occasion they may appear when not required, e.g. in white sauces, fruit juices and typically indicate over-heating. Although typical of prepared foods these reactions may occur in, for example, cooked meat, and make an important and desirable contribution to the colour particularly of the paler meats after cooking, e.g. pork and chicken.

One typical reaction in which proteins may participate is called non-enzymic or *Maillard browning*. This reaction gives the characteristic brown colouring and flavour of cooked foods, meat in particular, and although some nutritive value is lost in the process, it is offset by the increased attractiveness of the food and, therefore, its greater palatability.

4

Thickening and Binding Mechanisms

The mechanisms by which culinary products are thickened to varying degrees can be subdivided into three separate processes: starch thickening; protein coagulation; and emulsification.

Starch Thickening

Starches may be isolated from many plants, and when pure they are white, odourless, tasteless powders. Often instead of pure starches, starch-rich materials, e.g. cereals and pulses, are used as thickeners and these may be slightly coloured and have characteristic but acceptable odours and flavours. Because starch is a major component these starch-rich materials behave similarly but not identically to pure starches. Starches are commonly available from the kitchen stores in the following forms.

The nature of commodities commonly used as sources of starch

White flour	Produced from wheat. Also contains protein and fat
Cornflour	Purified maize starch
Arrowroot	A powdered root consisting almost exclusively of starch. Sometimes referred to as a fécula or fécule
Tapioca	Powdered cassava root, also a fécula and as a thickening agent very similar to arrowroot.
Fécule	Potato powder, perhaps the commonest fécula
Starchy vegetables	Potato as a fresh vegetable has a much higher moisture content and therefore lower starch content than the powder described above.
Split peas ⎱ Lentils ⎰	Starch-rich pulses also containing protein and a little fat.
Farinaceous materials	Also known as cereals; include barley and rice grains. Protein and fat are also present
Special starches	Starches isolated from plants which in some cases are chemically treated to meet particular requirements. Almost pure starches. Examples include waxy maize starch, waxy rice starch, pregelatinized starches, freeze-thaw resistant starches

---

The Use of Starches and Starch-rich Materials as Thickeners

As previously stated, various starches are used as thickening agents in many culinary instances. For example starch-rich materials in the form of pulses, cereal (rice) or starchy vegetables (potato) are used in the making and thickening of pulse and purée soups. Alternatively starch-rich materials are added to boiling liquids in the form of rice grains or barley when producing broth-type soups. In some cases dry forms of starch granules are added directly to boiling liquids, e.g. semolina, wheatflour or potato powder in the production of pasta, pastry, and potato mixes. However the practice of adding dry starch granules to boiling liquids is the exception rather than the rule, and it should be noted that in these instances starch clumping can easily occur resulting in lumpy, indigestible products. In most cases *raw* starch granules are dispersed and separated in oil, fat or cold liquid before they come into contact with heated liquids. Once starches are heated in a plentiful supply of liquid certain reactions occur, which effect the release of starch molecules from starch-rich materials and starch granules. These reactions, when controlled by the skilled cook, result in products taking on varying degrees of consistency, both when the product is hot and when it is cooled e.g. basic béchamel has a coating consistency when hot but sets firm when cooled in readiness for storage.

The role of the skilled cook when preparing starch-thickened products is an important one. The aim is to achieve overall product quality in terms of texture, consistency, appearance, flavour, temperature, and yield. The techniques used are many and include adequate dispersal of raw starch grains in the roux, manipulated butter or cold liquid. These processes should ensure that each granule is free to take part in the thickening/gelatinization process. Using the correct recipe balance and method, and thorough stirring (agitation) at all stages of preparation and cooking should prevent starch clumping and lumpiness as these techniques permit each granule to gelatinize freely. In the case of roux production further complications can arise:

(a) If the fat used contains water as is the case with meat dripping or butter, it should be cooled to a moderate temperature before the flour is added. Water in the fat at a high temperature could cause rapid, partial gelatinization and lumpiness in exactly the same way as insufficient liquid.

(b) If fat, whether it contains water or not is used at too high a temperature or there is a delay in the subsequent addition of liquid, the starch could break-down (dextrinize) and lose some of its thickening power.

N.B.   There are some occasions where the 'browning' associated with dextrinization is desirable. The loss of thickening power in these instances is overcome either by adding more starch in relation to the liquid or cooking the product for longer periods. An apt example of the latter is the production of Espagnole where the longer cooking period allows the sauce to reduce (by evaporation) to the required consistency.

In order to produce thickened products using starch-rich vegetables, cereals, or sauces it is essential to release and/or disperse the starch available within these materials. This is usually achieved by passing the cooked products through manual or motorized mechanical devices: passing pulse, purée, cream and certain velouté-type soups through a mouli, liquidizer, or vertical cutter/mixer in order to extract and or disperse the gelatinized starch.

Essentially these processes can be seen as the cook extracting gelatinized starch from a commodity to achieve thickening (consistency) and in some cases to establish a predominant flavour.

Flavours

Starches also have the ability to bind chemical components, which are responsible for flavour. This can be seen when strong-flavoured stock is tasted before and after the addition of a starch thickener. These effects can be overcome by adding more flavour contributing agents e.g. stock concentrates, and by using well balanced formulae (recipes). The quantity of starch or starch-rich material in any recipe should be dependent upon:

(a) the consistency aimed at in any finished product;
(b) the influence of the starch upon a product's flavour;
(c) the amount of starch available in the commodities used.

Consistency

Throughout the practical studies it will be seen that often different quantities of starch-rich materials in relation to similar amounts of liquid are used to achieve a like consistency. For example, when preparing purée soups from aqueous (watery) vegetables a similar consistency is achieved by using either $\frac{1}{20}$ rice to 1 unit stock, or alternatively $\frac{1}{10}$ raw potato to 1 unit stock (*see* p. 117). This illustrates that the quantities of starch-rich materials, e.g. rice or potatoes used in recipes to achieve similar consistencies may vary because the starch-rich materials themselves vary in the percentage of starch they contain. Therefore, different amounts of starch-rich materials may be used to provide similar amounts of starch in order to achieve the required consistency. The table below shows the approximate percentages of starch contained in various starch-rich commodities.

Commodity	Approximate percentage of starch
Arrowroot	90
Cornflour	90
Barley	80
Rice	80
Wheat flour (white)	78
Semolina	70
Lentils	50
Split-peas	50
Potato	17

It is worth noting that when certain types of thickened soups are produced using mainly aqueous vegetables (vegetables which are mainly comprised of water and contain little or no starch), the starch is introduced into the product by another ingredient. A good example is the addition of béchamel sauce in the production of aqueous vegetable cream soups (*see* p.119). The table below illustrates the approximate starch content of some common aqueous vegetables.

Commodity	Approximate percentage of starch
Onion	0.5
Asparagus	0.4
Cauliflower	0.4
Carrot	nil
Cucumber	nil
Lettuce	nil
Mushroom	nil

Comments on Consistencies Achieved when Using Wheat Flour, Cornflour, and Arrowroot as Starch Thickeners

When added to, and cooked with foods correctly, the consistencies achieved using these components will be chiefly determined by the relative proportions of starch and liquid employed. The table below is intended as an approximate guide to illustrate ratios commonly used in many traditional recipes. The starches referred to are those commonly used in daily kitchen practice but others could well be substituted. The ratios given are meant as guidelines only and not as exactitudes because the quantities required depend upon the specific properties of the different starches.

Approximate ratios of starch to liquid used to achieve varying sauce consistencies

	Basic Pouring Unit	Basic Coating Unit	Basic Binding Unit
Liquid	1	1	1
Starch	$\frac{1}{20}$	$\frac{1}{10}$	$\frac{1}{5}$

In practical sauce making the starch is commonly used in the form of a roux, a manipulated mixture, e.g. beurre manié (*see* p. 82) or as a temporary suspension, and the basic consistencies may well be adjusted (usually by adding more liquid) to suit culinary requirements.

Other Ingredients

The behaviour of starches and starch-rich ingredients is modified if other materials are present, and it makes no difference whether they are natural components of the starch-rich ingredients or a separate ingredient in the recipe.

Sugars

Sugars are available in the form of sucrose (cane or beet sugar), glucose, invert sugar, confectioner's glucose, golden syrup, etc. These ingredients may be used to sweeten starch-based products such as sauces, puddings, and fillings but these sugars also reduce the rate of gelatinization and give a softer and more liquid texture on cooling. The rate of gelatinization is reduced because the sugar 'removes' some of the water. Because of the slower gelatinization the viscosity is lower at a given degree of cooking and full cooking requires a longer period than in the absence of sugars. The magnitude of the effect is proportional to the amount of sugar added to the starch and many recipes advocate where possible the addition of sugar after gelatinization has been achieved, e.g. sugar added to sauces after they have been thickened. Although the various sugars show similar effects, they are not identical and it is not always a simple matter to change the sweetening agent in a recipe.

Acids

Acids modify the behaviour of starch-based products if present in sufficient quantity and will normally be encountered in the form of vinegars, wines, fruit juices or fruit purées. These acidic ingredients break down (hydrolyse) the large starch molecules and reduce the thickening power. This thinning effect can be overcome by using a greater amount of starch or starch-rich ingredient or by using a starch that is resistant, e.g. the starch from waxy maize or other type of modified starch. A simpler traditional way is to add the acidic component after the gelatinization stage, e.g. adding lemon juice to lemon meringue pie filling once the sauce base has gelatinized, using prepared demi-glace sauce with acids as in many derivative brown sauces. Some highly spiced oriental dishes contain starch and acidic fruit juices (typically lemon or another citrus juice). Once again the fruit juice is added towards the end of the cooking period.

Proteins

Proteins have quite marked effects upon starch-water mixtures and this is well illustrated by comparing the results of stirring cornflour (maize starch) in cold water with the result of treating wheat flour (starch 80%, proteins approximately 10%) similarly. The former (cornflour) separates out and the latter absorbs water to form a sticky elastic paste making it ideal for use with batters.

Proteins are added to starch-based formulations in many ways including egg, milk, gelatin or flesh foods. It should be noted that the incorporation of such ingredients will, by adding other materials further modify the behaviour of the starch. Usually the addition of proteins will yield some improvement in freeze-thaw stability (*see* below). Milk proteins for example help to stabilize white sauces and gelatin can be used to stabilize thick custard-based trifles. This property is associated with the ability of proteins to form three-dimensional gels and to bind water very strongly. However proteins alone are insufficient to impart freeze-thaw stability to products.

Chemically Modified Starches

When naturally occurring starches have not provided the properties required for certain catering operations food scientists have been able to obtain the desired properties by chemically modifying the natural starch. Examples include the following.

Freeze-thaw Resistant Starches

These are manufactured for use as a thickening agent in products, which are to undergo freezing and frozen storage for determined periods of time, prior to reconstitution. These starches may be used in recipes to replace natural starches or starch-rich materials and in some instances are used in conjunction with natural starches. The introduction of freeze-thaw resistant starches acts to prevent the separation of the starch from the liquid which would leave a lumpy, curdled product.

Pregelatinized or Cold-water Soluble Starches

The basis of this modification is to pre-cook the starch, to dry the product and grind it to a powder. This process can be applied to natural or modified starches and some very useful water-soluble starches are available. Perhaps the greatest use of these is in packaged instant puddings.

Syneresis (weeping)

On standing many gelatinized products release liquid and the gel structure shrinks. Commonly this phenomena is known as weeping. It can be recognized when the liquid collects around the edge of, for example, custard or a mould of gelatin products.

Protein Gelation and Coagulation

One of the most familiar but least understood changes which food proteins undergo is the change of state from a liquid to a solid. To understand this process it is necessary to know something of the nature of proteins, the causes and effects of protein breakdown (denaturation) and the associative reactions that may follow.

Denaturation (Protein Breakdown)

Proteins, which are present in plant and animal tissue, are referred to as native proteins. The application of heat and indeed other operations related to catering e.g. freezing, drying, foaming and exposure to acids also cause proteins to denature. Denaturation and the associative reactions that follow allow the proteins to take part in changes of state commonly referred to as gelling, setting, and coagulation. Many culinary products illustrate these changes, which result in their taking on a firm or relatively rigid texture. The following products illustrate these points:

(a) Baked egg custard – egg proteins coagulate during the cooking process giving the finished product a relatively rigid texture.
(b) Cooked meringues – egg white proteins are partially broken down during the whisking process and the meringues made firm by the application of gentle heat.
(c) Aspic jelly – aspic sets firm once the gelatin within it has been sufficiently heated and cooled to encourage gelation.

N.B.   For the use of proteins as an emulsifier *see* p. 67 on emulsifications.

Binding Agents

Culinary binding agents seem to have been little studied from a scientific point of view. They must however be cohesive (shape-retaining) and in some cases adhesive materials (i.e. able to bind). Those in common use are based upon either cooked (gelatinized) starches, or proteins or mixtures of both. The starch-based binders often take the form of thick binding sauces, breadcrumbs, cooked potato, etc. The commonest protein-based binder is egg, heating is required to coagulate the egg proteins and produce a permanent shape-retaining effect. An extensively used starch and protein-based binder is known as a panada. Wheatflour could also be included in this category, but it should be noted that the initial binding ability is derived from the proteins (gluten) but the final shape-retaining ability is derived in part from the gelatinized starch as well as the gluten.

Emulsification (Emulsions and foams)

An emulsion represents a more or less stable association between two substances (ingredients), which would not normally mix together, e.g. oil and water, gas and solids (foams). These substances are normally immiscible. To clarify this concept examples of emulsions foams encountered in catering are listed on pp. 68 – 9. These can be described as being:

(a) oil-in-water emulsions, e.g. mayonnaise;
(b) water-in-oil/fat emulsions, e.g. butter;
(c) gas-in-solid/liquid foams e.g. cakes, breads, soufflés, meringues.

All emulsions (foams) consist of a *continuous phase* throughout which a *dispersed* phase is distributed. For example when producing sauce mayonnaise oil (the dispersed phase) is distributed throughout the vinegar/lemon juice (the water-based continuous phase). Alternatively when butter and margarine are produced, water (the dispersed phase) is distributed throughout the plastic-like butter fat (the continuous phase). Meringue is a good example of air (the dispersed gas phase) being distributed throughout a network of egg albumen (the continuous phase) that has been mixed with sugar. Cakes, breads, hot soufflés also illustrate the dispersion of air throughout a plastic-type network of protein (gluten), starch and perhaps fat. The examples in which a gas (air) is dispersed throughout a solid are referred to as *foams*.

Emulsion Breakdown

When an emulsion breaks it is because the once dispersed phase, e.g. oil droplets in mayonnaise, has associated to such an extent that it can no longer be contained in the continuous phase, which in this example is vinegar. Breakdown or separation is seen as the curdled appearance of mayonnaise as the oily layer separates and rises to the surface, or as a foam collapsing. In order to produce a stable emulsion it is necessary to distribute one phase throughout the other (or in practical terms one ingredient throughout the other) and to inhibit or prevent their separation. This distribution and stability is achieved by whisking/agitation and where necessary by introducing an emulsifying agent into the recipe.

The Presence of Emulsifying Agents

Emulsifying agents can be seen as molecules having two parts, one of which is soluble in oil and the other in water. These emulsifying agents act to reduce the tension between the water and the oil by forming a bridge at the junction of the oil and water phases. For example in mayonnaise production this process allows the emulsifiers to form a film around each oil droplet which prevents the oil from running together and associating.

Proteins are one of the most common emulsifying agents and are used in the form of egg yolk, milk, wheatflour, or gelatin. Their use favours the production of oil in water emulsions.

Phospholipids (fat-like substances concentrated in the yolk of egg), which include the substance known as lecithin, are potent emulsifying agents generally used in the form of egg yolks but are available as commercial extracts.

Perhaps the best known commercially available synthetic emulsifying agent is GMS – glyceryl monostearate.

Notes on Emulsion Breakdown

As previously stated emulsions break because the dispersed phase, be it oil, water, or air, associates. Some of the factors and/or conditions common to catering practices which may influence such breakdown are commented on below.

Temperature and its Effects

In an emulsion such as butter the continuous fat phase is solid at ordinary temperatures and the dispersed water droplets cannot move at all. When butter is warmed the fat melts and the water droplets become free to move more easily. Consequently they associate and the emulsion breaks. The spattering of butter in the frying pan is a result of the water droplets sinking through the melted butter oil and coming into contact with the heated base of the pan. At this point they boil violently and explode through the oil layer.

In the production of Hollandaise sauce the skill of the cook when applying heat is critical if a stable emulsion is to be produced. Overheating of the egg yolks in the early stages can cause them to coagulate and curdle. Adding the melted butter at too high a temperature could lead to the same result. If this sauce is held at too high a temperature for any length of time its consistency becomes runny, the oil droplets are then free to associate, which results in the breakdown of the emulsion. Alternatively if this particular sauce is stored at too low a temperature the butter fat solidifies and once again there is a breakdown in the emulsion. When producing mayonnaise the oil is often warmed to ensure that any semi-congealed oil caused by cool temperatures is reversed to an oily consistency. This facilitates the coating of oil droplets with emulsifying agent – egg yolk.

Chilling and freezing of some emulsions e.g. mayonnaise but not butter can lead to separation of the phases during chill storage or on thawing. Whether or not separation occurs during chill storage is largely determined by the freezing characteristics of the oil. Even a so-called pure oil consists of many oil fractions that have separate freezing points, for example pure olive oil will cloud at chill temperatures because some of the oil fractions have frozen. These easily freezable fractions may be removed by filtering (sieving) and an oil so treated is said to be winterized. Winterized oils are better suited for use in salad dressings, sauces etc. that are to be chilled or frozen.

Oils differ in their requirements for winterization. Safflower oil is stable to $-7°C$ but must be winterized for use at $-12°C$. It cannot be economically winterized for use at $-18°C$ because too great a percentage of oil solidifies at this temperature. Corn oil and soyabean oil do not require winterization for use at refrigeration temperatures. Groundnut oil is suitable for use at frozen storage temperatures because it forms a non-crystalline (amorphous) mass on freezing rather than crystalline structures. To minimize crystal formation freezing must be rapid, i.e. by blast freezer and not in a frozen storage cabinet. Freezing may damage the emulsifying agent layer on the dispersed phase, particularly in the case of proteins, which may be denatured. Frozen egg yolks therefore are less successful for mayonnaise production than are fresh egg yolks.

N.B. See pp. 98 and 101 for practical information concerning the preparation of Hollandaise and mayonnaise sauces.

The nature of some common emulsions and foams

Emulsion (foam)	
Milk	Oil (approximately $3\frac{1}{2}\%$) dispersed in a continuous phase of water containing proteins, sugar, acids and salts. Proteins are the main emulsifying agent. Emulsion not indefinitely stable (cream collects at the surface) unless homogenized.
Butter	Water (not exceeding 16% by law), which may contain salt, dispersed in a continuous phase of semi-solid (plastic) butter fat. Stabilized mainly by rigidity of the continuous phase.
Margarine	Essentially as butter but incorporating non-dairy fats
Dairy cream (natural)	Milk fat and air dispersed in a continuous phase of water containing proteins, acids, sugar and salts. The fat content is controlled by law; single cream 18% fat; double cream 48% fat; whipping cream 35% fat. Proteins act as emulsifiers
Non-dairy cream (synthetic)	Essentially as dairy cream but incorporating non-dairy fats.
Ice-cream	Oil and air dispersed in sugar, syrup or cornflour starch paste and ice. Air content may be 50% or more *by volume*. Fat content controlled by law and typically not less than 5%. Type of fat (dairy/non-dairy) also controlled by law. Emulsifying agent depends on type but may be milk or egg proteins or added synthetic emulsifier

Mayonnaise	Oil (not less than 25% by law and typically 70–80% by weight) and air (10% by volume) dispersed in vinegar or lemon juice and emulsified by egg-yolk proteins or lecithin
Hollandaise	Similar to the above but typically 40–50% oil by weight
Choux pastry	Oil dispersed in wheat dough containing eggs. The proteins of egg and flour function as emulsifying agents
Some sauces, gravies, soups	Oil fat dispersed in water containing salt and starch or various vegetables, meat, etc. For example the addition of a liaison to soup, sauce, white stews
Cakes and breads (including unleavened breads)	Air dispersed in a plastic network of protein, starch and perhaps fat. The air volume varies considerably and may have been whipped in, generated by yeast action or by chemical action using baking powder or baking soda and cream of tartar
Meringue	Air dispersed in a network of egg albumen (egg white protein) that has been mixed with sugar

Illustrative Kitchen-scale Science Experiments

The experiments outlined below have been chosen to illustrate some of the points made in this section. They can all be performed in a kitchen.

1 To Show the Stability of an Emulsion

Mix equal volumes of oil and water.
Whisk briskly and put aside.
Repeat using milk and 2% gelatine or liquid egg instead of water.
Compare the time required for the emulsion to break and note where appropriate the formation of a foam.

2 To Show the Effect of Synthetic Emulsifier on Emulsion Stability

Repeat experiment 1 with the addition of available synthetic emulsifiers (or a few drops of washing-up liquid). Note how effective these agents are in producing stable emulsions.

3 To Show Spattering

Heat butter or margarine gently in a saucepan.
Transfer to a glass vessel and note the separation of the dispersed aqueous phase.
Heat butter or margarine in a frying pan and cautiously note the tendency to spatter.
Repeat using fresh lard and note that this does not spatter since it does not contain water.

4 To Show Winterizing

Place samples of the available pure oils and mayonnaise in a refrigerator.
Similarly place samples in a deep freeze.
After one day's storage check for signs of cloudiness. If you now chill a sieve you will be able to remove the solid fat (a sieve at room temperature might remelt the solid fat) and thus winterize the oil.
This filtered oil on storing in the same conditions for a further day will show much less cloudiness than the original oil.

5 To Show that Different Starches Behave Differently when Heated in Water

Prepare pouring consistency sauces (1 in 20 or 5%) using e.g. cornflour (maize starch), fécule (potato starch), arrowroot, tapioca, and any chemically modified starches available.

Treat all in the same way. Note and compare the thickness of the hot gels or pastes and the nature of the gels or pastes on cooling, i.e. colour, consistency, odour, and taste.

6   To Show the Effect of other Ingredients on Starch Behaviour

(a)   Prepare pouring consistency sauces using cornflour (maize starch) in:

  (i)   water;
  (ii)   water containing 1% citric acid, lemon juice or vinegar;
  (iii)   water containing 5% sugar;
  (iv)   milk.

Critically examine the products for thickness of the hot sauce, nature of sauces on cooling, i.e. colour, consistency, odour, and taste.

   (b)   Stir cornflour into cold water and allow to stand. Using the same proportions similarly treat wheat flour. Compare the appearance and consistency of these products. If a cold-water soluble pregelatinized starch is available the behaviour of this is worth comparing with cornflour and wheat flour.

7   Comparison of Freeze-thaw Stability

Prepare pouring consistency sauces using any available starches or starch-rich ingredients. Those sauces prepared in experiment 5 are ideal. Place individually into convenient containers and freeze. Leave in frozen storage for a week, then remove and allow to thaw. Examine for signs of weeping and curdling and where these changes are detected try to regenerate the sauce by the use of heat alone. If this is unsuccessful then try heating plus stirring. Decide which starches are most convenient for use in freeze-thaw recipes.

5

Basics of Culinary Practice

Mise-en-place translated means 'put in place', in kitchen terms it refers to organized advanced preparation of basic materials in both a raw and cooked state. Such mise-en-place enables the kitchen staff to cook and present food for service with the minimum of difficulty and in good time.

Organized working methods, partnered by knowledge, skill and innate talent are the chef's roadway to successful cookery. Whether the culinary delight be simple or exotic, well planned mise-en-place is essential if a smooth operation is to be achieved.

Basic mise-en-place for stove work is divided into the following groups:

1. basic flavourings in common use;
2. basic garnishes and other common preparations;
3. basic stocks essences and glazes. Thickening and binding agents;
4. basic sauces,—foundation and non-derivative types.

Basic Flavourings and their Uses

Flavourings are used to enhance the taste of a variety of savoury preparations. During the production of food for the table there are a number of basic flavourings that are frequently employed. They may be added in good measure, or in small amounts, according to the strength of the flavouring desired in the completed dish. A flavouring, therefore, may play a major role in the taste of a product or be used to savour delicately. For example:

(a) thyme is used to predominate when preparing thyme and parsley stuffing, but is used more delicately in stews and soups as part of the bouquet garni.
(b) garlic is used to predominate when preparing garlic flavoured butter, but used more delicately as a flavouring in French onion soup. Flavourings are infused, extracted or added just prior to service.

Flavourings in Common use

Bouquet Garni (an infused flavouring)

Consists of a variety of selected herbs and vegetables, neatly secured in a leek leaf or piece of muslin. The flavouring is used delicately, as over use would result in the bouquet garni predominating.

1 sprig of thyme
1 bay leaf
1 small piece of celery
few parsley stalks, few crushed peppercorns

Other herbs may be used to complement a particular flavour, e.g. basil with tomato, rosemary with lamb. The bouquet can be purchased commercially in made-up sachets.

Onion Clouté (piqué) — an infused flavouring

A peeled onion into which a selected number of cloves are pressed, one of which impales a bay leaf to the onion.

1 medium onion
4 cloves
1 bay leaf

Also referred to as a studded onion.

1
MIREPOIX (AN EXTRACTED FLAVOUR)

Mirepoix in a culinary sense indicates the use of a basic preparation of roughly cut vegetables, sometimes with pieces of streaky bacon, and a pinch of aromates.

Unit	Ingredient	Metric (g)	Imperial (oz)
1	Onion	400	16
1	Carrot	400	16
$1/2$	Celery	200	8
$1/4$	Streaky bacon ⎫ optional Aromates ⎭	100	4

Method and Uses

Roughly cut the prepared vegetables to the selected size. *A fine cut* is used when a speedy extraction of flavour is required, e.g. in sauce reductions, this ensures maximum extraction of flavour in the shortest possible time. *A medium cut* is employed when a lengthy 'sweating' process is used in the initial cooking stage, e.g. soups and stews. This larger size reduces the risk of over-cooking (burning). The full extraction of flavour is completed by the end of the cooking period. *A large cut* is often used when the mirepoix is employed as a base upon which pieces of meat are braised or pot-roasted. The large cut reduces the risk of the vegetables burning and full extraction of flavour is achieved by the end of the cooking time.

fine cut — brunoise
medium cut — 1 cm ($1/2$ in) approximately.
large cut — size determined by size of cooking vessel

Vegetable Adjunct (an extracted flavour)

Used and prepared as for mirepoix but omitting one or more of the ingredients, e.g. carrot would be omitted where a white colour is required in a finished product, e.g. cream of cauliflower soup. During the preparation of curry sauce, onion is used as a vegetable flavouring.

Scorched Mirepoix/Vegetable Adjunct

Vegetables browned on a hot griddle plate.

Preserved Garlic (an added flavour)

Crush the cloves of garlic with the flat side of a chopping knife and remove the outer skin. Sprinkle the crushed cloves liberally with salt and chop this mixture finely. Put into a suitable container and cover the preserved garlic with edible oil for storage. The oil acts as a seal and reduces the risk of discoloration. Garlic is chopped in salt

(a) to facilitate ease of chopping;
(b) to absorb the 'oil' from the garlic released during chopping;
(c) to act as a preservative.

Due to the high concentration of salt in this preparation, care must be exercised when seasoning foods to which preserved garlic has been added. Correctly stored, the prepared garlic will keep in good condition for a long period. It may be used to enhance the flavour of selected soups, stews, sauces, entrées, etc.

Garlic Pellets (an added flavour)

Finely chop or mince fat bacon and combine with chopped parsley. Add a hint of freshly chopped or preserved garlic and shape into small pellets. Used to flavour minestrone.

2
DUXELLE (AN ADDED FLAVOUR)
A savoury mixture used for stuffings, fillings and sauces.
Yield: 400 g (1 lb)
Cooking time: 5 min

Unit	Ingredient	Metric (g)	Imperial (oz)
1	Mushroom trimmings (brunoise)	400	16
1/2	Onion brunoise	200	8
1/8	Butter/oil	50	2
	Chopped parsley		
	Hint of garlic		
	Pinch of nutmeg		
	Salt and pepper		

To Prepare as a Stuffing

Add 1/4 unit (100 g [4 oz]) fresh breadcrumbs to the basic cooked duxelle and sufficient tomatoed demi-glace to develop a suitable texture.

Method

Place the onions and mushrooms into the melted butter and oil, sweat over a gentle heat without colouring. Season the ingredients during the cooking process. Once the ingredients are cooked, remove from the heat, add the parsley, seasonings, herbs and spices.

Use immediately or place into a covered container to cool, store in refrigerator.

Tomato Concassé (an added flavour)

Yield: 400 g (1 lb) tomatoes
gives 200 g (8 oz) concassé approximately

Method

Remove 'eye' from tomatoes.
Place into a perforated basket and plunge into boiling water for 5 – 10 seconds, withdraw
and plunge immediately into cold water. This blanching and refreshing process prevents
the tomatoes from over cooking and at the same time allows the skins to be removed with
ease. Cut the skinned tomatoes in half, remove seeds and juice and keep for use. Roughly
chop the remaining tomato flesh to form concassé.

   Use as an added flavour, garnish or filling.

3
TOMATES CONCASSÊES (AN ADDED COOKED FLAVOURING)

Yield: 400 g (1 lb)
Cooking time: 3 – 5 min

Unit	Ingredient	Metric (g)	Imperial (oz)
1	Tomato concassé	400	16
$1/8$	Onion brunoise	50	2
$1/16$	Butter/oil	25	1
	Hint of garlic		
	Pinch of salt		
	Pepper and sugar		

Method

Sweat the onions in butter/oil without colouring. Add remaining ingredients and continue
to sweat for a few seconds. Remove from the heat, use immediately, or place into a container to cool, cover and store in a refrigerator.

   Use as a savoury filling or garnish.

Basic Garnishes and Other Common Preparations

Decorative garnishes are frequently added to food preparations immediately prior to service. They enhance the appearance of the finished products making them more interesting and appetising. Indeed in many instances it is the garnish which enables a basic
preparation to appear on a menu under a number of different guises, for example,

(a) Consommé *Célestine* (small julienne of savoury pancake)
Consommé *Brunoise* (cooked brunoise of spring vegetables)
(b) Poulet Sauté *Bonne Femme* (bacon lardons, button onions, cocotte potatoes)
Poulet Sauté *Doria* (cooked shaped cucumber)
(c) Contrefilet de Boeuf Rôti *à l'Anglaise* (Yorkshire pudding, horseradish sauce, roast
gravy and watercress)
Contrefilet de Boeuf *Bouquetière* (cooked vegetables presented as small bouquets)

In order to effect an efficient service, and present a high quality product it is necessary to have garnishes prepared in advance, without their flavour or appearance having been adversely affected. Garnishes are prepared from a variety of foods. Some are used in a raw state, e.g. fresh watercress, whereas others are par-cooked and refreshed in readiness for speedy reheating at service time, e.g. vegetables for bouquets. Whatever the nature of the garnish advanced preparation is essential.

Points for Consideration when Garnishing Foods

(a) Attractively presented food acts as a sales incentive by stimulating the diner's appetite (e.g. food display in a self-service unit).
(b) The size and arrangement of the garnish needs to be in proportion to the size of the culinary product that it is to decorate.
(c) Garnishes need to be seasoned independently.
(d) Garnishes need to be arranged to facilitate ease of service and also to ensure adequate portioning.

Garnishes in Common Use

Green vegetables

(French beans, cauliflower bouquets, garden peas) Usually par-boiled, refreshed (*see* p. 178) and stored in readiness for reheating as required.

'Turned' vegetables

(Turnips, carrot, cucumber—*Légumes tourné*) Portions of raw vegetables 'turned' i.e. cut into barrel shape using an office knife. Usually simmered, refreshed, then reheated as required.

Shaped vegetables

Classical cuts.
A variety of vegetables may be prepared in the following shapes:

Brunoise   Vegetables cut to a very fine dice. The name is attributed to the Brunoy district of France renowned for the growing of fine spring vegetables.

Macédoine   Vegetables cut into small cubes—$\frac{1}{2}$ cm ($\frac{1}{4}$ in). The name is said to be derived from Macedonia, a country formed by small states which were conquered by Alexander the Great.

Julienne   Vegetables cut into very thin strips—2–3 cm (1–1$\frac{1}{2}$ in long). The name is said to be associated with the eighteenth century French chef, Jean Julienne who bequeathed his fortune to the poor of Paris.

Jardinière   Vegetables cut to a 'baton' shape approx 2$\frac{1}{2}$ cm × $\frac{1}{2}$ cm × $\frac{1}{2}$ cm (1 in × $\frac{1}{4}$ in × $\frac{1}{4}$ in). Jardiner translates as 'gardener' associating this garnish with garden vegetables

Paysanne   Vegetables cut into small thin triangles, circles and squares. Paysanne means 'peasant style' and originally indicated roughly cut vegetables, the above shapes have been refined from these origins.

N.B.   The sizes mentioned are meant only as a guide and may be varied as required.

Potato Garnishes in Common Use

Straw potatoes	— Pommes pailles	
Matchstick potatoes	— Pommes allumettes	
Game chips (crisps)	— Pommes chips	see pp. 213 – 14
Game chips (perforated)	— Pommes gaufrettes	
Turned potatoes	— Pommes tourné shaped as for turned vegetables, usually cooked just prior to service. The method of cookery will vary according to requirements.	

Skinned Tomatoes

Remove eye from tomato then plunge into boiling water for approximately 5 – 10 seconds, plunge immediately into cold water to prevent further cooking. Remove skins, drain off water and store in refrigerator for use.

Button Onions (Oignons Bouton)

May be cooked with or without colour and used for garnishing purposes.

With Colour (browned—glacés à brun)   Sauté the raw onions in cooking oil/butter, add a pinch of sugar to facilitate browning (i.e. sugar caramelises). Lightly season and cook to a golden brown. When browned cover with lid to complete cooking, use immediately.

The browned onions can be par-cooked, cooled and stored for use at a later stage. They are reheated by tossing in heated oil/butter.

Without Colour (kept white—glacés à blanc)   Par-cook in sufficient seasoned acidulated water (squeeze of lemon), allow to cool in liquor and store in refrigerator for use at a later stage. Complete cooking and preparation for service by:

(i)   Re-heating in the liquor.
(ii) Straining, then reheating by tossing onions in heated butter/margarine without colour.

N.B.   May be cooked 'à blanc' (*see* p. 179)

Par-cooked Mushrooms

Place the mushrooms into sufficient simmering acidulated water (squeeze of lemon) and a knob of butter. Cook to 'just done', and store in cooking liquor. The resultant liquor may be used in other culinary preparations e.g. sauces. The par-cooked mushrooms may be reheated with or without colour in melted butter.

Artichoke Bottoms (Fonds d'artichauts)

To prepare, hold the globe artichoke at the stalk end and peel away all the leaves until the base and fibrous matter are visible. Using a stainless steel knife remove the stalk, rub the base with a squeeze of lemon juice to prevent discoloration, trim to shape.

The fibrous matter is more easily removed once the base is cooked. Simmer the base in a 'blanc' (*see* p. 179) to 'just done', allow to cool, remove the fibrous matter with a stainless steel spoon. The artichoke bottoms can be used immediately or stored for a short while in the cooking liquor. The fonds can be reheated by tossing in melted butter (sliced or whole).

Lemon Garnishes

Using a stainless steel knife

Wedges   Trim the pointed ends of the lemon and leave a covering of pith to facilitate handling. Cut the lemon in half lengthways and then each half into wedges. Remove pips and pith to ensure that juice can be easily extracted.

N.B.   A stainless knife is used in preference to steel because it does not stain when in contact with the acid of lemon.

The skin of the lemon may be decorated with a 'channel cutter' before being cut into wedges. Used with deep fried fish, etc.

Rounds/fillets   Trim the pointed ends of the lemon until the fruit is visible. Using a stainless steel knife remove the outer skin and pith completely. Slice the skinned lemon into rounds and remove pips. Rounds are often dipped into chopped parsley or lightly dipped into paprika in order to add colour to the garnish. Remove fillets by cutting between pith segmentation and the fruit.
They are used to garnish shallow fried fish, cooked escalopes of veal/pork, etc.

N.B.   A stainless steel knife avoids staining of knives and foods.

Chopped Parsley

Wash the parsley before removing the leaves from the stalks. Dry well by squeezing out the excess moisture and complete the drying in a clean cloth. Remove stalks, squeeze the parsley leaves into a tight ball and chop finely.

Bouquets of Parsley or Watercress (small bunches)

Wash and store in a shallow trough of iced water until required for use. The iced water acts to keep the bouquets as crisp and fresh looking as possible.

Bread Garnishes and Preparations

Stale bread is used for the following preparations (staleness ensures ease of cutting).

Shapes   Croûtons or sippets — small to medium dice of bread
Croûtes/croûtons   — usually cut round or heart shaped.

Browned Breadcrumbs (White breadcrumbs cooked to a golden brown colour.)

All the above are shallow fried in oil or clarified butter/margarine to a golden brown colour, crisp texture, drained well and placed on absorbent kitchen paper to remove excess grease.

Flûtes   Toasted slices cut from thin French sticks.

N.B.   The above garnishes are used to decorate or accompany soups, entrées, roasts, etc.

Lardons of Bacon

Usually streaky bacon cut into bâton shapes, blanched for a few minutes in boiling water, strained and finished by colouring quickly in a sauté or frying pan. The lardons are often stored after blanching and later reheated for service.

Used as a garnish with various entrées.

Other Basic Preparations

Browned Flour

A preparation used in the making of a brown roux. The browned flour speeds up the browning process and develops a characteristic flavour of its own. Ideally suited for the production of Espagnole.

To brown, spread the plain flour evenly on to a suitably sized baking tray and place in a moderate oven to colour golden brown. During the browning process it is necessary to agitate the flour from time to time. This ensures even browning. Once the flour is sufficiently browned, sift through a cane sieve and store in a dry container in readiness for use.

Breadcrumbs and Raspings

Stale white bread minus the crusts is passed through a machine or a cane sieve to produce fresh white breadcrumbs. For raspings the whole loaf including the crusts is dried then passed through a fine mincer.

Clarified Butter

Heat the butter slowly until the whey has completely evaporated and the fat is separated from the milk solids. Pour off the butter fat into a container and store for use. Used chiefly as a cooking medium.

The reason for clarifying butter is to remove the possibility of the butter burning during cooking and spoiling the food. It is the milk solids that easily burn.

Dripping (rendered fat)

An economic means of utilizing fat trimmings.

Mince the trimming and place into a friture with a little water (this prevents the fat from sticking to the friture and burning in the early stages of cooking). Render over a slow heat until the fat is fully extracted and the water content has evaporated. This is indicated when fat ceases to bubble.

Strain clear fat into clean friture or pour into containers for storage. Store in cold room. Used as a frying medium.

N.B.   First class dripping is produced from beef fat only. Second class is produced from a variety of animal fats.

Basic Stocks, Essences and Glazes

Fonds de Cuisine (foundations of the kitchen)

Stock forms the essential basis for many culinary products including soups, sauces, gravies and main courses. Stock, therefore, is a premier basic culinary requirement, adding flavour and body to various dishes.

Stock liquor is a base of water into which flavour from selected bones and vegetables is extracted by a gentle boiling process. Other flavours are infused into the stock from such basic flavourings as a bouquet garni and onion clouté. Once the cooking time is complete the resultant strained liquor is termed stock.

Guidelines for Stock Production

(a) Choose fresh ingredients to ensure a longer life for the stock and to avoid unpleasant flavours, a result of using tainted ingredients.
(b) Scrape the bones to remove fat. This reduces the grease content of the stock.
(c) Chop the bones to facilitate full extraction of flavour.
(d) At the onset of the cooking process place the ingredients into cold rather than hot water, boiling water seals in, rather than extracts the flavour in the early stages.
(e) Use clean equipment to prevent food spoilage from harmful bacteria and dirt.
(f) On boiling, skim, degrease and simmer the stock. These practices prevent the stock from clouding, becoming greasy and losing volume due to rapid boiling and excessive evaporation.
(g) It is wise to leave the stock without seasoning. The stock will be utilized in the preparation of culinary products which will be seasoned at a later stage.
(h) Convenience stocks are of a highly seasoned nature and care must be employed when seasoning products with which they are used.
(i) Once the stock is cooked and full extraction of flavour achieved, strain into a clean stock pot. It is a mistake to leave bones and vegetables in the pot as they will begin to break up, re-absorb some of the stock flavour, cause obstruction and result in a cloudy stock.

Means of Preventing Stock from Souring

(a) Prepare regular quantities of fresh stock to cater for kitchen requirements, usually on a weekly basis.
(b) Store stock by cooling quickly for refrigeration. Reheat amounts as required.
(c) Reduce to concentrated form, i.e. stock glaze and store in a covered container 'on refrigeration'.
(d) Keep stock at boiling point and use as required.

4
BROWN STOCK
WHITE STOCK

(Fond Brun)
(Fond Blanc)

Yield: 5 l (1 gal)
Cooking time: see chart below

Unit	Ingredient	Metric	Imperial
1	Cold water	5 l	1 gal
½	Selected bones (trimmed and chopped)	2.5 kg	5 lb
1/10	Mirepoix (left whole)	500 g	1 lb
	for white stocks and sliced for brown to increase surfaces available for browning		
	Flavourings: bouquet garni mushroom and tomato trimmings		

Method for Brown Stocks

Place the chopped bones into a roasting tray and brown in a moderately hot oven. Brown the sliced mirepoix by scorching the vegetables on a hot griddle plate, take care not to over brown the mirepoix or bones otherwise a bitter flavour may result.

Once browned, place the bones and mirepoix into a clean stock pot, cover the contents with the water, place on the heat and bring the contents slowly to the boil. On boiling skim and degrease the stock, add bouquet garni and any trimmings, simmer gently.

Throughout the cooking process remove scum and grease as they rise to the surface. At the same time clean the inside of the pot from any scum sediment sticking to the upper sides, using a clean, damp cloth. After full extraction strain the stock for use.

Method for White Stocks

The same method as above omitting the browning process. As already mentioned it is unnecessary to slice the mirepoix.

Stocks prepared using the above formula

English	French	Selected bones	Cooking time (hr)
Beef stock	Fond de Boeuf	Beef	6—8
Veal stock	Fond de Veau	Veal	6—8
Mutton stock	Fond de Moûton	Mutton/lamb	4
Game stock	Fond de Gibier	Stewing game and selected game bones	4
Chicken stock	Fond de Volaille	Boiling fowl, chicken carcasses, necks and giblets	2—4

The above stocks may be prepared as brown or white. For example brown beef stock (fond de boeuf brun) or white beef stock (fond de boeuf blanc).

5
ESTOUFFADE (an enriched brown stock)

Yield: 5 l (1 gal)
Cooking time: until meat is cooked

Unit	Ingredient	Metric	Imperial
1	Beef/veal stock (brown)	5 l	1 gal
$\frac{1}{2}$	Beef/veal shin	2.5 kg	5 lb

Method

Place the meat into a hot oven to seal and colour to a golden brown, place into a stock pot, cover with the stock, bring slowly to the boil, skim and degrease. Simmer the contents until the meat is cooked. Strain the estouffade for use. The cooked meat may be further utilized in a variety of made-up dishes.

Store as for stocks (see p. 79)

6
FISH STOCK   **Fumet de Poisson**

Yield: 5 l (1 gal)
Cooking time: 20–30 min from simmering point

Unit	Ingredient	Metric	Imperial
1	Cold water	5 l	1 gal
$\frac{1}{2}$	White fish bones and trimmings (chopped)	2.5 kg	5 lb
$\frac{1}{20}$	Sliced onions	250 g	8 oz
$\frac{1}{20}$	Butter	250 g	8 oz
	Flavourings:		
	parsley stalks		
	few milled peppercorns		
	bay leaf		
	squeeze of lemon juice		

Method

Sweat the onions and chopped fish bones in melted butter for a few minutes over gentle heat. Do not allow the ingredients to take on colour. Add peppercorns, lemon juice, and water, bring contents slowly to the boil and skim the stock. At this stage introduce the remaining ingredients and simmer the stock for a further 20 minutes. Strain immediately and use as required. Over cooking of the fish bones may result in a bitter stock.

Essences and Glazes

Stock essence is the result of stock reduced by half to a more concentrated form. A stock glaze (glace de fond) describes the essence further reduced to a gelatinous consistency. The liquid glaze is poured into containers, allowed to cool, then stored in a refrigerator. On cooling the glaze sets firm.

Essences and glazes are used to strengthen the flavour of culinary products, e.g. stocks, sauces, stews, etc.

Stock Glazes

Chicken glaze (*Glace de Volaille*)
Meat glaze (*Glace de Viande*)
Fish glaze (*Glace de Poisson*)

General Comments

Kitchens working along traditional lines continue to make use of freshly prepared stocks, in the main two general stocks are prepared from a variety of selected bones, e.g. white and brown stock for general use. In addition to those two main stocks other stocks of a specific flavour are produced for use in particular culinary preparations, e.g. fish, veal, chicken, game, and mutton stocks.

Convenience preparations may be used as a substitute for traditional stocks. They may also be added to freshly prepared stock to strengthen flavour.

Practical Applications of Thickening and Binding Agents

As previously stated starch is employed as a thickening and binding agent in a number of culinary products. Many items are thickened to varying degrees of consistency and common examples include; soups, sauces, gravies, stews and braises, etc. When using fat/oil as the medium to disperse starch for use as a thickener the most common methods are as follows.

Roux

A mixture of melted fat or oil and flour which is cooked to achieve varying degrees of colour.

Beurre Manié (manipulated butter)

Butter and flour mixed together to form a soft paste.

Roux

An example of roux proportions is given.

Unit	Ingredient	Metric (g)	Imperial (oz)
1	Flour	50	2
1	Fat or oil	50	2

White Roux   Roux Blanc

Melt the fat over gentle heat, add the flour and mix well. Cook gently for a few minutes without allowing the roux to take on any apparent change of colour. Use for white sauces, soups, white stews, and white braised preparations, etc.

Blond or Fawn Roux   Roux Blond

As above but cooked for a longer period without allowing the roux to undergo any significant change in colour. Used in the preparation of sauces and soups, etc.

Brown Roux   Roux Brun

As above, but continue to cook over gentle heat until the roux takes on a rich brown colour. Take care not to burn the roux as this will create a bitter flavour in the final product. N.B. *Browned flour* (p. 78) can be used for this preparation and it has the advantage of colouring more quickly. This reduces the risk of burning by shortening the cooking time. Used in the preparation of Espagnole (basic brown sauce).

N.B.   Generally butter or margarine are used for the preparation of white and blond roux; oil, dripping or lard for brown roux.

Beurre Manié (manipulated butter)

Mix together equal quantities of butter and flour to form a soft paste. Add small amounts to boiling liquids stirring or whisking to achieve the required consistency.

N.B.   In order to ensure that starch-thickened products do not have a 'raw' starch flavour it is necessary to simmer/boil the products for a period of time.

Temporary Suspensions

When using a cold liquid medium to disperse starch for use as a thickening agent, the selected starch e.g. cornflour, arrowroot or modified, is mixed thoroughly in sufficient liquid before being used.

Panadas (binding agents)   Panade

As previously stated in Chapter 4 binding agents are based on either cooked starches or proteins, or mixtures of both. The principal panadas are listed below. They play a prominent part in the *larder preparations* of various products, which are despatched to the kitchen for cooking. Their main function in recipes is to act as a binding/shape-retaining/extending commodity.

Types of Panada

Bread, flour, frangipane, potato, and rice panadas. Thick basic sauces are also used as binding agents and sometimes referred to as sauce panadas.

    N.B. For recipes and methods of the listed panadas see *The Larder Chef* by M. J. L. Leto and W. K. H. Bode (London: Heinemann, 1975).

    Another thickening agent which is also used to enrich products is known as a liaison.

Liaison Oeuf et Crème

This is a liaison of egg yolks and fresh cream. The quantities of egg yolks and cream vary in accordance with the recipe in which the liaison is to be used. Whatever the amounts the cream and yolks are thoroughly mixed together for use. They are added to the product just prior to service and care must be taken not to boil the product once the liaison has been added otherwise it will curdle.

Liaison au Sang

This is a more obscure thickening using blood. This liaison is used in the thickening of certain speciality items, such as game stew, jugged hare, and coq au vin. In these instances the blood is collected from the evisceration and cleaning process of game and poultry. It is then whisked together with cold water in a ratio of approximately 1 part blood to $\frac{1}{4}$ part water. As with the egg and cream liaison it is added just prior to service and removed from the direct heat to prevent boiling and curdling.

Basic Sauces — foundation and non-derivative types

When a full kitchen brigade is employed a great number of sauces are the responsibility of the Chef Saucier. He/she is a prominent member of the brigade whose work requires a vast amount of culinary expertise and artistic flair. Sauces are also prepared by other members of the brigade as part of their general responsibilities. Fish sauces for example are the responsibility of the Chef Poissonier, and sauces to accompany most meats would be prepared by the Chef Rôtisseur. In smaller brigades the preparation of sauces may be carried out by other members of the kitchen staff.

    In some instances sauces date back over a century and many owe their identity to a particular continent, country, region or person. Examples of these associations are illustrated in the following list:

(a) Sweet and sour sauces of the Orient;
(b) Chilli sauces from Latin America;

(c) Curry sauces from India;
(d) Espagnole sauce from Spain;
(e) Tomato sauce from Italy (Salsa Pomodori);
(f) Béchamel sauce from France.

The functions of sauces in culinary work are to:

1. introduce harmony and contrast to culinary products;
2. add to the nutritive value of the food, often cheaply;
3. create more interesting ways of enjoying food;
4. add contrast in taste, texture and colour;
5. aid digestion, complement and counteract foods which they accompany, e.g. sharp flavoured sauces with fatty foods—apple sauce with roast pork.

Sauces may be classified as follows:

(a) basic foundation sauces and their derivatives;
(b) non-derivative sauces.

Basic Sauces

Basic foundation sauces are those from which many derivative sauces are produced.

Sauce Béchamel

A white coloured savoury sauce made from infused milk and a white roux (*see* p. 82).

Sauce Veloutée

A blond coloured savoury sauce made from white stock and a blond roux (*see* p. 82).

Espagnole

A brown sauce made from brown stock and a brown roux (*see* p. 82).

Demi-Glace or Half-Glaze

A refined Espagnole sauce.

N.B. The above sauces are all starch thickened.

Basic Emulsified Foundation Sauces

Sauce Hollandaise

This sauce is an emulsification of egg yolk, melted butter and a vinegar reduction.

Sauce Béarnaise

This is an emulsification of egg yolks, melted butter, and an aromatic vinegar reduction.

Sauce Mayonnaise

This sauce is an emulsification of egg yolk, edible oil and flavoured vinegar (larder preparation).

Non-derivative/Independent Sauces and Gravies

Foreign

Jus Lié	Thickened gravy
Sauce Kari	Curry sauce
Sauce Tomate	Tomato sauce
Sauce Portugaise	Portuguese sauce
Sauce Provençale	
Sauce Bigarade	Orange flavoured sauce
Sweet and Sour Sauce	
Sauce Homard	Lobster sauce
Sauce Smitane	Sour cream sauce
Sauce Bolognaise	Savoury meat sauce.

N.B.   For roast gravies (jus rôti) *see* p. 301.

English

Apple sauce	Sauce Pommes
Bread sauce	Sauce Pain
Cranberry sauce	Sauce Airelles Coussinette
Cumberland sauce	
Mint sauce	Sauce Menthe

Butter Sauces

Hot butter sauces	
Hard butter sauces	Beurre Composé

Independent à la Carte Sauces

Many sauces used in à la carte work, are either derivatives of the foundation sauces or are independently prepared in their own right, e.g. Sauce Provençale. In addition, other sauces for à la carte purposes are often prepared using cream, butter, wine, spirit or liqueur, etc.

General Faults in Sauce Production

The aim in sauce production is to prepare sauces of correct consistency, colour, texture and gloss, coupled with a distinct flavour pertaining to the particular sauce.
This ideal is not always achieved. Some of the more common faults are listed below.

Lumpiness

This may be caused by the following:

   (a) roux too dry when liquid is added. The dry roux is a result of using incorrect roux balance, i.e. insufficient fat to flour;
   (b) adding the liquid too quickly to the roux and not stirring continuously to the boil. A smooth textured sauce is achieved by adding the liquid slowly to the roux and mixing thoroughly and continuously to boiling point;

(c) insufficient mixing of a temporary starch suspension before stirring into a boiling liquid, e.g. thickening of Jus Lié with arrowroot starch. Unless the suspension is sufficiently blending with cold liquid, dry starch granules will form lumps once added to the boiling liquid.

(d) allowing a skin to form which later could be stirred into the sauce before its completion. The skin is formed when the surface of the sauce comes into contact with air. This skin formation is prevented by covering the completed sauce with one of the following:

   (i)   a film of melted butter;
   (ii) a greased paper (cartouche);
   (iii) a lid covering

(e) by allowing sauce to congeal on the sides of the cooking vessel which later could be stirred into sauce. This is prevented by clearing the sauce from the pan sides once sauce is completed or by re-straining the sauce.

Poor Gloss

This is caused by insufficient cooking of the sauce or using a sauce which has not been passed, tammied or liquidized. A tammied sauce is one that has been passed through a lightly moistened fine cloth. High gloss is achieved by preparing the sauce correctly and aided by the addition of butter just prior to service; technically this process is termed 'monter au beurre' (mounting with butter).

Incorrect Consistency

This is a result of incorrect formula balance. Over or under cooking of the sauce results in too thick a sauce due to excessive evaporation or too thin a sauce due to insufficient cooking around boiling point. Around boiling point the starch molecules effect full thickening (see p. 62).

Greasiness

This is caused by incorrect formula balance, i.e. too much fat in roux or failure to skim off surface grease as it rises. The use of greasy stock may cause this fault.

Poor Colour

Poor colour is a result of incorrect cooking of the roux in the early stages, using dirty cooking vessels or unsuitable utensils, e.g. using a metal whisk when preparing a white sauce in an aluminium saucepan. The sauce turns grey when the metal whisk comes into contact with the sides of the saucepan, removing the grey film from the aluminium, which then discolours the sauce.

Raw Starch Flavour

This is a result of insufficient cooking of the starch. Starch needs to reach boiling point, and be simmered for a further period to avoid raw starch flavour.

Bitter Flavour

This is caused by over browning or burning of the roux.

N.B. For faults in emulsified sauces (see p. 100).

Starch Thickened Foundation Sauces

7
BASIC WHITE SAUCE (made from milk and a white roux)   Béchamel

Yield: 1 l (1 qt)
Cooking time: 30 min

Unit	Ingredient	Metric	Imperial
1	Milk (heated)	1 l	2 pt
¹/₁₀	Butter/margarine	100 g	4 oz
¹/₁₀	Flour (plain)	100 g	4 oz
	Onion clouté		

Method

Form a white roux using butter and flour. Gradually add the heated milk to the roux stirring thoroughly and continuously to the boil. Add onion clouté and simmer gently for approximately 30 minutes. Remove onion clouté, strain sauce through fine chinois. Cover to prevent skin formation (*see* p. 86). Place in bain-marie to keep hot, use as required. The prepared sauce may be cooled, refrigerated, then reheated and finished as required at a later stage.

This sauce can be used as a thickening agent in cream soups, or extended into suitable derivative sauces as shown in following table.

Examples of sauces derived from sauce béchamel: (Added ingredients in relation to 1 unit ½ l (1 pt) basic sauce)

English term	Unit	Ingredient	Metric	Imperial	French term	Examples of uses
Anchovy sauce		Flavour with anchovy essence to taste			Sauce aux Anchois	Poached, boiled, grilled fish
Cheese sauce	¹/₁₀ ¹/₂₀	Grated Cheddar cheese Egg yolk when being glazed or gratinated Add ingredients to basic sauce (do not re-boil after yolk has been added). Correct seasoning	50 g 25 g	2 oz 1 oz	Sauce Mornay	Poached/ boiled eggs and fish. Boiled vegetables, cooked pasta
Cream sauce	¹/₅	Fresh cream Add to basic sauce. Correct seasoning	100 ml	4 fl.oz	Sauce Crème	Poached/ boiled fish and eggs. Boiled vegetables

English term	Unit	Ingredient	Metric	Imperial	French term	Examples of uses
Egg sauce	¹/₅	Chopped hard boiled egg	100 g	4 oz	Sauce aux Oeufs	Poached/ boiled fish
		Add ingredients to basic sauce. Correct seasoning				
Mustard sauce		Sufficient diluted English mustard to flavour. Correct seasoning			Sauce Moutarde	Grilled herrings and mackerel
Onion sauce	¹/₅	Onion brunoise sweated without colour, add to basic sauce. Correct seasoning	100 g	4 oz	Sauce aux Oignons	Boiled eggs, roast mutton
Refined onion sauce		As above passed through fine chinois			Sauce Soubise	Roast mutton, roast veal, poached/ boiled eggs
Parsley sauce		Sufficient chopped parsley to garnish and flavour. Correct seasoning			Sauce Persil	Poached/ boiled fish, vegetables, and ham

N.B.   All the above sauces are seasoned with salt and pepper to taste, and adjusted for consistency to suit requirements.

8
BASIC BLOND SAUCE
(made from white stock and a blond roux)   Sauce Veloutée or Velouté

Yield: 1 l/1 qt
Cooking time: 45 min

Unit	Ingredient	Metric	Imperial
1	White stock (chicken, veal, fish, mutton)	1 l	2 pt
¹/₁₀	Butter/margarine	100 g	4 oz
¹/₁₀	Flour	100 g	4 oz
	Bouquet garni and mushroom trimmings		

Method

Form a blond roux using butter and flour. Gradually add the stock to the roux stirring thoroughly and continuously to the boil. Add remaining ingredients and simmer gently for 45 minutes. Strain through a fine chinois. Cover to prevent skin formation (*see* p. 86).

Place in bain-marie to keep hot, use as required. The prepared sauce may be cooled and refrigerated, then reheated and finished as required.

This sauce can be used as a thickening agent in velouté soups or extended into suitable derivative sauces as shown in following chart.

N.B.   The name of the velouté is determined by the flavour of the stock used, i.e.

Stock	English	French
Chicken	Chicken Velouté	Velouté de Volaille
Fish	Fish Velouté	Velouté de Poisson
Mutton	Mutton Velouté	Velouté de Mouton
Veal	Veal Velouté	Velouté de Veau

N.B.   All the following sauces are seasoned with salt and pepper to taste and adjusted for consistency to suit requirements. The following sauces, other than caper sauce, are often served with poached chicken preparations, vegetable and egg courses.

Examples of Sauces Derived from Chicken/Veal Velouté

English term	Unit	Ingredient	Metric	Imperial	French term
		Added ingredients in relation to 1 unit ½ l (1 pt) basic sauce			
Supreme sauce	$\frac{1}{5}$	Cream	100 ml	4 oz	Sauce Suprême
	$\frac{1}{20}$	Butter	25 g	1 oz	
		Squeeze of lemon juice			
		Combine ingredients with basic sauce, season to taste			
		Added ingredient in relation to 1 unit ½ l(1 pt) of supreme sauce—Sauce Suprême			
Tomatoed supreme sauce	$\frac{1}{5}$	Tomato sauce	100 ml	4 fl.oz	Sauce Aurore
		Combine with supreme sauce to flavour and colour. Season to taste			
Curry flavoured supreme sauce	$\frac{1}{10}$	Onion brunoise	50 g	2 oz	Sauce Indienne
	$\frac{1}{10}$	Apple diced	50 g	2 oz	
	$\frac{1}{10}$	Coconut milk (see p. 103)	50 ml	2 fl.oz	
	$\frac{1}{20}$	Butter	25 g	1 oz	
	$\frac{1}{40}$	Curry powder	12.5 g	½ oz	
		Sweat onions and apple in butter without colour. Add curry powder and sweat a further few minutes. Add coconut milk and supreme sauce. Simmer for 20 minutes, correct seasoning, pass through fine strainer or liquidize and use as required			

English term	Unit	Ingredient	Metric	Imperial	French term
		Added ingredients in relation to 1 unit ½ l (1 pt) – Sauce Suprême			
Paprika sauce	$\frac{1}{5}$	White wine (dry)	100 ml	4 fl.oz	Sauce Hongroise
	$\frac{1}{20}$	Onion brunoise	25 g	1 oz	
	$\frac{1}{20}$	Butter	25 g	1 oz	
	$\frac{1}{40}$	Paprika	12.5 g	½ oz	
		Sweat onion in butter without colour. Add paprika, swill out with wine, reduce by a half. Add supreme sauce, correct seasoning, and simmer for 20 minutes. Pass through fine strainer or liquidize for use			
Mushroom sauce	$\frac{1}{5}$	Button mushrooms (sliced)	100 g	4 oz	Sauce Champignon (blanc)
	$\frac{1}{20}$	Butter	25 g	1 oz	
		Sweat mushrooms in butter without colour, add supreme sauce, correct seasoning and use as required			
German sauce	$\frac{1}{10}$	Egg yolks (mix with a few drops of cold water)	50 g	2 oz	Sauce Allemande
		Combine yolks with supreme sauce, correct seasoning, *do not reboil*			
Poulette sauce	$\frac{1}{10}$	Egg yolks (mix with few drops cold water)	50 g	2 oz	Sauce Poulette
	$\frac{1}{10}$	Mushroom essence Chopped parsley	50 ml	2 fl.oz	
		Combine ingredients with supreme sauce, correct seasoning, do not reboil			

Ivory sauce/Sauce Ivoire (Albufera). Add 1 fl oz (25 ml) meat glaze (glace de viande) to taste to the Sauce Suprême.

Examples of Sauces Derived from Velouté de Mouton: Added ingredients in relation to 1 unit ½ l (1 pt) basic sauce

	Unit	Ingredient	Metric	Imperial	
Caper Sauce	$\frac{1}{10}$	Cream	50 ml	2 fl.oz	Sauce aux Câpres
	$\frac{1}{10}$	Whole capers	50 g	2 oz	
		Add ingredients to basic sauce, season to taste adjust consistency			
		Serve with boiled mutton			

Examples of Sauces Derived from Velouté de Poisson: Added ingredients in relation to 1 unit ½ l (1 pt)

English term	Unit	Ingredient	Metric	Imperial	French term
Cheese sauce for fish	$\frac{1}{10}$ $\frac{1}{10}$ $\frac{1}{20}$	Grated Cheddar cheese Cream Egg yolk when being glazed or gratinated	50 g 50 ml 25g	2 oz 2 fl.oz 1 oz	Sauce Mornay de Poisson
		Add ingredients to basic sauce, season to taste (do not reboil after adding egg yolk)			
Mushroom sauce for fish	$\frac{1}{5}$ $\frac{1}{10}$	Sliced mushrooms (sweated without colour) Cream Squeeze lemon juice	100 g 50 ml	4 oz 2 fl.oz	Sauce Champignon de Poisson
		Add ingredients to basic sauce, season to taste			
Shrimp or prawn sauce	$\frac{1}{10}$ $\frac{1}{10}$	Picked prawns/shrimps Cream Cayenne pepper	50 g 50 ml	2 oz 2 fl.oz	Sauce aux Crevettes/ Crevettes Roses
		Add ingredients to basic sauce, season to taste			
White wine sauce	$\frac{1}{5}$ $\frac{1}{10}$	Dry white wine Cream Squeeze of lemon juice	100 ml 50 ml	4 fl.oz 2 fl.oz	Sauce Vin Blanc
		Reduce white wine by half add basic sauce, cream and lemon juice. Season to taste			
Bercy sauce	$\frac{1}{20}$	Shallots (brunoise)	25 g	1 oz	Sauce Bercy
		As for white wine sauce with shallots added to wine reduction. Finish with chopped parsley			
Granville sauce	$\frac{1}{10}$ $\frac{1}{10}$	Button mushrooms (sliced and sweated) Picked shrimps	50 g 50 g	2 oz 2 oz	Sauce Granville
		As for white wine sauce with the addition of the above ingredients. Garnish with finely chopped truffle			

Thermidor sauce	As for white wine sauce with addition of			Sauce Thermidor
$^{1}/_{10}$	Grated Cheddar cheese	50 g	2 oz	
$^{1}/_{10}$	Cream	50 g	2 oz	
$^{1}/_{20}$	Egg yolk when being glazed or gratinated	25 g	1 oz	
	English mustard (diluted)			

Lightly flavour with diluted English mustard. (Do not reboil after egg yolk has been added.) Season to taste

Paprika sauce	$^{1}/_{5}$	White wine (dry)	100 ml	4 fl.oz	Sauce Hongroise
	$^{1}/_{10}$	Onion brunoise	50 g	2 oz	
	$^{1}/_{10}$	Butter	50 g	2 oz	
	$^{1}/_{40}$	Paprika (flavour to taste)	12.5 g	$^{1}/_{2}$ oz	

Sweat onion in butter without colour, add wine and reduce. Add paprika, basic sauce, simmer for 10 − 15 minutes, season to taste, pass through a fine chinois or liquidize

N.B. The above sauces are served with fish/shellfish dishes and various fish preparations. They are seasoned to taste with salt and pepper and adjusted for consistency to suit requirements.

   Whenever any of the above sauces are to be used for a glazed dish, egg yolks or a sabayon should be added to the sauce just prior to glazing. The proportions are 1/10 (50 g [2 oz]) egg yolk/sabayon to 1 unit ($^{1}/_{2}$ l [1 pt]) completed sauce. Once egg has been added do not reboil otherwise the sauce will separate.

Sabayon

Mix yolks of egg with a few drops of water and whisk over bain-marie to ribbon stage. Use to enrich sauces and assist when a glazed appearance is required.

9
BASIC BROWN SAUCE (Spanish origin)   Espagnole

Yield: $^{1}/_{2}$ l (1 pt) (approximately)
Cooking time 4 − 6 hr
Cooking temp: 120 − 150°C (250 − 300°F)

Unit	Ingredient	Metric	Imperial
1	Brown stock	1 l	2 pt
$^{1}/_{5}$	Mirepoix (large and scorched)	200 g	8 oz
$^{1}/_{20}$	Flour (white or browned *see* p. 78)	50 g	2 oz
$^{1}/_{20}$	Dripping	50 g	2 oz
$^{1}/_{40}$	Tomato purée	25 g	1 oz
	Bouquet Garni, mushroom and tomato trimmings		

Method

Form a brown roux with the flour and dripping, allow to cool, add tomato purée and mix in thoroughly. Gradually add the stock, stirring thoroughly and continuously to the boil, skim and degrease, add scorched mirepoix, trimmings and bouquet garni.
Cover with greased cartouche and a tight fitting lid, cook gently:

(a) in the oven;
(b) on the stove top.

On completion of cooking strain through a fine chinois, in readiness for extension into demi-glace.

10
HALF-GLAZE
Demi-Glace (a refined Espagnole)

Yield: 1 l (1 qt)
Cooking time: 2 – 3 hr approximately or until sauce is sufficiently reduced

Unit	Ingredient	Metric (l)	Imperial (qt)
1	Espagnole	1	1
1	Estouffade/brown stock	1	1

Method

Combine the above preparations and reduce by half to form a smooth glossy sauce of pouring consistency. Strain through a fine chinois and tammy (optional). Cover to prevent skin formation (*see* p. 86), place in a bain-marie to keep hot, use as required.
The prepared sauce may be cooled and refrigerated then reheated, and finished as required.

Examples of Sauces Derived from Sauce Demi-Glace: Added ingredients to 1 unit demi-glace (½ l (1 pt))

English term	Unit	Ingredient	Metric	Imperial	French term	Examples of uses
Bercy sauce	$1/_5$	White wine (dry)	100 ml	4 fl.oz	Sauce	Grilled
	$1/_{10}$	Shallots (brunoise)	50 g	2 oz	Bercy	meats
		Milled peppercorns/				
		Pinch of salt				
		Chopped parsley				
		Beef marrow				
		(poached and diced)				
		Form a reduction with wine, shallots, peppercorns, add demi-glace and simmer 10 minutes. Correct seasoning. Garnish with parsley and marrow				

English term	Unit	Ingredient	Metric	Imperial	French term	Examples of uses
Bordelaise sauce	$^1/_5$ $^1/_{10}$	Red wine Shallots (brunoise) Milled peppercorns/ Pinch of salt Pinch of thyme Bay leaf Beef marrow (poached) Form a reduction with wine, shallots, peppercorns and aromats. Add basic sauce, simmer 20 minutes, pass through fine chinois. Correct seasoning, garnish with slices of beef marrow	100 ml 50 g	4 fl.oz 2 oz	Sauce Bordelaise	Grilled and sautéed meats
Burgundy sauce	$^1/_5$ $^1/_{10}$	Burgundy wine (red) Shallots (brunoise) Milled peppercorns/ Pinch of salt Pinch of thyme Bay leaf Form a reduction with shallots, wine, aromats and seasonings, add basic sauce, simmer 20 minutes, strain through fine chinois, correct seasoning and consistency	100 ml 50 g	4 fl.oz 2 oz	Sauce Bourguig-nonne	Sautéed meats, poultry
Chateau-briand sauce	$^1/_5$ $^1/_{10}$	White wine (dry) Shallots (brunoise) Pinch of thyme Tarragon Milled pepper Chopped parsley Bay leaf Squeeze of lemon juice Form reduction with wine, shallots, bay leaf, seasoning and thyme. Add basic sauce, simmer 10 minutes, pass through fine chinois, add lemon juice, parsley and tarragon, correct seasoning	100 ml 50 g	4 fl.oz 2 oz	Sauce Chateau-briand or Sauce Crapau-dine	Grilled meats, poultry

Chasseur sauce	$^1/_5$	White wine (dry)	100 ml	4 fl.oz	Sauce	Sautéed
	$^1/_5$	Sliced button mushrooms	100 g	4 oz	Chasseur	meats,
	$^1/_{10}$	Shallots (brunoise)	50 g	2 oz		poultry
	$^1/_{10}$	Tomato concassé	50 g	2 oz		
	$^1/_{10}$	Butter	50 g	2 oz		

Chopped parsley and tarragon
to garnish

Sweat shallots and mushrooms in
butter without colour, add wine and
form a reduction. Add basic sauce
and simmer for 10 minutes.
Add chopped tarragon, tomato concassé and parsley. Correct seasoning

Devilled sauce	$^1/_5$	White wine (dry)	100 ml	4 fl.oz	Sauce	Grilled
	$^1/_{10}$	Shallots (brunoise)	50 g	2 oz	Diable	meats,
						poultry

Milled peppercorns
Pinch of cayenne pepper
Chopped parsley

Form a reduction, with wine, shallots,
and peppercorns. Add basic sauce,
simmer 10 minutes and strain
through fine chinois. Add parsley,
cayenne pepper to garnish and
flavour. Correct seasoning

Italian sauce	$^1/_5$	Mushroom (brunoise)	100 g	4 oz	Sauce	Meat and
	$^1/_{10}$	Shallots (brunoise)	50 g	2 oz	Italienne	poultry
	$^1/_{10}$	Cooked ham (brunoise)	50 g	2 oz		
	$^1/_{10}$	Butter/oil	50 g	2 oz		

Flavoured with hint of garlic and
pinch of fine herbs.

Form a duxelle (*see* p. 73) with
shallots, mushrooms, butter and
garlic. Add ham, basic sauce and
flavourings. Simmer 10 minutes.
Correct seasoning

Brown onion sauce	$^2/_5$	Onion (shredded)	200 g	8 oz	Sauce	Liver, made-
	$^1/_{10}$	Butter	50 g	2 oz	Lyonnaise	up dishes
	$^1/_{10}$	Wine vinegar	50 ml	2 fl.oz		

Sweat onions in butter to light colour,
swill out (deglaze) with vinegar to
form a reduction. Add basic sauce
and simmer for 10 minutes. Season
to taste

English term	Unit	Ingredient	Metric	Imperial	French term	Examples of uses
Madeira sauce	¹/₁₀	Madeira	50 ml	2 fl.oz	Sauce Madère	Sautéed meats, cooked ham, meat fillings
		Add to basic sauce just prior to service. Season to taste				
Périgueux sauce		Garnish Madeira sauce with brunoise of truffle			Sauce Périgueux	Sautéed meats
		Truffle essence may be added to flavour. Season to taste				
Wine merchants sauce	¹/₅ ¹/₁₀	Red wine (claret) Shallots (brunoise) Squeeze of lemon juice	100 ml 50 g	4 fl oz 2 oz	Sauce Marchand de Vin	Grilled, sautéed meats
		Form a reduction with wine and shallots. Add basic sauce and simmer for 10 minutes. Flavour with lemon juice				
Piquant sauce	¹/₅	Shallots ⎫ Capers ⎬ brunoise Gherkins ⎭	100 g	4 oz	Sauce Piquante	Grilled meats, made-up dishes
	¹/₁₀	Wine vinegar Pinch of fine herbs	50 ml	2 fl oz		
		Form a reduction with all ingredients, add demi-glace sauce and simmer for 10 minutes. Correct seasoning				
Pepper sauce	¹/₅ ¹/₁₀ ¹/₁₀ ¹/₁₀	Mirepoix (brunoise) Red wine Vinegar (malt) Oil/butter Pinch of thyme Bay leaf Few milled peppercorns	100 g 50 ml 50 ml 50 g	4 oz 2 fl oz 2 fl oz 2 oz	Sauce Poivrade	Grilled, sautéed meats/ game
		Sweat mirepoix in butter to light colour. Swill out (deglaze) with wine/vinegar, add aromats, peppercorns and form a reduction. Add demi-glace, simmer 20 minutes, correct seasoning. Strain through fine chinois				

Port wine sauce	$\frac{1}{10}$	Port wine	50 ml	2 fl oz	Sauce Porto	Meats, game
		Add wine to demi-glace just prior to service. Correct seasoning and serve				
Réform sauce		Add the following to Sauce Poivrade			Sauce Réform	Sautéed lamb cutlets
	$\frac{1}{5}$	Julienne of cooked { Ham, Tongue, Mushroom, Egg white, Beetroot, Gherkin	100 g	4 oz		
	$\frac{1}{10}$	Port wine	50 ml	2 fl oz		
	$\frac{1}{20}$	Redcurrant jelly	25 g	1 oz		
Tomatoed demi-glace	$\frac{1}{2}$	Tomato sauce	250 ml	10 fl oz	Demi-glace Tomate	Sautéed meat, poultry
		Add to basic demi-glace				
Tarragon sauce	$\frac{1}{5}$	White wine (dry) Chopped tarragon	100 ml	4 fl oz	Sauce Estragon	Sautéed, grilled meats, poultry
		Form a reduction with above, add basic sauce, simmer 10 minutes. Season to taste				
Sherry sauce	$\frac{1}{10}$	Sherry	50 ml	2 fl oz	Sauce Xérès	Sautéed, grilled meats, offal
		Add to basic sauce just prior to service. Season to taste				
Brown mushroom sauce	$\frac{1}{5}$	Button mushrooms (sliced, sweated)	100 g	4 oz	Sauce Champignon Brun	Grilled, sautéed meats
		Add to sherry sauce. Season to taste				
Robert sauce	$\frac{1}{5}$	White wine (dry)	100 ml	4 fl oz	Sauce Robert	Grilled meats, fish
	$\frac{1}{10}$	Onion (brunoise)	50 g	2 oz		
	$\frac{1}{10}$	Butter Diluted English mustard to flavour	50 g	2 oz		
		Sweat onions in butter without colour. Form a reduction with wine, add basic sauce, flavour with mustard. Season to taste				
Charcutière sauce		As for Sauce Robert, garnished with 1/20 unit (25 g/1 oz) julienne of gherkins			Sauce Charcutière	Grilled pork

Notes on Above Sauces

(a) Where the method indicates the use of a *reduction*, this implies that the liquid, e.g. wine/vinegar, is reduced by a half.

(b) All the sauces are seasoned with salt and pepper to taste and adjusted for consistency to suit requirements.

(c) In order to improve the flavour, gloss and consistency of a sauce the relevant 'Glace de Fond' e.g. chicken, fish, meat, etc., and knobs of butter, i.e. monter au beurre (*see* p. 86), may be added. Reducing the sauce will improve its flavour and gloss. It will also act to thicken the sauce by the process of evaporation.

Emulsified Foundation Sauces

11
HOLLANDAISE SAUCE   Sauce Hollandaise

Yield: ½ l (1 pt)

Unit	Ingredient	Metric	Imperial
1	Melted butter (unsalted)	400 g	1 lb
¼	Egg yolks	100 g	4 oz
¹⁄₁₆	Vinegar/lemon juice	25 ml	1 fl oz
	1 Tablespoon of cold water		
	Few milled peppercorns		
	Pinch of cayenne		
	Pinch of salt to season		

Method

Form a reduction with vinegar/lemon and peppercorns in a sauteuse, reduce completely. Swill out with cold water, allow to cool. Place egg yolks and strained reduction into a mixing bowl and whisk to ribbon stage over a bain-marie.

Gradually whisk in the melted butter until an emulsion is formed (sauce thickens and becomes stable).

Add salt and cayenne pepper to season.

A squeeze of lemon juice may be added if a more piquant flavour is required.

Pass through a tammy (*see* p. 86) and keep warm.

This sauce can be served with poached fish and vegetables.

Examples of Sauces Derived from Sauce Hollandaise: Added Ingredients to 1 unit ½ l (1 pt) Hollandaise sauce

Unit	Ingredient	Metric	Imperial	French term	Examples of uses
¹⁄₁₀	Whipped cream	50 ml	2 fl oz	Sauce Divine	Poached fish
¹⁄₁₀	Sherry (reduce by half)	50 ml	2 fl oz		
	Fold into basic sauce				

Unit	Ingredient	Metric	Imperial	French term	Examples of uses
	Lightly flavoured with the juice and grated zest of blood oranges			Sauce Maltaise	Boiled asparagus
$^1/_{10}$	Whipped cream	50 ml	2 fl oz	Sauce Mousseline	Poached fish vegetables
	Fold into basic sauce				
$^1/_{10}$	Beurre noisette (*see* p. 110)	50 g	2 oz	Sauce Noisette	Boiled vegetables and grilled meats
	Cool and stir into basic sauce				

12
BÉARNAISE SAUCE   Sauce Béarnaise

Yield: $^1/_2$ l (1 pt)

Unit	Ingredient	Metric	Imperial
1	Melted butter (unsalted)	400 g	1 lb
$^1/_4$	Egg yolks	100 g	4 oz
$^1/_{16}$	Shallots (brunoise)	25 g	1 oz
$^1/_{16}$	Tarragon vinegar/lemon juice	25 ml	1 fl oz
	1 Tablespoon of cold water		
	Milled peppercorns		
	Tarragon stalks		
	Chopped chervil and tarragon		
	Pinch of cayenne		
	Salt to season		

Method
Form a reduction with vinegar/lemon juice, peppercorns and tarragon stalks in a sauteuse, reduce completely. Swill out with the cold water, and allow to cool. Place the egg yolks and strained reduction into a mixing bowl and mix to ribbon stage over a bain-marie. Gradually mix in the melted butter until the emulsion is formed (sauce thickens and becomes stable). Add salt and cayenne pepper to season. Pass through tammy, add chopped tarragon and chervil. A squeeze of lemon juice may be added if a more piquant flavour is required. Keep warm for service.

This sauce can be served with grilled meats and fish.

Examples of Sauces Derived from Sauce Béarnaise: Added ingredients to 1 unit ½ l (1 pt) Sauce Béarnaise

Unit	Ingredient	Metric	Imperial	French term	Examples of uses
¹/₁₀	Tomato purée	50 g	2 oz	Sauce Choron	Grilled steaks
	Blend purée with béarnaise sauce				
	Flavour delicately with warm meat glaze			Sauce Foyot/ Valoise	Eggs and sweetbreads

Technical Points to Consider when Preparing Warm Emulsified Sauces

Fault

Scrambled appearance of sauce due to coagulation, shrinking and hardening of egg protein at around 55°C (158°F) so care must be taken to:

(a) ensure that egg yolks do not become too hot when whisking to ribbon stage over the bain-marie;
(b) prevent the melted butter overheating before adding to the eggs;
(c) prevent the sauce from overheating before service.

Fault

Curdled sauce which may be a result of one, or more of the following:

(a) insufficient agitation (manual or mechanical) during mixing;
(b) too much mechanical agitation which breaks down the protective layer of emulsifying agent;
(c) adding melted butter too quickly to the egg yolks;
(d) using incorrect formula balance;
(e) using egg yolks which lack sufficient emulsifying agent, e.g. stale yolks.

Therefore care must be taken to:

(a) ensure the melted butter is not added too quickly to the egg yolks;
(b) whisk briskly when adding the melted butter;
(c) prepare sauce just before service;
(d) ensure fresh eggs are used.

Correcting a Curdled Sauce

(a) Place a small amount of boiling water into a clean mixing bowl. Gradually whisk the curdled mixture on to the water.
(b) Place fresh egg yolks into clean mixing bowl. Gradually whisk the curdled mixture on to the yolks over a bain-marie.

Cold Emulsified Sauces

13
MAYONNAISE SAUCE
Sauce Mayonnaise

Yield: 600 ml (1¼ pt)

Unit	Ingredient	Metric	Imperial
1	Oil	500 ml	1 pt
⅕	Egg yolk	100 g	4 oz
	Vinegar (tablespoon)		
	Squeeze of lemon juice		
	Pinch of English mustard		
	Pinch salt/cayenne pepper		

Method
Thoroughly whisk together egg yolk, half of the vinegar, mustard, salt and cayenne pepper. Add the oil gradually; whisking thoroughly and continuously until a stable emulsion is formed. Whisk in lemon juice and correct seasoning. Extra vinegar may be added to adjust flavour as required.

Examples of Sauces Derived from Mayonnaise: Added ingredients to 1 unit ½ l (1 pt) mayonnaise

Unit	Ingredient	Metric	Imperial	French term	Uses
⅕	Gherkins	100 g	4 oz	Sauce Tartare	Deep fried fish
⅒	Capers	50 g	2 oz		
	Fines herbes (pinch)				
	Chop ingredients finely and combine with mayonnaise. Adjust consistency				
	As for sauce Tartare but lightly flavoured with anchovy essence			Sauce Rémoulade	Deep fried fish

N.B.   Other derivatives are prepared from this sauce for use in the larder.

Technical Points to Consider when Preparing Mayonnaise
Fault
Unstable emulsion caused:

(a)   when the ingredients have been at too low a temperature, thus preventing the emulsifying agents from coating the oil droplets successfully. (Oil congeals at low temperatures.)

(b) by using stale egg yolks which consequently provide insufficient emulsifying agent
(c) by inadequate whisking when adding oil to the egg yolks, thus preventing even distribution of oil into egg.
(d) by adding oil too quickly in the initial stages of preparation. This prevents a thorough mixing of yolks and oil resulting in the sauce separating.
(e) by using incorrect formula balance, therefore providing insufficient emulsifying agent in relation to oil.

Correcting Unstable Mayonnaise

Mix the unstable emulsion on to fresh egg yolks or on to a few drops of boiling water. Use a clean bowl and proceed as for making mayonnaise.

Foreign Non-Derivative Sauces

14
THICKENED GRAVY   Jus Lié

Yield: ½ l (1 pt)
Cooking time 2 to 3 hours

Unit	Ingredient	Metric	Imperial
1	Stock chicken/veal	1 l	2 pt
½	Chopped bones chicken/veal	500 g	1 lb
⅕	Mirepoix (medium)	200 g	8 oz
1/40	Arrowroot	25 g	1 oz
1/40	Tomato purée	25 g	1 oz
	Mushroom and tomato trimmings		
	Bouquet garni		
	Seasoning		

Method

Brown the bones and mirepoix in a hot oven then place into a suitable cooking vessel. Add tomato purée and cover with the stock. Bring to the boil, skim, add trimmings, bouquet garni and seasoning. Cover with a lid and simmer until extraction of flavour is complete. Strain off the stock, blend arrowroot with a little cold water and stir into the boiling stock to form a thickened gravy. Pass through a fine chinois, tammy, correct consistency and season to taste.

This can be used as a sauce accompaniment to meat dishes.

15
CURRY SAUCE
Sauce Kari/Cari

Yield: ½ l (1 pt)
Cooking time: 45 min to 1 hr

Unit	Ingredient	Metric	Imperial
1	Stock (white or brown)	500 ml	1 pt
$\frac{1}{5}$	Onion (brunoise)	100 g	4 oz
$\frac{1}{10}$	Apple (diced)	50 g	2 oz
$\frac{1}{10}$	Margarine	50 g	2 oz
$\frac{1}{20}$	Flour	25 g	1 oz
$\frac{1}{20}$	Curry powder	25 g	1 oz
$\frac{1}{40}$	Tomato purée	12.5 g	½oz
	Added flavourings		
$\frac{1}{20}$	Coconut milk*	25 ml	1 fl oz
$\frac{1}{20}$	Diced chutney	25 g	1 oz
	Seasoning		

* Coconut milk is dessicated coconut, soaked in milk for 30 minutes and then strained.

Method

Sweat onions in margarine without colour. Add curry powder and apples and cook gently for a few minutes. Add flour to form a roux, cool slightly, add tomato purée. Mix in the stock stirring thoroughly and continuously to the boil, skim and simmer for 30 minutes. Add coconut milk and chutney, simmer a further 10 minutes. Season to taste.

This sauce can be served with vegetables, eggs, meats, fish, poultry etc.

16
TOMATO SAUCE
Sauce Tomate

Yield: 1 l (1 qt)
Cooking time: 2 hr

Unit	Ingredient	Metric	Imperial
1	White stock	1 l	2 pt
$\frac{1}{5}$	Mirepoix - medium	200 g	8 oz
$\frac{1}{10}$	Tomato purée	100 g	4 oz
$\frac{1}{20}$	Margarine	50 g	2 oz
$\frac{1}{20}$	Flour	50 g	2 oz
	Flavourings:		
	bacon scraps		
	tomato trimmings		
	bouquet garni		
	hint of garlic		
	basil, clove		
	seasoning		

Method

Sweat mirepoix and bacon scraps in fat without colour. Add flour to form a blond roux, cool slightly, add tomato purée. Gradually add stock stirring thoroughly and continuously to the boil. Skim, add remaining flavourings, simmer to complete cooking. Strain through fine chinois, correct seasoning and consistency.

This sauce can be served with fish, pasta and meat dishes, etc.

17
PORTUGUESE SAUCE   Sauce Portugaise

Yield: $\frac{1}{2}$ l (1 pt) (approx.)
Cooking time: 15 – 20 min

Unit	Ingredient	Metric	Imperial
1	Tomato sauce	250 ml	10 fl oz
$\frac{4}{5}$	Tomato concassé	200 g	8 oz
$\frac{2}{5}$	White wine (dry)	100 ml	4 fl oz
$\frac{1}{5}$	Shallots (brunoise)	50 g	2 oz
$\frac{1}{10}$	Oil/butter	25 g	1 oz
	Chopped garlic (hint)		
	Pinch of basil		
	Chopped parsley		
	Milled peppercorns		
	Pinch salt		

Method

Sweat shallots in oil without colour, déglacé with wine, add garlic, basil, parsley and seasoning.
Reduce by half, add tomato sauce and tomato concassé.
Simmer for approximately 5 minutes, correct seasoning and consistency and use as required.
DO NOT STRAIN
This sauce can be used for fish, poultry and pasta preparations.

18   Sauce Provençale

Yield: $\frac{1}{2}$ l (1 pt)
Cooking time: 5 – 10 min

Unit	Ingredient	Metric	Imperial
1	Tomato concassé (*see* recipe 3) (tinned tomatoes often used)	500 g	1$\frac{1}{4}$ lb
$\frac{1}{10}$	White wine	50 ml	2 fl oz
$\frac{1}{10}$	Shallots (brunoise)	50 g	2 oz
$\frac{1}{20}$	Oil/butter	25 g	1 oz
	Flavourings:		
	hint of chopped garlic		
	pinch of fine herbs and basil		
	Seasoning to taste		

Method

Sweat shallots and garlic in butter/oil without colour, déglacé with wine, and reduce by a half. Add tomato concassé, herbs and seasoning to taste. Simmer for a few minutes.

This sauce can be used with fish, poultry, pasta etc.

19
ORANGE SAUCE
Sauce Bigarade

Yield: ½ l (1 pt)
Cooking time: 30 to 45 min

Unit	Ingredient	Metric	Imperial
1	Thickened duck's gravy or Jus lié	500 ml	1 pt
⅕	Orange juice	100 ml	4 fl oz
1/20	Lemon juice	25 ml	1 fl oz
	Blanched julienne of orange and lemon zest to garnish. Season to taste		

Method

Combine Jus lié with orange/lemon juice and reduce by a quarter. Strain through fine chinois and tammy. Add garnish and season to taste.

N.B. A pinch of sugar may be added if the sauce is too sharp in flavour. A glass of curaçao may be added to enhance the flavour.

This sauce is served with braised and poêled ducklings.

20
SWEET AND SOUR SAUCE

Yield: ½ l (1 pt)
Cooking time: 30 min

Unit	Ingredient	Metric	Imperial
1	Jus lié	500 ml	1 pt
1/10	Onion brunoise	50 g	2 oz
1/10	Red or green pepper (brunoise)	50 g	2 oz
1/10	Butter	50 g	2 oz
1/10	Sugar (soft brown)	50 g	2 oz
1/10	Vinegar	50 ml	2 fl oz
1/20	Carrot (grated)	25 g	1 oz
1/20	Lemon juice	25 ml	1 fl oz
1/40	Tomato purée	12.5 g	½ oz
	Flavourings: grated ginger root dash of soy sauce grated orange zest, all added to taste. Seasoning		

Method

Sweat onion, peppers, carrot in butter without colour for a few minutes, add sugar and lightly caramelize. Add vinegar and lemon juice, reduce by half. Add tomato purée and jus lié, mix well bring to the boil and skim. Add flavourings and seasonings then simmer to complete cooking. Cover with lid to prevent excess evaporation. Adjust seasoning and use as required. Acidity or sweetness may be adjusted according to taste.

This sauce can be used with pork, chicken, kebabs, etc.

21
LOBSTER SAUCE   Sauce Homard (Americaine)

Yield: 1 l (1 qt)
Cooking time: 1 – 1¼ hr

Unit	Ingredient	Metric	Imperial
	1 hen lobster (live)		
1	Fish stock	1 l	2 pts
1/10	White wine	100 ml	4 fl oz
1/10	Tomato concassé	100 g	4 oz
1/10	Mirepoix (brunoise)	100 g	4 oz
1/20	Flour	50 g	2 oz
1/20	Butter	50 g	2 oz
1/20	Brandy	50 ml	2 fl oz
1/20	Tomato purée	50 g	2 oz
	Hint of garlic		
	Bouquet garni		
	Pinch of salt and pepper		

Preparation of Live Lobster

Place live lobster on to chopping board, pierce head with point of knife and split head lengthways (leave tail whole). Separate tail from head and cut tail into thick slices. Remove claws and crack claw shell with back of a heavy chopping knife. Remove cream of lobster from head and any coral and set aside ready for use. Discard sack from the head.

Preparation of Sauce

Heat butter in cooking vessel, add lobster shell/flesh, and cook until shell turns red. Add mirepoix, garlic and continue cooking for a few minutes and add flour to form roux. Add tomato purée, moisten with white wine and fish stock stirring thoroughly and slowly to the boil. Skim, add bouquet garni, tomato concassé and seasoning. Cover with a lid and simmer until lobster is cooked. Remove from heat and separate lobster from cooking liquor. Pick lobster meat from the shells and cool to store for future use. Replace shells into cooking liquor, add cream and coral of lobster and continue cooking to extract full flavour. Strain sauce through chinois, correct consistency and seasoning, add brandy and use as required.

This sauce can be used with fish, shellfish and egg preparations.

22
SOUR CREAM SAUCE

Sauce Smitane

Yield: $\frac{1}{4}$ l ($\frac{1}{2}$ pt approx.)
Cooking time: 5 – 8 min

Unit	Ingredient	Metric	Imperial
1	Sour cream (double)	500 ml	1 pt
$\frac{1}{10}$	Onion brunoise	50 g	2 oz
$\frac{1}{20}$	Butter	25 g	1 oz
	Squeeze of lemon juice		
	Pinch of cayenne pepper		
	Seasoning		

Method

Sweat onions in butter to light brown colour, add cream, lemon juice and reduce to required consistency. Season to taste.

This sauce can be served with bitoks, pojarskis, etc.

23
SAVOURY MEAT SAUCE

Sauce Bolognaise

Yield: 4 portions
Cooking time 1 – 1$\frac{1}{2}$ hr

Unit	Ingredient	Metric	Imperial
1	Demi-glace	500 ml	1 pt
1	Lean minced beef	500 g	1$\frac{1}{4}$ lb
$\frac{1}{5}$	Red wine	100 ml	4 fl oz
$\frac{1}{5}$	Onion brunoise	100 g	4 oz
$\frac{1}{5}$	Tomato concassé	100 g	4 oz
$\frac{1}{10}$	Oil	50 ml	2 fl oz
$\frac{1}{20}$	Tomato purée	25 g	1 oz
	Seasoning		
	Hint of chopped garlic		

Method

Sweat onions in oil to light brown, add meat, seal, colour brown. Add tomato purée, deglacé with wine and reduce. Add sauce to cover meat, bring to boil, skim and season, simmer until the meat is cooked (cover with lid to prevent excessive evaporation), stir occasionally to prevent meat adhering to bottom of saucepan. Add tomato concassé, and garlic. Correct seasoning and consistency, use as required.

This sauce can be used with pasta preparations.

24
APPLE SAUCE
Sauce Pommes

Yield: ¼ l (½ pt approx.)
Cooking time: 10 min

Unit	Ingredient	Metric (g)	Imperial (oz)
1	Cooking apples (sliced)	400	16
⅛	Margarine	50	2
⅛	Sugar	50	2
	Squeeze of lemon juice to taste		

Method

Sweat apples in margarine, without colour, cook to purée. Add sugar and lemon juice to taste.
　　N.B.　To produce a smooth textured sauce pass through sieve or liquidizer.
　　This sauce can be used as an accompaniment with roast pork, duckling, goose, etc.

25
BREAD SAUCE
Sauce Pain

Yield: ¼ l (½ pt approx)
Cooking time: 30 min

Unit	Ingredient	Metric	Imperial
1	Milk	250 ml	10 fl oz
1/10	White breadcrumbs	25 g	1 oz
1/10	Butter	25 g	1 oz
	Studded onion (clouté)		
	Seasoning		
	Pinch of nutmeg		

Method

Simmer onion clouté with milk for approximately 15 minutes. Remove clouté and add breadcrumbs to milk, mix thoroughly. Simmer for a few minutes, season, adjust consistency and finish with a knob of butter.
　　This sauce accompanies roast poultry and game.

26
CRANBERRY SAUCE   Sauce Airelles Cousinettes
Yield: $\frac{1}{4}$ l ($\frac{1}{2}$ pt approx.)
Cooking time 15 min

Unit	Ingredient	Metric (g)	Imperial (oz)
1	Cranberries	300	12
$\frac{1}{8}$	Sugar	37.5	$1\frac{1}{2}$
	Squeeze of lemon juice		

Method

Place all ingredients in a stainless steel or copper cooking vessel and simmer to a purée. Pass through sieve/liquidizer when smooth sauce is required.

This sauce is used as an accompaniment to roast turkey.

27
CUMBERLAND SAUCE

Yield: $\frac{1}{2}$ l (1 pt)
Cooking time 15 min

Unit	Ingredient	Metric	Imperial
1	Redcurrant jelly	500 ml	1 pt
$\frac{1}{5}$	Port wine	100 ml	4 fl oz
$\frac{1}{5}$	Orange juice	100 ml	4 fl oz
$\frac{1}{10}$	Lemon juice	50 ml	2 fl oz
$\frac{1}{20}$	Blanched chopped shallots	25 g	1 oz
	Seasonings—pinches of:		
	Salt		
	Cayenne pepper		
	English mustard		
	Ginger to taste		
	Garnish of blanched		
	julienne of orange zest		

Method

Melt jelly over heat, add wine, fruit juices, shallots and seasonings. Bring to boiling point, strain, correct seasoning and add garnish. Remove from heat and allow to cool.

This sauce is classically served cold to accompany cold meats, e.g. game, duck, ham. May also be served hot with baked or grilled ham, in which case sauce may require further thickening with arrowroot.

Mint Sauce   Sauce Menthe

Pick, wash and chop mint leaves with a little sugar. Place into china bowl and moisten with malt vinegar. Sweeten with sugar to taste.

N.B.   Sugar acts to absorb moisture from mint leaves and to facilitate chopping. Vinegar may be slightly diluted with water.

This sauce is served with roast lamb.

Hot Butter Sauces

Hot butter sauces are often used with vegetables, fish, meat, offal, and poultry dishes. They can be served to complete a dish or as a accompaniment e.g. Poisson Meunière (*see* recipe 107) beurre meunière to complete, beurre fondu to accompany asparagus, etc.

Sauce	Unit	Ingredient (4 portions)	Metric	Imperial	Method (Degree of Cooking)
Beurre Fondu (melted butter)	1	Butter Squeeze of lemon juice	100 g	4 oz	Melt butter, pour off oil leaving the whey, flavour oil with lemon juice
Beurre Noisette (brown butter)	1	Butter Squeeze of lemon juice	100 g	4 oz	Add butter to pre-heated frying pan and cook until golden brown. Remove from heat, add lemon juice. Stir to use
Beurre Meunière	1	Butter Squeeze of lemon juice Chopped parsley	100 g	4 oz	As for Beurre Noisette, garnish with chopped parsley
Beurre Noir (black butter)	1	Butter Flavour with few drops vinegar Squeeze of lemon juice Chopped parsley	100 g	4 oz	Add butter to pre-heated frying pan and cook until black. Remove from heat, add lemon juice, vinegar, garnish chopped parsley. Stir to use
Beurre Noir aux Câpres (black butter with capers)		As for Beurre Noir, plus whole capers to garnish			As for Beurre Noir, garnish with capers

The above sauces are usually prepared as required, but may be prepared in advance and kept hot in the bain-marie. The flavouring and colour of butter sauces is achieved by the varying degrees to which the butter solids are cooked.

Hard Butter Sauces—Beurre Composé

These preparations are used to accompany a variety of grilled meat or fish dishes and as such add interest and flavour to various products. They are easily prepared in advance and stored refrigerated in readiness for use.

28
HARD BUTTER SAUCES   Beurre Composé

Unit	Ingredient	Metric	Imperial
1	Butter	200 g	8 oz
★	Main flavouring (prepared)		
	Squeeze of lemon juice		
	Seasoning		

★ *See* chart below

Method

Cream butter until soft, combine with flavouring and seasoning to taste. Roll in dampened greaseproof paper to cylindrical shape, approximately 2½ cm (1 in) wide. Store refrigerated.

To use cut into slices ½ cm (¼ in) thick and:

(a) place in sauceboat of iced water (keeps butter solid in hot atmosphere), e.g. to accompany grilled fish, or;

(b) place on to hot food for service, e.g. grilled steak or;

(c) in the preparation of a culinary product, e.g. snails in garlic butter or;

(d) add to sauces to enhance their flavour.

Added ingredients in relation to 1 unit butter i.e. 200 g (8 oz)

Name	Unit	Ingredient	Metric	Imperial	Additional directions
Beurre d'Anchois (anchovy butter)		Anchovy essence Pinch of cayenne pepper			Combine ingredients together with the butter
Beurre d'Ail (garlic butter)		Garlic (chopped) Parsley (chopped) Pinch of pepper			Finely chop the garlic, parsley and combine with the butter
Beurre aux Crevettes (shrimp butter)	½	Picked shrimps Pinch of cayenne pepper Chopped parsley	100 g	4 oz	Pound shrimps with sufficient of the butter to form a paste. Pass through fine cane sieve, add cayenne and chopped parsley
Beurre aux Fines Herbes (herb butter)		Fine herbs to flavour (chervil, chives, parsley, tarragon) Pinch of pepper			Finely chop the fresh herbs, mix all ingredients with the butter

Name	Unit	Ingredient	Metric	Imperial	Additional directions
Beurre d'Homard (lobster butter)	$\frac{1}{8}$	Cooked spawn and coral of lobster Pinch of cayenne pepper	25 g	1 oz	Pound coral and spawn with sufficient of the butter to form a paste. Pass through fine cane sieve. Mix all ingredients with the butter
Beurre Maître d'Hôtel (parsley Butter)		Chopped parsley to flavour Squeeze of lemon juice Pinch of pepper			Combine all ingredients with the butter
Beurre Moutarde (mustard butter)		Dry English mustard to flavour Pinch of pepper			Sift mustard into butter and mix well

Ancillary Pastry Items

Strictly classified the following items are pastry products and would therefore be prepared by the pastry department. Throughout kitchen operations certain basic pastries are in common use and to facilitate users of this book they are outlined below. For more detailed information see specialist pastry books.

29
SHORT PASTRY
Pâte à Foncer

Unit	Ingredient	Metric	Imperial
1	Flour (soft)	200 g	8 oz
$\frac{1}{2}$	Fat (lard or margarine)	100 g	4 oz
$\frac{1}{8} - \frac{1}{4}$	Water (cold) Pinch of salt	25 – 50 ml	1 – 2 fl oz

Method

Sift flour and salt together. Rub in the fat to form a sandy texture. Form a well, add sufficient water to bind and form a smooth short pastry.

N.B. Water content may vary according to the water absorption rate of the flour.

30
SUET PASTRY

Unit	Ingredient	Metric	Imperial
1	Flour	200 g	8 oz
$\frac{1}{2}$	Beef suet (finely chopped)	100 g	4 oz
$\frac{1}{2}$	Water (cold)	100 ml	4 fl oz
$\frac{1}{16}$	Baking powder	12.5 g	$\frac{1}{2}$ oz
	Pinch of salt to taste		

N.B.   If using fresh beef suet, remove sinew and skin, mix with a little flour, chop finely.

Method

Sift flour, salt and baking powder together. Add suet and mix thoroughly. From a well, add sufficient water to bind and form a pastry dough.

Suet Dumplings

Scale off suet pastry into 25 g (1 oz) balls and simmer in stock for approximately 15–20 minutes. Alternatively when being served with a brown stew they may be cooked in the stew's sauce 15–20 minutes before required for service.

31
PUFF PASTRY (full puff English method)   Pâte à Feuilletage

Unit	Ingredient	Metric	Imperial
1	Flour (strong)	200 g	8 oz
1	Butter or margarine*	200 g	8 oz
$\frac{5}{8}$	Water (cold)	125 ml	5 fl oz
	Salt to taste		
	Squeeze of lemon juice		

* When pastry margarine is used take $\frac{1}{8}$ ordinary margarine or butter for rubbing in.

Method

Sift flour and salt together and rub in $\frac{1}{8}$ [25 g (1 oz)] of fat content. Form a well, add water and squeeze of lemon juice and mix to a smooth elastic dough. Rest dough for approximately 10 minutes allowing it to relax prior to rolling.

Roll out dough 1 cm ($\frac{3}{8}$ in) thick and, twice as long as wide keeping the corners square. Disperse pastry margarine evenly over two-thirds of rolled-out dough to incorporate fat. Leave outer edges and remaining one third of dough clear. Fold the clear one-third on to half of covered portion and fold over once more to form two fat and three dough layers. Press down to secure edges. Roll out and fold again into three as previously described. At this stage *one half turn* has been completed.

Brush all surplus dusting flour from pastry before continuing to roll. Repeat rolling and folding process until *six half turns (3 full turns)* have been completed allowing the pastry to rest and relax between each turn. Rest completed pastry then use as required.

N.B.   Lemon juice (citric acid) is employed in the ingredients to render the gluten in the flour ductile.

32
CHEESE STRAWS   Paillettes au Fromage

Yield: 4 portions
Cooking time: 10 min
Cooking temp: 205°C (400°F)

Unit	Ingredient	Metric (g)	Imperial (oz)
1	Puff pastry	100	4
½	Parmesan cheese (grated)	50	2
	Cayenne pepper (pinch)		
	Pinch of salt		

Method

Roll out puff pastry into rectangular shape 3 mm (⅛ in) thick. Lightly egg wash and sprinkle evenly with cheese, pinch of cayenne and salt. Cut into lengths of 6 mm (¼ in) wide. Twist to curl and place firmly on to lightly greased baking sheet. Rest before baking then cook in the oven until crisp and golden brown. Remove from oven and whilst still hot cut into 10 cm (4 in) lengths ensuring that the ends are neatly trimmed. Allow to cool and store for use.

33
SAVOURY EGG CUSTARD   Royale

Yield: 4 portions
Cooking time: 30 – 40 min
Cooking temp: 150°C (300°F)

Unit	Ingredient	Metric	Imperial
1	Whole egg	50 g	2 oz
1	White stock	50 ml	2 fl oz
	Seasoning, salt and pepper		

Method

Whisk together egg and stock, season to taste. Pour mixture through a fine chinois into a buttered mould. Place the mould into a bain-marie and cook in the oven until completely set. Allow to cool, carefully turn out of mould and cut into diamonds, circles, squares, etc. Store moistened with stock or consommé.

N.B.   Royale is most commonly used to garnish consommé. It may be coloured and flavoured prior to cooking as required, e.g.

Green royale — colour and flavour with purée of spinach;
Red royale — colour and flavour with tomato purée.
For choux pastry *see* p. 158.

6

Soups: Les Potages

Soups are a common feature offered on many types of menu in a wide variety of catering establishments. Such units range from fast food operations to the more traditionally based luxury catering systems.

Where a large 'Brigade de Cuisine' is employed the 'Chef Potager' is responsible for the preparation of soups and their garnishes.

The function of soup on the menu is to stimulate the customer's appetite rather than act as a complete meal. For this reason many soups are of a light and delicate nature. Hot soups are a welcome feature on winter menus, conversely cold soups are ideal in the summertime.

Soups may be classified in the following manner: *thickened* and *unthickened*.

Thickened Varieties

1. *Purée soups* — a type of soup thickened either by the main ingredient or a starch-based additive.
2. *Cream soups* — passed soups that have béchamel sauce as their main thickening agent.
3. *Velouté soups* — passed soups that have a velouté sauce or blond roux as their main thickening agent.
4. *Brown soups* — passed soups produced from flavoured brown stock thickened by a brown roux.
5. *Bisques* — passed shellfish soups that are traditionally thickened with starch in the form of rice, but may be thickened by the roux method.

Unthickened Varieties

6. *Broths* — unstrained soups prepared from a stock base flavoured and garnished by vegetables, meats, fish and cereals.
7. *Consommés* — Refined, clear soups prepared from a rich stock base.

Unclassified Varieties

Speciality soups that cannot be listed with the above types because of their unique mode of preparation.

Soups and the Menu

It is recommended that the more substantial types of soup be served at luncheon and those of a more delicate nature for dinner.
Luncheon — purées, creams, broths and brown soups;
Dinner — consommés, creams, veloutés and bisques.

Preparing and Cooking Soups

It is recommended that during the cooking of soups (except consommés) the cooking vessel be covered with a lid to avoid excessive evaporation (*see* p. 128 for consommé).

Vegetable trimmings are ideally suited for economic soup production e.g. mushroom stalks and peelings, celery tops, etc.

In the production of cream- and velouté-based soups it is taken for granted that basic béchamel and velouté sauces would be en place (hot or cold) for use.

Thickened Soups

1. Purées

This type of soup is produced from one of the following:

(a) Vegetables containing a high percentage of starch e.g. — pulse vegetables.
(b) Aqueous Vegetables i.e. watery vegetables e.g. celery, leaks onions etc.

Purée soups produced from *starchy vegetables* need no other thickening agent as starch based vegetables act as self-thickeners.

Alternatively, purée soups produced from aqueous vegetables need the assistance of a starchy food to effect cohesion. The ingredients most commonly used for this purpose are rice or potatoes.

34
(a) PURÉE SOUP

Potage Purée
(for pulse vegetables)

Yield: 4 portions
Cooking time. 1 – 1½ hr (approximately)

Unit	Ingredient	Metric	Imperial
1	White stock	1 l	2 pt
⅕	Pulse vegetable (main)	200 g	8 oz
¹⁄₁₀	Mirepoix (large including bacon)	100 g	4 oz
	Bouquet garni		
	Salt and pepper		

Method

Place stock, pulse vegetable and mirepoix in saucepan. Bring to the boil, skin and simmer. Add bouquet garni, cover with lid and continue cooking until pulse falls. Remove bouquet garni and bacon. Pass through soup machine and then through medium conical strainer. Reboil, correct consistency and seasoning, garnish as required. Serve accompanied with soup croûtons (*see* p. 77)

Extensions of Soups Using Above Formula: Garnish in relation to 1 unit stock i.e. 1 l (2 pt)

English term-main ingredient	Unit	Ingredient for garnish	Metric	Imperial	French term
Purée of haricot bean soup		Chopped parsley			Potage Soissonnaise
Purée of red bean soup	$1/20$	Finish with: dry red wine	50 ml	2 fl oz	Potage Condé
Purée of lentil soup		Chopped parsley			Potage de Lentilles
Purée of lentil soup	$1/20$	Diced cooked bacon Pinch of chopped chervil	50 g	2 oz	Potage Conti
Purée of lentil soup	$1/40$ $1/40$	Boiled rice Butter	25 g 25 g	1 oz 1 oz	Potage Esaü
Purée of green split pea soup					Potage St Germain
Purée of yellow split pea soup		Chopped parsley			Potage Égyptienne

N.B. For best results dried pulses should be soaked overnight in cold water, but they must be weighed *prior to soaking* to obtain correct consistency.

35
(b) PURÉE SOUP

Potage Purée
(for aqueous vegetables)

Yield: 4 portions
Cooking time: 1 hr (approximately)

Unit	Ingredient	Metric	Imperial
1	White stock	800 ml	$1\frac{1}{2}$ pt
$2/5$	Main vegetable (sliced)	320 g	12 oz
$1/10$	Mirepoix or vegetable adjunct	80 g	3 oz
$1/10$	Potato (sliced) or	80 g	3 oz
$1/20$	Patna rice	40 g	$1\frac{1}{2}$ oz
$1/20$	Margarine or butter Bouquet garni Salt and pepper	40 g	$1\frac{1}{2}$ oz

Method

Melt fat in saucepan, add main vegetable and mirepoix, sweat without colour and season lightly. Add the stock, bring to the boil, skim, add potato *or* rice, bouquet garni and continue to simmer until all the vegetables are cooked. Cover with lid to prevent excess evaporation.

Remove bouquet garni, liquidize or pass the soup through machine and then through a medium conical strainer. Reboil, correct seasoning and consistency, garnish as required. Accompany with soup croûtons.

Examples of Soups Using Above Formula

English term—main ingredient	Garnish for 4 portions	French term
Purée of carrot soup	Chopped parsley	Purée de Carottes
Purée of cauliflower soup	Small cauliflower sprigs (cooked) 50 g (2 oz) and chopped parsley	Purée Dubarry
Purée of celery soup	Chopped parsley	Purée de Céleri
Purée of Jerusalem artichoke soup	Chopped parsley	Purée Palestine
Purée of leek soup	Chopped parsley	Purée de Poireaux
Purée of onion soup	Chopped parsley	Purée d'Oignon
Purée of potato soup*	Chopped parsley	Purée Parmentier
Purée of pumpkin soup	Chopped parsley	Purée de Potiron
Purée of swede soup	Chopped parsley	Purée de Rutabaga
Purée of sprout soup		Purée Flamande
Purée of turnip soup		Purée Navet
Purée of vegetable soup (combined aqueous vegetables)		Purée de Légumes
Purée of watercress soup	As for potato soup, but cooked with a bunch of watercress — garnished with blanched watercress leaves	Purée Cressonnière

N.B.   Either thickening agent may be used when preparing the above soups with the exception of *purée of potato soup**. In this case the amount of main vegetable i.e. 320 g (12 oz) of potato is sufficient to both flavour and thicken this soup. Extra vegetable adjunct can therefore be added to improve the flavour in the amount of 80 g (3 oz). Generally, when using vegetables with a delicate flavour, as the main ingredient, best results are achieved by thickening with rice.

2. Creams   Crèmes

With only a few exceptions, the principal thickening element used in the production of cream soup is that of sauce béchamel. The predominant flavour of the soup is determined by the recipe balance.

The class of vegetables best suited to cream soup production are the aqueous type. Starchy vegetables, in general act as self-thickeners and need no other thickening element.

It is worth mentioning at this stage that there are many soups appearing on the menu as creams, which are basically velouté or purée soups to which cream has been added prior to service. The word 'cream' in these instances refers to the addition of cream rather than the underlying principle of cream soup production.

36
(USING AQUEOUS VEGETABLES)

Yield: 4 portions
Cooking time: 1 hr (approximately)

Unit	Ingredient	Metric	Imperial
1	White stock	800 ml	$1\frac{1}{2}$ pt
$\frac{2}{5}$	Main vegetable (sliced)	320 g	12 oz
$\frac{1}{5}$	Mirepoix or vegetable adjunct (sliced)	160 g	6 oz
$\frac{1}{5}$	Béchamel (*see* recipe 7)	160 ml	6 fl oz
$\frac{1}{20}$	Butter or margarine	40 g	$1\frac{1}{2}$ oz
$\frac{1}{20}$	Cream (optional)	40 ml	$1\frac{1}{2}$ fl oz
	Bouquet garni		
	Salt and pepper		

Method

Melt fat in saucepan, add all vegetables, season lightly and sweat without colour. Add stock, bring to boil, skim. Add bouquet garni, simmer until all vegetables are cooked (cover with lid).

Remove bouquet garni, add béchamel sauce, mix well and reboil. Liquidize or pass through soup machine and then through fine chinois. Reboil, correct seasoning and consistency, garnish as required.

N.B. If cream is used, add on service. Cream soups are often served accompanied with soup croûtons (*see* p. 77). N.B.B. This soup can be thickened by *replacing* béchamel with $\frac{1}{40}$ (20 g/$\frac{3}{4}$ oz) flour to form a white roux with sweated vegetables .

Extensions of Soups Using Above Formula: Garnish in relation to 1 unit stock i.e. 800 ml ($1\frac{1}{2}$ pt)

English term-main ingredient	Unit	Ingredient	Metric (g)	Imperial (oz)	French term
Cream of asparagus soup		4 Cooked asparagus tips			Crème d'Asperges/ Argenteuil
Cream of carrot soup		Chopped parsley			Crème de Carottes
Cream of carrot soup	$\frac{1}{20}$	As above plus: boiled rice	40	$1\frac{1}{2}$	Crème Crécy
Cream of cauliflower soup	$\frac{1}{20}$	Small cooked sprigs of cauliflower	40	$1\frac{1}{2}$	Crème de Chou-fleur / Dubarry
Cream of celery soup	$\frac{1}{20}$	Cooked julienne of celery	40	$1\frac{1}{2}$	Crème de Céleri
Cream of cucumber soup	$\frac{1}{20}$	Small cucumber balls	40	$1\frac{1}{2}$	Crème Concombre/ Doria
Cream of leek soup					Crème Poireaux
Cream of lettuce soup		Shredded lettuce lightly sweated			Crème de Laitue/ Judic

English term-main ingredient	Unit	Ingredient	Metric (g)	Imperial (oz)	French term
Cream of mushroom soup ($\frac{1}{5}$ main unit may be used 160 g (6 oz)	$\frac{1}{20}$	Julienne of cooked mushrooms	40	$1\frac{1}{2}$	Crème de Champignons
Cream of onion soup					Crème d'Oignon
Cream of spinach soup					Crème d'Épinards/ Florentine
Cream of sweetcorn soup	$\frac{1}{20}$	Cooked corn kernels	40	$1\frac{1}{2}$	Crème de Maïs/ Washington
Cream of vegetable soup					Crème de Légumes
Cream of watercress soup [$\frac{1}{5}$ main unit may be used 160 g (6 oz)]		Blanched watercress leaves			Crème Cressonnière

N.B.   Other aqueous vegetable soups may be prepared using the basic recipe. The above soups may be garnished with chopped parsley as required.

3. *Velouté Soups*   Veloutés

The French word velouté translated into English means velvety. This describes the finished texture and appearance of the soup. The principal thickening element is a blond roux or a velouté sauce, which may be flavoured using different stock bases according to requirements. When preparing meat, poultry, or fish veloutés the predominant flavour is determined by the stock used. Alternatively when producing aqueous vegetable velouté soups the flavour of the main vegetable predominates.

In order to achieve the velvety finish required, a liaison of egg yolks and cream is added just before service. Once this has been added the soup must not be allowed to reboil otherwise it will take on a curdled appearance, a result of egg yolk coagulation.

37
VELOUTÉ (for meat, poultry, fish soups)

Yield: 4 portions
Cooking time: 1 hr approximately

Unit	Ingredient	Metric	Imperial
1	Selected white stock	1 l	2 pt
$\frac{1}{10}$	Vegetable adjunct sliced (optional)	100 g	4 oz
$\frac{1}{20}$	Flour	50 g	2 oz
$\frac{1}{20}$	Butter	50 g	2 oz
$\frac{1}{20}$	Cream } liaison	50 ml	2 fl oz
$\frac{1}{20}$	Egg yolk }	50 g	2 oz
	Bouquet garni		
	Salt and pepper to season		

N.B. When a vegetable adjunct is used care must be taken to use vegetables that will enhance rather than impair the colour of the finished soup, e.g. omit carrots when a 'white' appearance is required.

Method

Melt fat in saucepan, add the adjunct, lightly season and sweat without colour. Add the flour to form a blond roux. Gradually pour in the stock, bring to the boil, stirring continuously, skim, add bouquet garni, simmer until cooked (cover with lid).

Once cooked remove bouquet garni, liquidize or pass through a soup machine, then through fine chinois. Reboil, correct seasoning and consistency, remove from heat and add liaison just before service (do not reboil).

Extensions of Velouté Soups Using Above Formula: Garnish in relation to 1 unit stock i.e. 1 l (2 pt)

Menu term	Main stock	Unit	Ingredient	Metric (g)	Imperial (oz)
Velouté de Volaille (chicken velouté)	Chicken	$^1/_{20}$	Julienne of cooked chicken	50	2
Velouté de Poisson (fish velouté)	Fish		Chopped parsley		
Velouté Dieppoise (mussel velouté)	Fish and mussel cooking liquor	$^1/_{20}$ $^1/_{20}$	Budded mussels Shrimps/prawns Chopped parsley	50 50	2 2
Velouté aux Huîtres (oyster velouté)	Fish and oyster cooking liquor		8 poached oysters Chopped parsley		

N.B. Many velouté soups may be prepared using the above recipe. By adding a more complex garnish to the basic soup the name of the soup changes, e.g. Velouté Germinal—chicken velouté flavoured with tarragon, garnished with asparagus tips and chervil.

Velouté Agnès Sorel

Using basic recipe prepare a chicken velouté replacing vegetable adjunct with unit [200 g (8 oz)] mushroom brunoise. Garnish completed soup with:

$^1/_{40}$ unit Julienne of cooked tongue 25 g (1 oz);
$^1/_{40}$ unit Julienne of cooked chicken 25 g (1 oz);
$^1/_{40}$ unit Julienne of cooked mushrooms 25 g (1 oz).

38
VEGETABLE VELOUTÉS

Veloutés des Légumes
(using a main flavouring of aqueous vegetables)

Yield: 4 portions
Cooking time: 1 hr (approximately)

Unit	Ingredient	Metric	Imperial
1	White stock	800 ml	$1\frac{1}{2}$ pt
$\frac{2}{5}$	Main vegetable (sliced)	320 g	12 oz
$\frac{1}{5}$	Vegetable adjunct (sliced)	160 g	6 oz
$\frac{1}{5}$	Chicken velouté (*see* p. 88)	160 ml	6 fl oz
$\frac{1}{10}$	Cream } mix to form liaison	80 ml	3 fl oz
	Egg yolk }		
$\frac{1}{20}$	Butter or margarine	40 g	$1\frac{1}{2}$ oz
	Bouquet garni		
	Salt and pepper		

Method

Melt fat in saucepan, add all vegetables, season lightly and sweat without colour. Add stock, bring to the boil and skim. Add bouquet garni and simmer until all vegetables are cooked (cover with lid).

Remove bouquet garni, add velouté, reboil, mixing well. Liquidize or pass through soup machine and then through fine chinois. Reboil, correct seasoning and consistency.

Add liaison just prior to service. *DO NOT REBOIL* soup once liaison has been added, otherwise soup will curdle. N.B. This soup can be thickened by *replacing* chicken velouté with $\frac{1}{40}$ (20 g/$\frac{3}{4}$ oz) flour to form a blond roux with sweated vegetables.

Extensions of Aqueous Vegetable Velouté Soups using Above Formula: Garnish in relation to 1 unit stock i.e. 800 ml (1½ pt)

English term-main ingredient	Unit	Ingredient	Metric	Imperial	French term
Asparagus velouté soup soup		8 cooked asparagus tips			Velouté d'Asperges
Cucumber velouté soup	$\frac{1}{20}$ {	Cucumber balls / Boiled rice	40 g	$1\frac{1}{2}$ oz	Velouté Doria
Mushroom velouté soup [($\frac{1}{5}$ main unit may be used 160 g (6 oz)]	$\frac{1}{20}$	Julienne of cooked mushroom	40 g	$1\frac{1}{2}$ oz	Velouté de Champignons
Watercress velouté soup [$\frac{1}{5}$ main unit may be used 160 g (6 oz)]		Blanched watercress leaves			Velouté Cressonnière

N.B. Other aqueous vegetable velouté soups may be prepared using the basic recipe. The above soups may be garnished with chopped parsley as required.

General Note   Many soups which are prepared by the velouté methods appear on menus as 'creams'. Generally in these instances the egg yolk is omitted.

4. *Thickened Brown Soups*   Potages Brun Lié

Soups prepared from a base of brown stock, flavoured with a mirepoix, selected meat and thickened with a brown roux.
This type of soup is traditionally served for luncheon or at suppertime.

39
THICKENED BROWN SOUP   Potage Brun Lié

Yield: 4 portions
Cooking time: 2 to 3 hr according to meat used, *see* below

Unit	Ingredient	Metric	Imperial
1	Brown stock	1 l	2 pt
$1/_5$	Selected meat (medium cut)	200 g	8 oz
$1/_5$	Mirepoix (medium cut)	200 g	8 oz
$1/_{20}$	Dripping	50 g	2 oz
$1/_{20}$	Flour	50 g	2 oz
$1/_{40}$	Tomato purée	25 g	1 oz
	Bouquet garni		
	Salt and pepper		

Method

Melt fat in cooking vessel, add meat and vegetables, lightly season, cook to brown colour.

Add flour and cook gently to form a brown roux. Cool, add tomato purée, brown stock, stir to boil, skim, add bouquet garni and simmer until meat is cooked. Cover with lid to minimize evaporation.

Remove meat and bouquet garni then pass the soup through a fine strainer. Adjust seasoning and consistency.

Dice the cooked meat, add to soup and reheat for service.

N.B.   Browned flour, (*see* p. 78) may be used when forming the roux.

Due to the long cooking process it is necessary to add extra stock to replace stock lost by evaporation over the long cooking periods.

Examples of Soups Prepared Using Above Formula

English term	Main meat	Flavouring at service	Cooking time approximate (hr)	French term
Kidney soup	Ox-kidney		$2^1/_2$	Soupe aux Rognons
Oxtail soup	Oxtail (tail ends only	Dry sherry (glass)	3	Queue de Boeuf Lié
Game soup	Assorted game	Port (glass)	$2^1/_2$	Soupe de Gibier

English term	Main meat	Flavouring at service	Cooking time approximate (hr)	French term
Hare soup	Hare	Port (glass)	2½	Soupe de Lièvre
Pheasant soup	Pheasant	Port (glass)	2½	Potage Faisan
Mock turtle soup	Calves head. N.B. Add *Turtle herbs* 20 minutes before completion of soup	Dry sherry (glass)	2½	Potage Fausse Tortue

5. *Shellfish Soups*   Bisques

Bisques may be defined as thickened, passed, classical seafood soups prepared from a base of fish stock flavoured with selected shellfish and mirepoix. They are enhanced with wine, brandy and thickened with starch usually in the form of rice. Due to the delicacy of their flavour and the high cost of production bisques are best suited to service at dinner.

40
SHELLFISH SOUP   Bisque

Yield: 4 portions
Cooking time: 45 min – 1 hr

Unit	Ingredient	Metric	Imperial
1	Fish stock	1 l	2 pt
²/₅	Shellfish (live where possible *see* p. 267)	400 g	1 lb
¹/₁₀	Mirepoix (brunoise)	100 g	4 oz
¹/₁₀	Dry white wine	100 ml	4 fl oz
¹/₂₀	Brandy	50 ml	2 fl oz
¹/₂₀	Cream	50 ml	2 fl oz
¹/₂₀	Butter	50 g	2 oz
¹/₂₀	Rice	50 g	2 oz
¹/₄₀	Tomato purée	25 g	1 oz
	Bouquet garni		
	Seasoning		

Method

Sweat prepared shellfish (*see* p. 125) and mirepoix in melted butter until shellfish adopts a cooked colour, e.g. lobster turns red. Add white wine and reduce, flame with brandy and lightly season.

Moisten with fish stock, bring to boil, skim, add bouquet garni and simmer for 20 minutes. Remove shellfish from the liquor and separate fish meat from shell. Set shellfish meat aside for garnish and other uses. Crush remaining shell and replace into the cooking liquor. Reboil for a further 10 minutes then pass liquor into a saucepan. Add rice and tomato purée to the liquor and simmer for approximately 20 minutes or until the rice is cooked. Liquidize and pass through a fine chinois to form a thickened soup.

Reboil, adjust seasoning and consistency, add cream and garnish with brandy flavoured diced lobster meat.

N.B.   When shellfish is unduly expensive it is possible to obtain an acceptable flavour by preparing the soup with the shells of certain shellfish along with rich fish stock, e.g. crushed lobster or crab shells.

Examples of Bisques Prepared Using Above Formula: Garnish in relation to 1 unit i.e. 1 l (2 pt) stock

Menu term	Main shellfish and preparation	Unit	Ingredient	Metric (g)	Imperial (oz)
Bisque de Crabe (crab bisque)	Crab claws (cracked)	$\frac{1}{20}$	White crab meat	50	2
Bisque de Homard (Lobster bisque)	Lobster, split (sack removed from head), claws cracked, remainder cut into pieces	$\frac{1}{20}$	Diced, cooked lobster meat flavoured with brandy.	50	2
Bisque de Crevettes (prawn or shrimp bisque)	Whole prawns or shrimps	$\frac{1}{20}$	Cooked prawns or shrimps	50	2

Unthickened Soups

Broths   Bouillons—Potages

Broth is comprised of savoury stock liquor, flavoured and garnished with a combination of vegetables, vegetables and meat, or vegetables and seafood.

In most cases broth contains a cereal ingredient, usually rice or barley. The flavour is enhanced by herbs, seasonings and occasionally spices. Often broth has the appearance of a thickened soup, a result of the starch content extracted from the cereal ingredient during cooking. However, because the soup remains unpassed, full thickening is not effected.

Broths are sub-divided into three types according to the method of preparation:

(a)   when the vegetables are added directly to a stock base which contains a meat ingredient, e.g. stewing mutton as for mutton broth;

(b)   when the vegetables are sweated in fat without colour in the initial stages of preparation just prior to the addition of stock;

(c)   fish flavoured broths e.g. chowders.

41 (a) UN-SWEATED BROTH TYPE

Yield: 4 portions
Cooking time: $1\frac{1}{2} - 2$ hr

Unit	Ingredient	Metric	Imperial
1	White stock	1 l	2 pt
$\frac{1}{5}$	Meat content (raw)	200 g	8 oz
$\frac{1}{5}$	Vegetable content (fine dice)	200 g	8 oz
	carrot – celery – leek – onion – swede – turnip		
$\frac{1}{40}$	Barley	25 g	1 oz
	Bouquet garni		
	Chopped parsley		
	Seasoning		

Method

Blanch and refresh meat to remove scum. Replace meat in cooking vessel and cover with the stock. Bring to the boil, skim, add bouquet garni, barley and seasoning. Simmer until meat and barley are almost cooked.

Add the prepared vegetables and continue to simmer until vegetables are cooked. Remove meat content and bouquet garni. Cut meat into small pieces and replace in the broth. Correct seasoning and consistency for service. Garnish with chopped parsley.

N.B. For large-scale production vegetables could be coarsely minced or passed through bowl cutter before cooking.

Examples of Soups Using Above Formula

English term	Meat content	Garnish	French term
Beef broth	Stewing beef	Chopped parsley	Bouillon de Boeuf
Chicken broth	Boiling fowl	Chopped parsley	Bouillon de Volaille
Game broth	Assorted stewing game	Chopped parsley	Bouillon de Gibier
Scotch mutton broth	Stewing mutton	Chopped parsley	Potage Eccossais

42 (b) SWEATED BROTH TYPE

Yield: 4 portions
Cooking time: 45 min – 1 hr

Unit	Ingredient	Metric	Imperial
1	White chicken stock	1 l	2 pt
$\frac{2}{5}$	Main vegetable (cut into selected shape *see* below)	400 g	1 lb
$\frac{1}{20}$	Garnishing vegetables (when required)	50 g	2 oz
$\frac{1}{40}$	Butter/margarine	25 g	1 oz
	Bouquet garni		
	Seasoning		

Method

Sweat main vegetables in fat content without colour, lightly season. Add the stock, bring to boil, skim, add bouquet garni and simmer until vegetables are almost cooked. Add additional garnish, complete cooking. Correct seasoning and consistency for service.

Extensions of Broths Using Above Formula: Garnish in relation to 1 unit i.e. 1 l (2 pt) stock

Menu term	Main vegetables	Unit	Ingredient	Metric	Imperial
Potage Bonne Femme (leek and potato soup)	Equal quantities of leek and potato cut into paysanne.	$1/20$	Cream Chopped parsley	50 ml	2 fl oz
Cocky-Leeky soup	Julienne of leek	$1/20$ $1/40$	Julienne cooked chicken Julienne cooked prunes Chopped parsley	50 g 25 g	2 oz 1 oz
Potage Paysanne	Paysanne of: carrot, leek, onion, potato, swede, turnip, green cabbage	$1/40$ $1/40$	Green peas Diced French beans Chopped parsley	25 g 25 g	1 oz 1 oz
Minestroni (minestrone)	As for Potage Paysanne	$1/40$ $1/40$	Tomato concassé Raw spaghetti Tomato purée (to colour) 8 Garlic pellets (*see* p. 73) Grated parmesan cheese to accompany	25 g 25 g	1 oz 1 oz

43
SHELLFISH BROTH   Chowder

Yield: 4 portions
Cooking time: 30 min

Unit	Ingredient	Metric	Imperial
1	Fish stock	1 l	2 pt
$1/5$	Budded shellfish (plus the cooking liquor)	200 g	8 oz
$1/5$	Vegetable adjunct (paysanne of leek and potato)	200 g	8 oz
$1/10$	Belly pork (blanched and diced)	100 g	4 oz
$1/10$	Tomato concassé	100 g	4 oz
$1/10$	Cream	100 ml	4 fl oz
$1/40$	Butter/margarine	25 g	1 oz
	Bouquet garni		
	Chopped parsley		
	Salt and pepper		

Method

Sweat pork and vegetable adjunct in the butter without colour until soft, lightly season. Add stock, shellfish and liquor, bring to boil, skim, add bouquet garni and simmer until vegetables are cooked.

Add tomato concassé, correct seasoning, finish with cream and garnish with chopped parsley.

N.B.   On service *crushed water biscuits or fresh breadcrumbs* may be added to soup to act as a thickener. Alternatively chowders may be thickened with beurre manié.

Examples of Soups Prepared Using Above Formula

English term	Main shellfish	Garnish
Clam chowder	Clams	Chopped parsley
Mussel chowder	Mussels	Chopped parsley
Oyster chowder	Oysters	Chopped parsley
Scallop chowder	Scallops	Chopped parsley
Seafood chowder	Assorted shellfish	Chopped parsley

Clear Soups   Consommés

Consommés are refined clear soups prepared from good quality stocks which are flavoured and clarified by a combination of ingredients.

Clarification Process

During cooking the protein content, derived mainly from the egg white and minced beef, coagulates, flocculates and rises to the surface of the consommé. This action results in a clarified liquid being produced. Once cooking is complete the clear liquid lies beneath the mass of coagulated protein and other ingredients.

Points For Consideration

(a) In order to allow the egg white to disperse thoroughly, mix all the ingredients and allow to stand for a period prior to cooking.

(b) Use fat-free stock in order to prevent excess fat causing a greasy product.

(c) Once the consommé has been brought to the boil it is important to ensure that it simmers gently, without stirring for the remainder of the cooking period as rapid boiling or stirring will result in a clouded consommé. For the same reason do not cover the soup with a lid as this would disturb and inhibit the formation of congealed protein.

(d) A tall, deep, thick bottomed cooking vessel is ideally suited for consommé production, this type of vessel is designed to prevent excessive evaporation during cooking and helps to maintain an even temperature throughout.

(e) When most of the grease has been skimmed away from the completed consommé, any remaining grease is removed by passing pieces of absorbent paper across the surface of the consommé.

(f) The desired colour of consommé is amber.

44
BASIC CONSOMMÉ

Consommé Ordinaire

Yield: 4 portions
Cooking time: 1½ hr

Unit	Ingredient	Metric	Imperial
1	Cold stock (white or brown)	1 l	2 pt
⅕	Beef shin (minced)	200 g	8 oz
⅕	Mirepoix (scorched *see* recipe 1)	200 g	8 oz
1/20	Egg white	50 g	2 oz
	Bouquet garni		
	Salt and pepper		

N.B.   The type of stock used is determined by the flavour required in the consommé. In addition browned game, poultry carcasses, etc. may be added to appropriate consommés to enhance the flavour.

Method

Thoroughly mix all ingredients in cooking vessel and allow to stand approximately 30 minutes prior to cooking.

Commence cooking by bringing slowly to simmering point, stirring occasionally. Once boiling point is reached allow to simmer gently without any further stirring or undue agitation.

On completion strain carefully through wet muslin, degrease and correct seasoning. Reheat and garnish for service.

Examples of Consommés Prepared Using Above Formula
Garnish in relation to 1 unit i.e. 1 (2 pt)

Menu Term	Unit	Ingredient	Metric	Imperial
Consommé en Tasse (consommé served in a cup)				
Consommé Brunoise (consommé with vegetables)	1/20	Cooked brunoise of vegetables: carrot turnip leek celery	50 g	2 oz
Consommé Célestine (consommé with savoury pancake)	1/40	Julienne of savoury pancake	25 g	1 oz
Consommé Julienne (consommé with vegetables)	1/20	Cooked julienne of vegetables: carrot turnip leek celery	50 g	2 oz

Menu Term	Unit	Ingredient	Metric	Imperial
Consommé Madrilène (consommé with celery and tomato	$\frac{1}{5}$	Celery (add to consommé throughout cooking period)	200 g	8 oz
	$\frac{1}{20}$	Tomato purée (add to consommé throughout cooking period)	50 g	
		Garnish:		
	$\frac{1}{20}$	tomato concassé	50 g	2 oz
	$\frac{1}{40}$	small celery batons (cooked)	24 g	1 oz
	$\frac{1}{40}$	diced pimento (cooked)	25 g	1 oz
		shredded sorrel (sweated in butter)		
	$\frac{1}{40}$	vermicelli (cooked)	25 g	1 oz
Consommé Alphabétique (consommé with shaped pasta)	$\frac{1}{40}$	Cooked alphabet pasta	25 g	1 oz
Consommé Vermicelle (consommé with vermicelli)	$\frac{1}{40}$	Cooked vermicelli pasta	25 g	1 oz
Consommé au Porto (consommé with port wine)	$\frac{1}{20}$	Port wine	50 ml	2 fl oz
Consommé au Xérès (consommé with sherry)	$\frac{1}{20}$	Sherry	50 ml	2 fl oz
Consommé Tortue (consommé with turtle flavour)		1 sachet of turtle herbs		
	$\frac{1}{20}$	*Diced cooked turtle meat	50 g	2 oz
	$\frac{1}{20}$	Sherry	50 ml	2 fl oz
		Add turtle herbs to prepared consommé and infuse for 20 minutes before removing sachet.		
Consommé Royale (consommé with savoury egg custard)	$\frac{1}{20}$	Cooked egg custard (savoury *see* recipe 33)	50 g	2 oz

* When using dried turtle meat it must be soaked for at least 24 hr and then boiled for 6–8 hr in water until tender.

Jellied Consommé   Consommé en Gelée

In summertime consommés are often served cold in a light jellied form. If necessary the gelatinization may be assisted by the addition of $\frac{1}{40}$ unit gelatine in relation to the completed amount of consommé. Consommé au Porto en Gelée (*see* above) or Consommé Madrilène en Gelée (*see* above but omit vermicelli garnish).

Miscellaneous Soups

A selection of common soups, which cannot be strictly grouped under the former classifications, due to the method of preparation adopted.

45
FRENCH ONION SOUP   Soupe à l'oignon Française

Yield: 4 portions
Cooking time: 30 – 45 min

Unit	Ingredient	Metric	Imperial
1	Brown stock	1 l	2 pt
$\frac{1}{2}$	Onions (shredded)	500 g	20 oz
$\frac{1}{20}$	Margarine/butter	50 g	2 oz
	Chopped garlic (1 to 2 cloves)		
	Salt and pepper		
$\frac{1}{40}$*	Flour (when thickened soup is required)	25 g	1 oz
	Toasted flûtes (p. 77)		
	Grated cheese for garnish		

*N.B. This soup may be served thin or slightly thickened. In the latter case the flour forms a roux with the browned onions.

Method
Fry onions in melted fat until lightly browned. Season lightly, add stock, bring to the boil and skim. Simmer until onions are cooked, add garlic and correct seasoning. Serve in earthenware soup dish. Garnish with cheese-flavoured gratinated flûtes (p. 77).

46
MULLIGATAWNY

Yield: 4 portions
Cooking time: 1 hr

Unit	Ingredient	Metric	Imperial
1	Chicken stock	1 l	2 pt
$\frac{1}{10}$	Onion (chopped)	100 g	4 oz
$\frac{1}{20}$	Apple (chopped)	50 g	2 oz
$\frac{1}{20}$	Butter/margarine	50 g	2 oz
$\frac{1}{20}$	Flour	50 g	2 oz
$\frac{1}{40}$	Curry powder	25 g	1 oz
$\frac{1}{40}$	Tomato purée	25 g	1 oz
$\frac{1}{40}$	Chutney (chopped)	25 g	1 oz
$\frac{1}{40}$	Cooked patna rice	25 g	1 oz
	Chopped garlic		
	Salt and pepper		

Method
Sweat onions and apples in melted fat until soft, lightly season, add curry powder and cook gently for a few minutes, add flour to form a roux.

Cool, add tomato purée and gradually add stock stir to boil, skim and add remaining ingredients. Simmer until cooked. Liquidize or pass through soup machine and then through medium chinois. Re-boil, correct seasoning and consistency and lightly garnish with cooked patna rice.

N.B. Soup may be finished with cream on service.

47
TOMATO SOUP

Potage de Tomates

Yield: 4 portions
Cooking time: 1½ hr

Unit	*Ingredient*	*Metric*	*Imperial*
1	White stock	1 l	2 pt
$^1/_5$	Mirepoix (medium cut – include bacon scraps)	200 g	8 oz
$^1/_{10}$	Tomato purée	100 g	4 oz
$^1/_{20}$	Butter/margarine	50 g	2 oz
$^1/_{20}$	Flour	50 g	2 oz
	Bouquet garni (to include basil, clove, crushed garlic)		
	Salt and pepper		

Method

Sweat mirepoix in melted fat without colour and lightly season. Add flour to form a blond roux. Cool and then add tomato purée. Add stock, gradually stirring to the boil, skim add bouquet garni and simmer until soup is cooked. Cover with lid.

Pass through medium chinois, adjust seasoning and consistency, reboil and serve accompanied with soup croûtons.

The flavour of tomato soup may be made more piquant (sharp) by the addition of 'a gastric'. A gastric is a mixture of vinegar and sugar (usually half sugar to vinegar) and is used in small quantities.

N.B. Tomato soup is usually prepared from tomato purée rather than fresh tomatoes mainly in the interests of economy and culinary method. The soup has been classified miscellaneous as a result of this mode of preparation.

Extensions of Tomato Soup Prepared Using Above Formula: Garnish in relation to 1 unit i.e. 1 l (2 pt) stock

Menu term	*Unit*	*Ingredient*	*Metric*	*Imperial*
Crème de Tomates (cream of tomato soup)	$^1/_{10}$	Cream	100 ml	4 fl oz
		Chopped parsley		
Crème Portugaise	$^1/_{10}$	Cream	100 ml	4 fl oz
	$^1/_{20}$	Boiled patna rice	50 g	2 oz

48
CRÈME SOLFÉRINO

Yield: 4 portions
Cooking time: 10–15 min

Unit	Ingredient	Metric	Imperial
1	Cream of tomato soup	500 ml	1 pt
1	Purée Parmentier (*see* p. 118)	500 ml	1 pt
$^1/_{10}$	Small potato and carrot balls (cooked)	50 g	2 oz
	Chopped parsley		
	Seasoning		

Method

Combine tomato and potato soups in a saucepan, bring to boil and correct seasoning and consistency. Garnish with pre-cooked potato and carrot balls and decorate with chopped parsley for service.

49
FISH SOUP (MODERN STYLE) — Soupe de Poissons Moderne

Traditionally this soup is prepared from a variety of Mediterranean fish which, because of their small size and boney structure, are unsuitable for many culinary operations. The traditional method requires that the cooked soup is pressed through a sieve in order to remove the fish flesh from the bones and obtain maximum flavour. The ingredients and method shown below is a modification which simplifies the process by using filleted fish so that the soup can be liquidized.

Yield: 4 portions
Cooking time: 30 – 45 min

Unit	Ingredient	Metric	Imperial
1	Fish stock	1 l	2 pt
$^2/_5$	Small rock fish filleted (cut in pieces)	400 g	1 lb
$^1/_{10}$	Dry white wine (optional)	100 ml	4 fl oz
$^1/_{10}$	Potato (roughly diced)	100 g	4 oz
$^1/_{20}$	Tomato purée	50 g	2 oz
$^1/_{20}$	Vegetable adjunct (onion roughly chopped	50 g	2 oz
$^1/_{20}$	Gruyère cheese (grated)	50 g	2 oz
$^1/_{40}$	Oil	25 ml	1 fl oz
	Bouquet garni		
	Freshly chopped parsley		
	2 cloves of garlic (finely chopped)		
	Pinch of saffron		
	Freshly ground black pepper		
	Salt to season		
	4 croûtes of French bread (toasted)		
	Garlic dressing★		

★Garlic Dressing	Egg yolk	*50 g (2 oz)*	Seasoning	*to taste*
	Chopped garlic	*2 cloves*	Lemon juice	*squeeze*
	Saffron	*pinch*	Oil	*100 ml (4 fl oz)*

Method

Whisk together egg yolk, garlic, saffron, seasoning and lemon juice. Whisk the oil in gradually, as in the making of mayonnaise, to form an emulsified garlic dressing.

Method (soup production and service)

Heat oil in the saucepan, add adjunct, chopped garlic and sweat gently until the vegetables are softened. Add fish and tomato purée and continue gentle cooking for 2 minutes. Stir in the wine, fish stock, bring to the boil and skim. Add potato, bouquet garni, saffron and seasoning. Simmer gently for approximately 30 – 45 minutes. Remove Bouquet garni, liquidize the soup and pour into clean saucepan. Reheat, correct seasoning and consistency.

Spread toasted croûtes with garlic dressing and sprinkle with grated gruyère cheese. To serve ladle soup into dishes, garnish with croûtes and chopped parsley.

Bouillabaisse

A type of soup/stew (*see* recipe 130).

50
RUSSIAN BORTSCH   Bortsch à la Russe

Yield: 4 portions
Cooking time: 30 min

Unit	Ingredient	Metric	Imperial
1	Duck consommé (made from duck stock)	1 l	2 pt
$^1/_5$	Julienne of: leek, celery, carrot, onion, cabbage	200 g	8 oz
$^1/_{10}$*	Beetroot juice	100 ml	4 fl oz
	Julienne of:		
$^1/_{20}$	cooked beef	50 g	2 oz
$^1/_{20}$	cooked breast of duck	50 g	2 oz
$^1/_{40}$	cooked beetroot	25 g	1 oz
$^1/_{40}$	Butter	25 g	1 oz
	Seasoning		

*To prepare beetroot juice grate some raw beetroot, wrap in muslin and squeeze to extract the juice.

Method

Sweat vegetables in butter without colour, add duck consommé, bring to boil, skim and simmer until vegetables are cooked. Add beetroot juice, reboil and correct seasoning. Garnish with julienne of cooked beef, duck and beetroot, degrease and serve.

Bortsch Accompaniments

(a) Sauceboat of cold beetroot juice;
(b) sauceboat of soured cream;
(c) sauceboat of tiny duck patties (small choux or puff pastry cases filled with duck forcemeat).

51
POTAGE GERMINY

Yield: 4 portions
Cooking time: 15 – 20 min

Unit	Ingredient	Metric	Imperial
1	White chicken stock	800 ml	1½ pt
⅕	Egg yolks ⎫ liaison	160 g	6 oz
⅕	Cream (double) ⎭	160 ml	6 fl oz
¹⁄₂₀	Butter	40 g	1½ oz
¹⁄₄₀	Sorrel (julienne)	20 g	¾ oz
	Seasoning		

Method

Sweat sorrel in half of the butter without colour, add stock and simmer briskly for 10 minutes to extract flavour. Remove from heat, stir in liaison of yolks and cream to effect a light thickening, do not allow to reboil otherwise egg yolks will curdle and spoil the appearance of the soup. Blend in remaining butter, correct seasoning and serve with an accompaniment of cheese straws (p. 114).

52
CREAM OF GREEN PEA SOUP (USING FRESH/FROZEN PEAS)
Crème St Germain

Yield: 4 portions
Cooking time: 45 min – 1 hour

Unit	Ingredient	Metric	Imperial
1*	White stock	500 ml	1 pt
⅘	Shelled peas	400 g	1 lb
⅕	Cream	100 ml	4 fl oz
¹⁄₁₀	Diced onion	50 g	2 oz
¹⁄₁₀	Butter	50 g	2 oz
	Sprig of mint		
	Pinch of sugar		
	Seasoning		
	Soup croûtons (*see* p. 77)		

*Extra stock may be required to adjust consistency.

Method

Sweat onions in butter without colour, add peas, sugar, mint, stock and seasoning cover with a lid and simmer until peas are tender. Liquidize or pass through soup machine and medium conical strainer. Adjust consistency, blend in cream, correct seasoning and serve with soup croûtons.

Extensions of Crème St Germain Using Above Formula: Garnish in relation to 1 unit i.e. 500 ml (1 pt) stock

Menu term	Unit	Ingredient	Metric (g)	Imperial (oz)
Crème Lamballe/Cream of pea soup with tapioca	$1/20$	Cooked tapioca	25	1
Crème Longchamp/Cream of pea soup with vermicelli and sorrel	$1/20$ $1/40$	Cooked vermicelli Sorrel (julienne-sweated)	25 12.5	1 $1/2$
Crème St Cloud/Cream of pea soup with lettuce and chervil	$1/20$	Julienne of lettuce and chervil (sweated)	25	1

53
GAZPACHO (A COLD SPANISH SOUP)

Yield: 4 portions

Unit	Ingredient	Metric	Imperial
1	Tomato juice	500 ml	1 pt
$1/4$	Iced water	125 ml	5 fl oz
$1/4$	Tomato concassé	125 g	5 oz
$1/4$	Peeled cucumber (small dice)	125 g	5 oz
$1/4$	Green pepper ⎫ brunoise	125 g	5 oz
$1/10$	Onion ⎭	50 g	2 oz
$1/20$	Mayonnaise	25 ml	1 fl oz
$1/20$	Wine vinegar	25 ml	1 fl oz
	Flavourings: hint of chopped garlic dash of Worcester sauce dash of Tobasco sauce squeeze of lemon juice seasoning		

Method

Combine all ingredients other than cucumber and season to taste. Allow to stand for 2 hours in a cool place. Correct seasoning, add cucumber and serve chilled.

N.B. This soup may be prepared by the Chef Garde-Manger.

54
VICHYSSOISE (COLD LEEK AND POTATO SOUP)

Yield: 4 portions
Cooking time: 1 hr

Unit	Ingredient	Metric	Imperial
1	Chicken stock	800 ml	1½ pt
²/₅	White of leek ⎫ sliced	320 g	12 oz
¹/₅	Potato ⎭	160 g	6 oz
¹/₁₀	Cream	80 ml	3 fl oz
¹/₂₀	Butter	40 g	1½ oz
	Bouquet garni		
	Chopped chives (garnish)		
	Seasoning		

Method
Sweat leeks and potato in butter without colour and lightly season. Add stock bring to the boil, skim, add bouquet garni, cover with lid and simmer until vegetables are cooked. Remove bouquet garni, liquidize or pass through a soup machine and through a fine conical strainer. Correct seasoning, stir over ice until cold, add cream, garnish with chives and serve chilled.

55
PETITE MARMITE

Yield: 4 portions
Cooking time: 45 min

Unit	Ingredient	Metric	Imperial
1	Beef consommé	1 l	2 pt
¹/₅	Carrot and turnip (small, turned)	200 g	8 oz
¹/₅	Julienne of: leek, cabbage, celery	200 g	8 oz
¹/₁₀*	Blanched beef and chicken dice	100 g	4 oz
	4 Slices of beef marrow		
	Toasted flûtes		
	Chopped parsley		
	Seasoning		

*Meat content is blanched to remove congealed blood particles and scum which would impair the appearance of the soup.

Method

Add the blanched beef and chicken dice to the consommé, bring to the boil and skim. Simmer until the meat is almost cooked, add carrot and turnip and simmer for 5 minutes, add remaining julienne of vegetables. Continue simmering until meat and vegetables are cooked, correct seasoning and add marrow just before service. Serve in small earthenware marmite pots accompanied with toasted flûtes of bread and grated parmesan cheese.

Extensions of Petite Marmite Using Above Formula: Garnish in relation to 1 unit i.e. 1 l (2 pt) stock

Menu term	Unit	Ingredient	Metric (g)	Imperial (oz)
Petite Marmite Béarnaise	¹⁄₄₀	Boiled patna rice	25	1
	¹⁄₄₀	Julienne of cooked potato	25	1
Croûte au Pot		As for Petite Marmite omitting beef and chicken dice		

7

Basic Egg Cookery and Extensions

Throughout culinary work eggs are employed in a number of ways. Examples of their general use may be listed as follows:

(a) to aerate — soufflés, batters;
(b) to bind — potato dishes, stuffings;
(c) to coat — coating foods with breadcrumbs;
(d) to enrich and thicken — sauces, soups, and white stews;
(e) to emulsify — hollandaise, béarnaise, mayonnaise sauces;
(f) to glaze and colour — used as egg wash on goods for baking and browning under the salamander.

In addition egg dishes appear on the traditional menu as a course in their own right and are often chosen as a preliminary item prior to the main dish. However, they may also be selected as a main course item, e.g. omelets, curried eggs.

Egg dishes are ideal for use in the more modern type of fast-food operation, e.g. hotel buttery, bistro, snack bar, motorway operation, etc. In these circumstances they may be served as a meal 24 hours a day and in most instances are cooked to order.

When a traditional kitchen brigade is employed, all cold egg dishes are the responsibility of the Chef Garde-Manger (Larder Chef), hot egg dishes for luncheon and dinner the responsibility of the Chef Entremettier (Vegetable Chef), and egg dishes for breakfast prepared by the Breakfast Chef. The allocation of these duties may vary from one establishment to another according to the size and nature of the brigade.

Eggs
Les Oeufs

Egg dishes may be classified according to the method of cookery used. They are as follows:

Method I: Poached Eggs
Oeufs Pochés

Prepare a shallow pan or tray containing lightly acidulated (vinegar), seasoned (salt) water. Bring to simmering point, break in eggs and poach gently until white sets firm and yolks remain soft.

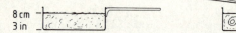

8 cm
3 in

Remove eggs with perforated spoon and drain well, use immediately or 'refresh' and store in iced water for later use. *To re-heat* plunge into simmering seasoned water for approximately 30 seconds to 1 minute.

Method II: Poached en Bain-Marie   Oeufs Moulés

Half fill cooking vessel with water to form bain-marie. Bring to boiling point, prepare egg moulds with seasoning (salt and pepper) and knob of butter to flavour and prevent eggs from sticking to moulds.

Break eggs one at a time into individual moulds, cover with lid and cook gently en bain-marie until white sets firm and yolk remains soft (approximately 3–5 minutes). Turn out from moulds and serve.

Lid to cover
Lightly seasoned buttered moulds
Steam vents
Half-filled with water

Examples of Dishes Prepared Using Oeufs Pochés: Ingredients for 4 Portions Using 4 Poached Eggs (1 per portion)

English term	Unit	Ingredient	Metric	Imperial	French term
Egg with asparagus served in pastry cases	1	Cream sauce 8 Asparagus spears (cooked) 4 small savoury pastry cases	250 ml	10 fl oz	Oeuf Poché Argenteuil
		Trim 4 small asparagus tips for garnish. Finely chop remaining asparagus and cohere with a little of the sauce. Heat the mixture and place in base of pastry case. Sit hot eggs into cases, napper with sauce, garnish with hot asparagus tips and serve			
Egg with muffins, tongue and hollandaise sauce	1 2/5	Hollandaise sauce Sliced cooked tongue 4 croûtes toasted (muffins buttered) 4 slices truffle for garnish	250 ml 100 g	10 fl oz 4 oz	Oeuf Poché Bénédictine
		Place heated tongue on to croûtes of muffin. Sit heated egg on to tongue and napper with sauce, garnish with truffle			

English term	Unit	Ingredient	Metric	Imperial	French term
Egg with rice and curry sauce	1 $^1/_5$	Curry sauce Patna rice (boiled)	250 ml 50 g	10 fl oz 2 oz	Oeuf Poché Bombay or Indienne
		Put a bed of hot rice into buttered egg dish. Sit heated egg on to rice and napper with sauce and serve			
Egg in cheese sauce	1 $^1/_5$	Mornay Sauce Grated cheese	250 ml 50 g	10 fl oz 2 oz	Oeuf Poché Mornay
		Place heated eggs in buttered and sauced egg dish. Coat with sauce, sprinkle with grated cheese and gratinate for service. N.B. May be presented in pastry cases			
Egg in cheese sauce with spinach	$^2/_5$	Cooked leaf spinach	100 g	4 oz	Oeuf Poché Florentine
		Prepare as for Oeuf Poché Mornay but placing eggs on a bed of heated spinach			
Egg in pastry case with cooked chicken	1 $^2/_5$	Supreme sauce Diced cooked chicken 4 small savoury pastry cases	250 ml 100 g	10 fl oz 4 oz	Oeuf Poché à la Reine
		Cohere chicken with a little sauce. Heat the mixture and place in base of pastry cases. Sit heated eggs on to bed of chicken, napper with sauce and serve			
Egg in pastry case with cooked sweetcorn		As for Oeuf Poché à la Reine but replace chicken with sweetcorn			Oeuf Poché Washington

Boiled Eggs   Oeufs Bouillis

Eggs are boiled to varying degrees according to requirements and may be served with or without shell.

Method

Place eggs into metal basket and plunge into simmering water, reboil and simmer for required time. Commence timing once water has reboiled.
The stages of boiling are:

(1) *Soft boiled (in shell)*   *Oeuf à la Coque*   *Boiling Time (3–4 min)*

Served in shell, timed to the customer's personal requirements.

(2) *Soft boiled and shelled*   *Oeuf Mollet*   *Boiling Time (5 min)*

On completion of boiling 'refresh' in cold water, remove shells carefully and reheat in boiling water ($\frac{1}{2}$ min) as required. Prepare and garnished as for poached eggs (*see* above).

(3) *Hard boiled*   *Oeuf Dur*   *Boiling Time (8–10 min)*

Served with or without shell. Often refreshed and shelled immediately in readiness for use.

Examples of Dishes Prepared Using Oeufs Durs (Hard Boiled Eggs): Ingredients for 4 portions using 4 hard boiled eggs (1 per portion)

English term	Unit	Ingredient	Metric	Imperial	French term
Egg with rice and curry sauce	1 $\frac{2}{5}$	Curry sauce Patna rice (boiled)	250 ml 100 g	10 fl oz 4 oz	Oeuf Dur Bombay or Indienne
		Place a bed of hot rice into buttered egg dish. Sit halved or quartered egg on to rice, napper with sauce and serve			
Egg in white onion sauce	1	White onion sauce Chopped parsley	250 ml	10 fl oz	Oeuf à la Tripe
		Place halved or quartered eggs into buttered sauce egg dish. Napper with sauce and garnish with parsley and serve			
Stuffed egg in cheese sauce	1 $\frac{2}{5}$ $\frac{1}{5}$	Cheese sauce Duxelle Grated cheese	250 ml 100 g 50 g	10 fl oz 4 oz 2 oz	Oeuf Chimay
		Halve eggs lengthways, remove yolk and sieve finely. Mix sieved yolk with duxelle and cohere with a little sauce. Replace mixture into egg white cavity to form a mound. Place in buttered sauced egg dish, napper with sauce, sprinkle with cheese. Bake in hot oven till golden brown 205°C (400°F)			
Stuffed egg with aurore sauce		Prepare as for Oeuf Chimay, but substitute cheese sauce with Sauce Aurore. N.B. Béchamel coloured and flavoured with tomato purée may be used			Oeuf Aurore

Egg in Cocotte

Oeuf en Cocotte

Indicates egg cooked in a small glazed earthenware dish (cocotte), garnished in various ways. When served as a preliminary course one egg per person is the accepted portion. These dishes are served for luncheon or dinner and are presented in and eaten from the cocotte dish in which they are cooked. All these items are cooked to order.

Glazed earthenware cocotte dishes

Prepared en bain-marie for cooking

Lid to cover.

Whole egg   Garnish   Water

Method

Butter and season cocotte dishes, break in eggs one at a time. Place cocottes in prepared bain-marie (only sufficient water to half cover cocotte). Cover with lid and cook on stove top until white of egg is set but yolk remains soft. Once cooked pour away the condensation that has formed on egg surface. Serve immediately.

N.B.   When a garnish is employed it is usually placed in the base of the cocotte before the egg is put in position. Upon completion of cooking the eggs may be finished with a cordon of sauce or cream and decorated with parsley.

Examples of Dishes Prepared Using Oeuf En Cocotte: Ingredients for 4 portions using 4 eggs (1 per portion)

English term	Unit	Ingredient	Metric	Imperial	French term
Egg garnished with mushroom and cooked mutton	1	Jus lié	100 ml	4 fl oz	Oeuf en Cocotte Bergère
	½	Minced mutton (cooked)	50 g	2 oz	
	½	Chopped mushroom (cooked)	50 g	2 oz	
		Cohere mushrooms and mutton with a little sauce and place in base of cocotte before adding eggs to cook. Once cooked finish with a cordon of sauce			
Egg garnished with poached beef marrow and bordelaise sauce	1	Bordelaise sauce	100 ml	4 fl oz	Oeuf en Cocotte Bordelaise
		8 thin slices of poached beef marrow			
		Garnish base of each cocotte with one slice of marrow before adding eggs to cook. Once cooked finish with a cordon of sauce and a slice of marrow			
Egg with cream	1	Double cream	100 ml	4 fl oz	Oeuf en Cocotte à la Crème
		Once egg is cooked finish with a cordon of cream			

English term	Unit	Ingredient	Metric	Imperial	French term
Egg with thickened veal gravy	1	Jus lié	100 ml	4 fl oz	Oeuf en Cocotte Jus Lié
		Once egg is cooked finish with cordon of sauce			
Egg garnished with foie gras and Périgueux sauce	1	Périgueux sauce	100 ml	4 fl oz	Oeuf en Cocotte Périgourdine
		4 Thin slices of foie gras			
		Garnish base of each cocotte with one slice of foie gras before adding eggs to cook. Once cooked finish with a cordon of sauce			
Egg garnished with asparagus and Périgueux sauce	1	Périgueux sauce	100 ml	4 fl oz	Oeuf en Cocotte Petit-Duc
		8 Asparagus spears heated			
		Trim 4 small asparagus tips for garnish. Chop remaining asparagus and place in base of each cocotte before adding eggs to cook. Once cooked garnish with asparagus tips and cordon of sauce			
Egg garnished with tomatoes	1 $^1/_2$	Tomato sauce Tomatoes concassées	100 ml 50 g	4 fl oz 2 oz	Oeuf en Cocotte Portugaise
		Garnish base of each cocotte with tomato before adding eggs to cook. Once cooked finish with a cordon of sauce			
Egg garnished with creamed chicken	1 $^1/_2$	Double cream Minced cooked chicken	100 ml 50 g	4 fl oz 2 oz	Oeuf en Cocotte à la Reine
		Cohere chicken with half cream and place in the base of each cocotte before adding eggs to cook. Once cooked finish with a cordon of cream			
Egg garnished with onions and soubise sauce	1 $^1/_2$	Soubise sauce Sliced onion (sweat without colour)	100 ml 50 g	4 fl oz 2 oz	Oeuf en Cocotte Soubise
		Cohere onion with a little sauce and place in the base of each cocotte before adding eggs to cook. Once cooked finish with a cordon of sauce			

Egg Baked in China Plate (dish)   Oeuf Sur le Plat

China plate:
Sur le Plat dish

Indicates an egg baked in a buttered ovenproof china dish which may be garnished in a variety of ways. When served as a preliminary course one egg per person is the accepted portion. These dishes may be served at lunch or dinner and are presented in and eaten from the dish in which they are cooked. All these dishes are cooked to order.

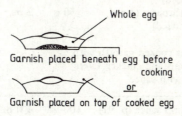

Whole egg

Garnish placed beneath egg before
                                    cooking

or

Garnish placed on top of cooked egg

Method

Butter and season sur le plat dish, place on stove top to heat. Break in eggs one at a time and cook until white begins to set. Place in moderately hot oven to complete cooking. This is complete when white is set firm and yolk remains soft. Serve immediately.

N.B.   When a garnish is employed it may be placed in the base of the dish before egg is added or used to garnish once egg is cooked. These dishes are often finished with a cordon of sauce or cream and decorated with parsley.

Examples of Dishes Prepared Using Oeuf Sur Le Plat: Ingredients for 4 portions using 4 eggs (1 per portion)

English term	Unit	Ingredient	Metric	Imperial	French term
Egg with grilled ham and tomato sauce	1	Tomato sauce	100 ml	4 fl oz	Oeuf Sur le Plat Américaine
		4 Thin slices grilled ham			
		Garnish base of dish with ham before adding egg to cook. Once cooked finish with a cordon of tomato sauce			
Egg with grilled chipolata sausage and tomato sauce	1	Tomato sauce	100 ml	4 fl oz	Oeuf Sur le Plat Bercy
		8 Grilled cocktail chipolata sausages			
		Once egg is cooked garnish with sausage and finish with a cordon of tomato sauce			

English term	Unit	Ingredient	Metric	Imperial	French term
Egg with cream	1	Double cream	100 ml	4 fl oz	Oeuf Sur le Plat à la Crème
		Once egg is cooked finish with cordon of double cream			
Egg with chicken livers, mushrooms, and Madeira sauce	1 ½	Madeira sauce Chicken livers (diced, sautéed)	100 ml 50 g	4 fl oz 2 oz	Oeuf sur le Plat Chasseur
	½	Mushrooms (diced, sautéed)	50 g	2 oz	
		Once egg is cooked garnish with mushrooms and chicken livers cohered with sauce			
Egg garnished with shrimps and shrimp sauce	1 ½	Shrimp sauce (p. 91) Picked shrimps (heated)	100 ml 50 g	4 fl oz 2 oz	Oeuf sur le Plat aux Crevettes Grises
		Once egg is cooked garnish with shrimps and finish with cordon of sauce			
Egg with grilled bacon		4 Slices of grilled bacon			Oeuf sur le Plat au Lard
		Garnish base of dish with bacon before adding egg to cook			
Egg with grilled bacon, gruyère cheese and cream	1 ½	Double cream Gruyère cheese (grated) 4 Slices of grilled bacon	100 ml 50 g	4 fl oz 2 oz	Oeuf sur le Plat Lorraine
		Garnish base of dish with bacon and cheese before adding egg to cook. Once cooked finish with cordon of cream			
Egg with spinach and cheese sauce	1 ½ ¼	Cheese sauce Leaf spinach (cooked) Grated cheese	200 ml 100 g 50 g	8 fl oz 4 oz 2 oz	Oeuf sur le Plat Florentine
		Garnish base of dish with spinach before adding egg to cook. Once cooked napper with sauce, sprinkle with cheese and gratinate under salamander			

Shallow Fried Eggs   Oeufs Frits

Indicates eggs gently cooked with oil/bacon fat/lard in a shallow frying vessel until white is firm while yolk remains soft. These eggs may be cooked to customer requirements e.g. well cooked yolk. Fried eggs are served at breakfast and are also served in fast food operations as snack meals 24 hours a day. In addition they are used as a garnish when preparing certain entrées, e.g. Escalope de Veau Holstein and Vienna Steaks.

Method

Cover the base of a shallow cooking vessel with clean frying oil or selected fat. Heat gently, break in eggs one at a time and fry steadily until the white sets firm and yolk remains soft. During frying baste eggs frequently with fat/oil to ensure even cooking. Remove with egg slice, drain well and serve.

   N.B.   Ensure at the onset that the cooking fat/oil is not too hot, otherwise egg white will over-cook, become crisp, brown and indigestible.

Turned Egg

As above but fried on both sides until well cooked.

Deep Fried Egg   Oeuf Frit à la Française

Egg which is deep fried in oil, shaped during cooking by enveloping the yolk with the white. Chiefly used as a garnish, e.g. Poulet Sauté Marengo.

Method

Half fill omelette pan with oil and heat to frying temperature. Break in the egg, then using an oiled wooden spatula manipulate the white around the yolk as the egg begins to set. Continue cooking to light brown colour. Using perforated spoon remove cooked egg, drain well and serve.

56
SCRAMBLED EGGS   Oeufs Brouillés

Indicates seasoned, beaten eggs cooked in butter until eggs coagulate to become firm and fluffy in texture. Scrambled eggs may be served for breakfast, garnished and served as a course at luncheon, dinner or as a snack meal in fast food establishments.

Yield: 4 portions
Cooking time: 5 – 10 min approx.
(will take longer with larger quantities)

Unit	Ingredient	Metric	Imperial
1	Beaten whole egg	400 g	1 lb
$\frac{1}{8}$	Milk	50 ml	2 fl oz
$\frac{1}{8}$	Butter	50 g	2 oz
	Seasoning: salt and white pepper to taste		

Method

Mix eggs, milk and seasoning together.
Melt butter over gentle heat in saucepan, add eggs and mix thoroughly with wooden

spoon until eggs lightly set (coagulate). Correct seasoning and serve immediately. N.B.

(a) May be enriched before service with a little cream.

(b) When using aluminium pan do not mix with metal whisk during cooking otherwise eggs will discolour.

(c) Large quantities are best cooked en bain-marie as they take a longer time to cook and the chance of burning is reduced by this method.

Examples of Dishes Prepared Using Oeufs Brouillés: Ingredients for 4 portions using 8 eggs (2 per portion)

English term	Unit	Ingredient	Metric	Imperial	French term
Scrambled eggs with ham, mushrooms, and asparagus	1 ½	Cooked diced ham Cooked diced mushrooms 4 Asparagus tips (heated)	100 g 50 g	4 oz 2 oz	Oeufs Brouillés Archiduchesse
		Heat ham, mushrooms in a little butter, combine carefully with scrambled egg. Place in selected service dish, garnish with asparagus and serve			
Scrambled eggs with mushrooms	1	Cooked sliced mushrooms	100 g	4 oz	Oeufs Brouillés aux Champignons
		Combine hot mushrooms with scrambled egg and serve			
Scrambled eggs with diced fried croûtons	1	Diced croûtons (shallow fried)	100 g	4 oz	Oeufs Brouillés aux Croûtons
		Surround scrambled egg with croûtons and serve As above finished with chopped parsley			Oeufs Brouillés Grand' Mère
Scrambled eggs with chicken livers and Madeira sauce	1 1	Madeira sauce Chicken liver (diced, sautéed in butter	100 ml 100 g	4 fl oz 4 oz	Oeufs Brouillés aux Foies de Volaille
		Cohere chicken livers with half sauce. Place in centre of scrambled egg, finish with cordon of sauce			
Scrambled eggs with tomatoes	1	Tomato concassé	100 g	4 oz	Oeufs Brouillés Portugaise
		Heat tomato in a little butter and combine with scrambled egg			

All garnishes are seasoned to taste.

Omelets   Les Omelettes

To the layman the making of an omelet appears to be a simple operation, however if a satisfactory product is to be achieved a great deal of skill is required.

Omelets are served for breakfast, luncheon, dinner and frequently as a meal in fast food establishments. In general 2 – 3 eggs are used per omelet according to portion control requirements and sizes of eggs used. Omelets are generally served in one of two ways either flat or folded (cigar shaped).

The garnish or flavouring may be added in a variety of ways:

(a) combined with egg before cooking;
(b) placed into centre of omelet before it is folded;
(c) placed on top of omelet, in a cavity after folding is complete.

General Points Concerning Omelet Preparation

Omelet Pans

These are made from heavy gauge wrought iron or steel. When the pans are new or sticking they need to be *'proved'* before use. This is achieved by filling the pan with plenty of salt and heating them on the stove top or in a moderate oven for 2 to 3 hours. The salt is then removed and the pan wiped clear with a clean dry cloth. At this stage the pan is half filled with cooking oil and steadily heated on the stove top for a further period until the pan is smooth, black and shiny in appearance. Once in general use the omelet pans should on no account be washed but instead wiped clean with a dry cloth after use. If the pan is washed it will lose its non-stick characteristic, will need re-proving and may also rust from contact with the water. Always store omelet pans clean and brushed with a film of oil to prevent bacterial infection and rusting.

Degree of Cooking Omelets

The texture of the completed omelet should be soft, with a firm exterior and a moist centre, this is termed *baveuse*. Ideally the exterior of the completed omelet should have just begun to colour. However, the texture and colour of an omelet may vary according to customer requirement and also when a glazed finish is required. Omelets are generally cooked to order.

Service of Omelet

For service omelets are placed on lightly buttered flats, then brushed gently with melted butter. This gives the omelet a shiny appearance.

General Mise-en-place for Omelet Production

1. Collect eggs required.
2. Small bowl and fork for mixing eggs.
3. Seasonings, fillings, flavourings and garnishes.
4. Jug of cooking oil and knobs of butter.
5. Prepared heated omelet pan half filled with oil.
6. Service dishes.
7. Clean dry cloth for wiping pan clean after use.
8. Melted butter and brush to butter service dishes and cooked omelet.

Plain Omelet   Omelette Nature

Yield: 2 – 3 eggs = 1 portion
Cooking time: approximately 1 min

Method

Break eggs into bowl, season and beat with a fork, mix thoroughly to disperse white and
yolk evenly. This ensures an omelet of even colour and texture. Remove oil from heated
omelet pan, place pan directly over heat, add knob of butter and allow to melt.

Pour in the eggs, shake pan briskly whilst gently stirring with the fork to distribute egg
evenly around base of the pan.

Once egg begins to set, remove pan from heat, loosen around edge with fork, tilt pan
downwards slightly, fold nearside of omelet to centre, tap pan handle briskly to move
omelet to far edge of pan. Fold far side of omelet to centre to form cigar (oval) shape, seal
quickly with fork and turn out on to buttered service dish. Brush surface with melted
butter and serve.

Flat Omelet

Add garnish to egg before making the omelet, turn out without folding, coloured side
uppermost.

Stuffed and Folded Omelet

Place filling in centre of omelet before folding.

Folded and Stuffed Omelet

Slit turned out omelet along centre of top surface, place in the filling.

Folded Omelet

Add garnish to egg before cooking.

Examples of Omelet Extensions: Ingredients for 4 portions of filling (2/3 eggs per omelet)

English term	Unit	Ingredient	Metric	Imperial	French term
Flat Omelets					
Spanish omelet	1	Diced pimento (cooked)	100 g	4 oz	Omelette Espagnole
	1	Tomato concassé	100 g	4 oz	
	1	Diced onion (sweated without colour	100 g	4 oz	
		4 Anchovy fillets ⎱ garnish for decoration 4 Stoned olives ⎰			
		Hint of chopped garlic			
		Chopped parsley			
		Combine all ingredients with egg omitting garnish. Cook and serve flat. Garnish with olive wrapped in anchovy fillet			

English term	Unit	Ingredient	Metric	Imperial	French term
Omelet farmer's style	1	Finely diced cooked ham Chopped parsley	100 g	4 oz	Omelette Fermière
		Combine ingredients with egg, cook and serve flat			
Omelet peasant style	1	Finely diced potato (cooked)	100 g	4 oz	Omelette Paysanne
	1	Diced cooked bacon Chopped fine herbs and sorrel	100 g	4 oz	
		Combine ingredients with egg, cook and serve flat			
Potato omelet	1	Diced sautéed potatoes Chopped parsley	100 g	4 oz	Omelette Parmentier
		Combine ingredients with egg, cook and serve flat			

Stuffed Omelets (folded)

The omelets listed below are stuffed according to service style.

English term	Unit	Ingredient	Metric	Imperial	French term
Turkish omelet	1	Diced cooked chicken livers cohered in Madeira sauce	100 g	4 oz	Omelette à la Turque
		Cordon of Madeira sauce to garnish			
Shrimp omelet	1	Picked shrimps cohered with shrimp sauce	100 g	4 oz	Omelette aux Crevettes Grises
	1	Mornay sauce	250 ml	10 fl oz	Omelette Arnold Bennett
	$^2/_5$	Cooked smoked haddock flaked and cohered with double cream	100 g	4 oz	
	$^1/_5$	Grated cheese	50 g	2 oz	
		Stuff omelet with haddock, turn out on to service dish, napper with sauce, sprinkle with grated cheese and gratinate to serve			

English term	Unit	Ingredient	Metric	Imperial	French term
Tomato omelet	1	Tomates concassées	100 g	4 oz	Omelette aux Tomates/ Portugaise
		Cordon of tomato sauce garnish			

Folded Omelets

For the omelets below the garnish is mixed with eggs prior to cooking.

English term	Unit	Ingredient	Metric	Imperial	French term
Mushroom omelet	1	Sliced mushrooms sweated in butter	100 g	4 oz	Omelette aux Champignons
Herb omelet		Fine herbs to garnish and flavour			Omelette Fines Herbes
Cheese omelet	1	Grated cheese	100 g	4 oz	Omelette au Fromage
Ham omelet	1	Finely diced cooked ham	100 g	4 oz	Omelette au Jambon
Ham and potato omelet	1	Finely diced potato	50 g	2 oz	Omelette Limousine
	1	Finely diced ham	50 g	2 oz	
		Toss garnish in butter until cooked, combine with eggs			
Bacon and cheese omelet	1	Small diced fried bacon	50 g	2 oz	Omelette Lorraine
	1	Gruyère cheese (grated)	50 g	2 oz	
		Chopped chives			

8

Farinaceous Cookery and Extensions

The word farinaceous is derived from 'farine' meaning flour, and is used to classify culinary products prepared from rice, pasta and various types of gnocchis (small dumplings)

Where a traditional kitchen brigade is employed, farinaceous preparations are usually the responsibility of the 'Chef Entremettier' (Vegetable Chef), this responsibility may vary according to the nature and size of the brigade.

Farinaceous products may be served for luncheon or dinner and appear in a variety of guises:

(a) as a menu course e.g. spaghetti bolognaise;
(b) as an accompaniment e.g. boiled rice and curries;
(c) as a garnish e.g. gnocchi with goulash;
(d) as a substitute for vegetables e.g. braised rice to replace potatoes.

Farinaceous dishes are ideal for use in modern units as explained for egg dishes (p. 139). They may be classified as follows:

1. Rice   – Riz
2. Gnocchi – Noques
3. Pasta   – Pâtes alimentaires

Rice Products

The types of rice commonly used in the kitchen are broadly classified as 'long grain (patna, piedmont) and 'short' grain (carolina), the latter being used for rice-based sweet preparations.

All the products in this study are prepared using long-grained rice which on cooking remains intact, dry and fluffy without the grains sticking together.

Points for Consideration when Cooking Rice

(a) When boiling rice, use plenty of lightly seasoned water to allow the rice grains freedom of movement during cooking. An approximate guide is 10 units water to 1 unit rice.

(b) At the commencement of boiling, the rice should be stirred to prevent clogging or sticking. Once the grains are cooked care must be taken, when stirring, not to damage the softened grains, as this would spoil the appearance of the finished product. Likewise in the cooking of pilaff and risotto a double pronged cook's fork is used for stirring, after the initial cooking period.

(c) The appearance and texture of cooked rice should be fluffy and firm. Overcooked rice becomes soggy, taking on an unpleasant watery texture and flavour.

(d) When Piedmont rice is not available for risotto other long-grained varieties are used.

(e) The main differences between a pilaff and a risotto are:

(1) the mode of cookery used, pilaff is braised in the oven, risotto is stewed on the stove top;

(2) less stock is used when cooking a pilaff, and as a result the stock is fully absorbed into the rice giving a drier appearance than that of the more moist risotto.

(f) The stock proportions used in both the pilaff and risotto may vary according to the absorption rates of rice and the length and speed of the cooking period.

57
PLAIN BOILED RICE

Riz Nature

Yield: 200 g or 8 oz = 4 portions
Cooking time: 15–20 min

Unit	Ingredient	Metric	Imperial
1	Rice patna	200 g	8 oz
	Salt to taste		
*	Water (boiling)	2 l	4 pt

* 10 units *water* to 1 unit *rice* approximately 10:1.

Method

Season boiling water, add rice grains, stir to the boil, reduce heat and simmer until just cooked (*al dente*). Once the rice is cooked place the vessel under slow running cold water to cool rice and remove excess starch. This is indicated when water clears. Drain well in colander. At this point the grains should separate readily.

Spread grains on to lightly greased shallow trays, cover with a clean cloth and place in slow oven/hot cupboard to dry and reheat. Stir occasionally with fork to prevent sticking. Use as required.

Fried Rice

Quickly shallow fry dried boiled rice in a film of cooking oil, margarine or butter. The rice is fried without colour and seasoned to taste. A garnish may be added to improve appearance and flavour, e.g. cooked pimentoes, cooked sliced mushrooms, saffron, etc.

58
STEWED SAVOURY RICE (ITALIAN STYLE)   Rizotto

Yield: 200 g or 8 oz = 4 portions
Cooking time: 20–30 min

Unit	Ingredient	Metric	Imperial
1	Rice (piedmont/patna)	200 g	8 oz
1/4	Onion (brunoise)	50 g	2 oz
1/8	Butter/margarine	25 g	1 oz
	Seasoning to taste		
	Bouquet garni		
*	White stock (heated usually chicken)	600 ml	1 1/4 pt

* 3 units *stock* to 1 unit *rice* approximately 3:1.

Method

Sweat onions in butter without colour, add rice, mix well. Add stock, stir to the boil, add bouquet garni and seasoning. Cover with lid and simmer gently on stove top until rice is cooked. Stir occasionally to prevent rice from sticking to bottom of cooking vessel. Using a fork stir in a knob of butter and any further seasoning. Remove bouquet garni and serve as required.

59
BRAISED SAVOURY RICE (INDIAN STYLE)   Pilaff/Pilaw/Pilau

Yield: 200 g or 8 oz of rice = 4 portions
Cooking time: 15–20 min
Cooking temperature: 205°C (400°F)

Unit	Ingredient	Metric	Imperial
1	Rice patna	200 g	8 oz
1/4	Onion brunoise	50 g	2 oz
1/8	Butter/margarine	25 g	1 oz
	Seasoning to taste		
	Bouquet garni		
*	Heated white stock (usually chicken)	400 ml	16 fl oz

* 2 units *stock* to 1 *unit* rice approximately 2:1.

Method

Sweat onions in butter without colour, add rice and mix well. Add stock, stir to the boil, add bouquet garni and seasoning. Cover with greased cartouche and lid. Braise in oven until rice is cooked and all stock has been absorbed. Stir occasionally with a fork to keep rice grains separated. Once cooked stir in knob of butter and any further seasoning. Remove bouquet garni and use as required.

Examples of Rice Dishes Using Basic Risotto/Pilaff: Added ingredients in relation to 1 unit i.e. 200 g (8 oz) rice

English Term Risotto/Pilaff	Unit	Ingredient	Metric (g)	Imperial (oz)	French Term Rizotto/Pilaff
Chicken	1	Diced cooked chicken	200	8	à Volaille
Ham	1	Diced cooked ham	200	8	au Jambon
Liver	1	Sautéed chicken livers	200	8	au Foie de Volaille
Mushroom	1	Sliced cooked mushrooms	200	8	aux Champignons
Prawn	1	Cooked prawns (other shellfish may be used)	200	8	aux Crevettes Roses
		Garnish:			Créole
	½	sliced cooked mushrooms	100	4	
	¼	diced cooked pimento	50	2	
	¼	tomato concassé	50	2	
Piedmont style		As for Créole, flavoured:			Piémontaise
	¼	grated parmesan cheese diced truffle	50	2	
Italian style		Flavoured:			Italienne
	¼	grated parmesan cheese	50	2	
Milan style		Flavoured and garnished:			Milanaise
	½	sliced cooked mushrooms	100	4	
	¼	tomato concassé	50	2	
	¼	grated parmesan cheese	50	2	
		N.B. Use saffron flavoured/coloured stock			

Other combinations may be prepared as required. The quantities indicated may be halved when the rice dish is served as a garnish.

Alternatively, when serving pilaff/risotto products the meat is prepared separately, often in a sauce and acts to accompany the rice. An example would be chicken in white sauce served with risotto/pilaff.

60
PAELLA (SPANISH STEWED RICE)

Yield: 200 g or 8 oz rice = 4 portions
Cooking time: 20–30 min

Unit	Ingredient	Metric	Imperial
1	Rice (long grain)	200 g	8 oz
1	Chicken (raw pieces off bone)	200 g	8 oz
½	Prawns (picked)	100 g	4 oz
½	Mussels (budded leave in half shell and retain liquor)	100 g	4 oz
¼	Garlic sausage (sliced)	50 g	2 oz
¼	Onion (chopped)	50 g	2 oz
¼	Tomato concassé	50 g	2 oz
¼	Pimento (diced)	50 g	2 oz
¼	Green peas (cooked)	50 g	2 oz
⅛	Cooking oil	25 ml	1 fl oz
	Seasoning		
	Garlic chopped (hint)		
	Bouquet garni		
★	White stock (chicken) flavoured and coloured with saffron		

★ 3 units *stock* to 1 *unit* rice approximately i.e. 3:1 = 600 ml (24 fl oz)

Method

Sweat onions, pimento, chicken in oil to light brown colour. Add rice and mix well. Add stock, stir to the boil, add bouquet garni, seasoning and garlic. Cover with lid and simmer gently until rice is half cooked. Using a fork mix in remaining ingredients to include mussel liquor. Complete cooking and correct seasoning.

Notes

The word *paella* refers to a two-handled shallow iron pan in which the dish is cooked and served. The ingredients for paella will vary according to region of origin.

Gnocchi (Tiny Dumplings)   Noques

Gnocchi products are in the main of Italian peasant origin and are prepared using a starch base of flour, potatoes, semolina or maize flour.
The types of gnocchi are:

(a) *Gnocchi Parisienne* — Paris style made from a base of choux pastry;
(b) *Gnocchi Romaine* — Roman style made from a base of semolina with milk as the liquid;
(c) *Gnocchi Piémontaise* — Piedmont style made from a base of potatoes;
(d) *Polenta* — Made from a base of maize flour with water as the liquid.

N.B.   All gnocchis are served with an accompaniment of grated parmesan.

61
CHOUX PASTRY FOR SAVOURY PREPARATIONS   Pâte à Choux

Cooking time: 15 – 20 min

Unit	Ingredient	Metric	Imperial
1	Whole egg	200 g	8 oz
⁵/₈	Water	125 ml	5 fl oz
¹/₂	Flour (strong)	100 g	4 oz
¹/₄	Butter/margarine	50 g	2 oz
	Salt to season		

Method

Combine water and butter, bring to the boil, add sifted flour, stir continuously and thoroughly to the boil. Continue cooking until mixture cleans the sides of the saucepan and is of a smooth texture. This ensures adequate cooking of starch. Cool slightly then beat the eggs in gradually until a smooth pipeable mixture is achieved. Use as required.

  N.B.   All the egg may not be required as this will vary according to the strength of the flour.

62
ROMAN STYLE DUMPLINGS   Gnocchi Romaine
(cheese flavoured)

Yield: 4 portions
Cooking time: 5 – 10 mins
Cooking temperature: 205°C (400°F)

Unit	Ingredient	Metric	Imperial
1	Milk	500 ml	1 pt
¹/₄	Semolina	120 g	5 oz
¹/₂₀	Butter	25 g	1 oz
¹/₂₀	Grated parmesan cheese	25 g	1 oz
¹/₂₀	Egg yolk	25 g	1 oz
	Seasoning		
	Pinch of nutmeg		
	Hint of garlic		
	Parmesan to gratinate		

Method

Butter a shallow tray and line with greased greaseproof paper, put aside. Combine milk, garlic, nutmeg and seasoning, pour into saucepan and bring to the boil. Sprinkle semolina into milk and whisk briskly to boiling point. Using a wooden spatula continue mixing to achieve a smooth consistency. Beat in butter, egg yolk, cheese and mix well. Spread the hot mixture evenly into the prepared tray approximately 2 cm (³/₄ in) deep. Allow to cool, refrigerate to set firm.

Turn out mixture on to board, remove paper. Cut into required shapes, e.g. discs or crescents. Place into buttered gratin dish, sprinkle with parmesan and a little melted butter. Place into hot oven for 5–10 minutes, until golden brown and gratinate under salamander if required.

N.B. Gnocchi Romaine may be served with a cordon of tomato sauce, or may be lightly masked with mornay sauce prior to being baked in the oven.

63
PARIS STYLE DUMPLINGS IN MORNAY SAUCE   Gnocchi Parisienne

Yield: 4 portions
Cooking time: 15 min

Unit	Ingredient	Metric	Imperial
1	Mornay sauce (*see* p. 87)	250 ml	10 fl oz
⋆⁴/₅	Choux pastry (savoury)	200 g	8 oz
	Nutmeg to taste		
	Grated parmesan to gratinate		

⋆N.B. Indicates amount of egg used when making choux pastry.

Method

Using 1 cm plain tube and bag, pipe small dumplings into plenty of simmering seasoned water (use a sharp wet knife to cut dumplings away from the tube). Poach gently for 8–10 minutes until the dumplings have increased in volume and have taken on a lighter colour. Strain dumplings and place in buttered gratin dishes. Flavour sauce with a pinch of nutmeg and napper (coat) dumplings. Sprinkle with parmesan cheese and gratinate to golden brown for service.

64
POTATO DUMPLINGS   Gnocchi Piémontaise

Yield: 4 portions
Cooking time: 10–15 min

Unit	Ingredient	Metric (g)	Imperial (oz)
1⋆	Mashed potatoes	200	8
1/4	Plain flour	50	2
1/8	Whole egg (beaten)	25	1
1/8	Butter	25	1
1/8	Grated parmesan cheese	25	1
	Seasoning		
	Pinch of nutmeg		
	Hint of garlic		
	Parmesan and melted		
	butter to gratinate		

⋆ Mashed potato is weighed at cooked weight.

Method

Dry the potato over heat and place into a mixing bowl. Add egg, butter, parmesan, nutmeg, garlic, seasoning, and combine with flour to form a stable mixture. Allow to cool and set. Divide into 16 portions and shape into tiny dumplings. Mould on to a floured tray and depress lightly with a fork.

To Cook   Place into plenty of seasoned simmering water and poach for 5 minutes until the dumplings float. Drain well and place in buttered gratin dishes. Sprinkle with parmesan and a little melted butter, gratinate golden brown.

N.B. Gnocchi piémontaise may be finished with a cordon of tomato sauce, or may be lightly masked with mornay sauce prior to being gratinated.

65
CORN MEAL DUMPLINGS   Polenta

Yield: 4 portions
Cooking time: 3 – 5 min

Unit	Ingredient	Metric	Imperial
1	Water	500 ml	1 pt
$\frac{1}{4}$	Corn meal (or semolina)	125 g	5 oz
$\frac{1}{10}$	Oil	50 ml	2 fl oz
	Seasoning		
	Pinch of nutmeg		
	Hint of garlic		

Method

Butter a shallow tray and line with greased greaseproof paper, put aside. Combine water, garlic, nutmeg and seasoning, pour into saucepan and bring to the boil. Sprinkle corn meal into water and whisk briskly to boiling point. Using a wooden spatula continue mixing to achieve a smooth consistency. Spread the hot mixture evenly into the prepared tray approximately 2 cm (¾ in) deep. Allow to cool, refrigerate to set firm. Turn out the mixture on to a board, remove paper. Cut into required shapes (discs, crescents) and sauté in oil and a little garlic until golden brown.

Place into buttered gratin dish, sprinkle with parmesan cheese and gratinate. Finish with beurre noisette.

Pasta Products   Pâtes Alimentaires

These are prepared from dried commercial preparations or freshly made pasta dough.

The commercial products are made from stiff dough which is forced through machines from which the dough emerges in a variety of designs and shapes. The pastas are then dried before packing for sale.

Common examples of pasta include:

Dry	*Fresh*
Spaghetti	Ravioli
Macaroni	Canneloni
Lasagne	Lasagne
Noodles	Noodles
Vermicelli	

Numerous varieties of pasta are available many of which may be prepared from a fresh dough or bought commercially as a dried preparation. These pastas may vary in flavour and colour, e.g. plain, egg, spinach and tomato.

Points for consideration when boiling pasta

1. Plunge pasta into plenty of seasoned boiling water to ensure even cooking and prevent the pasta from clogging together.
2. In the initial stages of boiling, stir the pasta to separate and prevent clogging.
3. Cook pasta to '*al dente*' stage (firm and with a bite) 12 – 15 minutes.
   Over cooking will cause pasta to become soggy and unappetising.
4. Once cooked, drain pasta well in colander and use immediately or 'refresh' carefully and store in iced water ready for use. The iced water keeps pasta fresh and also prevents clogging during storage.
5. When placing filling into pasta it is piped with a plain tube or put into place with a spoon.
6. It is traditional to accompany pasta products with grated parmesan cheese.
7. When using dry pasta allow 50 g (2 oz) per portion.

(a) Basic Pasta Doughs (fresh made)

66
NOODLE DOUGH
Pâte à Nouilles

Yield: 4 portions

Unit	Ingredient	Metric	Imperial
1	Strong flour	200 g	8 oz
⁵/₈	Whole egg (beaten)	125 g	5 oz
¹/₈	Oil	25 ml	1 fl oz
	Pinch of salt to taste		

Method

Sift flour and salt and form a well. Pour oil and egg into well, combine with flour to form a smooth and developed dough. Cover with damp cloth and rest in a cool place for at least 30 minutes before use.

To make Noodles   Roll pastry into 36 cm (18 in) wide thin sheet, dust with semolina or strong flour. Roll each sheet into a cylindrical shape and cut immediately into 3 mm (⅛ in) widths. Unroll strips immediately and partly allow to dry on floured trays. Use as required.

67
RAVIOLI PASTE   Pâte à Ravioli

Yield: 4 portions

Unit	Ingredient	Metric	Imperial
1	Strong flour	120 g	4 oz
½	Water	60 ml	2 fl oz
⅛	Oil	15 ml	½ fl oz
	Pinch of salt to taste		

Method

Sift flour and salt and form a well. Pour oil and water into well, combine with flour, form a smooth and developed dough. Cover with damp cloth, rest in a cool place for at least 30 minutes before use.

(b) Basic Savoury Stuffings for Pasta Products

68
SPINACH STUFFING   Farce à la Florentine

Yield: 4 portions
Cooking time: 10 min

Unit	Ingredient	Metric (g)	Imperial (oz)
1	Spinach (cooked purée)	200	8
¼	Onion brunoise	50	2
⅛	Egg yolk	25	1
⅛	Butter	25	1
	Pinch of nutmeg		
	Hint of chopped garlic		
	Seasoning to taste		

Method

Sweat onions without colour in butter, add spinach and dry thoroughly over heat (drive off moisture by evaporation). Add remaining ingredients, mix thoroughly, season to taste.

69
ITALIAN STUFFING   Farce Italienne

Yield: 4 portions
Cooking time: 10 min

Unit	Ingredient	Metric (g)	Imperial (oz)
1	Spinach (cooked, purée)	100	4
1	Beef (cooked, minced)	100	4
1/4	Brains (cooked)	25	1
1/4	Onion brunoise	25	1
1/4	Egg yolk	25	1
1/4	Butter	25	1
	Pinch of nutmeg		
	Hint of chopped garlic		
	Seasoning to taste		

Method

Sweat onion without colour in butter, add spinach and dry thoroughly over heat (drive off moisture by evaporation). Add remaining ingredients, mix thoroughly, season to taste.

70
RAVIOLI OR CANNELONI

Yield: 4 portions
Cooking time: 20 – 25 min

Unit	Ingredient	Metric	Imperial
1	Selected sauce	250 ml	10 fl oz
4/5	Selected stuffing	200 g	8 oz
4/5*	Ravioli paste	200 g	8 oz
	Grated parmesan and melted butter to gratinate		

N.B.   *Indicates amount of flour used when making ravioli paste.

Method for Ravioli

Roll out ravioli paste into a large paper-thin rectangle. Dust with strong flour or semolina during rolling. Lightly mark pastry into two halves using back of knife. Do not cut.

Space small mounds of selected filling across and down half of the rolled out paste. Water wash the clear half.

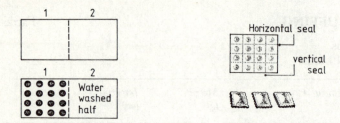

Carefully fold the second half of pastry on top of the filled half, pressing down firmly around fillings to seal. Avoid air pockets.

Using a ravioli cutter or knife cut pasta into squares along the sealed lines.

Separate ravioli squares and place on greaseproof paper for cooking. Simmer gently in boiling water to '*al dente*' stage. Drain well in colander, place in buttered gratin dish, napper with sauce, sprinkle with grated parmesan and bake in hot oven (5 – 10 min) to colour golden brown. Serve immediately.

N.B.   This dish may be gratinated under salamander.

Method for Canneloni

Roll out the ravioli paste into a large paper-thin square. Dust with strong flour or semolina during rolling. Cut into 8 cm or 3 in squares. Cook gently in boiling salted water to '*al dente*' stage. Refresh in cold water and drain well in colander. This facilitates handling. Spread drained pasta squares on to clean cloth to dry.

Place portion of filling across bottom third of square and roll up neatly into cylindrical shape. Place in buttered gratin dish, napper with sauce, sprinkle with grated parmesan and bake in hot oven (5 – 10 min) to colour golden brown. Serve immediately.

Examples of Dishes Prepared Using Recipe 70

Name of dish	Stuffing used	Sauce used
Ravioli/Canneloni Florentine	Florentine stuffing	Mornay
Ravioli/Canneloni Italienne	Italian stuffing	Tomate or Jus lié
Ravioli/Canneloni au Gratin	Either stuffing	Mornay

Other preparations may be created using suitable stuffings to include fish stuffings, e.g. lobster, crab, etc.

71
LASAGNE

Yield: 4 portions
Complete cooking time: 45 min

Unit	Ingredient	Metric	Imperial
1	Mornay sauce (thin)	400 ml	16 fl oz
1*	Bolognaise sauce	400 g	1 lb
½**	Ravioli paste	200 g	8 oz
	Grated parmesan and		
	melted butter to gratinate		

N.B. *Indicates amount of meat used when preparing bolognaise sauce
     **Indicates amount of flour used when making ravioli paste.

Method

Roll out ravioli paste in large thin rectangle 20 cm (8 in) wide. Cut rectangle in strips
20 cm × 6 cm (8 in × 2½ in). Cook gently in boiling salted water to 'al dente' stage.
Refresh in cold water and drain well in colander. This facilitates handling. Place on clean
cloth to dry.
   Butter a gratin dish and napper base with a layer of bolognaise sauce. Follow with a thin
layer of mornay sauce and a layer of pasta. Repeat this process until all pasta is used and
complete with a final layer of pasta masked with a thin coat of mornay sauce. Sprinkle
with grated parmesan and melted butter. Bake in hot oven for 20–30 minutes until hot
and golden brown. Serve immediately.

72
BOILING, REFRESHING AND REHEATING PASTA — SPAGHETTI, NOODLES, MACARONI ETC.

Yield: 4 portions
Boiling time: fresh pasta, 7–12 min
Boiling time: dry pasta, 12–15 min
Reheating time: 3–5 min

Unit	Ingredient	Metric (g)	Imperial (oz)
1	Selected pasta (cooked)	200	8
⅛	Butter/oil	50	2
	Seasoning		

Method

Boiling   Plunge pasta into plenty of lightly salted boiling water. Simmer until cooked
to 'al dente'. Drain and use immediately or refresh in cold water, drain well in colander
and store in iced water ready for reheating.

Reheating   Drain pasta well in colander. Heat butter/oil in sauté pan, add pasta, seasoning and toss continuously until thoroughly heated. Garnish as required, see below.

Pasta Extensions Using Above Formula: Added ingredients in relation to 1 unit, i.e. 200 g (8 oz) pasta

Name of dish	Unit	Ingredient	Metric	Imperial
au Beurre (with butter)		As in formula using butter only		
Italienne (Italian style)	$\frac{1}{4}$	Cream	50 ml	2 fl oz
	$\frac{1}{8}$	Grated parmesan cheese	25 g	1 oz
		Hint of garlic		
		Flavour with parmesan and garlic, cohere with cream		
Napolitaine (Naples style)		As for Italienne with:		
	1	tomato sauce	200 ml	8 fl oz
	$\frac{1}{2}$	tomato concassé	100 g	4 oz
		Add to pasta when reheating		
Milanaise (Milan style)		As for Napolitaine with:		
	$\frac{1}{2}$	Cooked julienne { ham tongue mushroom	100 g	4 oz
		Julienne of truffle to garnish		
		Add to pasta when reheating		
Bolognaise (with meat sauce)		As for Italienne with: Sauce Bolognaise (*see* recipe 23)		
Niçoise (Nice style)		As for Italienne with:		
	$\frac{1}{2}$	tomates concassées	100 g	4 oz
		Add when reheating pasta.		
au Gratin (gratinated with cheese)		As for Italienne with:		
	1	Mornay sauce	200 ml	8 fl oz
	$\frac{1}{8}$	Grated parmesan cheese	25 g	1 oz
	$\frac{1}{8}$	Melted butter	25 g	1 oz
		Combine sauce with pasta Italienne. Place into buttered gratin dishes, sprinkle with parmesan and melted butter. Gratinate in hot oven 230°C/450°F until golden brown.		
aux Moules (with mussels)		As for au Beurre with:		
	1	budded mussels with liquor	200 g	8 oz
	$\frac{1}{4}$	cream	50 ml	2 fl oz
		hint of chopped garlic		
		chopped parsley		
		Add mussels, cream and garlic when reheating pasta. Garnish with chopped parsley		

N.B. All the above are seasoned with salt and pepper to taste.

Spetzli (Alsatian cookery)

This pasta appears as short, thin strips, which on cooking remain intact with a soft texture. Spetzli or Spätzle (German) is best bought commercially in a dried form for cooking. It is cooked as in recipe 72 and best used immediately after cooking.

Spetzli is used as a garnish or accompaniment with main course items (e.g. pork and veal sautés) or specifically to garnish a goulash in replacement of Gnocchi Parisienne. It can also be used in its own right as a pasta course and integrated with selected flavours and garnish.

73
SPETZLI (SPÄTZLE)

Yield: 4 portions
Cooking time: 5 min

Unit	Ingredient	Metric	Imperial
1	Flour (cake)	200 g	8 oz
$5/8$	Whole egg	125 g	5 oz
$1/2$	Milk	100 ml	4 fl oz
	Salt to taste		
	Pinch of nutmeg		

Method

Sift flour, salt, nutmeg together and form a well. Whisk milk and eggs together and pour into well. Combine ingredients to form a slack mixture. Pass mixture through coarse colander and gently simmering seasoned water and simmer until cooked.

Drain well and use immediately or refresh and store for use.

Spetzli Provençale

Toss drained Spetzli quickly in melted butter, season with a pinch of salt, pepper and a hint of garlic. Place into gratin dish, sprinkle with chopped parsley and serve.

9

The Principle and Practice of Boiling

To Boil Bouillir

To Simmer Mijoter

Strictly speaking there are only a few occasions when food is actually boiled for long periods of time. In most instances food is simmered rather than boiled. Normally, rapid boiling takes place at around 100°C (212°F) whereas simmering requires a slightly lower temperature. Simmering is identified when the surface of the liquid is barely agitated as a result of the convection current set in motion during cooking.

On many, but not all occasions, simmering is preferred to rapid boiling because:

(a) evaporation loss and shrinkage are minimized;
(b) the texture and colour of products are not unduly impaired.

The liquids most commonly used as mediums for boiling are: water, stock, milk, and court-bouillon which usually remain unthickened during cooking. An exception is when a thickened 'blanc' *see* recipe 82 is used for boiling certain vegetables, e.g. artichoke bottoms.

Boiling is begun in one of two ways:

1. By placing food into cold liquid which is gradually brought to boiling point. This method is adopted when the primary purpose is to:

   (a) extract the flavour from the product, e.g. stocks;
   (b) gradually soften hard fibrous materials, e.g. carrots and parsnips;
   (c) prevent damage to items which would lose their shape if plunged into boiling liquid, e.g. whole fish.

2. By plunging food directly into boiling liquid. This method is adopted when it is necessary to:

   (d) seal in the food's flavour, e.g. small cuts of fish, leg of mutton;
   (e) set the protein and colour of foods, e.g. green vegetables;
   (f) reduce the overall cooking time, e.g. boiled eggs, green vegetables.

Notes Concerning Boiling

The technique of boiling may be used for the cooking of a wide variety of commodities including animal protein, vegetables, farinaceous products and eggs. When a traditional kitchen brigade is employed the following Chefs de Partie are involved with the preparation and cooking of boiled products:

Chef Saucier	— butcher's meats, offal, poultry. etc.
Chef Poissonnier	— fish preparations
Chef Entremettier	— vegetables to include potatoes
Chef Garde-manger	— involved with initial preparation of meats and fish prior to cooking.

Selected Cooking Vessels

The size and shape of cooking vessels will be determined by the volume of food being cooked. Steam jacket boilers of various sizes are often used for commercial boiling when large quantities are involved. On most occasions boiling vessels are covered with a lid, which helps to retain heat and speed-up the cooking process.

Preparing and Boiling Vegetables

Many vegetables contain water-soluble vitamins and minerals which are easily lost during preparation and cooking. It is therefore expedient to prepare, wash and cook vegetables quickly, and at no time allow them to soak for long periods in cold water.

Speedy cooking is also essential if vegetables are to remain crisp, nutritious, flavoursome and colourful. Over-cooking of vegetables results in:

(a) loss of flavour;
(b) poor colour;
(c) watery textures;
(d) low nutritive value.

Boiling Meats

It is important to ensure that meats are adequately covered with water/stock during boiling. When the resultant liquor is to be prepared as a sauce the stock level must not be excessive otherwise the cooking liquor will lack strength and flavour.

Skimming and Degreasing (for meat, etc.)

In order to ensure that the cooking liquor remains clear and grease-free it is necessary to skim away scum and grease as they rise to the surface.

Boiling of Butcher's Meat and Poultry

Although all meat can be cooked by boiling, it is not a satisfactory method of cooking tender cuts as it is difficult to retain the flavour of meat cooked in this way. Preserved meats, offal, and poultry however, are ideally suited to the boiling technique as they are often of a tougher structure. Certain meats need to be soaked in cold water prior to cooking to remove the excess salt, e.g. gammons and pickled beef. The time for soaking will vary according to the saltiness of the meat.

This saltiness will be determined by the following:

(a) the weight, thickness, fattiness, and texture of the meat in question;
(b) the strength of the brine used and the length of time the meat has been pickled in the solution.

It is therefore difficult to determine an exact soaking time for the cuts of meat before boiling, but they are usually soaked overnight. When boiling uncured meats or poultry initial soaking is eliminated. On some occasions the resultant cooking liquor is served as part of the dish in an unthickened or thickened form, e.g. boiled beef and carrots moistened with the liquor, or boiled leg of mutton served with caper sauce made from the cooking liquor.

Selection and Preparation of Meats for Boiling

Meat	*Preparation*
Beef joints	
Silverside, brisket, thin flank, topside, plate, Ox-tongue	Where necessary trim excess fat and sinew, roll and tie if required, e.g. brisket, thin flank. If joints have been pickled in brine, soak overnight in cold water before cooking
Bacon joints	*Gammon/shoulder*
Whole gammon, shoulder joints, hock, middle, corner of gammon. Collar, fore hock of shoulder	Left whole or boned, rolled and secured with string. Soak overnight in cold water before cooking. May be dissected into smaller cuts
*Ham**	Left whole, trim end of knuckle bone, remove any mould. Soak overnight in cold water before cooking
Mutton Joints	
Leg of mutton	Remove pelvic bone, trim end of leg bone, leave whole for use. If necessary secure chump end of leg with string

* Ham is the hind leg of a porker pig that has been cut from the side of pork (banjo shaped) and is then cured in a number of ways according to the region/country of origin, e.g. York ham, Parma ham. This should not be confused with gammon, which is the hind leg from a side of bacon.

74
BOILED MEATS   Viandes Bouillies

Yield: 4 portions 600 g (1¼ lbs) meat off the bone
          1 kg (2 lb) meat on the bone
Cooking times: beef/mutton 25 min per 400 g (1 lb) and 25 min over
                  Gammon/ham/tongue 20 min per 400 g (1 lb) and 20 min over

Unit	Ingredient	Metric (g)	Imperial (oz)
1	Selected meat	600	20
²/₅	Mirepoix (left whole)	240	8
	Bouquet garni		
	Seasoning (not required for pickled meats)		
*	Water		

* Sufficient water to cover adequately meat being boiled.

Method I: for Pickled Meats

Place meat in cooking vessel, cover with cold water, bring to the boil, skim add vegetables and bouquet garni. Cover with lid and simmer gently until meat is tender. Use as required.

Method II: for Fresh Meats

As above but commence cooking in boiling water.

Service   After carving moisten meat with cooking liquor and decorate with garnish for service.

Examples of Dishes Prepared Using Above Formula—garnish, in relation to 1 unit 600 g (1¼ lb) meat

English term-main ingredient	Unit	Ingredient	Metric	Imperial	French term
Boiled pickled beef English style	²/₅	Turned carrots 4 Whole onions (small) *8 Suet dumplings	240 g	8 oz	Boeuf Bouilli à l'Anglaise
		Cook garnish in cooking liquor			
Boiled beef French style	⁴/₅	Cabbage (quartered and tied)	480 g	16 oz	Boeuf Bouilli à la Française
	²/₅	Celery ⎱ tied in neat	240 g	8 oz	
	²/₅	Leek ⎰ bundles	240 g	8 oz	
	¹/₅	Turned carrots	120 g	4 oz	
	¹/₅	Turned turnips	120 g	4 oz	
		Cook garnish in cooking liquor			
Boiled ham or gammon with parsley sauce	¹/₂	Parsley sauce	300 ml	10 fl oz	Jambon Bouilli à Sauce Persil
		Serve sauce separately in a sauceboat			
Boiled leg of mutton with caper sauce	¹/₂	Caper sauce	300 ml	10 fl oz	Gigot de Mouton Sauce aux Câpres
		Prepare sauce from cooking liquor and serve separately in a sauceboat			
Boiled ox-tongue English style		As for boiled beef English style			Langue de Boeuf Bouillie à l'Anglaise
Boiled ox-tongue with Madeira sauce	¹/₂	Madeira sauce	300 ml	10 fl oz	Langue de Boeuf Bouillie à sauce Madère
		Serve sauce separately in a sauceboat			
Boiled ox-tongue with spinach and Madeira sauce	¹/₂ ²/₅	Madeira sauce Cooked leaf spinach	300 ml 240 g	10 fl oz 8 oz	Langue de Boeuf Bouillie Florentine
		Dress sliced tongue on bed of cooked leaf spinach, serve sauce separately in a sauceboat			

N.B.   Other suitable garnishes may be served with boiled meat.

* For 8 suet dumplings (4 portions) use 100 g (4 oz) flour when making suet pastry.

Calf's Head   Tête de Veau

Preparation Prior to Cooking

Remove any hairs from the head. To remove flesh from bone make an incision down centre of head to the nostrils. Keeping close to the bone carefully ease away flesh from bone and remove tongue from jaw. Wash the flesh and tongue and place into acidulated water until required. Saw across crown of head and carefully remove brains. Soak the brains in gently running cold water, remove membrane and wash away any blood. Blanch and refresh tongue and flesh to set protein and remove any scum. Trim the tongue and cut the flesh into 5 cm (2 in) squares.

Sauce Vinaigrette for Calf's Head

Garnish $\frac{1}{4}$ l ($\frac{1}{2}$ pt) vinaigrette with onion brunoise, chopped capers and chopped parsley.

75
CALF'S HEAD WITH VINAIGRETTE SAUCE   Tête de Veau Vinaigrette

Yield: 4 portions
Cooking time:
For tongue and flesh $2\frac{1}{2}$ hr
For brains 5 – 10 min

Unit	Ingredient	Metric	Imperial
	1 Calf's head (brains, tongue and flesh)		
1	Blanc (*see* recipe 82)	4 l	1 gal
$\frac{1}{8}$	Court-bouillon (*see* recipes 78 and 79)	$\frac{1}{2}$ l	1 pt
$\frac{1}{10}$	Mirepoix (left whole)	400 g	1 lb
$\frac{1}{20}$	Vinaigrette sauce	200 ml	8 fl oz
	Salt and pepper to taste		
	Bouquet garni and picked parsley		

Method

Place tongue, flesh, mirepoix and bouquet garni into simmering blanc. Skim, lightly season and cover with greased cartouche and continue simmering until tongue and flesh are cooked. Gently simmer brains in court-bouillon until cooked. Remove tongue, flesh and brains from cooking liquors. Skin the tongue.

Service   Place cooked meat from calf's head into serving dish with slices of tongue and brains. Moisten lightly with cooking liquor and accompany with sauce vinaigrette.

76
BOILED PIGS' TROTTERS   Pieds de Porc Bouillis
Yield: 4 portions
Cooking time: 2½ hr

Unit	Ingredient	Metric (g)	Imperial (oz)
	4 Pig's feet (singed and trimmed)		
1	Mirepoix (left whole)	200	8
	Bouquet garni		
	Seasoning		
	Squeeze of lemon juice		
★	Water		

★ Sufficient to cover pig's feet during boiling.

Method

Blanch and refresh pig's feet to remove scum. Place in clean cooking vessel, with vegetables, seasoning and squeeze of lemon juice. Cover with water, bring to the boil, skim, add bouquet garni, cover with a lid and simmer until tender. Serve whole or remove bone if required, accompanied with a suitable sauce, e.g. Sauce Poulette, Vinaigrette, etc.

77
Boiled Chicken   Poulet Bouilli/Poché

On the menu, boiled chicken dishes are often referred to as being poached, they are in fact simmered very gently and as such closely relate to the poaching method of cookery.

Yield: 4 portions 1 medium chicken
Cooking times: chicken 1 – 1½ hr
              boiling fowl 2 – 3 hr

Unit	Ingredient	Metric (g)	Imperial (lb)
	1 Whole trussed chicken or fowl		
1	Mirepoix (left whole)	400	1
	Seasoning		
	Bouquet garni		
★	Water or white chicken stock		

★ Sufficient liquid to cover adequately chicken being boiled.

Method

Place the chicken in cooking vessel, cover with cold water or stock, bring to the boil, skim, add vegetables and bouquet garni. Cover with lid and simmer gently until chicken is tender. Remove chicken from stock and allow to stand and set. Remove skin, joint or carve into required portions. Prepare Sauce Suprême (*see* p. 89) from cooking liquor. Keep sauce ready for use. See chart below.

Extensions of Dishes Using Above Formula: Sauce and Garnish for 4 portions

English term	Unit	Ingredient	Metric	Imperial	French term
Boiled chicken with rice and supreme sauce	1 $\frac{2}{5}$	Sauce Suprême Rice pilaff	500 ml 200 g	1 pt 8 oz	Poulet Poché au Riz Sauce Suprême
		Dress chicken portions on a bed of rice, napper with sauce and serve			
Boiled chicken with rice and asparagus sauce	1 $\frac{2}{5}$ $\frac{1}{5}$	Sauce Suprême Rice pilaff Purée asparagus 12 Asparagus tips	500 ml 200 g 100 g	1 pt 8 oz 4 oz	Poulet Poché Argenteuil
		Add asparagus purée to Sauce Suprême. Arrange chicken portions on bed of rice, napper with sauce and garnish with asparagus tips			
Boiled chicken with rice and mushroom sauce	1 $\frac{2}{5}$ $\frac{1}{5}$	White mushroom sauce (*see* p. 90) Rice pilaff Button mushrooms (glacés à blanc)	500 ml 200 g 100 g	1 pt 8 oz 4 oz	Poulet Poché au Riz Sauce Champignons
		Dress chicken portions on a bed of rice, napper with sauce and garnish with mushrooms			
Boiled chicken with rice and paprika sauce	1 $\frac{2}{5}$ $\frac{1}{5}$	Sauce Hongroise Rice pilaff Tomato concassé	500 ml 200 g 100 g	1 pt 8 oz 4 oz	Poulet Poché Hongroise
		Garnish rice with tomato concassé. Arrange chicken portions on to bed of rice and napper with sauce			
Boiled chicken with rice and curry-flavoured sauce	1 $\frac{2}{5}$ $\frac{1}{5}$	Sauce Indienne (*see* p. 89) Rice pilaff Mushrooms } Tongue } Julienne Truffle }	500 ml 200 g 100 g	1 pt 8 oz 4 oz	Poulet Poché à la Stanley
		Dress chicken portions on bed of rice, sprinkle with julienne garnish and napper with sauce for service			

N.B.   Amount shown for pilaff in recipe indicates amount of rice used to prepare pilaff.

Service   As an alternative to serving the chicken on a bed of rice, it may be presented surrounded by rice pyramids which have been shaped in buttered dariole moulds and turned out for service.

Boiled Fish   Poisson Bouilli

When boiling fish either whole or in portions, great care is required to ensure that the fish keeps its shape and texture throughout cooking. Fish flesh is composed of muscle, divided into flakes, which vary in size according to the type of fish. The composition of fish protein is similar to meat except there is far less connective tissue present. Therefore, the fish muscle is not held together as firmly as in meat protein.

The connective tissue in fish is collagen, which when heated in moist conditions changes into gelatin causing the flakes to separate easily on cooking (*see* p. 55). For this reason fish usually cooks more quickly than meat and is more tender, but great care is needed during cooking to prevent it from breaking up on service.

The liquids commonly used for boiling fish are termed court-bouillons, which vary according to the type of fish being cooked. When boiling whole fish it is recommended that the fish is placed into COLD bouillon and brought slowly to the boil to simmer gently. This enables the fish to retain its shape and prevents the skin from splitting. Alternatively small cuts of fish (usually on the bone) are immersed in simmering court-bouillon to cook. This sets the fish protein and speeds up the cooking time. In all cases the fish is cooked until tender, indicated when flesh begins to leave the bone and the flakes to separate.

Menu Term for Boiled Fish

On the menu, boiled fish dishes are often referred to as 'poached'. They are in fact simmered very gently and as such are closely related to the poaching method of cookery.

Court-Bouillons

These fall into two main categories:

  (a) for oily fish, e.g. salmon, trout, mackerel, salmon trout, etc;
  (b) for white fish, e.g. halibut, turbot, cod, brill etc.

N.B.   Court-bouillons may also be used for cooking some meat dishes e.g. calf's brains.
    A combination of milk and water may be used when cooking white fish for invalids.

78
COURT—BOUILLON (FOR OILY FISH)

Yield: 1 l (2 qt) approx.
Cooking time: 30 min

Unit	Ingredient	Metric	Imperial
1	Water	$1\frac{1}{2}$ l	3 pt
$\frac{1}{10}$	Vinegar	150 ml	6 oz
$\frac{1}{20}$	Carrots (sliced)	75 g	3 oz
$\frac{1}{20}$	Onion (sliced)	75 g	3 oz
	6 crushed peppercorns		
	Parsley stalks		
	Bouquet garni		
	Salt to season		

Method

Combine all ingredients, bring to the boil, skim and simmer for 30 minutes. Strain through a muslin in readiness for use.

79
COURT—BOUILLON (FOR WHITE FISH)

Yield: 1 l (2 qt) approx.

Unit	Ingredient	Metric	Imperial
1	Water	1 l	2 pt
$1/_{20}$	Lemon juice (1 large lemon)	50 ml	2 fl oz
	Salt to season		
	Parsley stalks		

Method

Combine all ingredients together in readiness for use.

80
BOILED FISH   Poisson Bouilli/Poché

Yield: 4 portions
Cooking time: Small cuts 5 – 10 mins. Whole fish according to size.

Unit	Ingredient	Metric (g)	Imperial (lb)
*	Selected court-bouillon		
1	Selected fish (whole piece, or cuts on the bone, e.g. Darne, Tronçon) Seasoning	800	2

* Sufficient court-bouillion to cover fish during cooking.

Method 1: For Whole or Large Pieces of Fish

Lightly season the prepared fish and allow to stand for 10 minutes to absorb the seasoning. Place in cooking vessel and cover with selected cold court-bouillon. Bring slowly to the boil and allow to simmer gently until fish is cooked. Drain well, remove skin and serve lightly moistened with the cooking liquor. Whole or large pieces of fish are usually trimmed and portioned in the restaurant for service.

Method 2: For Small Cuts of Fish on the Bone

Lightly season the prepared cuts of fish and allow to stand for 10 minutes to absorb the seasoning. Bring selected court-bouillon to boiling point, place the fish portions into the bouillon and simmer gently until cooked. Drain well, remove skin and centre bone of darnes. For flat fish cuts leave bone intact to prevent fish portion from breaking up unless its removal would not impair appearance of fish on presentation.

When fish is to be served cold remove from heat just prior to completion of cooking and allow to cool in the court bouillon. This allows the flavours in the bouillon to impregnate the fish.

N.B. All hot boiled fish dishes are served with a garnish of plain boiled shaped potatoes, sprig of parsley, lemon wedge and an accompanying sauce/liquor after which the dish is named. Turbot poché hollandaise/Saumon poché hollandaise are common examples.

Examples of Accompanying Sauces for Selected White or Oily Fish

à Sauce Hollandaise	— Sauceboat of hollandaise sauce
à Sauce Mousseline	— Sauceboat of mousseline sauce
au Beurre	— Sauceboat of melted butter
au Court-Bouillon	— Moistened with cooking liquor, garnished with button onions and decorated carrot rondels (cooked in the bouillon)

For Selected White Fish Only

à Sauce Anchois	— Sauceboat of anchovy sauce
à Sauce Crème	— Sauceboat of cream sauce
à Sauce aux Oeufs	— Sauceboat of egg sauce
à Sauce Persil	— Sauceboat of parsley sauce
à Sauce Crevettes Grises/Roses	— Sauceboat of shrimp or prawn sauce

Miscellaneous Boiled Fish Dishes

Skate with Black Butter   Raie au Beurre Noir

Simmer fish in court-bouillon (for white fish), until cooked, drain and place on to service dish. Lightly cover with black butter [100 g (4 oz)] for four portions. Garnish with capers and chopped parsley. N.B. If cooked with skin on, remove before flavouring with black butter.

81
BLUE TROUT   Truite au Bleu

Yield: 4 portions 4 live trout 150 g (6 oz) each
Cooking time: 5 – 10 min

Unit	Ingredient	Metric	Imperial
	4 Selected live trout		
1	Prepared bouillon (for oily fish *see* recipe 78)	1 l	2 pt
$^1/_{10}$	Button onions (sliced into rings)	100 g	4 oz
$^1/_{10}$	Carrot (grooved and thinly sliced)	100 g	4 oz
$^1/_{10}$	Malt vinegar (to colour trout)	100 ml	4 fl oz
$^1/_{10}$	Turned boiled potatoes	100 g	4 oz
	Sprigs of parsley to garnish		

Method: Preparation of Trout

Stun trout, slit belly to remove gut, membrane and blood, remove gills and wash inside the trout with cold running water. Pour vinegar over trout and turn continuously until blue.

Cooking of Trout   Bring bouillon with vegetable garnish to the boil and simmer for 3 – 4 minutes to soften vegetables. Add trout and simmer gently for 5 minutes. Serve moistened with cooking liquor, garnish with onion and carrot slices, shaped boiled potatoes, wedge of lemon and sprigs of parsley. Accompany with sauce hollandaise or melted butter.

N.B.   This dish is cooked and served to order and may be presented in the room in a small copper fish kettle in which the fish has been cooked. In this case the garnish of potatoes, lemon and parsley are served separately with the sauce. When cooked the shape of the fish is distorted and its skin broken. The head and skin are removed for service.

Boiling Live Shellfish (in the shell)   Although live shellfish may be boiled in court-bouillon (*see* recipe 79) they are more commonly cooked by plunging into plenty of boiling salted water, simmered for a specified time, drained and allowed to cool for use.

Boiling Times for Live Shellfish (Crustaceans)

Name	French	Cooking times from boiling point (min) (approx)
Crab	Crabe	15 – 25
Crayfish	Écrevisse	8 – 10
Crawfish	Langouste	20 – 25
Lobster	Homard	20 – 25
Prawns	Crevettes Roses	5 – 8
Scampi	Langoustine	8 – 10
Shrimps	Crevettes Grises	5 – 8

Boiled shellfish are served both cold and hot. The hot shellfish dishes are often prepared from pre-boiled items which have been allowed to cool.

Boiling of Vegetables

In general vegetables are boiled in seasoned water with the exception of those that are boiled in a 'blanc' preparation (*see* recipe 82), or acidulated water i.e. (water and squeeze of lemon juice), in order to keep them white.

As a rule, vegetables grown above the ground and frozen vegetables are plunged into boiling water at the commencement of cooking and boiled briskly until cooked. Those grown beneath the ground are placed into cold water, brought to boiling point, and simmered more gently.

Vegetables Grown Above the Ground or Frozen Vegetables

Cooking commences in boiling water which acts to:

(a) speed up the cooking time;
(b) set the natural colour of the vegetable;
(c) eliminate the enzymic action which destroys vitamin C (the enzymic action is eliminated by high temperatures);
(d) keep vegetables crisp and of fresh appearance.

Most green vegetables lose their appetizing colour if left too long in a hot cupboard and this deterioration is a problem when cooking for large numbers. A technique used in the trade to minimize this effect is the process of *blanching and refreshing* when the vegetables are cooked to *al dente* or just done, cooled immediately in cold water and drained. Later the vegetables can be quickly re-heated for service in a number of ways. This process prevents overcooking and maintains the fresh colour and crisp texture of the vegetables. After being well drained, blanched and refreshed, vegetables may be stored chilled in readiness for use. When this technique is not adopted staggered cooking times should be used.

Vegetables Grown Beneath the Ground

Cooking starts in cold water which is heated to boiling/simmering point. This acts to:

(a) extract the starch from certain root vegetables, e.g. potatoes;
(b) tenderize the fibrous structure of certain vegetables to aid digestion and palatability, e.g. turnips;
(c) prevent vegetables from breaking up during cooking, e.g. potatoes and swedes.

Boiled Vegetables   Légumes Bouillis

Method 1

(For vegetables that are plunged into boiling salted water) –
   Yield: 400 g (1 lb) prepared vegetables = 4 portions.
   Plunge vegetables into boiling salted water. Boil until tender. Drain well and serve as required.

Method 2

(For vegetables that are plunged into boiling seasoned acidulated water) –
   As for above but flavour water with lemon juice in order to keep vegetables white.

Method 3

(For vegetables that commence cooking in cold water) –
   Cover vegetables with cold water, season, bring to boil simmer gently until tender. Drain well and serve as required.

Method 4

(For vegetables cooked in a blanc – 'à blanc') –

82
PREPARATION OF BLANC   Blanc

Unit	Ingredient	Metric	Imperial
1	Water	1 l	2 pt
1/40	Flour	25 g	1 oz
	Squeeze of lemon juice		
	Salt to season		

Combine ingredients, stir to boil, strain and use. Plunge vegetables into boiling blanc, simmer until cooked, drain and serve as required.
N.B.   For boiling times and service of vegetables see respective charts.

1 Vegetables That are Plunged into Boiling Salted Water: Cooking times from boiling point

English	French	Preparation for Boiling	Cooking times (approx.) (min)	Examples of methods of Presentation
Asparagus	Asperges	Scrape stems lightly towards the base, tie into even bundles and trim the bases	12–20	au Beurre, au Beurre Fondu, Amandine, Hollandaise, Nature, Purée
Broad beans	Fèves	Pod the beans	15–20	au Beurre, à la Crème, à Sauce Persil, Nature
Brussel sprouts	Choux de Bruxelles	Remove decaying leaves, make a small incision at the base of each sprout, wash well in cold water	5–10	au Beurre, Milanaise, Nature, Polonaise
Broccoli	Brocolis	Remove outer leaves, trim base of stem, wash well	10–15	au Beurre, Amandine Hollandaise, Milanaise, Mornay, Nature, Polanaise
Cabbage Cabbage (spring)	Chou Chou de Printemps	Trim away decaying leaves, quarter to remove stalks, wash well	10–15	au Beurre, Nature
Chicory	Endive	Wash leaves very thoroughly	20–25	au Beurre, à la Crème Mornay, Nature, Purée
Cauliflower	Choufleur	Remove green leaves, trim base and hollow out the stem at the base. Wash well	12–15	au Beurre, Amandine aux Fines Herbes Hollandaise, Milanaise, Mornay, Nature, Polonaise
Cucumber	Concombre	Remove outer peel, cut into 3 cm (1½ in) cylinders and then into neat wedges. (may be turned)	5–10	au Beurre, à la Crème, Glacé, Milanaise, Nature, Persillé
Curly kale	Chou Frisé	Remove course stalks, wash well	15–20	au Beurre, Nature
French beans	Haricots Verts (Fins)	Top and tail, wash well	8–10	au Beurre, à la Crème, Nature, Tourangelle
Ladies' fingers or gumbo	Okra	Wash well. Do not remove stem	10–15	au Beurre, Hollandaise, Nature

English	French	Preparation for Boiling	Cooking times (approx.) (min)	Examples of methods of Presentation
Leeks	Poireaux	Discard damaged outer leaves, trim tops (retain for soups, etc.) Lightly trim the root, half split lengthways, leaving root intact wash well. Tie into neat bundles for cooking	15–20	au Beurre, à la Crème Mornay, Nature
Marrow (baby)	Courgette	Peel, trim stalk, wash well. Leave whole or slice or shape	8–10	au Beurre, à la Creme, aux Fines Herbes, Mornay, Nature, Persillée
Marrow	Courge	Remove outer skin, cut in half lengthways, remove seeds with a spoon, cut into 5 cm (2 in) squares, wash well	8–10	
Peas (garden)	Petits Pois	Pod the peas	15–20	au Beurre, à la Menthe, Nature, Purée
Young peas in the pod	Mange Tout (eat all)	Top and tail, leave peas in pod	8–10	au Beurre, Glacés Hollandaise, Nature
Pumpkin	Potiron	As for marrow	20–30	As for marrow
Runner beans		Top and tail, remove strings of the beans from sides. Wash well and slice into strips	10–15	au Beurre, Nature
Sea kale	Chou de Mer or Chou Marin	Trim away damaged stalks and roots, wash well, tie in bundles	20–25	au Beurre, à la Crème, Hollandaise, Nature
Leaf spinach	Épinards en Branches	Remove leaves from stems and wash well	8–10	au Beurre, à la Crème, Mornay, Nature, Purée
Sweetcorn (on the cob)	Maïs	Remove outer green leaves and fibres, wash well, trim ends	10–15	au Beurre Fondu, Nature
Sweetcorn (off the cob)	Maïs	Prepare as above, when cooked remove kernels with a spoon	10–15	au Beurre, à la Crème, Nature

See pp. 184–5 for methods of presentation.

2 Vegetables that are Plunged into Boiling, Seasoned, Acidulated Water Cooking Times from Boiling Point

English	French	Preparation	Cooking times (min)	Examples of methods of presentation
Artichokes (globe)	Artichauts	Cut across the top removing quarter of leaves. Trim points of leaves, remove stem at the base. Place slice of lemon on base and secure with string. Place into water with base uppermost. When cooked, remove string, lemon, heart and choke	40–45	au Beurre Fondu, Hollandaise
Artichokes (Jerusalem)	Topinambours	Wash well, peel and place in acidulated water before cooking	20–25	au Beurre, à la Crème, aux Fines Herbes, Nature, Persillés, Purée
Celeriac	Céleri-rave	Wash and peel, cut to required shape (cubes, strips, etc.) Place into acidulated water before cooking	25–30	au Beurre, à la Crème, aux Fines Herbes, Nature

See pp. 184–5 for methods of presentation.

3 Vegetables that Commence Cooking in Cold Water

English	French	Preparation for Boiling	Cooking time from boiling point (min)	Examples of methods of presentation
Beetroot	Betterave	Trim off tops and wash well	60–120	au Beurre, à la Crème, Nature
Carrots	Carottes	Top and tail, peel, wash well, cut into selected shape (wedges, slices, turned, cubed)	10–25	au Beurre, à la Crème, Glacées, Persillées, Purée Vichy
Kohlrabi	Chou-rave	Remove leaves from bulb and trim roots. Wash well in cold water and remove thick peel. Leave whole, slice, dice or cut to shape according to requirements	30–60	au Beurre, à la Crème, Nature, Persillés

English	French	Preparation	Cooking times (min)	Examples of methods of presentation
Onions	Oignons	Peel, trim root leaving intact	20–30	à la Crème, Nature
Parsnips	Panais	Wash, peel and re-wash, cut into wedges lengthways. Remove fibrous root from the centre if tough	20–30	au Beurre, à la Crème, Nature, Persillés, Purée
Swedes	Rutabaga	Wash, trim ends and remove thick peel. Slice or cut to desired shape (cubes, bâtons or turned)	15–20	au Beurre, Nature, Persillés, Purée
Turnips	Navets	As for swedes	25–30	au Beurre, Nature, Persillés, Purée

See pp. 184–5 for methods of presentation.

4 Vegetables Cooked in a Blanc 'à Blanc' Cooking Times from Boiling Point

English	French	Preparation	Cooking times (min)	Examples of methods of presentation
Artichoke bottoms	Fonds d' Artichauts	Cut away stalk from base, using a stainless steel knife, rub base lightly with lemon juice. Pluck away all the leaves until artichoke bottom is clear of leaves, place in acidulated water in readiness for cooking. Choke remains during cooking and is removed by using a stainless steel spoon. Leave whole, quarter or slice for service.	20–25	au Beurre, à la Crème, aux Fines Herbes, Hollandaise, Mornay, Nature, Persillés
Fennel	Fenouil	Trim stalks and root, wash well, cook whole or in quarters according to size of fennel	60–90	au Beurre, à la Crème, aux Fines Herbes, Milanaise, Mornay, Nature, Persillés, Poulette
Salsify (Oyster plant)	Salsifi	Wash well, peel, section into 5 cm (2 in) cylinders. Place in acidulated water ready for cooking	40–45	au Beurre, à la Crème, aux Fines Herbes, Nature, Persillés, Poulette, Tourangelle

See pp. 184–5 for methods of presentation.

Boiled Pulse Vegetables

Yield: 250 g (10 oz) of dried vegetable = 4 portions

Method

Soak vegetables overnight in cold water. Drain and wash thoroughly. Cover with cold water and season. Bring gradually to the boil and simmer gently until tender. Drain well and serve as required.

Cooking times from boiling point.

English	French	Cooking time (hr)	Presentation style
Butter beans		$1\frac{1}{2} - 2$	Nature, à la Menthe, au Beurre
Haricot beans	Haricots Blancs	$1\frac{1}{2} - 2$	Nature, Bretonne, au Beurre
Kidney beans (green)	Haricots Flageolets	$1\frac{1}{2} - 2$	Nature, au Beurre
Kidney beans (red)	Haricots Rouges	$1\frac{1}{2} - 2$	Nature, au Beurre
Lentils	Lentilles	$1\frac{1}{2} - 2$	Purée, Purée à la Crème
Marrowfat peas		$\frac{3}{4} - 1$	Nature, au Beurre, à la Menthe. These peas may be cooked until they 'fall' and thicken the cooking liquor

See below for methods of presentation.

Common Modes of Vegetable Presentation

au Beurre	Brush with melted butter
au Beurre Fondu	Accompany with sauceboat of melted butter
à la Crème	Lightly napper or cohere vegetable with cream sauce or fresh cream
à la Menthe	Add fresh mint leaves during cooking to flavour. Garnish with blanched mint leaves
Amandine	Sauté some almonds in a little butter, sprinkle over vegetables. Garnish with chopped parsley
aux Fines Herbes	Brush with butter and sprinkle with fine herbs
Bretonne	Cohere with tomato sauce to complete cooking
Glacés/ées (f)	Boil in minimum of water with knob of butter, pinch of sugar. At end of cooking period reduce liquor to give vegetables glossy appearance
Hollandaise	Accompany with sauceboat of Hollandaise sauce or lightly mask vegetable for presentation
Maltaise	Accompany with sauceboat of Maltese sauce
Milanaise	Sprinkle with parmesan cheese, gratinate and finish with Beurre Noisette
Mornay/au Gratin	Coat with cheese sauce, sprinkle with cheese and gratinate

Nature	Serve plain boiled
Persillées/és (m)	Brush with melted butter and sprinkle liberally with chopped parsley
au Sauce Persil	Cohere with parsley sauce
Polonaise	Sprinkle with sieved hard boiled egg, chopped parsley, fried breadcrumbs and beurre noisette to finish
Poulette	Cohere with poulette sauce (*see* p. 90)
Purée	*See* method (below)
Tourangelle	Cohere with cream sauce flavoured with garlic
Vichy	Cook as for glacé using Vichy Water (French mineral water)

Other Boiled Vegetable Dishes

Yield: 400 g (1 lb) total weight for 4 portions

Bouquetière	A selection of vegetables served in bouquets. This usually includes: cauliflower, shaped carrots, shaped turnips, French beans, etc., serve au beurre. Cauliflower is coated with hollandaise sauce when used in this garnish
Jardinière	Bâtons of carrots and turnip, garden peas and French beans, serve au beurre
Macédoine	As above but cut carrots and turnips into small cubes, serve au beurre
Primeurs	As for Bouquetière but using new/spring vegetables, serve au beurre
Haricots Panaches	Selection of beans mixed together e.g. French beans, kidney beans, broad beans, etc., serve 'au beurre'
Petits Pois Flamande	Combine selected quantity of garden peas with half as many shaped carrots (bâtons or cubes)

Vegetable Purées   Purées de Légumes

Method

Pass boiled, drained vegetables through a medium sieve or mouli. Place into a saucepan and dry out excess moisture over heat. Correct seasoning and finish with knob of butter and cream if required. Serve dome-shaped in a vegetable dish. Decorate using palette knife. (Often used as a garnish.)

83
BOILED POTATOES   Pommes de Terre Bouillies

Yield: 400 g (1 lb) prepared potatoes = 4 portions
Cooking time: 20 min from boiling point, approximately.

Method

Old Potatoes   Cut potatoes to even size or required shape (to ensure even cooking), place in cooking vessel, cover with cold water, season, bring to boil and simmer until tender. Drain and use as required.

New Potatoes   Lightly scrape or scrub potatoes clean. Cook as above but commence in boiling salted water.

When scrubbed and not scraped or peeled, remove peel after cooking.

Examples of Dishes Prepared from Plain Boiled Old Potatoes: Added Ingredients and Preparation to 1 unit i.e. 400 g (1 lb) boiled potatoes

English term	Preparation	French term
Plain boiled potatoes	Boiled cut or turned potatoes served plain	Pommes Nature
Parsley potatoes	As for Pommes Nature, brush with melted butter, garnish liberally with freshly chopped parsley	Pommes Persillées
	Boiled potatoes (large noisette shape). Finish as for Pommes Persillées	Pommes Quelin
Boiled in jackets	Small to medium sized potatoes boiled whole in their jackets (skins). Served plain	Pommes en Robe de Chambre

English term	Unit	Ingredient	Metric	Imperial	French term
Potatoes with cream	1/8	Cream (fresh)	50 ml	2 oz	Pommes à la Crème
	1/16	Butter	25 g	1 oz	
		Milk (to barely cover potatoes)			
	Peel potatoes that have been boiled in their jackets, slice into 1/2 cm (1/4 in) rondels, barely cover with milk and cream, add butter and seasoning. Reboil, simmer for 3–4 minutes and serve				
	As for Pommes à la Crème, sprinkle with chopped parsley				Pommes Maître d'Hôtel
Snow potatoes	Pass boiled potatoes through a masher into service dish. Serve immediately				Pommes à la Neige
Mashed potatoes	1/8	Boiled milk	50 ml	2 fl oz	Pommes Purée
	1/16	Butter	25 g	1 oz	
	Pass boiled potatoes through masher return to clean pan, add milk and butter over heat. Season to taste. Serve as required, e.g. dome shaped				
Mashed potatoes with a cordon of cream	1/8	Fresh cream	50 ml	2 fl oz	Pommes Purée à la Crème
	As for Pommes Purée but finished with a cordon of cream				

English term	Unit	Ingredient	Metric	Imperial	French term
Creamed potatoes	⅛	Fresh Cream	50 ml	2 fl oz	Pommes Mousseline
		As for Pommes Purée, combine with cream			
Mashed potatoes with cheese	⅛	Grated cheese	50 g	2 oz	Pommes Purée au Gratin
		As for Pommes Purée sprinkle with grated cheese and gratinate			
Mashed potatoes with ham, pimentoes and parsley	⅛	Finely chopped cooked ham	50 g	2 oz	Pommes Biarritz
	1/16	Finely diced pimento Chopped parsley	25 g	1 oz	
		Combine ingredients with Pommes Purée, serve as required			

Examples of Dishes Prepared from Plain Boiled New Potatoes

English term	Presentation for service	French term
Plain boiled new potatoes	Serve plain boiled	Pommes Nouvelles
Minted new potatoes	During boiling add bunch of mint to flavour. Brush with butter and garnish with blanched mint leaves	Pommes Nouvelles à la Menthe
New potatoes with parsley	Plain boil new potatoes, brush with butter and sprinkle liberally with chopped parsley	Pommes Nouvelles Persillées
New potatoes boiled in their jackets	Cook in jackets (skins), serve plain boiled	Pommes en Robe de Chambre

10

The Principle and Practice of Poaching

To Poach
Pocher

Poaching may be defined as cooking in a minimum amount of liquid, which ideally should never be allowed to boil, but rather maintain a temperature of almost simmering intensity, i.e. just below boiling point.

Foods suitable for poaching vary, as does the length of cooking time, the latter being determined by the type and structure of the product. Examples of foods commonly cooked by this method include fish, poultry, fruits, eggs, and certain offal.

Poaching Fish

Fish may be poached in various poaching liquors. The choice of the poaching medium is determined by the dish being prepared, the type of fish, its size and texture.

Examples of poaching liquors in common use with fish include wine, milk, fish stock or a combination of such liquors. Throughout the cooking process the poaching liquor remains unthickened and only partly covers the fish. The resultant liquor is usually used to form a coating sauce which completes the dish. Many fish dishes that appear on the menu as poached are in fact boiled and are explained and outlined in Chapter 9 concerning boiling.

Poaching Chicken

This usually involves the poaching of chicken breasts, i.e. suprêmes with white chicken stock used as the poaching liquor. At times the stock may be flavoured with wine. As with fish certain chicken dishes appear on the menu as poached but are in fact boiled, these are also explained in Chapter 9.

Quenelles

N.B. Finer forcemeats of chicken, veal, and fish are also poached and presented in the same manner as for classical poached fish and suprêmes of chicken (*see* recipes 86 and 84 respectively).

In general when poaching any of the above products the poaching liquor is cool at the commencement of the process, being heated gradually to the temperature required. If the products were placed into hot stock or liquor there would be a possibility of some distortion or breaking up, particularly in the case of fish.

Poached Offal

The offal most commonly poached is brains (sheeps' or calves') and the poaching liquor used is a type of court bouillon flavoured with lemon juice.

For explanation of poached eggs and fruits see Chapters 7 and 13 respectively.

Points for Consideration

Short Poaching

This study is concerned with 'short poaching', a term used to describe the poaching of small, tender cuts of fish, poultry, meat and offal. Due to the size and structure of the foods being poached the cooking time is short, enabling the chef to cook and present items quickly for service.

Foods poached by this method require speedy and gentle poaching, which is best achieved by *oven poaching*. Alternatively many dishes that appear on the menu as poached are in fact boiled. In these cases the cooking time involved is usually longer, requiring a gentle simmering action on the stove top. this ensures that the food is thoroughly cooked. These types of dishes are explained in Chapter 9.

Covering Foods for Poaching

During the process many foods are only part covered with liquid and therefore a paper and/or lid covering is required. This ensures that even heat is maintained within the cooking vessel and that steam generated is retained to ensure complete cooking of the food in the shortest possible time. Over-cooking results in excessive shrinkage and dry, unpalatable foods.

Draining Poached Items

Once cooked, poached items need to be well drained otherwise the undrained liquor mixes with the resultant masking sauce spoiling both appearance and consistency. Draining is assisted by placing poached items on to a clean cloth or absorbent paper before completing the dish for service.

Service

Before arranging food for service, the service dish is lightly sauced to prevent items adhering to the base of the dish. This facilitates ease of service. When presenting a glazed/gratinated items the service dish may be decorated with a border of duchess potato. In addition to improving appearance, the border prevents sauce spilling over on to the rim of service dish. Speed of operation and organized methods are essential if a good class product is to be achieved.

When a traditional kitchen brigade is employed the preparation of foods for poaching would be the responsibility of the Chef Garde-manger. The poaching of foods outlined in this study would be the responsibility of:

Chef Poissonnier — Fish products and fish sauces
Chef Saucier   — Entrées

Chicken and Offal   Volaille et Abats

84
POACHED BREAST OF CHICKEN   Suprême de Volaille Poché

Yield: 4 portions
Cooking time: 12–15 min
Cooking temperature: 175°C (350°F)

Unit	Ingredient	Metric (ml)	Imperial (pt)
	4 Suprêmes of chicken (prepared)		
1	Selected sauce (*see* chart)	500	1
	Squeeze of lemon juice		
	Seasoning		
*	White chicken stock (cold)		

* Sufficient just to cover chicken portions during cooking.

Method

Lightly season chicken suprêmes and place into buttered cooking vessel. Add squeeze of lemon juice and just cover with chicken stock. Bring steadily to boiling point, cover with buttered cartouche and place in oven or stove top to poach until cooked. Remove suprêmes from stock and drain well. Lightly sauce the base of service dish, neatly arrange suprêmes on to the dish, napper with sauce, garnish and complete as required for service.

N.B.   Cooking liquor may be reduced to a glace de volaille and added to selected sauce to enhance the flavour.

Examples of Dishes Prepared Using Above Formula: Selected Sauce and Garnish for 4 Portions in Relation to Formula

English term	Unit	Ingredient	Metric	Imperial	French term
Poached chicken	1	Supreme sauce	500 ml	1 pt	Suprême de Volaille
breasts with	$^1/_5$	Grated cheddar cheese	100 g	4 oz	Poché Florentine
spinach and	$^1/_5$	Cooked leaf spinach	100 g	4 oz	
cheese		Parmesan to gratinate			

Combine grated Cheddar cheese with
sauce. Lightly sauce base of service
dish, lay in bed of spinach and place
in poached suprêmes. Napper with
sauce, sprinkle with parmesan and
gratinate

English term	Unit	Ingredient	Metric (g)	Imperial (oz)	French term
Poached chicken breasts with mushroom sauce	1	White mushroom sauce (Velouté based) 8 Mushroom heads (à blanc) Chopped parsley	500 ml	1 pt	Suprême de Volaille Poché aux Sauce Champignons
		Garnish poached chicken with mushrooms, napper with sauce and decorate delicately with chopped parsley			
Poached chicken breasts with supreme sauce and vegetables	1 ⅕	Supreme sauce Cooked julienne of vegetables (carrot – celery – leek – mushroom)	500 ml 100 g	1 pt 4 oz	Suprême de Volaille Poché Polignac
		Add garnished to sauce and napper for service			
Poached chicken breasts with asparagus	1	Supreme sauce 12 Asparagus tips (cooked) 4 slices of truffle 4 Heart shaped croûtons (fried)	500 ml	1 pt	Suprême de Volaille Poché Princesse
		Napper poached suprêmes with sauce, garnish with asparagus, slices of truffle and croûtons			

85
POACHED CALVES'/LAMBS' BRAINS
Cervelles de Veau/d'Agneau Pochées

Yield: 4 portions
Cooking time: 15 – 20 min
Cooking temperature: 175°C (350°F)

Unit	Ingredient
	4 Brains (remove membrane and wash gently to remove blood
★	Court-bouillon (*see* recipe 79)

★ Sufficient bouillon just to cover brains during poaching.

Method

Place brains in cooking vessel, add court-bouillon barely to cover. Bring slowly to the boil cover with greased cartouche and lid. Place in oven to poach until cooked. Once cooked remove brains, drain well, serve with sauce and garnish as required (*see* below).

Examples of Poached Brain Dishes Using Above Formula: Sauce and Garnish for 4 portions

English term	Unit	Ingredient	Metric (g)	Imperial (oz)	French term
Poached brains with nutbrown butter	1	Beurre noisette Chopped parsley	100	4	Cervelles Pochées au Beurre Noisette
		Pour butter over poached brains, sprinkle with chopped parsley and serve			
Poached brains with black butter and capers	1 ¼	Beurre noir Capers Chopped parsley	100 25	4 1	Cervelles Pochées au Beurre Noir
		Add capers to beurre noir and pour over poached brains. Sprinkle with chopped parsely and serve			

Poached Fish   Poisson Poché

Poaching is employed in the cooking of a wide variety of fish and shellfish, some are left whole whilst others are prepared into smaller cuts.

The items most commonly used are as follows.

Whole Fish/Shellfish

English term	French term	Yield for 4 portions
Dover sole	Sole Douvres	4 × 300 g (12 oz)
Oysters	Huîtres	16 to 24
Scallops	Coquilles St. Jacques	400 g (1 lb) shelled weight
Scampi	Langoustine	400 g (1 lb) shelled weight

Fish Cuts in Common Use for Short Poaching in the Oven

English term	French term	Yield for 4 portions	Explanation & Illustration
Fillet	le Filet	4–8 according to size and requirements	A cut of flat fish free from bone

Supreme	le Suprême	4 × 125 g (5 oz) portions	A cut on the slant taken from large fish fillets

	le Délice	4 – 8 according to size and requirements	Small fillets of fish neatly folded

	la Paupiette	4 – 8 according to size and requirements	Small fillets of fish rolled into cylindrical shape. Paupiettes are often filled with a fish stuffing before rolling

Fish Commonly Prepared into Small Cuts for Poaching

English term	French term	Type of cut
Brill	Barbue	Suprêmes
Cod	Cabillaud	Suprêmes
Dover sole	Sole Douvres	Filet-délice- paupiettes
Frogs' legs	Cuisse de Grenouilles	Left whole
Haddock	Aigrefin	Suprêmes
Hake	Colin	Suprêmes
Halibut	Flétan	Suprêmes
Lemon sole	Sole Limande	Filets-délice-paupiettes
Plaice	Plie	Filet-délice-paupiettes
Salmon	Saumon	Suprêmes
Salmon trout	Truite Saumonée	Suprêmes
Turbot/young turbot	Turbot/Turbotin	Suprêmes

N.B.   For explanation of cuts *see* above.

Classical Poached Fish Dishes Using Small Cuts of Fish and Whole Dover Sole

86

Yield: 4 portions
Cooking time: 5 – 10 min
Cooking temperature: 205°C (400°F)

Unit	Ingredient	Metric	Imperial
	Selected fish portions (*see* pp. 192 – 3)		
1	Fish velouté	250 ml	10 fl oz
$^2/_5$	Cream (double)	100 ml	4 fl oz
$^2/_5$	White wine (dry)	100 ml	4 fl oz
$^1/_5$	Butter	50 g	2 oz
$^1/_{20}$	Shallots/onion brunoise	12.5 g	$^1/_2$ oz
	Squeeze of lemon juice		
*	Fish stock		

*Fish stock — sufficient to adjust consistency of sauce and $^2/_3$ cover fish for poaching.

Method

Lightly butter base of poaching vessel, sprinkle with shallots. Lay fish portions neatly on to bed of shallots, lightly season and flavour with squeeze of lemon juice. Pour on wine and stock to part cover fish portions. Cover with buttered cartouche and poach in hot oven until fish is just cooked. Once cooked pour cooking liquor into sauteuse and reduce quickly to form a glace de poisson. Add velouté, cream, bring to the boil, adjust consistency and seasoning. If necessary strain through fine chinois.

Service

1. *Not glazed:* Lightly sauce the base of service dish, neatly arrange well-drained fish on to dish, napper with sauce, garnish as required and serve.
2. *Glazed:* Enrich sauce with egg yolk or sabayon (do not reboil). Lightly sauce base of service dish, neatly arrange well-drained fish on to dish, napper with sauce, glaze under hot salamander and serve.
3. *Gratinated:* Proceed as for glazed fish but sprinkle with grated parmesan cheese before gratinating under hot salamander. Garnish as required and serve.

N.B. When using whole dover sole, on completion of poaching remove side bones. Gently ease upper fillets away from backbone and snip main part of backbone to remove. Reshape fish ready for service.

When adding egg yolk or sabayon to the sauces which are to be glazed or gratinated use $^1/_{10}$ unit egg yolk to 1 unit sauce (e.g. 25 g [1 oz] egg yolk to 250 ml [$^1/_2$ pt] sauce).

Alternative Method of Preparing Sauce for Classical Poached Fish Dishes

Where a richer sauce is required the velouté content is replaced with additional double cream. Cream is reduced to coating consistency. This method is particularly suited where a speedy à la carte service is required. Obviously the cost of the dish is substantially increased.

Examples of Dishes Prepared Using Above Formula: Added Ingredients and Garnish for 4 Portions in Relation to Above Formula

English term	Unit	Ingredient	Metric (g)	Imperial (oz)	French term
1 Poached Fish Dishes — not glazed					
Fish in white wine sauce		8 fleurons			Poisson Vin Blanc
		Garnish completed dish with fleurons			
	¹/₅	Julienne of cooked mushrooms and truffle 8 fleurons	50	2	Poisson Polignac
		Combine mushrooms and truffle with the sauce before coating the fish Garnish with fleurons			
	¹/₅	Julienne of cooked vegetables and truffle (carrot, leek, celery)	50	2	Poisson Suchet
		Combine above with sauce before coating the fish			
Poached fish Granville style	¹/₅	Sliced cooked mushrooms Picked shrimps Finely chopped truffle	50	2	Poisson Granville
		Combine above with sauce before coating the fish			
Poached fish Dieppe style	¹/₅	Budded mussels	50	2	Poisson Dieppoise
	¹/₁₀	Picked shrimps	25	1	
	¹/₁₀	Cooked button mushrooms (à blanc)	25	1	
		Chopped parsley			
		Garnish completed dish with above			
	²/₅	Tomato concassé	100	4	Poisson Dugléré
		Chopped parsley			
		Prior to poaching add tomato to fish. Finish sauce with chopped parsley before coating the fish			

English term	Unit	Ingredient	Metric (g)	Imperial (oz)	French term

2 Poached Fish Dishes — glazed

		Chopped parsley			Poisson Bercy
		Garnish sauce with parsley before coating fish for glazing			

	1/5	Sliced mushrooms	50	2	Poisson Bonne Femme

Chopped parsley
Place sliced mushrooms on to fish prior
to poaching. Finish sauce with chopped parsley before glazing

	1/5	Tomato concassé	50	2	Poisson Bréval/
	1/5	Sliced mushrooms	50	2	d'Antin

Chopped parsley
Place mushrooms and tomatoes on to
fish prior to poaching. Finish sauce
with chopped parsley before glazing

	1/5	Sliced mushrooms	50	2	Poisson Saint-Valéry
	1/10	Picked shrimps	25	1	

Place mushrooms and shrimps on to
fish prior to poaching. Coat with
sauce for glazing

	2/5	Muscat grapes (green) (skinned de-pipped and chilled)	100	4	Poisson Véronique

Place chilled grapes on to cooked fish
portions prior to masking with sauce
for glazing

3 Poached Fish Dishes — glazed or gratinated

Poached fish in cheese sauce	1/5	Grated cheddar cheese	50	2	Poisson Mornay

Add cheese to sauce before coating to
glaze or gratinate

$^2/_5$	Duxelle	100	4	Poisson Cubat
$^1/_5$	Grated cheddar cheese	50	2	
	8 slices truffle			

Place poached fish on a bed of duxelle.
Add cheese to sauce, mask fish and
gratinate or glaze. Garnish with slices
of truffle

| $^2/_5$ | Cooked leaf spinach | 100 | 4 | Poisson Florentine |
| $^1/_5$ | Grated Cheddar cheese | 50 | 2 | |

Place poached fish on a bed of spinach.
Add cheese to sauce, mask fish and
glaze or gratinate

$^1/_5$	Grated Cheddar cheese	50	2	Poisson Walewska
	8 Slices of cooked			
	lobster tail			
	8 slices of truffle			

Add cheese to sauce, decorate cooked
fish with slices of lobster. Mask with
sauce, glaze or gratinate

87
POACHED SHELLFISH DISHES, using Scallops (Coquilles St Jacques), Oysters (Huîtres), Scampi (Longoustines) and Frogs Legs (Cuisses de Grenouilles)

Yield: 4 portions
Cooking time: 5 – 10 min
Cooking temperature: 205°C (400°F)

Unit	Ingredient	Metric	Imperial
1	Selected shellfish (free from shell)	400 g	1 lb
1	Selected sauce (*see* chart)	400 ml	16 fl oz
	Squeeze of lemon juice		
	Seasoning		
*	Fish stock		

* Sufficient stock to barely cover shellfish during poaching.

Method

Place shellfish in cooking vessel, season and flavour with lemon juice. Barely cover with stock, bring to boiling point, cover with buttered cartouche and place in a hot oven to poach until just done. Drain shellfish well, lightly sauce base of service dish, neatly arrange shellfish on to dish, napper with sauce and glaze or gratinate as for poached fish (*see* p. 194).

Examples of Poached Shellfish Dishes Prepared Using Above Formula

English term	Selected sauce and garnish	Metric	Imperial	French term
In white wine sauce with parsley	Bercy sauce (fish based) (p. 93) Glazed for service			Bercy
In white wine sauce with truffle	Sauce vin blanc Garnish of chopped truffle Glazed for service			Parisienne
In cheese sauce	Fish mornay sauce Parmesan cheese to gratinate for service			Mornay
With spinach and cheese sauce	Fish mornay sauce Cooked leaf spinach	100 g	4 oz	Florentine
	Place poached shellfish on a bed of spinach mask with sauce and gratinate or glaze			

N.B. Other suitable sauces and garnishes may be used for the above dishes.

88
POACHED SMOKED FISH
(Smoked cod, haddock)

Yield: 4 portions
Cooking time: 10 – 12 min
Cooking temperature: 205° (400°F)

Unit	Ingredient	Metric (g)	Imperial (oz)
1	Selected smoked fish (cut into portions)	500	20
$^1/_{10}$	Butter	50	2
	Pepper to season		
*	Milk		

* Sufficient milk to cover the fish during cooking.

Method

Lay portions of fish (skin down) in a buttered cooking vessel. Lightly season with pepper and cover with milk and a knob of butter. Cover with a greased cartouche and place in the oven until cooked. Once cooked remove from oven, drain fish portions and remove any bone. Arrange fish on to service dish, moisten with a little cooking liquor and serve.

N.B.   Alternatively smoked fish may be cooked by simmering on stove-top in milk or milk and water.

89
HADDOCK MONTE CARLO

Yield: 4 portions
Cooking time: 15 min
Cooking temperature: 205°C (400°F)

Unit	Ingredient	Metric	Imperial
1	Smoked haddock (cut into portions)	500 g	1$\frac{1}{4}$ lb
$\frac{1}{5}$	Tomato concassé (heated)	100 g	4 oz
$\frac{1}{10}$	Cream	50 ml	2 fl oz
$\frac{1}{10}$	Butter	50 g	2 oz
	4 Poached eggs		
*	Beurre manié		
†	Milk		
	Pepper to season		

* Sufficient to thicken lightly cooking liquor.
† Sufficient milk to cover the fish during cooking.

Method

Cook as for poached smoked fish. Once cooked remove from oven, drain fish portions, remove any bone and place in service dish, keep hot. Lightly thicken the cooking liquor with beurre manié and enrich with cream. Crown each fish portion with a poached egg, napper with sauce and surround each egg with hot tomato concassé to garnish. Serve immediately.

11

The Principle and Practice of Steaming

To Steam   Vapeur

Commercial steaming involves cooking with water vapour (steam), under varying degrees of pressure. The minimum pressure generally used in trade operations is around 0.35 kg/cm^2 (5 psi). The boiling point of water at normal atmospheric pressure is 100°C (212°F), a temperature that will not increase no matter how long boiling continues. If however atmospheric pressure is increased the boiling temperature may be raised. This is the underlying principle of steaming under pressure.

During steaming heat is transferred from the water vapour to the food, which acts to cook and tenderize the products concerned. Many foods may be cooked successfully by this method, e.g. vegetables, fish, butcher's meat, offal, poultry, and various puddings. The steaming process reduces the risk of overcooking protein. Therefore, steamed products are easily digested and thus suitable for service to invalids. In addition there is less loss of the soluble nutrients from foods than with the other moist methods of cookery.

When a traditional kitchen brigade is employed the following Chefs de Partie may be involved with the preparation and cooking of steamed products:

Chef Garde-Manger   — involved with initial preparation of meats and fish prior to
                                       cooking
Chef Saucier   — butcher's meat, poultry, etc.
Chef Pâtissier   — preparation of suet pastry and sweet puddings for steaming
Chef Poissonnier   — fish products
Chef Entremettier   — vegetables to include potatoes.

Points for Consideration

Safety

Where a water-well is an integral part of a steamer it is essential to check for sufficient water prior to igniting. If this routine safety measure is ignored the steamer is liable to be seriously damaged.

Once foods are placed in the steamer ensure that the doors are sealed firmly to achieve correct pressure within. Before opening the doors release steam pressure as indicated by manufacturer's recommendations. On opening, use the door as a shield from escaping steam. When steaming puddings always cover with greased greaseproof paper and a pudding cloth to protect foods from condensed steam.

Where high pressure steamers are used check the cooking times as recommended by the manufacturer. Ensure that steamers are cleaned thoroughly after use and maintained frequently according to manufacturer's recommendations.

Steaming of Butcher's Meat, Offal, and Poultry

Pieces of meat, offal, and poultry that are suitable for boiling may also be steamed. When steaming at low pressure the cooking times for meats are similar to boiling times per equal unit of weight. Where pressure is increased cooking times are reduced.

Steamed meats may lack some of the colour and flavour associated with other methods of cooking but this may be counteracted by serving them with flavoursome sauces and colourful garnishes.

Steaming is ideally suited to bulk catering and for meat products where significant amounts of stock are *not* required.

Preparation of Meats for Steaming

Lightly season meat and secure with string as required:

(a) when no stock is required place meat on perforated steamer tray;
(b) when stock is required place the meat in a deep steaming vessel.

Set meat to steam until cooked.
Steamed meats may be served and garnished similarly to boiled meats (*see* Chapter 9).

Steaming of Fish

Whole fish and smaller cuts of fish may be cooked by this method. Steaming of small cuts may be adopted when cooking for large numbers, e.g. banqueting. This method facilitates ease of preparation and cooking without undue loss of colour or flavour. Where a sauce is required it would be prepared independently. Cooking times similar to boiled/poached fish unless they are reduced by high pressure steaming.

Preparation of Fish for Steaming

Lightly season and flavour with lemon juice and steam as for meats. Steamed fish may be served and garnished similarly to boiled and poached fish dishes (*see* Chapters 9 and 10).

Steaming of Vegetables to Include Potatoes

Vegetables suitable for boiling may also be steamed although when steaming at low pressure green vegetables tend to lose their fresh green appearance. As for meats and fish, steaming is an ideal method for cooking vegetables and potatoes when catering for large numbers. Preparation and cooking times are similar to those for boiled vegetables unless they are reduced by high pressure steaming.

Preparation of Vegetables and Potatoes for Steaming

Lightly season vegetables and place into perforated steamer tray. Set to steam until cooked. Steamed vegetables and potatoes may be prepared and served similarly to their boiled counterparts.

Steaming of Eggs

Where large numbers of hard boiled eggs are required they may be steamed in their shell then treated as for boiled eggs. At low pressure, steaming time is approximately 15 minutes.

90
STEAMED BEEFSTEAK PUDDING

Yield: 4 portions
Cooking time: 3 – 4 hr

Unit	Ingredient	Metric (g)	Imperial (oz)
1	Stewing beef diced [1½ cm (¾ in)]	500	20
⅕	Onion brunoise	100	4
*	Brown stock		
	Seasoned flour		
	Salt and pepper to taste		
	Chopped parsley (optional)		
	Few drops of Worcester sauce		
†	Suet pastry		

* Sufficient stock barely to cover meat.
† Sufficient for 4 portions approximately 150 g (6 oz) flour prepared into suet pastry (*see* recipe 30).

Method

Roll out two-thirds of suet pastry and line greased pudding basin. Lightly season the meat and roll through seasoned flour. Combine meat with onion, parsley and Worcester sauce. Place filling into lined basin, moisten with stock and roll out remaining pastry to form sealed lid. Cover with greased greaseproof paper and pudding cloth. Set to steam until cooked. Once cooked, clean the basin, surround with clean serviette and present for service.

Extensions of Basic Formula: Added Ingredients to 1 Unit – 500 g (1¼ lb) of Meat

Name of dish	Unit	Ingredient	Metric (g)	Imperial (oz)
Steak and mushroom pudding	¹⁄₁₀	Sliced mushrooms Add to filling	50	2

Name of dish	Unit	Ingredient	Metric (g)	Imperial (oz)
Steak and kidney pudding	$^{1}/_{5}$	Diced ox-kidney	100	4
		Add to filling		
Steak, kidney and oyster pudding	As for steak and kidney with the addition of oysters to filling 2 oysters per portion			
Steak, kidney and mushroom pudding	$^{1}/_{5}$	Diced ox-kidney	100	4
	$^{1}/_{10}$	Sliced mushrooms	50	2
		Add to filling		

N.B.   For steak puddings using cooked fillings *see* Chapter 18 on combined methods.

12

The Principle and Practice of Frying

There are two methods of frying:

(a) deep frying
(b) shallow frying

In both cases foods are cooked in heated fat or oil, either by submerging the food completely (deep frying) or by cooking in the minimum of oil/fat (shallow frying). All manner of foods may be cooked by these methods, e.g. animal protein, vegetables, fruits, etc.

To Fry (Deep)   Frire

Deep frying is cooking in selected oil or clarified fat in a friture. The cooking medium selected must be capable of being heated to high temperatures without burning. Temperatures will vary according to the food being fried and are determined by the extent of cooking and colouring required. Frying temperatures may vary from 160–195°C (320–380°F) approximately. As a guide fat/oil is ready for use when it is quite still and gives off a faint bluish haze. Examples of frying mediums in common use are as follows: cotton seed oil, palm, vegetable oil, and first class dripping.

How Food is Cooked by the Deep-Frying Process

During the process food is immersed in the heated frying medium. The exterior of the product may or may not be protected with a coating (e.g. batter, flour, breadcrumbs), but whatever the case the high temperature seals the exterior of the food. At this stage the moisture content within the food takes in heat, steam is then created which in turn acts as a cooking medium.

When deep frying *battered products*, they are best placed directly into a friture without a frying basket. Battered products tend to adhere to the baskets making them difficult to handle when removing from the friture on cooking. During frying many foods require turning to ensure even cooking, e.g. fish, meats, beignets, etc. When starting to fry it may be necessary to agitate foods gently to prevent their sticking together, e.g. battered foods, potato dishes.

Draining Foods for Service

On completion of frying the products should be drained well before service to remove excess grease. This may be achieved by:

(a) draining the food well over the fryer;
(b) placing cooked articles on to absorbent paper;
(c) always serving deep-fried foods on dish papers to absorb any remaining grease.

Care of Friture

After *each* fry the fat is cleaned with a fine mesh strainer to remove fried scraps and particles *before* continuing the next fry. After an extensive frying period the fat is drained from the friture and strained. The friture is cleaned and the strained fat/oil carefully replaced.

Items Required for Deep-Frying Operation

Frying baskets and fine-mesh sieves
Trays for scraps, fat drips, blanched and cooked foods
Cloth for cleaning hands
Seasonings
Foods to be fried
Protective coatings (flour, batter).

Operational Layout

Food $\longrightarrow$ Coating $\longrightarrow$ Friture $\longrightarrow$ Drip and scraps trays $\longrightarrow$ Food trays
(*Utensils to hand as required*)

Notes Concerning Deep Frying

Where a traditional kitchen brigade is employed all deep frying other than for pastry goods, is the responsibility of the Chef Rôtisseur.

Cooking Times

As indicated in the charts, this will vary according to size, structure, and nature of the product being fried and the temperature used.

Preparation for Frying

When using the various coatings for frying it is essential to cover the food completely and at the same time ensure a light even coating. This is achieved by:

(a) passing foods lightly through seasoned flour and shaking off excess flour before coating with batter;
(b) panéing food lightly and shaking off excess crumbs before patting the food into shape. Ensure the crumbs used for coating are finely sieved (not coarse) and re-sieved when required.
(c) where batter is used, test that the consistency for coating is correct (not too heavy) and that on coating only a light covering is applied.

N.B. Do not allow foods that have been coated in flour to stand for any length of time prior to cooking. The flour absorbs moisture from the food, becomes sticky and results in the food being difficult to handle. If fried in this condition the quality of the end-product would be impaired. This may be corrected by washing away sticky exterior, drying the article and re-flouring just before cooking.

Safety Factors

Deep frying can be a hazardous operation unless carried out with the utmost care and skill. It must be noted that *smoking fat is burning fat,* and if left unattended may reach flash point and burst into flames.

Care must be taken in the preparation of foods for deep frying:

(a) Wet foods need to be 'well drained' before frying otherwise the excess water boils when in contact with the hot fat often causing some of the fat to spill over the sides of the friture. This may result in serious accidents to staff and premises, e.g. burns and fire.

(b) Overloading the friture with food will displace the oil causing it to overflow – as a result accidents may occur. This is prevented by ensuring that the level of the frying medium in the friture does not exceed two thirds full (often indicated by a safety marker), and that the amount of food to be fried is not excessive at any one time. *NOTE*: In the event of a fat fire, extinguish with a foam extinguisher. *DO NOT USE WATER* as this causes further danger by spreading the fire.

(c) Whenever possible use a frying basket to ensure safe handling of food.

(d) *Organizational factors*. It is important that food and equipment are at hand and organized if a safe efficient system is to operate.

(e) When placing food into the fryer, dip items gently away from the body to prevent fat splashing, which could result in skin burns.

Protective Coatings for Deep-Fried Foods

Due to the high temperatures used when deep frying it is often necessary to surround foods with a protective coating prior to cooking. Such coatings are used to:

(a) prevent the surface of foods from being burnt or overcooked, which would make them indigestible;

(b) prevent moisture escaping from foods and spoiling the frying medium;

(c) to protect food from oil which would otherwise be absorbed by the food resulting in a greasy product;

(d) to seal in the food's moisture, which on heating turns to steam and cooks the food;

(e) offer variety in flavour, colour, and texture to the finished product.

91
FRYING IN BATTER
YEAST BATTER

Frit
Pâte à Frire

Yield: 1 l (2 pt) approx.

Unit	Ingredient	Metric	Imperial
1	Water (tepid)	500 ml	1 pt
4/5	Flour	400 g	1 lb
1/40	Yeast	12.5 g	1/2 oz
	Pinch of salt		

Method

Sift flour and salt into basin and form a well. Cream yeast in water thoroughly and pour into the well. Gradually beat in the flour to form a smooth batter. Cover with a damp cloth and allow to ferment in warm place for approximately 45 minutes to 1 hour.

Before use beat thoroughly and adjust to light coating consistency.

92
EGG BATTER   Pâte à Frire

Yield: 1 l (2 pt) approx.

Unit	Ingredient	Metric	Imperial
1	Water	500 ml	1 pt
4/5	Flour	400 g	1 lb
1/5	Whole egg	100 g	4 oz
1/40	Baking powder	12.5 g	1/2 oz
	Pinch of salt		

Method

Sift flour, baking powder and salt into basin and form a well. Whisk water and egg together thoroughly and pour into well. Gradually beat in the flour to form a smooth batter. Allow batter to stand in cool place to rest the gluten and enable the starch to effect full thickening. Before use adjust to light coating consistency.

N.B.   Before coating with batter items are passed lightly through seasoned flour to form a dry surface which enables the batter to adhere to the food. If the batter is allowed to rest in a warm area the baking powder would begin to work thus reducing its ability to aerate successfully when used at a later stage.

ENGLISH STYLE   à l'Anglaise (pané)

Coated in seasoned flour, egg wash and breadcrumbs.
Prepare food, pass through seasoned flour, egg-wash (eggs beaten with a little milk) and breadcrumbs. Lightly pat food to remove any excess crumbs. Re-shape items where required.

FRENCH STYLE   à la Française

Coated with milk and seasoned flour.
Prepare food, pass through milk and seasoned flour, shake well to remove excess flour and fry immediately.

N.B.   On no account allow foods coated in flour to stand for any length of time prior to cooking. This results in the flour absorbing moisture from the food and becoming soggy, which consequently spoils the appearance of the finished article.

ORLY STYLE   à l'Orly

Applied only to fish. Fish is lightly marinated, passed through seasoned flour and batter for deep frying, and served with tomato sauce, lemon and parsley (*see* p. 211).

Deep-Fried Chicken/Pork/Veal (raw)

Yield: 4 portions take: (a) One medium chicken (cut for sauté) or (b) 4 chicken suprêmes as required or (c) 500 g (1¼ lb) raw chicken/pork off bone cut into 2½ cm (1 in) chunks or (d) 8 chicken drumsticks (e) 4 × 150 g (6 oz) escalopes of veal.

Name of dish	Preparation and cooking	Frying temperature °C (°F)	Frying time (min)
Deep-fried chicken southern style	Season chicken, cut for sauté, pass through seasoned flour and frying batter. Deep fry until cooked and golden brown. Serve garnished with: 4 slices of grilled bacon 4 pineapple fritters 4 corn cakes 250 ml (½ pt) tomato sauce	175–190 (350–375)	8–10
Pilon de Volaille Frit (deep-fried chicken drumsticks)	Season drumsticks, pané, deep fry and serve garnished with deep fried parsley, dress with cutlet frills.	175–190 (350–375)	8–10
Suprême de Volaille Kiev (supreme of chicken Kiev)	Stuff the chicken supremes with garlic butter (*see* p. 111), season and pané. Deep fry until cooked and golden brown, serve garnished with deep fried parsley and dress with cutlet frills	175–190 (350–375)	8–10
Suprême de Volaille Cordon Bleu (supreme of chicken cordon bleu)	As for Kiev but replace garlic butter with: 4 thin slices of cooked ham 100 g (4 oz) grated gruyère cheese	175–190 (350–375)	8–10
Fritots de Volaille/Pork (deep-fried chicken/ pork (off bone)	Season chunks of chicken, pass through seasoned flour and frying batter. Deep fry until cooked and golden brown. Garnish with deep fried parsley. May be accompanied with sweet and sour sauce and rice pilaff	175–190 (350–375)	5–8

Name of dish	Preparation and cooking	Frying temperature °C (°F)	Frying time (min)
Wiener Schnitzel (deep-fried veal escalopes)	Season and pané veal. Deep fry until cooked and golden brown. Serve garnished with deep fried parsley and lemon wedge or rondel	175–190 (350–375)	5–6

N.B. Drain deep-fried products well and place on dish papers to absorb any excess grease.

DEEP-FRIED FISH
Poisson Frit

Deep frying is employed for cooking a wide variety of fish and shellfish, some are prepared and left whole and others prepared into smaller cuts. The whole fish/shellfish and cuts most commonly deep fried are listed below.

Whole Fish (prepared for cooking)

English term	French term	Yield 4 portions
Smelts	Éperlans	16 smelts
Dover sole	Sole Douvres	4 × 300 g (12 oz) approx.
Whiting	Merlan	4 × 200 g (8 oz) approx.
Whitebait	Blanchailles	400 g (1 lb)
Sprats	Melettes	8–12 sprats

Shellfish

English term	French term	Yield 4 portions
Oysters	Huîtres	16–24 oysters
Scallops	Coquilles Saint Jacques	400 g (1 lb) shelled weight
Scampi	Langoustine	400 g (1 lb) shelled weight

Fish That are Commonly Prepared into Small Cuts for Deep Frying (see overleaf)

English term	French term	Common cuts for deep frying (see overleaf)
Cod	Cabillaud	Filet-Suprême-Goujon
Dover sole	Sole Douvres	Filet-en Tresse-Goujon/ettes
Haddock	Aigrefin	Filet-Suprême-Goujon
Hake	Colin	Filet-Suprême-Goujon
Lemon sole	Sole Limande	Filet-en Tresse-Goujon/ettes
Monk		Goujon/ettes
Plaice	Plie	Filet-en Tresse-Goujon/ettes
Whiting	Merlan	Filet

Fish Cuts in Common use for Deep Frying

English term	French term	Yield 4 portions	Explanation and illustration
Fillet	le Filet	4 – 8 fillets according to size and requirements	A cut of fish free from the bone, taken from flat fish (4 fillets), round fish (2 fillets)
Supreme	le Suprême	4 × 125 g (5 oz) pieces	A cut (on the slant) taken from large fish fillets
Platted	en Tresse	4 – 8 fillets according to size and requirements	Platted fillets of fish (using small fillets only)
Thin strips	les Goujons	500 g (1¼ lb) cut into strips	Fillets cut into thin strips approximately 6 cm (2½ in) long by ½ cm (¼ in) thick
Tiny thin strips	les Goujonettes	500 g (1¼ lb) cut into strips	Fillets cut into very small thin strips as for goujons but cut smaller

Styles of Deep Frying

Name of dish	Preparation and cooking	Suggested accompanying sauce	Frying temperature °C (°F)	Frying time (min)
Poisson Frit à l'Anglaise (fried fish English style)	Pané prepared fish, deep fry until cooked and golden brown. Garnish with lemon wedge and deep fried picked parsley	Tartare sauce Sauce Tartare	175 – 190 (350 – 375)	3 – 6
Poisson Frit à la Française (fried fish French style)	Pass prepared fish through milk and seasoned flour, deep fry until cooked and golden brown. Garnish as above	Tartare/Rémoulade sauces Sauce Rémoulade	175 – 190 (350 – 375)	3 – 6
Poisson à l'Orly (fried fish Orly style)	Marinate prepared fish for 15 – 30 minutes in oil, lemon juice and chopped parsley. pass through seasoned flour and batter. Deep fry until cooked and golden brown. Garnish as above.	Tomato Sauce Sauce Tomates	175 – 190 (350 – 375)	3 – 6
Sole Douvière Colbert (Dover sole Colbert)	Take whole prepared soles (minus skin, eyes, fins, gut). Cut down the backbone on one side of the fish. Commence filleting to within 3 cm (1 in) of the sides, leave fillets attached. Fold fillets towards the sides. Snip the backbone in three places, pané and deep fry steadily until cooked. Remove backbone and garnish cavity with the parsley butter and wedge of lemon.	Parsley butter/Beurre Maître d'Hôtel	175 – 190 (350 – 375)	6 – 10
Merlan en Colère (deep-fried curled whiting)	Take whole prepared whiting (minus skin, eyes guts and gills). Place tail in mouth to secure, pané, deep fry until cooked and golden brown. Serve garnished with fried picked parsley and wedge of lemon	Tartare/Rémoulade Sauces	175 – 190 (350 – 375)	6 – 10

Name of dish	Preparation and cooking	Suggested accompanying sauce	Frying temperature °C (°F)	Frying time (min)
Blanchailles Diable (devilled white-bait*)	Pass whitebait through milk and seasoned flour. Place on to cane sieve and shake well to remove excess flour and to separate fish. Deep fry until crisp and golden brown. Drain and lightly sprinkle with salt and cayenne pepper. Garnish with lemon wedges and deep fried picked parsley		190 (375)	1–2
Blanchailles Frites (fried whitebait)	As above omitting cayenne pepper.			1–2
Fritto Misto Mare (Italian) (fried sea-food mixture)	A selection of fish/shell fish, prepared for frying, passed through *milk and seasoned flour* or *seasoned flour and batter*. Deep fry until crisp and golden brown, garnish with lemon wedges and deep-fried picked parsley, drain well and serve	Tartare/Rémoulade	175–190 (350–375)	3–6

* When handling whitebait in a hot atmosphere it is necessary to keep it in iced water to prevent the fish from decomposing and breaking up. The cold temperature keeps the whitebaits natural oil congealed and retards growth of micro-organisms.

Deep-Fried Vegetables   Légumes Frits

Using Raw Vegetables
Yield: 4 portions 300 g (12 oz) prepared weight

Name of dish	Preparation and cooking	Frying temperature C° (°F)	Frying time (min)
Aubergine Frite à la Française (deep-fried egg plant)	Trim ends of egg plant, decorate with channel cutter or peel away skin. Cut into ½ cm (¼ in) slices, pass through milk and seasoned flour, deep fry until golden brown and crisp. Drain, sprinkle lightly with salt and serve	190 (375)	2–3

Courgettes Frites à la Française (deep-fried baby marrows)	Trim ends, cut into ½ cm (¼ in) slices on the slant or lengthways. Continue as for egg plant	190 (375)	2-3
Oignons Frits à la Française (deep-fried onion rings)	Trim and peel onions, thinly slice into rings and separate. Omit small rings. Continue as for egg plant	190 (375)	2-3
Champignons Frits (deep fried mushrooms)	Select medium sized mushrooms, wash well, trim stalk and (peel if necessary) Pass through seasoned flour, lightly batter and deep fry until crisp and golden brown. Drain well, sprinkle with salt and serve	190 (375)	2-3

N.B. Drain deep-fried products well and present on dish papers to absorb any excess grease.

Using Par-Cooked Vegetables (Par-boiled, Refreshed and Drained)
Yield: 4 portions 300 g (12 oz) prepared weight

Name of dish	Preparation and cooking	Frying temperature °C (°F)	Frying time (min)
Beignets de Chou-fleur (cauliflower fritters)	Cut cauliflower into neat fleurettes, pass through seasoned flour and lightly batter. Deep fry until cooked and golden brown. Drain well, sprinkle lightly with salt and serve	175-190 (350-375)	3-5
Beignets de Panais (parsnip fritters)	Pass parsnip fingers through seasoned flour and lightly batter. Continue as for cauliflower	175-190 (350-375)	3-5

Deep-Fried Potatoes   Pommes de Terre Frites

Using prepared raw potatoes
Yield: 4 portions 400 g (1 lb) prepared weight

Name of dish	Preparation and cooking	Frying temperature °C (°F)	Frying time (min)
Pommes Chips (crisps)	Cut into very thin slices on a mandolin. Cover with cold water and stand for 30 minutes to remove excess starch, change water after 15 minutes. Too much starch causes crisps to stick together during cooking. Drain well, deep fry until golden brown and crisp. Agitate potatoes during frying to keep separated. Drain well, lightly sprinkle with salt and serve.	190 (375)	3-4

Name of dish	Preparation and cooking	Frying temperature °C (°F)	Frying time (min)
Pommes Gauffrettes (perforated crisps)	Cut into very thin perforated slices on a mandolin. Proceed as for crisps	190 (375)	3–4
Pommes Pailles (straw potatoes)	Cut into fine julienne on a mandolin or with a knife. Proceed as for crisps	190 (375)	1–2
Pommes Allumettes (matchstick potatoes)	Cut into large julienne. Proceed as for crisps	190 (375)	2–3
Pommes Mignonnette (potato bâtons)	Cut into small neat bâtons. Proceed as for crisps	190 (375)	3–4
Pommes Frites (chipped potatoes)	Cut potatoes into large bâtons by machine or manually	165–190 (330–375)	5–10
	Blanch in friture 165°C (330°F) without colour and until chips begin to soften. Drain and place on trays until required. To complete cooking submerge in hot friture 190°C (375°F) until crisp and golden brown. Drain, sprinkle lightly with salt and serve		
Pommes Pont Neuf (thick chipped potatoes)	Cut potatoes as for chipped potatoes but approximately twice as thick. Proceed as for chipped potatoes	165–190 (330–375)	10–15
Pommes Bataille (potato cubes)	Cut potatoes in 1 cm (½ in) dice. Proceed as for chipped potatoes	165–190 (330–375)	5–8

Drain deep-fried products well on dish papers to remove any excess grease

Deep-Fried Soufflé Potatoes   Pommes Soufflées

Trim potatoes into cylindrical shape. Cut into ¼ cm (⅛ in) slices and place in cold water to stand. Drain well and place into moderately hot fat [approximately 175°C (350°F)], agitate carefully throughout to prolong frying period, prevent colouring and lightly aerate in initial frying. When potatoes begin to souffle, remove from friture and place into second friture at a high temperature (190°C (375°F)) until potatoes soufflé completely are golden brown and crisp. Sprinkle lightly with salt and serve.

93
CHOUX PASTRY BASED FRITTERS

Beignets Soufflés

Yield: 4 portions
Frying time: 5 – 8 min
Frying temperature: 175 – 190°C (350 – 375°F)

Unit	Ingredient	Metric (g)	Imperial (oz)
1	*Choux pastry	100	4
1	Main flavouring	100	4
	Seasoning		

* Indicates amount of egg used when making choux pastry.

Method

Combine ingredients and season to taste. Shape into ovals using dessert spoons, place on to lightly oiled paper. Place into friture and fry steadily until fritters soufflé, become crisp and golden brown. Drain well, lightly sprinkle with salt and serve.

Examples of Dishes Prepared Using above Formula

English term	Main ingredient and garnish	French term
Cheese fritters	Grated cheese (Cheddar/parmesan)	Beignets au Fromage
Crab fritters	White crab meat, garnish with lemon wedges	Beignets de Crabe

N.B. Drain deep-fried products well and present on dish papers to absorb any excess grease.

94
DEEP-FRIED FRUITS (used to garnish meats)

Beignets de Fruits

Banana Fritters

Beignets de Banane

Yield: 4 portions 2 small bananas
Cooking time: 2 – 3 min
Frying temperature: 175 – 190°C (350 – 375°F)

Method

Peel bananas just before cooking (if peeled and left to stand for any length of time fruit turns black due to enzymic browning, *see* p. 57). Pané, or pass through milk and flour or flour and batter. Deep fry until cooked and golden brown, drain well and serve as required.

To Fry (Shallow)

Sauter

The French term used to describe foods that are shallow fried is sauter. Literally translated 'sauter' means to jump or leap, which seems far removed from the preparation and cooking of foods. There are times, however, when items being shallow fried are 'tossed' and give the appearance of leaping or jumping.

Shallow Fried in Butter   Sauté au Beurre

Denotes foods cooked or reheated by shallow frying in butter.

Meunière

A French term used to denote shallow-fried fish, which is garnished in a particular manner (*see* recipe 107).

Technique of Shallow Frying

Shallow frying can be simply defined as cooking in heated oil or selected fat. The initial starting temperature of the melted fat or oil needs to be near to smoking point in order to seal and cook the food quickly. Placing food into a cool frying medium would cause the food to absorb the fat/oil and consequently adversely affect the quality of the finished product. Various oils and fats attain smoking point at different temperatures, e.g. olive oil 250°C (480°F) and butter 140°C (280°F) approximately.

Shallow frying is carried out in frying or sauté pans according to the dish being cooked. Foods are cooked in the minimum of oil, on both sides with the presentation side being cooked first. This ensures ease of handling for presentation. On many occasions the meat juices form a sediment in the cooking vessel and are déglacéd with wine to form part of an accompanying sauce. The types of food suitable for this process are small pieces of tender meat, made-up dishes, fish, vegetables and fruits. The tougher cuts of meat are unsuitable for shallow frying.

Ensure that the cooking medium is at a sufficiently high temperature to seal and colour the food. At too low a temperature the fat/oil is absorbed by the food making it greasy and unpalatable. Also at a low temperature food is not adequately coloured or sealed and as a result the finished product may be of inferior quality.

When initial colouring and sealing of the food has been effected the cooking temperature is lowered to allow the food to cook through evenly. Continual cooking at a high temperature will result in overcooked, burnt, indigestible products.

When plain frying for large quantities it is necessary to change the frying medium and clean the pan before re-use. This is required because food particles burn and spoil the appearance of other fried foods. Care must be taken when handling certain foods during shallow frying because of their delicate structure, e.g. fish. Shallow-fried foods are lightly drained prior to service. When shallow frying those items that deteriorate on standing, e.g. steaks, and which also require an accompanying sauce/garnish, it is advisable to have the sauce and garnish prepared in advance of cooking.

Notes Concerning Shallow Frying

Where a traditional kitchen brigade is employed shallow frying is the shared responsibility of the following Chefs de Partie.

Chef Saucier   — Meat, poultry, game and offal entrées.
Chef Poissonier   — Fish dishes.
Chef Entremettier   — Vegetable and potato dishes.
Breakfast Cook   — Shallow fried breakfast dishes.

Cooking Times

These are indicated in the formulae and will vary according to the size, structure, and nature of the product being cooked.

Preparation for Shallow Frying

Season raw foods prior to cooking to ensure flavour. Do not allow foods which have been coated in flour to stand for any length of time prior to cooking (for reason *see* p. 205).

POULTRY   Volaille

Shallow-Fried Chicken   Sautés de Poulet

In readiness for shallow frying (sauter) chicken is usually prepared in one of three ways.

1   *Using Whole Chicken Cut into Joints (using medium/large chicken)*

	English term	French term
	Winglets	Ailerons
	Wing	Aile
	Breast	Blanc ou poitrine
 	Drumstick	Pilon de cuisse
	Thigh	Gras de cuisse

2 For Smaller Chicken Cut into Two Legs—Two Breasts

	English term	French term
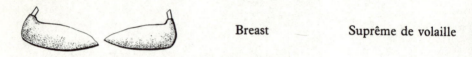	Breast	Suprême de volaille
	Leg	Cuisse de volaille

3 Using Chicken Breasts (Two per Chicken)

	English term	French term
	Breast	Suprême de volaille

95
SHALLOW-FRIED CHICKEN   Poulet Sauté

Yield: 4 portions
Chicken cut for sauté
Cooking time: 15–25 min

Method 1: Brown Sautés

Lightly season chicken pieces and shallow fry in a film of oil or clarified butter. Commence by cooking the leg joints, after a few minutes add breast and wing cuts. Sauté steadily until evenly browned, tender and cooked through. Remove chicken from sauté pan and keep hot. Drain off excess oil/fat leaving a thin film with which to prepare sauce. Form the sauce (*see* below) replace chicken into sauce and simmer to complete cooking. Portion chicken into service dish, cover with sauce, garnish as required and serve.

Method 2: White Sautés

Proceed as for Method 1 but use butter as the frying medium and cook chicken with the minimum of colour.

Name	Unit	Ingredient	Metric	Imperial	Method of sauté
Poulet Sauté	1	Chicken velouté	250 ml	10 fl oz	White
Archiduc	$^3/_5$	Cream	150 ml	6 fl oz	
	$^1/_5$	Onion (brunoise)	50 g	2 oz	
	$^1/_5$	Brandy	50 ml	2 fl oz	
	$^1/_{10}$	Madeira	25 ml	1 fl oz	
		Squeeze of lemon juice			
		Seasoning			
		Garnish—4 slices truffle			

Name	Unit	Ingredient	Metric	Imperial	Method of sauté

Sweat onions in sauté pan without colour, deglaze
with brandy and Madeira, add velouté and cream
to form a sauce. Flavour with lemon juice and
season to taste. Garnish completed dish

Name	Unit	Ingredient	Metric	Imperial	Method of sauté
Poulet Sauté Bercy	1	Demi-glace	400 ml	16 fl oz	Brown
	$\frac{1}{4}$	White wine (dry)	100 ml	4 fl oz	
	$\frac{1}{8}$	Shallots	50 g	2 oz	
		Milled peppercorns/salt			
		Garnish:			
	$\frac{1}{4}$	mushrooms (sliced sweated)	100 g	4 oz	
	$\frac{1}{4}$	chipolatas (grilled)	100 g	4 oz	

Sweat shallots without colour in sauté pan, deglaze
with wine and form a reduction. Add demi-glace,
correct seasoning. Garnish completed dish with
mushrooms and chipolatas

Name	Unit	Ingredient	Metric	Imperial	Method of sauté
Poulet Sauté Bonne Femme	1	Demi-glace	400 ml	16 fl oz	Brown
	$\frac{1}{4}$	White wine	100 ml	4 fl oz	
		Milled peppercorns/salt			
		Garnish:			
	$\frac{1}{4}$	button onions (glacés à brun)	100 g	4 oz	
	$\frac{1}{4}$	lardons of bacon (blanched and sautéd)	100 g	4 oz	
	$\frac{1}{4}$	cocotte potatoes (*see* p. 245)	100 g	4 oz	

Deglaze sauté pan with wine, reduce, add demi-glace.
Correct seasoning. Garnish completed dish

Name	Unit	Ingredient	Metric	Imperial	Method of sauté
Poulet Sauté Bourguignonne	1	Demi-glace	400 ml	16 fl oz	Brown
	$\frac{1}{4}$	Burgundy wine (red)	100 ml	4 fl oz	
	$\frac{1}{8}$	Shallots (brunoise)	50 g	2 oz	
		Milled peppercorns/salt			
		Pinch thyme and bay leaf			
		Garnish with:			
	$\frac{1}{4}$	button onions (glacés à brun)	100 g	4 oz	
	$\frac{1}{4}$	button mushrooms (glacés à brun)	100 g	4 oz	
	$\frac{1}{4}$	lardons of bacon (blanched and sautéd)	100 g	4 oz	
		4 heart-shaped croutons decorated with parsley			

Form a reduction in sauté pan with shallots, wine,
herbs, pepper. Add demi-glace, correct seasoning.
Garnish completed dish

Name	Unit	Ingredient	Metric	Imperial	Method of sauté
Poulet Sauté Champeaux	1	Demi-glace	400 ml	16 fl oz	Brown
	$\frac{1}{4}$	White wine (dry)	100 ml	4 fl oz	
		Seasoning			
		Garnish:			
	$\frac{1}{4}$	button onions (glacés à brun)	100 g	4 oz	
	$\frac{1}{4}$	cocotte potatoes (*see* p. 245)	100 g	4 oz	

Deglaze sauté pan with wine, reduce, add demiglace, correct seasoning. Garnish completed dish

Name	Unit	Ingredient	Metric	Imperial	Method of sauté
Poulet Sauté Chasseur	1	Demi-glace	400 ml	16 fl oz	Brown
	$\frac{1}{4}$	White wine (dry)	100 ml	4 fl oz	
	$\frac{1}{4}$	Button mushrooms (sliced)	100 g	4 oz	
	$\frac{1}{4}$	Tomato concassé	100 g	4 oz	
	$\frac{1}{8}$	Shallots (brunoise)	50 g	2 oz	
		Chopped parsley/tarragon/seasoning			

Sweat shallots and mushrooms, in sauté pan, deglaze with wine, reduce, add demi-glace, tarragon, parsley and tomato concassé. Simmer for 10 minutes

Name	Unit	Ingredient	Metric	Imperial	Method of sauté
Poulet Sauté Duroc		As for Chasseur garnished with cocotte potatoes			Brown

Name	Unit	Ingredient	Metric	Imperial	Method of sauté
Poulet Sauté Hongroise	1	Hongroise sauce (*see* p. 90)	400 ml	16 fl oz	White
	$\frac{1}{4}$	Tomato concassé	100 g	4 oz	
	$\frac{1}{4}$	Cream	100 g	4 oz	
	$\frac{1}{4}$	Onion (brunoise)	100 g	4 oz	
		Pinch of paprika			
		Chopped parsley			
		Seasoning			

Sweat onions in sauté pan without colour, flavour lightly with paprika. Swill out with cream, add hongroise sauce and tomato concassé, correct seasoning. Garnish complete dish with chopped parsley.
N.B. Usually served with braised rice

Name	Unit	Ingredient	Metric	Imperial	Method of sauté
Poulet Sauté Portugaise	1	Tomato sauce	250 ml	10 fl oz	Brown
	$\frac{4}{5}$	Tomato concassé	200 g	8 oz	
	$\frac{2}{5}$	White wine (dry)	100 ml	4 fl oz	
	$\frac{1}{5}$	Shallots (brunoise)	50 g	2 oz	
		Chopped garlic (hint)			
		Pinch of basil			
		Pinch of chopped parsley			
		Milled peppercorns/salt to taste			

Sweat shallots in sauté pan without colour, deglaze with wine, add garlic, basil, parsley and seasoning. Reduce by half, add tomato sauce and tomato concassé. Simmer for 2 – 3 minutes, correct seasoning.

Poulet Sauté Provençale	1	Tomato concassé	400 g	1 lb	Brown
	⅛	White wine (dry)	50 ml	2 fl oz	
	⅛	Shallot (brunoise)	50 g	2 oz	
		Pinch of salt/milled peppercorns			
		Chopped garlic (hint)			
		Pinch of fine herbs and basil			

Sweat shallots and garlic without colour in sauté pan, deglaze with wine and reduce by half. Add tomato concassé, herbs, season to taste. Simmer for a few minutes

N.B. The above sauces are adjusted to correct consistency.

96
SHALLOW-FRIED CHICKEN BREASTS   Suprêmes de Volaille Sautés

Yield: 4 portions 4 suprêmes (*see* p. 218)
Cooking time: 10 – 15 min

Method 1: Brown Sautés Using Panéd Chicken Suprêmes

Shallow fry prepared chicken (presentation side first), in a film of oil/clarified butter until cooked and golden brown on both sides. Remove chicken from sauté pan, garnish (*see* below) lightly moisten with beurre noisette and a cordon of sauce jus lié. Dress with cutlet frills.

Method 2: White Sautés Using Lightly Floured and Seasoned Suprêmes of Chicken

Shallow fry chicken in clarified butter (presentation side first) with the minimum of colour. When cooked remove suprêmes from sauté pan and keep hot. Drain off excess butter from pan leaving a thin film with which to prepare a sauce. Form the sauce (*see* below) napper, garnish as required and serve.

Examples of Chicken Sautés using Suprêmes: Preparation of Sauce and Garnish for Four Portions

Name	Unit	Ingredient	Metric	Imperial	Method of saute
Suprême de Volaille Sauté Archiduc		As for 'Poulet Sauté Archiduc' (*see* p. 218) using chicken suprêmes			White
Suprême de Volaille Sauté à la Crème	1	Cream (double)	300 ml	10 fl oz	White
	⅕	Sherry	60 ml	2 fl oz	
		Pinch of cayenne			
		Pinch of salt			

Deglaze sauté pan with sherry, reduce, add cream and simmer to required consistency. Season with salt and cayenne pepper

Name	Unit	Ingredient	Metric	Imperial	Method of sauté
Suprême de Volaille Sauté à la Crème aux Champignons	1 $^2/_5$ $^1/_5$	Cream (double) Mushrooms white (sliced) Sherry Squeeze of lemon juice Pinch of salt/cayenne pepper	300 ml 120 g 60 ml	10 fl oz 4 oz 2 fl oz	White
		Sweat mushrooms in sauté pan without colour, deglaze with sherry and lemon juice and reduce. Add cream and simmer to required consistency, season with salt and cayenne pepper			
Suprême de Volaille Sauté Doria	1	Cucumber (turned and cooked in butter)	100 g	4 oz	Brown panéd
		Garnish with cucumber			
Suprême de Volaille Sauté Hongroise		As for Poulet Sauté Hongroise (*see* p. 220)			White
Suprême de Volaille Sauté Maréchale		12 Cooked asparagus tips 4 Truffle slices			Brown panéd
		Garnish with above			
Suprême de Volaille Sauté Maryland		4 Small corn cakes (*see* recipe 218) 4 Small bananas (remove top half of skin) } shallow fried in butter			
		4 Grilled bacon rolls 4 Grilled tomatoes			Brown panéd
		Horseradish sauce (hot or cold)			
		Garnish with above, serve horseradish sauce separately.			
Suprême de Volaille Sauté Sandeman	1 $^2/_5$ $^1/_5$ $^1/_{10}$	Cream (double) Sweet peppers (julienne) Sherry Whisky Pinch of salt and pepper	300 ml 120 g 60 ml 30 ml	10 fl oz 4 oz 2 fl oz 1 fl oz	White
		Sweat peppers in sauté pan without colour, deglaze with sherry and whisky, and reduce. Add cream and simmer to required consistency. Correct seasoning			

Beef Sautés   Sautés de Boeuf

Small cuts of beef commonly used for sauté.

English term	French term	Yield 4 portions	Explanation and illustration
			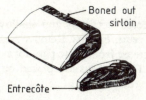
Sirloin steak	Entrecôte	4 × 200 g (8 oz)	Steaks cut from the boned out sirloin (contrefilet)
Minute steak	Entrecôte à la Minute	4 × 150 g (6 oz)	Sirloin steaks batted out thinly

	Tournedos	4 × 150 g (6 oz)	Small round steaks cut from middle of the fillet of beef secured with string

Tail of beef fillet cut into strips or slices	Émincé de Filet Mignon de Boeuf	500 g (1¼ lb)	Filet Mignon de Boeuf

Labels in illustrations:
- Boned out sirloin
- Entrecôte
- Sirloin steaks batted out thinly
- Heart of beef fillet
- Tournedos
- String
- Strips
- Slices

97
BEEF SAUTÉS

Sautés de Boeuf

(Using cuts shown above)
Yield: *see* chart above
Cooking time: According to requirements

Method

Season selected beef cuts and shallow fry on both sides in clarified butter/oil, to meet customers' requirements. Remove steaks from sauté pan and place aside for service. Drain off excess grease from sauté pan, form the sauce (*see* chart), napper and garnish for service.

   N.B. All tournedos are placed on croûtes of fried bread for service. Bread absorbs juices from the steak.

Examples of Beef Sautés: Preparation of Sauce an Garnish for 4 Portions

Name	Unit	Ingredient	Metric	Imperial	Examples of cuts used
au Beurre Noisette	1	Beurre noisette	100 g	4 oz	Entrecôte/ Entrecôte à la Minute
aux Champignons	1 $^1/_{10}$	Sauce Champignon (à brun) Sherry Chopped parsley	300 ml 30 ml	10 fl oz 1 fl oz	Entrecôte/ Entrecôte à la Minute/ Tournedos
		Deglaze sauté pan with sherry, add sauce champignon and garnish completed dish with chopped parsley			
au Poivre à la Créme	1 $^1/_{10}$	Cream (double) Brandy Crushed peppercorns	300 ml 30 ml	10 fl oz 1 fl oz	Entrecôte
		Press peppercorns into the raw meat, lightly season with salt. Cook as for sauté. *Sauce:* Deglaze sauté pan with brandy, add cream and simmer to required consistency. Season to taste.			
Bordelaise	1 $^1/_{10}$	Sauce Bordelaise Red wine 8 Slices of poached beef marrow Chopped parsley	300 ml 30 ml	10 fl oz 1 fl oz	Entrecôte/ Tournedos
		Deglaze sauté pan with wine, add sauce. Napper steaks with sauce and garnish with marrow and parsley			

Name	Unit	Ingredient	Metric	Imperial	Examples of cuts used
Chasseur	1	Sauce Chasseur	300 ml	10 fl oz	Entrecôte/
	$^1/_{10}$	White wine (dry)	30 ml	1 fl oz	Tournedos/
					Émincé de
		Deglaze sauté pan with wine and add sauce			Filet Mignon
à l'Estragon	1	Sauce Estragon	300 ml	10 fl oz	Entrecôte
	$^1/_{10}$	White wine (dry)	30 ml	1 fl oz	Tournedos
		Blanched tarragon leaves			
		Deglaze sauté pan with wine and add sauce. Napper steaks with sauce and garnish with tarragon leaves			
Fleuriste	1	Demi-glace	300 ml	10 fl oz	Tournedos
	$^1/_5$	White wine (dry)	60 ml	2 fl oz	
		4 Tomatoes filled with Jardinière garnish			
		Seasoning			
		Deglaze sauté pan with wine add demi-glace, correct consistency and seasoning. Napper tournedos and surround with cooked tomato garnish			
Hongroise	1	Sauce Hongroise (*see* p. 90)	300 ml	10 fl oz	Émincé de
	$^1/_{10}$	White wine (dry)	30 ml	1 fl oz	Filet Mignon
		Pinch of paprika			
		Season meat with paprika and cook as for sauté. Deglaze sauté pan with wine and add the sauce			
Marchand de Vin	1	Sauce Marchand de Vin	300 ml	10 fl oz	Entrecôte/
	$^1/_{10}$	Red wine	30 ml	1 fl oz	Entrecôte à la Minute
		Deglaze sauté pan with wine and add the sauce			
Périgordine	1	Sauce Madère	300 ml	10 fl oz	Tournedos
	$^1/_{10}$	Madeira	30 ml	1 fl oz	
		4 slices of truffle			
		Deglaze sauté pan with madeira and add the sauce. Napper steaks with sauce, garnish with truffle			
Rossini		As for Périgordine with the addition of 4 slices of Pâté de Foie Gras to garnish steaks			Tournedos

Name	Unit	Ingredient	Metric	Imperial	Examples of cuts used
Strogonoff	1	Cream (double)	300 ml	10 fl oz	Émincé de
	$1/5$	Mushrooms (sliced)	60 g	2 oz	Filet Mignon
	$1/5$	Tomato concassé	60 g	2 oz	
	$1/5$	Onion (brunoise)	60 g	2 oz	
	$1/10$	White wine (dry)	30 ml	1 fl oz	
		Squeeze of lemon juice			
		Pinch of tarragon			
		Chopped parsley			
		Seasoning			
		Sweat onions and mushrooms without colour, Deglaze with wine and lemon juice, add cream and simmer to required consistency. Add herbs, tomato concassé and season to taste			

Lamb Sautés   Sautés d'Agneau

Small cuts of lamb commonly used for sauté.

English term	French term	Yield 4 portions	Explanation and illustration

Lamb cutlets	Côtelettes d'Agneau	8 prepared cutlets	Cutlets cut from best-end of lamb
Lamb noisettes (nut)	Noisette d' Agneau	8 prepared noisettes	Noisettes cut from boned out loin of lamb

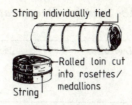

String individually tied

Rolled loin cut into rosettes/medallions

String

Lamb Rosettes/ Médaillons	Rosettes/ Médaillons d'Agneau	8 prepared rosettes/ médaillons	Rosettes cut from boned out loin of lamb tied into a cylinder

Filet Mignon

Slices of lamb's fillet

Fillet of lamb cut into slices	Émincé de Filet Mignon d'Agneau	500 g (1¼ lb)	Filet mignon taken from saddle of lamb May be left whole for certain dishes

98
LAMB SAUTÉS   Sautés d'Agneau
(Using cuts shown above)

Yield: *see* chart
Cooking time: 4 – 10 min
(according to customers' requirements)

Method 1: Prepared pané

Shallow fry prepared lamb on both sides in clarified butter/oil to meet customers' requirements. Remove from sauté pan garnish, lightly moisten with beurre noisette. Dress cutlets with frills.

Method 2: Left Plain

Season lamb, shallow fry on both sides in clarified butter/oil to meet customers' requirements. Remove from sauté pan and place aside for service. Drain excess grease from sauté pan, form the sauce (see chart), napper and garnish for service.

  N.B. Noisettes/rosettes are placed on croûtes of fried bread for service – the bread absorbs juices from the lamb.

Examples of Lamb Sautés: Preparation of Sauce and Garnish for 4 Portions

Name	Unit	Ingredient	Metric	Imperial	Examples of cuts used	Method of preparation for sauté
à l'Anglaise	1	Beurre noisette	100 g	4 oz	Côtelettes	Pané
Chasseur		As for Sauté of Beef Chasseur (p. 225)			Émincé de Filet Mignon	Plain
Clamart	1 $^1/_{10}$	Sauce Madère Madeira 4 Artichoke bottoms filled with cooked peas or peas purée (*see* p. 185) Deglaze sauté pan with Madeira and add sauce. Napper lamb and surround with cooked artichoke bottoms	300 ml 30 ml	10 fl oz 1 fl oz	Noisettes/ Rosettes	Plain
Fleuriste		As for Sauté of Beef Fleuriste (p. 225)			Noisettes/ Rosettes	Plain
Hongroise		As for Sauté of Beef Hongroise (p. 225)			Émincé de Filet Mignon	Plain
Maréchale		As for Suprême de Volaille Sauté Maréchale (p. 222)			Côtelettes	Pané
Masséna	1	Sauce Béarnaise 4 Artichoke bottoms (cooked *see* p. 76) 8 slices poached marrow Fill artichoke bottoms with bearnaise sauce to garnish cooked noisettes. Place a slice of marrow on each noisette	300 ml	10 fl oz	Noisettes/ Rosettes	Plain
Niçoise	1 $^2/_5$ $^2/_5$ $^2/_5$ $^1/_5$	Jus lié Tomato concassé French beans (reheated in butter) Cocotte potatoes White wine (dry) Deglaze sauté pan with white wine, add sauce correct seasoning. Napper lamb and garnish: place tomato on top of each rosette and surround with potatoes and French beans	300 ml 120 g 120 g 120 g 60 ml	10 fl oz 4 oz 4 oz 4 oz 2 fl oz	Rosettes/ Noisettes	Plain

Name	Unit	Ingredient	Metric	Imperial	Examples of cuts used	Method of sauté
Réform	1	Sauce Réform	250 ml	10 fl oz	Côtelettes	Pané
		Pané cutlets with the addition of finely chopped ham and parsley in the crumbs. Cook as for method 1, serve sauce Réform separately				

Veal and Pork Sautés

Sautés de Veau/Porc

Small cuts of veal and pork commonly used for sauté

English term	French term	Yield 4 portions	Explanation and illustration

Rib-bone ends

Back bone removed (chined) and rib-ends trimmed for cutlets (see pork cutlet)

Cutlet

Veal/pork cutlets	Côte de Veau/Porc	4 × 150 g (6 oz) cutlets	Cutlets taken from best-end of veal/pork

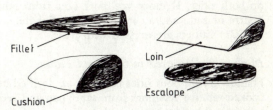

Fillet

Loin

Cushion

Escalope

| Veal/pork escalopes | Escalope de Veau/Porc | 4 × 150 g (6 oz) escalopes | Batted out slices of veal/pork taken from fillet or cushion of veal and fillet or boned-out pork loin |

Studded with fat

| Veal grenadins | Grenadin de Veau | 8 × 75 g (3 oz) grenadins | Thick escalopes from fillet or cushion of veal which are studded (piquéd with strips of bacon/pork fat) |

Studded with fat/truffle
String to keep in shape

| Veal médaillons | Médaillon de Veau | 4 × 150 g (6 oz) médaillons | Médaillons are round cuts (small tournedos) taken from fillet or cushion of veal, shaped like tournedos and secured with string. May be studded with fat or truffle. |

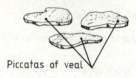

Piccatas of veal

| Veal piccata | Piccata de Veau | 12 × 50 g (2 oz) piccatas | Tiny escalopes taken from fillet of veal |

99
VEAL AND PORK SAUTÉS
(Using cuts shown above)

Sautés de Veau/Porc

Yield: 4 portions (*see* chart)
Cooking time: 3 – 10 min (according to cuts used)

Method 1: Prepared Pané

Shallow fry prepared cuts in a film of oil/clarified butter until cooked and golden brown on both sides. Remove veal/pork cuts from sauté pan, garnish (*see* chart) moisten with beurre noisette and a cordon of sauce Jus lié.

  N.B. Cutlets are dressed with frills.

Method 2: Prepared in Seasoned Flour

Shallow fry on both sides in a film of clarified butter, cook to light brown colour. When cooked remove veal/pork from sauté pan and keep hot. Drain off excess butter from pan, leaving a thin film with which to prepare a sauce. Form sauce (*see* chart), napper garnish as required and serve.

Examples of Veal/Pork Sautés: Preparation of Sauce and Garnish for 4 Portions

Name	Unit	Ingredient	Metric	Imperial	Examples of cuts used	Method of preparation for sauté
à l'Anglaise	1	Beurre noisette	100 g	4 oz	Escalopes/ Côtes	Pané

Name	Unit	Ingredient	Metric	Imperial	Examples of cuts used	Method of preparation for sauté
à la Crème		As for Suprême de Volaille à la Crème (p. 221)			Escalopes/ granadins/ médaillons/ piccatas	Floured
à la Crème aux Champignons		As for Suprême de Volaille à la Crème aux Champignons (p. 222)			Escalopes/ grenadins/ medaillons/ piccatas	Floured
au Madère	1 $^{1}/_{10}$	Sauce Madère Madeira	300 ml 30 ml	10 fl oz 1 fl oz	As above	Floured
		Deglaze sauté pan with Madeira and add sauce				
aux Champignons		As for Beef Sauté aux Champignon *see* p. 224			As above	Floured
Cordon Bleu		4 Slices of cooked ham 4 Slices of gruyère cheese 4 Rondels of peeled lemon			Escalopes	Pané
		Place ham and cheese in one half of raw escalope, fold over to seal, bat edges, pané and cook as for method one. Garnish with lemon				
Holstein		4 Shallow fried eggs 8 Slices of anchovy fillet 4 Rondels of peeled lemon			Escalopes	Pané
		Garnish cooked escalopes by placing eggs on top. Finish with criss-cross of anchovy and lemon slices				
Italienne		Garnish with Spaghetti Italienne (*see* p. 166)			Côtes/ escalopes	Pané
Maréchale		As for Suprême de Volaille Sauté Maréchale (*see* p. 222)			Côtes/ escalopes	Pané

Name	Unit	Ingredient	Metric	Imperial	Examples of cuts used	Method of preparation for sauté
au Marsala	1	Strong veal stock	100 ml	4 fl oz	Grenadin/ piccata	Floured
	1	Marsala (dry)	100 ml	4 fl oz		
	1/4	Butter	25 g	1 oz		
		Seasoning				
		Deglaze sauté pan with Marsala and veal stock, boil briskly and reduce until sauce takes on a glazing consistency. Add butter, season to taste.				
Milanaise		Garnish with Spaghetti Milanaise (*see* p. 166)			Côtes/ escalopes	Pané
Napolitaine		Garnish with Spaghetti Napolitaine (*see* p. 166)			Côtes/ escalopes	Pané
Viennoise		4 Stuffed olives 4 Anchovy fillets 4 Rondels of peeled lemon 1 Hard boiled egg (sieve white and yolk separately) Chopped parsley			Escalopes	Pané
		Place lemons on to cooked escalopes, wrap olives in anchovy fillets and place on to lemon. Decorate escalope with sieved egg and chopped parsley.				

Venison Sautées   Sautées de Venaison

Small cuts of venison commonly used for sauté

English term	French term	Yield 4 portions	Explanation and illustration
			Noisettes ⟶
Venison noisettes	Noisettes de Venaison	8 × 75 g (3 oz) noisettes	*Noisettes* are cut slantways from boned out loin of venison, lightly bat out to shape

Venison cutlets	Côtelettes de Venaison	8 × 75 g (3 oz) cutlets	Long saddle of venison with best-end

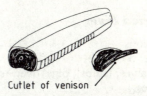

Cutlet of venison

Cutlets taken from best-end of venison, and lightly batted to shape

100
VENISON SAUTÉES
(Using cuts shown above)

Sautées de Venaison

Yield: 4 portions (*see* chart)
Cooking time: 8 – 10 min

Preparation for Cooking

Marinade cuts of venison in red wine for 24 hours before use.

Method

Season cuts of venison with salt and mill pepper. Shallow fry in a film of oil/clarified butter to saignant (underdone). Remove meat from sauté pan, keep hot, pour away excess grease and congealed blood, prepare sauce (see chart), napper and garnish as required. Dress cutlets with frills.

N.B. If sautéed venison is overcooked it becomes dry and tough.

Examples of Venison Sautées: Preparation of Sauces and Garnish for 4 Portions

Name	Unit	Ingredient	Metric	Imperial
au Porto	1	Sauce Porto	300 ml	10 fl oz
	1/10	Port	30 ml	1 fl oz
		Deglaze sauté pan with port and add sauce. Bring to boil and napper venison		
aux Cerises	1	Sauce Poivrade	300 ml	10 fl oz
	1	Poached stoned red cherries	300 g	10 oz
	1/10	Red wine	30 ml	1 fl oz
		Deglaze sauté pan with wine and add sauce. Add cherries, bring to the boil and napper venison		
Chasseur	As for Sauté of Beef Chasseur (*see* p. 225)			
Smitane	1	Sauce Smitane	300 ml	10 fl oz
		Napper venison with sauce		

101
SHALLOW-FRIED OFFAL   Sautés d'Abats

Shallow Fried Liver   Foie Sauté

Yield: 4 portions
Cooking time: 3–5 min
400 g (1 lb) calves, lambs', pigs' liver – skin liver remove tubes and gristle. Cut slantways
into thin slices.

Method

Pass liver through seasoned flour and shallow fry quickly in oil on both sides until sealed
and just cooked. Present for service with accompanying sauce and garnish (*see* chart).

Sauce and Garnish for 4 Portions

English term	French term	Unit	Ingredient	Metric	Imperial
Fried liver with onion sauce	Foie de Veau/ d'Agneau Sauté Lyonnaise	1	Sauce Lyonnaise	300 ml	10 fl oz
			Lightly napper liver with a little sauce and serve remainder in sauceboat		
Fried liver with bacon	Foie de Veau/ d'Agneau Sauté au Lard	1 1	Beurre noisette Sauce Jus lié 8 Thin rashers of grilled bacon	100 g 100 ml	4 oz 4 fl oz
			Garnish cooked liver with bacon, surround with a cordon of Jus lié and napper with beurre noisette		

102
SHALLOW-FRIED KIDNEYS   Rognons Sautés

Yield: 4 portions
8 Lambs kidneys – cut in half lengthways, remove skin and centre gristle.
Cooking time: 5–8 min

Method

Season kidneys and shallow fry in a film of oil or clarified butter until sealed and just
cooked. Remove from sauté pan and keep hot. Drain off excess fat and congealed blood,
leaving a thin film of oil/butter with which to prepare a sauce. Form sauce (*see* chart),
napper kidneys, garnish as required and serve.
     N.B.   The following dishes may be served with a rice pilaff.

Preparation of Sauce and Garnish for 4 Portions

Name	Unit	Ingredient	Metric	Imperial
Rognons Sautés Chasseur		Prepare sauce and finish as for Sauté de Boeuf Chasseur (*see* p. 225).		
Rognons Sautés au Madère	1 $^1/_{10}$	Sauce Madère Madeira Deglaze pan with Madeira and add sauce. Bring to boil and napper kidneys	300 ml 30 ml	10 fl oz 1 fl oz
Rognons Sautés Turbigo	1	As for Rognon Sauté au Madère garnished: Button mushrooms (glacés à brun) 8 small chipolatas 4 heart-shaped croûtes Chopped parsley	100 g	4 oz

103
SHALLOW-FRIED CHICKEN LIVERS IN MADEIRA SAUCE
Foie de Volaille Sauté à Sauce Madère

Yield: 4 portions
Cooking time: 4 – 6 min

Unit	Ingredient	Metric	Imperial
1	Chicken livers	400 g	1 lb
$^5/_8$	Sauce Madère	250 ml	10 fl oz
$^1/_8$	Madeira	50 ml	2 fl oz
$^1/_8$	Butter	50 g	2 oz
	Seasoning		

Method

Trim livers by removing gall bladders and stained liver. Cut in half, lightly season and sauté very quickly in hot butter until sealed and cooked. Remove livers into serving dish and keep hot. Remove excess grease from sauté pan, deglaze with Madeira, add sauce, correct seasoning and strain over liver to serve.

N.B.   Usually served with an accompaniment of braised rice.

104
SHALLOW-FRIED CALVES SWEETBREADS   Ris de Veau Sautés

Yield: 4 portions 600 g (1$^1/_4$ lb)
Cooking time: 5 – 8 min

Preparation of Sweetbreads Prior to Shallow Frying

Using white braised sweetbreads (p. 282) drain from unthickened cooking liquor), allow to cool and press gently between trays until set. Pressing ensures close texture and ease of handling. Slice into *thick* escalopes and prepare for shallow frying.

Method 1: Prepared Pané

Shallow fry in a film of oil/clarified butter until cooked and golden brown on both sides. Place in service dish and garnish (*see* chart). Serve moistened with beurre noisette and a cordon of Sauce Jus lié.

Method 2: Prepared in Seasoned Flour

Shallow fry on both sides in a film of clarified butter, cook to light brown. Remove from sauté pan and keep hot. Drain off excess butter from pan leaving a thin film with which to prepare sauce if required (*see* chart). Form the sauce, napper sweetbreads, garnish as required and serve.

Examples of Ris De Veau Sautés: Preparation of Sauce and Garnish for 4 Portions

Name	Unit	Ingredient	Metric	Imperial	Method of preparation for sauté
Escalope de Ris de Veau à l'Anglaise	1	Beurre noisette	100 g	4 oz	Pané
Escalope de Ris de Veau aux Champignons	1 $^{2}/_{5}$ $^{1}/_{10}$	Cream (double) Mushrooms (sliced) Brandy Squeeze of lemon juice Chopped parsley Seasoning	300 ml 120 g 30 ml	10 fl oz 4 oz 1 oz	Floured
		Sweat mushrooms in sauté pan without colour, deglaze with brandy and lemon juice. Add cream and simmer to coating consistency. Correct seasoning. Napper sweetbreads and garnish with chopped parsley			
Escalope de Ris de Veau Florentine	1 $^{4}/_{5}$ $^{1}/_{5}$	Sauce Mornay Cooked leaf spinach Grated cheese	300 ml 240 g 60 g	10 fl oz 8 oz 2 oz	Floured
		Place cooked escalopes on spinach in buttered serving dish. Napper with mornay sauce, sprinkle with grated cheese, gratinate and serve			
Escalope de Ris de Veau Maréchale		12 Cooked asparagus tips 4 Slices truffle			Pané
		Garnish sweetbreads with above			

Shallow-Fried Miscellaneous Dishes

105
BASIC RAW FORCEMEAT FOR BITOKS   Bitoks
(beef, veal or pork)

Yield: 4 portions
Cooking time: 8 – 10 min

Unit	Ingredient	Metric (g)	Imperial (oz)
1	Selected raw meat (lean, finely minced)	360	12
¼	White breadcrumbs (soaked in milk)	90	3
¼	Onion brunoise (sweated in butter)	90	3
⅛	Whole egg (beaten)	45	1½
	Seasoning		
	Chopped parsley		
	Oil (for shallow frying)		

Method
Squeeze breadcrumbs to remove milk. Re-mince meat with breadcrumbs then add onion, parsley, seasoning and mix thoroughly, binding with the egg. Refrigerate to set. Fry a small portion to test for seasoning. Correct seasoning if required. Divide the mixture into four portions and shape each into a medallion on a lightly floured board. Shallow fry steadily in oil on both sides until cooked and browned.

Drain, and present with a suitable sauce and garnish, *see* below. The sauce may be used to napper the bitoks or served in a sauceboat as an accompaniment.

Examples of Dishes Prepared Using the Above Formula

Menu term	Main ingredient	Garnish	Sauce
Bitok de Boeuf (hamburger steak)	Beef	French fried onions	Piquante
Vienna Steak	Beef	Shallow fried egg	Lyonnaise
Bitok de Porc (pork Bitok)	Pork	Chopped parsley	Smitane/Chasseur/ Hongroise
Bitok de Veau (veal Bitok)	Veal	Chopped parsley	As for pork

N.B.   Other suitable garnishes and sauces may be used for Bitoks.

106
BASIC RAW FORCEMEAT FOR POJARSKI (for veal or chicken)
Côtelette de Veau/Volaille Pojarski

Yield: 4 portions
Cooking time: 8 – 10 min

Unit	Ingredient	Metric	Imperial
1	Chicken or veal (lean and finely minced)	360 g	12 oz
¼	White breadcrumbs (lightly soaked in milk)	90 g	3 oz
⅛	Double cream	45 ml	1½ fl oz
⅛	Melted butter	45 g	1½ oz
	Squeeze of lemon juice		
	Pinch of nutmeg		
	Chopped parsley		
	Seasoning		

Method
Squeeze breadcrumbs to remove any excess milk. Combine minced meat with soaked breadcrumbs and pass through fine mincer to ensure even distribution. Add seasoning, nutmeg, and parsley. Place mixture in refrigerator or into a mixing bowl over ice to chill. Gradually work in the cream and melted butter and flavour with lemon juice. Mix until stiff. Fry off a small portion to test for seasoning and correct if necessary. Divide mixture into four equal portions and mould into cutlet shapes. Pané and shallow fry on both sides until cooked and golden brown. Drain well and present for service moistened with beurre noisette and accompanied by a selected sauce.

Examples of Dishes Prepared Using the Above Formula

Menu term	Main ingredient	Selected sauce
Côtelette de Veau Pojarski (veal Pojarski)	Lean veal (raw)	Chasseur/Smitane/Réform
Côtelette de Volaille Pojarski (chicken Pojarski)	Lean chicken (raw)	Chasseur/Smitane/Réform

N.B. Pojarskis may be served and garnished as for panéed veal escalopes/chicken suprêmes (*see* pp. 230 and 222 respectively).

Shallow-Fried Fish
Poisson Meunière

Shallow frying is employed for cooking a wide variety of fish and shellfish. Certain small fish are left whole whereas others are prepared into smaller cuts. The whole fish, shellfish and cuts most commonly used for shallow frying are listed below.

Whole Fish (prepared for cooking)

English term	French term	Yield 4 portions
Dover sole	Sole Douvres	4 × 300 g/12 oz
Herring	Hareng	4 × 200 g/8 oz
Mackerel	Maquereau	4 × 200 g/8 oz
Trout	Truite	4 × 200 g/8 oz
Whiting	Merlan	4 × 200 g/8 oz

Shellfish

Scallops	Coquilles St. Jacques	400 g/1 lb shelled wt
Scampi	Langoustine	400 g/1 lb shelled wt

Fish Commonly Prepared in Small Cuts for Shallow Frying

English term	French term	Common cuts (see pp.210 and 239)
Cod	Cabillaud	Filet – Darne – Suprême
Brill	Barbue	Suprême – Tronçon
Dover Sole	Sole Douvres	Filet – Goujons
Haddock	Aigrefin	Filet – Suprême – Darne
Hake	Colin	Filet – Suprême – Darne
Halibut	Flétan	Suprême – Tronçon
Lemon sole	Sole Limande	Filet – Goujons
Monk		Goujons
Plaice	Plie	Filet – Goujons
Red Mullet	Rouget	Filet
Salmon	Saumon	Suprême – Darne
Salmon Trout	Truite Saumonée	Suprême
Skate	Raie	Wing
Turbot	Turbot	Suprême – Tronçon

Fish Cuts in Common Use for Shallow Frying

Filet
Suprême } de Poisson—as for deep frying (*see* p. 210).
Goujons

English term	French term	Yield 4 portions	Explanation and illustration

Steak of round fish	Darne	4 × 150 g (6 oz)	A cut of round fish on the bone

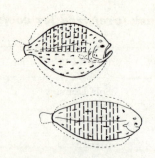

| Steak of flat fish | Tronçon | 4 × 150 g (6 oz) | A cut of flat fish on the bone |
| | | | (a) Cut in half lengthways then into tronçons |

(b) Cut across completely

107
SHALLOW-FRIED FISH
(using cuts shown above)

Poisson Meunière

Yield: 4 portions (*see* chart)
Cooking time: 3 – 10 min
according to cut used

Unit	Ingredient	Metric (g)	Imperial (oz)
	Selected fish (*see* chart above)		
1	Butter	100	4
½	Seasoned flour	50	2
½	Oil/clarified butter	50	2
	Garnish of 4 lemon slices/segments (without skin)		
	Chopped parsley		
	Squeeze of lemon juice		

Method

Pass fish through seasoned flour and shallow fry on both sides in oil (presentation side first) until cooked and golden brown. Remove fish to service dish, garnish with lemon. Prepare 'beurre meunière' (*see* p. 110) with butter and lemon juice, pour over fish and garnish with chopped parsley.

N.B.   Fish may be shallow fried in clarified butter and garnished with lemon wedge and sprig of parsley in place of beurre meunière. In these instances the term meunière would not be appropriate on the menu and the term doré could be used, e.g. Filet de Sole Doré (gilded sole).

Extensions of Fish Meunière: Garnish for 4 Portions

Menu term	Unit	Ingredient	Metric (g)	Imperial (oz)
Poisson Amandine	1	Flaked almonds	100	4
		Bake almonds brown, sprinkle over fish and finish à la meunière		
Poisson Belle Meunière		4 Mushroom heads 4 Slices of tomato 4 Soft roes		
		Shallow fry garnish and place on fish, finish à la meunière		
Poisson Bretonne à la Meunière	1 1	Picked shrimps Sliced mushrooms	50 50	2 2
		Shallow fry garnish, sprinkle over fish and finish à la meunière		
Poisson Cléopâtre à la Meunière	1 1	Picked shrimps Capers 4 Soft roes	50 50	2 2
		Shallow fry garnish and place on fish, finish à la meunière		
Poisson Doria	1	Shaped cucumber	100	4
		Cook cucumber in butter, garnish fish and finish à la meunière		
Poisson Grenobloise	1	Capers	50	2
		Sprinkle capers over fish and finish à la meunière		

N.B.   Generally with the exception of Poisson Grenobloise the above meunière preparations are garnished with lemon slices (without skin). Grenobloise is garnished with lemon segments (without skin).

Poisson Murat	1 1	Cooked artichoke bottoms (*see* p. 76) Potatoes (dice)	100 100	4 4
		Sauté potatoes until cooked and golden brown, slice artichoke and toss quickly with potatoes, sprinkle over fish and finish à la meunière		
		For goujons garnish and fish may be tossed in in butter together		

108
SHALLOW FRIED SCAMPI/SCALLOPS
WITH TOMATOES AND GARLIC

Scampi/Coquilles St. Jacques
Sautée Provençale

Yield: 4 portions
Cooking time: 5 – 8 min

Unit	Ingredient	Metric	Imperial
1	Scampi/scallops (shelled)	400 g	1 lb
3/4	Tomato concassé	300 g	12 oz
1/8	White wine (dry)	50 ml	2 fl oz
1/8	Shallots (brunoise)	50 g	2 oz
1/8	Seasoned flour	50 g	2 oz
1/8	Oil/butter	50 g	2 oz
	Hint of garlic		
	Pinch of fine herbs and basil		
	Pinch of salt/milled pepper		

Method

Sweat shallots in oil for a few minutes without colour, pass scampi through seasoned flour and add to shallots cook to light brown. Add garlic, déglacé with white wine reduce by half, add tomato concassé, herbs and simmer for 2 – 3 minutes. Correct seasoning and serve accompanied with rice pilaff.

109
SCAMPI NEWBURG

Langoustine Newburg

Yield: 4 portions
Cooking time: 5 – 8 min

Unit	Ingredient	Metric	Imperial
1	Scampi (shelled)	400 g	1 lb
3/4	Cream (double)	300 ml	12 fl oz
1/8	Butter	50 g	2 oz
1/8	Madeira	50 ml	2 fl oz
1/8	Egg yolk		
1/16	Brandy	25 ml	1 fl oz
	Seasoning		
	Rice pilaff for 4 portions (recipe 59)		

Method

Mix egg yolk with a little of the cream to form a liaison and put aside.
Season scampi and gently sauté in heated butter until cooked. Flame with brandy, add Madeira and reduce by half. Pour on the cream, bring to boil and simmer briskly to coating consistency. Correct seasoning, remove from heat, stir in liaison and do not reboil. Serve with an accompaniment of rice pilaff. Garnish scampi with slices of truffle which have been flavoured in brandy.

110
SCAMPI THERMIDOR   Langoustine Thermidor

Yield: 4 portions
Cooking time: 5 – 8 min

Unit	Ingredient	Metric	Imperial
1	Scampi (shelled)	400 g	1 lb
3/4	Sauce thermidor (*see* p. 92)	300 ml	12 fl oz
1/8	Butter	50 g	2 oz
	Seasoning		
	Parmesan to gratinate		
	4 Slices truffle		

Method

Season scampi and gently sauté in heated butter until cooked. Lightly sauce service dish, add cooked scampi, napper with sauce, sprinkle with parmesan cheese and gratinate. Garnish with slices of truffle.

Shallow-Fried Vegetables/Potatoes   Légumes/Pommes de Terre Sautés/ées

Vegetable and potato preparations in this study are shallow fried from raw. Other dishes that are pre-cooked then completed by shallow frying are outlined in Chapter 19 under combined methods.

111
SHALLOW FRIED EGG PLANT/   Aubergine/Courgette Sautée Provençale
BABY MARROW WITH TOMATO AND GARLIC

Yield: 4 portions
Cooking time: 10 – 15 min

Unit	Ingredient	Metric (g)	Imperial (oz)
1	Aubergine or courgette (peeled and sliced)	400	16
1/2	Tomato concassé	200	8
1/4	Onion (shredded)	100	4
1/8	Oil/butter	50	2
	Hint of chopped garlic		
	Pinch of fine herbs and basil		
	Pinch of salt/milled peppercorns		

Method

Sweat onion in oil without colour, add aubergine or courgettes. Add garlic, herbs and seasoning, cover with lid and sweat for 10 min. Add tomato concasse; correct seasoning, simmer for 1–2 minutes and serve.

112
SHALLOW-FRIED MUSHROOMS   Champignons Sautés

Yield: 4 portions
Cooking time: 3–5 min

Unit	Ingredient	Metric (g)	Imperial (oz)
1	Mushrooms (trimmed and washed)	400	16
1/8	Butter	50	2
	Chopped parsley		
	Pinch of salt/milled peppercorns		

Method

Place mushrooms in heated butter, lightly season and shallow fry until cooked and light brown. Drain well and serve sprinkled with chopped parsley.

Shallow-Fried Onions   Oignons Sautés

Peel and shred onions and proceed as for Champignons Sautés. Usually used as an accompaniment with hamburgers, sausages, liver, etc.

Shallow-Fried Button Onions   Oignons Bouton Sautés

Peel onions and continue as for Champignons Sautés. (Pinch of sugar may be added to effect browning.)

113
SHALLOW-FRIED POTATOES   Pommes de Terre Sautées

Yield: 4 portions
(using raw potatoes)
Cooking time: 15–20 min (according to shape of potato used)

Unit	Ingredient	Metric (g)	Imperial (oz)
1	Potatoes (peeled and cut to required shape)	400	16
1/8	Oil/butter	50	2
	Seasoning		
	Chopped parsley		

Method

Cut potatoes into required shape (*see* chart below). Sauté in oil/butter until cooked and golden brown. Drain off fat, lightly season and serve sprinkled with chopped parsley.

Potato Dishes Prepared using Sauté Method of Cookery

Name	Shape of potato cut and garnish
Pommes Sautées à Cru	Slice potatoes into even rondels
Pommes Sautées Columbine	Slice potatoes into even rondels add julienne of pimento during cooking
Pommes Parmentier	Cut potatoes into 1 cm ($^1/_2$ in) cubes
Pommes Sablées	As for Parmentier but sprinkle with breadcrumbs near end of cooking
Pommes Cocotte	Turn potatoes into small barrels
Pommes Noisette	Scoop potatoes into balls using a parisienne cutter
Pommes Parisienne	As for Pommes Noisette but roll in melted meat glaze for service

13

The Principles and Practice of Stewing and Braising

To Stew   Étuver

The French verb 'étuver' literally translated means 'to cook in its own juice'. In culinary terms stewing can best be defined as slowly cooking food in its own juices with the aid of a minimum amount of moistening agent in the form of stock, wine, beer, sauce, butter, etc. During cooking the liquid is flavoured by extractives from the stewed food, the result is a highly-flavoured liquor or sauce which forms an integral part of the stew. Throughout this process, which is generally a lengthy one, evaporation is kept to a minimum by covering the stewing vessel with a tight-fitting lid and by simmering the stew on the stove top or in an oven (oven stewing).

Condensation, which continually forms on the inside of the lid, acts as a self-basting process keeping the food moist. If the rate of evaporation is not kept to a minimum the stew will become dry and could burn. Therefore it may be necessary to add additional liquid as needed throughout the cooking period.

Once cooked the liquid and food are usually served together to form the complete dish.

Tougher cuts of meat may be made tender and palatable by this method (*see* Chapter 3 p. 52 concerning foods selected for stewing). Foods for stewing are cut into small pieces or cuts before cooking and may comprise of meats, fish, vegetables and fruit.

Notes concerning Stewing and Braising

The techniques of stewing or braising may be employed when cooking animal protein, vegetables or fruit. When a traditional kitchen brigade is employed the following Chefs de Partie are usually concerned with the preparation and cooking of braises and stews:

Chef Saucier   — butcher's meats, offal, poultry and game dishes
Chef Poissonnier   — fish dishes
Chef Entremettier   — vegetable dishes including potatoes
Chef Garde-Manger   — involved with initial preparation of
                         meats and fish prior to cooking

Breakfast Cook or
Chef Pâtissier — fruit dishes for breakfast.

Suitable Meats for Stewing and Braising

Item	Stewing Cuts	Braising cuts and joints
Lamb	Middle neck, breast, shoulder, chump	Shoulder (whole), chump, tongue, heart, sweetbreads
Beef	Shin, topside, silverside, thin and thick flank, chuck, sticking piece, plate, leg of mutton cut, ox kidney tripe	Topside, thick flank, middle rib, chuck, leg of mutton, ox liver, ox heart, ox tongue
Pork	Shoulder belly, spare rib	Shoulder
Veal	Neck, shoulder, breast, knuckle, kidney	Neck, shoulder, best end, saddle, leg cuts, sweetbreads, tongues
Poultry	Chicken	Duck, turkey winglets
Game	feathered game, furred game — rabbit, hare, venison, (neck, shoulder, breast)	Rabbit, hare, wild duck, feathered game, e.g. pheasant

Cooking times

These are indicated in the recipes and will vary according to the size, structure and nature of food being cooked.

Preparation

All the initial preparation of meats and fish would be carried out in the larder, under the direction of the Chef Garde-Manger. Certain joints for braising may be larded and/or marinaded prior to cooking (*see* p. 260) to ensure adequate portions.

Selecting the vessel

The size and shape of the cooking vessel will be determined by the volume of the food being cooked and whether cooking is carried out on the stove top or in the oven. The size of vessel used will also affect the amount of stock employed in the recipe and the degree of adjustment required to correct the consistency of the finished sauce.

Stock

The flavour and colour of stock used will be determined by the type of meat being cooked and the colour required in the finished dish, e.g. brown beef stew using brown beef stock.

Achieving Correct Colour And Flavour

When a *brown colour* is required the meat and vegetables are sealed and browned in oil/dripping at a high temperature to ensure correct colour and sealing of the meat. Colouring is also achieved by browning the roux (when employed) and by using brown stock. If a *white coloured* product is required less heat is applied to seal gently and without browning. The most suitable cooking mediums for this process are butter and margarine. Where a roux is employed it is cooked to the blond stage before being moistened with stock to effect a white colour. In some instances meats used for white stews are blanched and refreshed as a means of sealing the meat and also extracting the scum, which would otherwise discolour the resultant sauce.

Care during cooking

Throughout cooking, items need to be checked periodically to ensure that stock levels are maintained and that the food is not adhering to the base of the cooking vessel as this could result in a burnt stew. Over cooking results in unpalatable meat which breaks up, becomes stringy in texture and difficult to handle.

Adjusting the sauce

On completion of cooking the flavoursome liquor is adjusted for consistency. This is achieved by one of the following:
  (a) reducing the sauce;
  (b) whisking in beurre manié, arrowroot or cornflour, and reboiling to cook the starch and effect thickening;
  (c) adding demi-glace, jus lié or velouté sauce as required by the dish in question.

STEWING

Meat stews

Stewing meat is an economical method of cooking as it allows the use of the less expensive cuts of meat.
Generally meat stews can be categorised as follows:

Brown stews

The articles being cooked are browned, which results in the stew taking on a bronze colour.
  Examples of brown stews are:
Brown beef stew – Ragoût de Boeuf
Brown lamb stew – Navarin d'Agneau

White Stews

The article being stewed is kept white at the beginning of and throughout the cooking process.
  Examples of white stews:
White lamb stew – Blanquette d' Agneau
White chicken stew – Fricassée de Volaille

Miscellaneous Stews

This refers to stews that cannot be strictly classified as above.
Examples of such stews are:
Spiced stews – curries, goulashes, Chile Con Carne, Osso Bucco
Poultry and game stews – Coq au Vin, Salmis, Civet
Unthickened stews – Lancashire Hot Pot, Chop d'Agneau Champvallon, Irish Stew.

114
BROWN STEW   Ragoût Brun

Yield: 4 portions
Cooking time: 1½—2 hrs
Cooking temperature:
Moderate oven 150° C (300° F)

Unit	Ingredient		Metric (g)	Imperial (oz)
1	Stewing meat (prepared large dice)		600	20
¹/₅	{ Mirepoix (medium) or Onion (finely diced) }	According to requirements *see* chart	120	4
¹/₂₀	Flour		30	1
¹/₂₀	Oil or dripping		30	1
¹/₄₀	Tomato purée		15	½
	Bouquet garni			
	Seasoning			
	Hint of garlic			
*	Brown stock/liquid			

* Sufficient stock to cover meat during cooking and also form a lightly thickened sauce with the roux. An *approximate guide* is EQUAL QUANTITIES OF STOCK TO MEAT i.e. 1:1.

Method

Lightly season meat with salt and pepper and seal quickly in heated oil/dripping to colour light brown. Add mirepoix or onion and continue cooking to golden brown. Add flour and singe brown. Add tomato purée, stir in stock, bring to boil and skim. Add bouquet garni and additional flavourings.

Cover with tight-fitting lid, stew gently on stove top or in moderate oven, check periodically until meat is cooked. Once cooked remove meat into a clean vessel, correct consistency and seasoning of sauce, reboil and strain through fine chinois on to the meat. Garnish as required and serve.

Examples of Brown Stews Prepared from Above Formula:

Main ingredient and Garnish (in relation to 1-unit 600 g (1¼ lb) selected meat)

English term	Unit	Ingredient	Metric (g)	Imperial (oz)	French term
Lamb Stews					
Brown lamb stew		Stewing lamb (use mirepoix for formula)			Navarin d'Agneau
		As above garnished with:			Navarin d'Agneau:
	²⁄₅	{ glazed turned carrots, turnips and { button onions à brun	240	8	Printanier
Brown lamb stews with vegetables	²⁄₅	{ glazed paysanne { of vegetables	240	8	Paysanne
	²⁄₅	{ glazed julienne { of vegetables	240	8	Julienne
	²⁄₅	{ glazed jardinière } of vegetables	240	8	Jardinière
Brown lamb stew	¹⁄₅	Glazed turned carrots	120	4	Navarin
Bourgeoise	¹⁄₅	Glazed button onions à brun	120	4	d'Agneau
	¹⁄₁₀	Lardons of bacon	60	2	Bourgeoise
Brown Beef stews					
Brown beef stew		Stewing beef (use mirepoix for recipe)			Ragoût de Boeuf
Brown beef stew with vegetables		As for lamb stew, *see* chart above			
Brown beef stew Bourgeoise		As for lamb stew, *see* chart above			Ragoût de Boeuf Bourgeoise
Brown beef stew with dumplings		Garnish with 8 suet dumplings (*see* recipe 30)			
Brown beef stew in red wine		Replace half of the stock with red wine			Ragoût de Boeuf au Vin Rouge

English term	Unit	Ingredient	Metric (g)	Imperial (oz)	French term
Beef Burgundy style	$^1/_5$ $^1/_5$ $^1/_{10}$	As for Vin Rouge garnish with: glazed button onions à brun glazed button mushrooms à brun lardons of bacon 4 heart-shaped croûtons	120 120 60	4 4 2	Boeuf Bourguignonne
Savoury beef mince		Minced stewing beef (use onion in formula) N.B. Leave unstrained May be garnished with: Fried heart-shaped croûtons and a border of duchess potatoes			Hachis de Boeuf
Brown Veal Stews Brown veal stew		Stewing veal (use mirepoix in recipe)			Ragoût de Veau
Brown veal stew with vegetables		As for lamb stew, *see* chart above			
Brown veal stew with white wine		Replace quarter of the stock with white wine			Ragoût de Veau au Vin Blanc
Veal Marengo style	$^1/_5$ $^1/_5$ $^1/_5$	As for Ragoût de Veau au Vin Blanc but garnish with: glazed button onions à brun glazed button mushrooms à brun tomato concassé Add to the completed stew just prior to service and garnish with 4 heart-shaped croûtons and chopped parsley	120 120 120	4 4 4	Ragoût de Veau Marengo

Other Brown Stews Prepared Using Above Formula

Brown rabbit stew		Stewing rabbit (ready jointed) use mirepoix in recipe. Garnish as for lamb			Ragoût de Lapin
Stewed ox-kidney		Ox-kidney (use mirepoix in recipe)			Ragoût de Rognon de Boeuf

White Stew   Ragoût Blanc

Blanquette

This indicates a thickened white stew usually made from veal, lamb or rabbit. The meat is stewed in flavoured white stock from which a velouté sauce is produced at the end of cooking period. This forms part of the complete dish.

Fricassée

This indicates a thickened white stew usually made from veal, poultry or rabbit. The meat is stewed in a thickened sauce throughout the cooking period with the sauce forming part of the complete dish.

N.B. Both the above preparations are enriched with a liaison of egg yolk and cream just prior to service.

115
White Stew   Blanquette

Yield: 4 portions
Cooking time: 1-1½ hrs
For *rabbit* take 1 small rabbit

Unit	Ingredient	Metric	Imperial
1	Stewing meat (prepared large dice or jointed)	600 g	1¼ lb
1/5	Mirepoix (left whole)	120 g	4 oz
1/10	Cream ⎫ liaison	60 ml	2 fl oz
1/10	Egg yolk ⎭	60 g	2 oz
1/20	Butter	30 g	1 oz
1/20	Flour	30 g	1 oz
	Bouquet garni		
	Seasoning and squeeze of lemon juice		
*	White stock		

* N.B. Sufficient stock to cover meat during cooking, an *approximate guide* is EQUAL QUANTITIES OF STOCK TO MEAT i.e. 1:1

Method

Blanch and refresh meat to remove scum which would otherwise discolour sauce and spoil appearance of finished blanquette.

Season meat, place in saucepan with mirepoix, cover with stock, bring to boil, skim, add bouquet garni, seasoning and cover with tight-fitting lid. Stew gently on top of stove and check periodically until meat is tender. Once meat is cooked strain off the cooking liquor.

Prepare a blond roux with butter and flour, add stock to form a velouté, correct seasoning and consistency. Add lemon juice, re-heat the meat in the sauce, remove from heat, add liaison, garnish and serve as required.

N.B. Once liaison is added do not reboil otherwise egg will curdle in sauce.

116
White Stew   Fricassée

Yield: 4 portions
Cooking time: 1-1½ hr
Cooking temperature: moderate oven 150° C (300° F)
Poultry — 1 medium chicken
Game — 1 small rabbit

Unit	Ingredient	Metric	Imperial
1	Stewing meat (prepared large dice or jointed)	600 g	1¼ lb
¹/₁₀	Onion brunoise	60 g	2 oz
¹/₁₀	Cream ⎱ liaison	60 ml	2 fl oz
¹/₁₀	Egg yolk ⎰	60 g	2 oz
¹/₂₀	Butter	30 g	1 oz
¹/₂₀	Flour	30 g	1 oz
	Bouquet garni		
	Seasoning and squeeze of lemon juice		
	Mushroom trimmings		
*	White stock		

* N.B. Sufficient stock to cover meat during cooking and also to form a lightly thickened sauce with the roux. An *approximate guide* is EQUAL QUANTITIES OF STOCK TO MEAT i.e. 1:1.

Method

Season meat with salt and pepper, melt butter in sauté pan, add meat and onion, cover with lid and sweat gently without colour to seal. Add flour to form a blond roux, moisten with stock, bring to boil, skim, add bouquet garni, mushroom trimmings and seasoning.

Cover with tight-fitting lid and stew gently on stove top or in a moderate oven. Check periodically until meat is cooked. Once cooked, remove meat and place into clean vessel. Reduce sauce to pouring consistency, correct seasoning, add lemon juice, pass through fine chinois. Re-heat meat with sauce, remove from heat, add liaison, garnish and serve as required.

N.B. Once liaison is added do not reboil otherwise egg will curdle in the sauce.

Examples of Blanquettes and Fricassées Using Above Formula

English term	Main ingredient	French term
Blanquettes		
White lamb stew	Stewing lamb	Blanquette d'Agneau
White pork stew	Stewing pork	Blanquette de Porc
White veal stew	Stewing veal	Blanquette de Veau
White rabbit stew	Rabbit (jointed and trimmed)	Blanquette de Lapin
Fricassées		
White chicken stew	Chicken (cut for sauté)	Fricassée de Volaille
White pork stew	Stewing pork	Fricassée de Porc
White veal stew	Stewing veal	Fricassée de Veau
White rabbit stew	Rabbit (jointed and trimmed)	Fricassée de Lapin

Examples of Garnishes Used for Blanquettes and Fricassées

	Unit	Ingredient	Metric (g)	Imperial (oz)	
Ancient style	$1/5$	Glazed button onions à blanc	120	4	à l'Ancienne
	$1/5$	Glazed button mushrooms à blanc	120	4	
		4 Heart-shaped croûtons			
With asparagus		Garnish: 12 asparagus tips			Argenteuil
Finely chopped spring vegetables	$2/5$	Garnish: brunoise of vegetables sweated in butter without colour and mixed throughout sauce prior to service	240	8	Brunoise
Mother's style	$2/5$	Garnish: julienne of vegetable prepared and served as for brunoise	240	8	Bonne Maman
With mushrooms	$2/5$	Garnish: button mushrooms glazed without colour	240	8	aux Champignons

| With cucumber | $^2/_5$ | Garnish: cucumber (turned and poached) | 240 | 8 | Doria |

All the above dishes are usually garnished with freshly chopped parsley and shallow fried heart-shaped croûtons.

Miscellaneous Stews

(a) Spiced Stews

117
MEAT CURRY   Kari de Viande

Yield: 4 portions
Cooking time: 1 – 2 hr
Cooking temperature: moderate oven 150°C (300°F)

Unit	Ingredient	Metric	Imperial
1	Stewing meat (prepared large dice)	600 g	$1^1/_4$ lb
$^1/_5$	Onion (finely diced)	120 g	4 oz
$^1/_{10}$	Dripping or margarine	60 g	2 oz
$^1/_{20}$	Curry powder	30 g	1 oz
$^1/_{20}$	Flour	30 g	1 oz
$^1/_{40}$	Tomato purée	15 g	$^1/_2$ oz
*	Stock		
	Salt to season		
Flavourings			
$^1/_{10}$ †	Coconut milk	60 ml	2 fl oz
$^1/_{10}$	Diced apple	60 g	2 oz
$^1/_{20}$	Diced chutney	30 g	1 oz

---

* Sufficient stock to cover meat during cooking and also form a lightly thickened sauce with the roux. An approximate guide is *equal* quantities of *stock to meat*.
† Coconut milk — soak desiccated coconut in milk for 20 – 30 minutes, squeeze out for use.

Method

Season the meat lightly with salt and roll in a little of the curry powder. Melt fat in cooking vessel, add meat and onions and seal quickly. Add remaining curry powder and cook slowly for a few minutes. Add flour and colour to light brown, cool slightly, add tomato purée then moisten with stock.

Bring to boil, skim, add seasoning, cover with tight-fitting lid and stew gently on stove top or in moderate oven, check periodically until meat is almost cooked. At this stage add flavourings, continue cooking until meat is tender. Correct consistency and seasoning, serve with an accompaniment of plain boiled rice.

N.B. Varying quantities of curry powder may be added according to the type of powder used and *hotness* of curry required.

Examples of Curries Prepared Using Above Formula

English term	Main ingredient	French term
Beef curry	Stewing beef	Kari de Boeuf
Lamb curry	Stewing lamb	Kari d'Agneau
Mutton curry	Stewing mutton	Kari de Mouton
Veal curry	Stewing veal	Kari de Veau

In addition to rice it is usual to serve various accompaniments with the curry. These are presented attractively in small ravier dishes. They may include the following:

Deep fried or grilled popadums
Grilled bombay duck
Diced mango chutney
Browned coconut
Fried sultanas
Nuts

Diced apple/sliced banana in acidulated cream
Sliced fresh mango
Diced papaw
Fried plantain
Diced pineapple
Sliced tomato

118
HUNGARIAN GOULASH   Goulache Hongroise

Yield: 4 portions
Cooking time: 1½–2 hr
Cooking temperature: Moderate oven 150°C (300°F)

Unit	Ingredient	Metric (g)	Imperial (oz)
1	Stewing meat (prepared large dice)	600	20
⅕	Onion (finely diced)	120	4
¹⁄₂₀	Dripping	30	1
¹⁄₂₀	Paprika	30	1
¹⁄₂₀	Flour	30	1
¹⁄₄₀	Tomato purée	15	½
	Salt to season		
★	Stock		
	Garnish of:		
	8 small turned potatoes (blanched)		
	12 gnocchi parisienne (plain boiled)		
	chopped parsley		

★ Sufficient stock to cover meat during cooking and form a lightly thickened sauce. An *approximate guide* is EQUAL QUANTITIES OF STOCK TO MEAT i.e. 1:1.

Method

Season meat lightly and roll in a little paprika. Melt fat in cooking vessel, add meat and onions to seal quickly. Add remaining paprika and cook slowly for a few minutes. Add flour, colour light brown, cool slightly, add tomato purée then moisten with stock. Bring to the boil, skim, add seasoning, cover with tight-fitting lid and stew gently on stove top or in moderate oven, check periodically until meat is almost cooked. At this stage add blanched potatoes and continue cooking until meat is tender and potatoes are cooked.

Correct consistency and seasoning, garnish with plain boiled gnocchi and parsley for service.

Examples of Goulash Using Above Formula

English term	Main ingredient	French term
Beef goulash	Stewing beef	Goulache de Boeuf Hongroise
Lamb goulash	Stewing lamb	Goulache d'Agneau Hongroise
Mutton goulash	Stewing mutton	Goulache de Mouton Hongroise
Pork goulash	Stewing pork	Goulache de Porc Hongroise
Veal goulash	Stewing veal	Goulache de Veau Hongroise

119
STEWED BEEF MEXICAN STYLE

Chili Con Carne

Yield: 4 portions
Cooking time: $1\frac{1}{2} - 2$ hr
Cooking temperature: moderate oven 150°C (300°F)

Unit	Ingredient	Metric	Imperial
1	Coarse mince/small dice of lean beef	500 g	$1\frac{1}{4}$ lb
$\frac{1}{5}$	Dried red kidney beans* (soaked overnight)	100 g	4 oz
$\frac{1}{5}$	Onions (diced)	100 g	4 oz
$\frac{1}{5}$	Tomato concassé	100 g	4 oz
$\frac{1}{20}$	Oil	25 ml	1 fl oz
$\frac{1}{40}$	Tomato purée	12.5 g	$\frac{1}{2}$ oz
†	2 Chili peppers (finely chopped)		
	Salt to taste		
‡	Stock		

* Increase to $\frac{2}{5}$ unit when using processed beans.
† Only small amounts used approximately 1 – 2 chilis per 500 g ($1\frac{1}{4}$ lb) meat.
‡ Sufficient stock to cover meat. Approximately equal quantity of stock to meat.

Method

Sweat onions and chilis in oil for a few minutes, add meat to seal and colour, season lightly. Add tomato purée, soaked beans, tomato concassé and sufficient stock just to cover meat. Cover with tight-fitting lid and stew gently on stove top or in moderate oven. Check periodically until meat and beans are cooked. Correct seasoning and serve.

N.B.   Chili con carne is often served with plain boiled rice or pilaff. If using processed beans they will be added for the last 30 minutes of cooking time.

120
STEWED KNUCKLE OF VEAL MILAN STYLE   Osso-Bucco Milanaise

Yield: 4 portions
Cooking time: $2 - 2\frac{1}{2}$ hr
Cooking temperature: 150°C (300°F)

Unit	Ingredient	Metric	Imperial
1	Veal knuckle (cut into pieces on bone)	1 kg	$2\frac{1}{2}$ lb
$\frac{1}{5}$	Mirepoix (brunoise)	200 g	8 oz
$\frac{1}{5}$	Tomato concassé	200 g	8 oz
$\frac{1}{5}$	Dry white wine	200 ml	8 fl oz
$\frac{1}{20}$	Oil	50 ml	2 fl oz
$\frac{1}{40}$	Flour	25 g	1 oz
$\frac{1}{40}$	Tomato purée	25 g	1 oz
	Salt and pepper		
	Hint of chopped garlic		
	Squeeze of lemon juice		
	Chopped parsley – basil – thyme – bay leaf		
*	Stock (white chicken or veal)		

* Sufficient to cover meat during cooking and form a lightly thickened sauce.

Method

Season veal and pass through the flour. Seal quickly in heated oil to colour light brown, add mirepoix, cover with lid and sweat gently for a few minutes, add tomato purée and wine. Add stock, bring to boil, skim, add seasoning, garlic and herbs. Cover with tight-fitting lid and stew gently in moderate oven until meat is tender.

Add tomato concassé, squeeze of lemon juice, correct seasoning, simmer for $2 - 3$ minutes, garnish with chopped parsley and serve accompanied by Rizotto Milanaise (*see* p. 156).

(b)   *Poultry and Game Stews*

121
CHICKEN IN RED WINE   Coq au Vin

Yield: 4 portions
Cooking time: 45 min – 1 hr
Cooking temperature: 150°C (300°F)

Take a medium-sized chicken and cut for sauté.

Unit	Ingredient	Metric	Imperial
	One chicken (cut for sauté)		
1	Red wine	500 ml	1 pt
$1/5$	Chicken stock	100 ml	4 fl oz
$1/10$	Oil	50 ml	2 fl oz
$1/20$	Butter ⎫ beurre manié	25 g	1 oz
$1/20$	Flour ⎭	25 g	1 oz
$1/40$	Meat glaze	12.5 g	$1/2$ oz
	Bouquet garni		
	Seasoning/hint of chopped garlic		
	Garnish of:		
$1/5$	button onions	100 g	4 oz
$1/5$	button mushrooms	100 g	4 oz
$1/5$	blanched lardons of bacon	100 g	4 oz
	4 fried heart-shaped croûtons		
	Chopped parsley		

Method

Season chicken, seal and colour quickly in oil. Remove chicken and place in stewing vessel with bouquet garni and garlic. Sauté onions, mushrooms and lardons in chicken residue until lightly browned, put aside. Swill out (deglaze) sauté pan with red wine and stock, bring to boil, season and pour on to chicken. Cover with tight-fitting lid and stew in the oven until chicken is tender. Remove chicken and place into a clean cocotte or serving dish. Garnish with onions, mushrooms and lardons. Reduce cooking liquor by a third, add chicken glaze and thicken to required consistency using beurre manié, correct seasoning. Strain sauce on to chicken, replace in oven to re-heat thoroughly. Serve in cocotte garnished with croûtons and chopped parsley.

   N.B.   Fried croûtons may be spread with a purée of the cooked liver of the chicken. Traditionally this dish is prepared using a freshly killed bird, its blood being used to thicken the sauce. In this instance the sauce must not reboil otherwise it will curdle.

122
FEATHERED GAME STEW   Salmis de Gibier

Yield: 4 portions
Cooking time: 45 min – 1 hr
For 4 portions: 1 medium pheasant or   Faisan
                 2 wild ducks or   Canard Sauvage
                 2 grouse   Grouse
The above game birds are roasted underdone *see* p. 298 skinned and jointed into portions. Carcass retained for use in sauce.

Unit	Ingredient	Metric	Imperial
1	Demi-glace	500 ml	1 pt
$1/2$	Red wine	250 ml	10 fl oz
$1/10$	Onion brunoise	50 g	2 oz
$1/10$	Butter	50 g	2 oz
$1/20$	Brandy	25 ml	1 fl oz
	Seasoning		
	salt and crushed peppercorns,		
	bay leaf		
	Garnish of		
$1/5$	glazed button mushrooms		
	à brun	100 g	4 oz
	4 heart shaped croûtons		
	Chopped parsley		

Method

Chop the carcass and trimmings then sauté in butter with shallots, peppercorns and bay leaf until brown. Flame with brandy, déglacé with red wine and reduce by a half. Add demi-glace, simmer and reduce to extract game flavour from bones until sauce reaches required consistency, season to taste. Place jointed game in buttered cocotte, strain sauce through a fine chinois on to the game. Cover with a lid and reheat in hot oven. Serve garnished with mushrooms, heart shaped croûtons and chopped parsley.

Furred Game Stews   Civet de Gibier

For this type of game stew the raw meat is first of all placed in a red wine marinade and stored in a refrigerator for a minimum of eight hours. The marinade impregnates the meat during this period.

123
RED WINE MARINADE

Yield: 4 portions

Unit	Ingredient	Metric	Imperial
1	Red wine	500 ml	1 pt
$1/5$	Mirepoix (medium dice)	100 g	4 oz
$1/10$	Oil	50 ml	2 fl oz
	Seasoning		
	salt, crushed peppercorns		
	Hint of crushed garlic		
	Bouquet garni		

Method

Combine all ingredients together and place in bowl ready for use.

124
PREPARATION OF CIVET

Yield: 4 portions
Cooking time: 2½–3½ hr
Cooking temperature: 150°C (300°F)
For 4 portions — small hare (skinned)   Civet de Lièvre
                        800 g (2 lb) venison   Civet de Venaison

The above game is jointed or cut into pieces and placed in the marinade, retain blood to thicken the sauce.

Unit	Ingredient	Metric	Imperial
	Game and marinade		
1	Game stock	500 ml	1 pt
¹⁄₂₀	Flour	25 g	1 oz
¹⁄₂₀	Dripping	25 g	1 oz
¹⁄₂₀	Tomato purée	25 g	1 oz
	Seasoning		
	Retained blood (mixed with a little cold water)		

Method

Remove game and vegetables from marinade and fry in the dripping to seal and colour. Add flour and singe in hot oven, add tomato purée, moisten with liquor from marinade, add sufficient stock to cover the meat. Bring to the boil, skim cover with tight fitting lid and stew in a moderate oven. Check periodically until meat is cooked adjusting consistency if required. Remove meat from sauce, place in service dish and keep hot. Reboil the sauce remove from heat, add blood to thicken. Correct seasoning, strain sauce over the hare. Garnish as required and serve.

N.B.   Once blood liaison is added do not reboil or sauce will curdle.

Examples of Dishes Using Above Recipe: Garnish—in Relation to 1 Unit Game Stock i.e. ½ l (1 pt)

English term	Unit	Ingredient	Metric (g)	Imperial (oz)	French term
English style jugged hare		8 Forcemeat balls deep-fried: chop game liver and mix with a little sausage meat, roll in balls, pané and deep fry			Civet de Lièvre à l'Anglaise

English term	Unit	Ingredient	Metric g	Imperial oz	French term
Burgundy style jugged hare	$^1/_5$	Glazed button mushrooms à brun	100	4	Civet de Lièvre Bourguignonne
	$^1/_5$	Glazed button onions à brun	100	4	
	$^1/_{10}$	Cooked lardons of bacon 4 Heart-shaped croûtons	50	2	

N.B.   All civets are served with an accompaniment of red-currant jelly.

(c) Unthickened Stews

125
LANCASHIRE HOT-POT

Yield: 4 portions
Cooking time: $2 - 2^1/_2$ hr
Cooking temperature: 150°C (300°F)

Unit	Ingredient	Metric	Imperial
1	Middle neck lamb cutlets	600 g	$1^1/_4$ lb
1	Potatoes (peeled and sliced into thin rounds)	600 g	$1^1/_4$ lb
1	Onions (shredded)	600 g	$1^1/_4$ lb
$^1/_{20}$	Dripping	30 g	1 oz
	Seasoning of salt and pepper		
	Chopped parsley		
★	White stock		

★ Amount of stock will vary according to size of cooking vessel used.

Method

Lightly season the meat, potatoes, and onions. Fry meat in dripping to colour and seal on both sides. Place a layer of potatoes and onion on the base of an earthenware dish, follow with some of the fried meat. Repeat layering process and finish with a neat layer of overlapping potatoes.

Pour in sufficient stock to come just beneath surface of top layer of potatoes. Brush surface with melted dripping. Place in moderate oven until cooked and golden brown. Clean sides of dish, sprinkle with chopped parsley and serve. Accompany with pickled red cabbage.

126
LAMB CHOP CHAMPVALLON   Chop d'Agneau Champvallon

Yield: 4 portions
Cooking time: 2 hr
Cooking temperature: Moderate oven 150°C (300°F)

Unit	Ingredient	Metric (g)	Imperial (oz)
	4 chump chops (1 per portion)		
1	Potatoes (peeled and sliced into thin rounds)	500	20
²/₅	Onions (shredded)	200	8
²/₅	Tomatoes (skinned and sliced)	200	8
¹/₂₀	Dripping	25	1
	Bay leaf, pinch of thyme		
	Seasoning of salt and pepper		
	Hint of garlic and chopped parsley		
*	White stock		

* Amount of stock will vary according to size of cooking vessel used.

Method
Lightly season meat, potatoes and onions. Fry meat in dripping to colour and seal on both sides. Place a layer of onions and potatoes on the base of an earthenware dish, follow with the chops. Cover chops with the tomatoes, onions, garlic, bay leaf, and thyme. Finish with a neat layer of overlapping potatoes.

Pour in sufficient stock to come just beneath surface of top layer of potatoes. Brush surface with melted dripping and place in a moderate oven until cooked and golden brown. Clean sides of dish, sprinkle with chopped parsley and serve.

127
IRISH STEW

Yield: 4 portions
Cooking time: 1½ hr

Unit	Ingredient	Metric (g)	Imperial (oz)
1	Stewing lamb (large dice)	500	20
1	Potatoes (turned - keep trimmings)	500	20
¼	Celery (sliced)	125	5
¼	Onion (sliced)	125	5
¼	Leek (sliced)	125	5
¼	Button onions (to garnish)	125	5
	Bouquet garni		
	Seasoning of salt and pepper		
	Chopped parsley		
*	White stock		

* Amount of stock will vary according to size of cooking vessel used.

Method

Blanch, refresh and drain the lamb to remove scum (scum would impair the appearance of finished stew). Place in a stew pan with onions, leeks, celery, bouquet garni and barely cover with white stock. Bring to the boil and simmer for three-quarters of the stewing time. Add turned potatoes, potato trimmings and button onions, continue cooking until meat and vegetables are cooked. Correct seasoning, garnish with chopped parsley.

128
STEWED TRIPE AND ONIONS

Yield: 4 portions
Cooking time: 2 hr

Unit	Ingredient	Metric (g)	Imperial (oz)
1	White tripe (large trimmed pieces)	600	20
½	Onions shredded	300	10
½₀	Butter or margarine ⎱ white roux	30	1
½₀	Flour ⎰	30	1
*	Milk		
	Seasoning of salt and pepper		

* Sufficient milk to cover tripe. This will vary according to size and shape of cooking vessel.

Method

Blanch and refresh tripe to remove scum which would impair appearance of finished dish. Place tripe, onions, seasoning in stew pan and cover with milk. Bring to boil and stew gently until tripe is tender. Prepare a white roux with fat and flour, form a white sauce of coating consistency using the cooking liquor. Cook sauce for 10 minutes to ensure starch is cooked. Mix the sauce with the strained tripe and onion, reboil, correct seasoning and serve.

Stewed Fish   Matelote de Poisson

Matelote is the French culinary term for a fish stew. Strictly speaking matelotes are prepared from freshwater fish and in some instances are served as fish soups.

129
EEL STEW   Matelote d'Anguille

Yield: 4 portions
Cooking time: 30 min

Unit	Ingredient	Metric	Imperial
1	Freshwater eels (prepared skinned and jointed)	500 g	1¼ lb
³/₅	Red or white (dry) wine	300 ml	12 fl oz
¹/₅	Onion (brunoise)	100 g	4 oz
¹/₅	Cream	100 ml	4 fl oz
¹/₁₀	Butter	50 g	2 oz
¹/₂₀	Flour	25 g	1 oz
	Bouquet garni		
	Hint of garlic		
	Chopped parsley		
	Salt and pepper		
	Garnish with		
¹/₅	glazed button onions à blanc	100 g	4 oz
¹/₅	glazed button mushrooms à blanc	100 g	4 oz
	French bread		

Method

Sweat onion brunoise in half the butter without colour, add eels and continue to sweat and seal. Add bouquet garni, garlic, chopped parsley, seasoning and moisten with wine. Bring to boil, skim, cover with tight-fitting lid and stew until eels are tender. Place strained eel in serving dish and keep hot.

Prepare beurre manié with remaining butter and flour, thicken cooking liquor to pouring consistency, add cream, correct seasoning and strain over eels. Garnish with button onions, mushrooms and chopped parsley and serve accompanied with slices of French bread.

N.B.   Other fish stews (matelotes) may be similarly prepared using other types of fish and shellfish.

French Fish Soup/Stew   Bouillabaisse

Strictly defined, bouillabaisse is a type of fish soup prepared by the stewing method. Many varieties of this dish are found in the Mediterranean region where they are served as a soup or stew, but the most popular is that from Marseilles. The recipe below produces a generally acceptable culinary adaptation.

130
                                                               Bouillabaisse

Yield: 4 portions
Cooking time: 30 min
For 4 portions use a combination of the following prepared fish:

whiting, red mullet, conger eel, John Dory, squid (cut into sections free from skin and bone), crayfish and mussels (both in shell)

Unit	Ingredient	Metric	Imperial
1	Selected fish	500 g	1¼ lb
⅕	White wine (dry)	100 ml	4 fl oz
⅕	Onion (shredded)	100 g	4 oz
⅕	Leek (julienne)	100 g	4 oz
⅕	Tomato concassé	100 g	4 oz
¹/₁₀	Olive oil	50 ml	2 fl oz
	Bay leaf		
	Pinch of fennel		
	Hint of garlic		
	Pinch of saffron		
	Chopped parsley		
	Salt and milled pepper		
*	Fish stock		
	Garnish of French bread		

* Sufficient stock to cover fish for cooking. This will vary according to whether the bouillabaisse is to be served as a soup or stew.

Method

Sweat onions and leeks in oil without colour. Add all fish (other than shellfish), bay leaf, garlic, fennel, parsley and seasoning. Cover with lid and sweat for a few minutes to extract flavours. Moisten with wine and sufficient stock to just cover the fish. Bring to the boil, skim, add shellfish then saffron to flavour and colour. Cover with tight-fitting lid and stew gently until cooked. Adjust seasoning and serve with an accompaniment of sliced French bread.

N.B. French bread may be flavoured with cut garlic and served with bouillabaisse. Slices of French bread may be piquéd with garlic strips and then toasted or baked to a golden colour.

131
LOBSTER AMERICAINE   Homard Américaine

Yield: 4 portions
Cooking time: 20 – 30 min

Unit	Ingredient	Metric	Imperial
	2 Hen lobsters (live)		
1	Fish stock	250 ml	½ pt
⅗	White wine	150 ml	6 fl oz
⅖	Tomato concassé	100 g	4 oz
⅖	Mirepoix brunoise	100 g	4 oz
⅕	Oil	50 ml	2 fl oz
⅕	Butter	50 g	2 oz
⅕	Brandy	50 ml	2 fl oz
¹/₂₀	Tomato purée	12.5 g	½ oz
	Chopped parsley		
	Hint of garlic		
	Squeeze of lemon juice		

Preparation of Live Lobster

Place live lobster on chopping board, pierce head with point of knife and split head lengthways (leave tail whole). Separate tail from head and cut tail into thick tronçons. Remove claws and crack claw shell with back of heavy chopping knife. Remove liver (cream of lobster) from head and any coral, mix with butter ready for use. Discard sack from head. Retain carapace (head) and tail-fan shell for decoration.

Cooking of Lobster

Heat oil in cooking vessel, add lobster and cook until shell turns red. Add mirepoix brunoise, garlic and sweat to soften. Flame with brandy, add wine, fish stock, tomato purée, tomato concassé, squeeze of lemon juice and seasoning. Bring to boil, skim, cover with lid and stew gently for 15 minutes. Remove from heat, separate lobster from cooking liquor. Remove lobster meat from shell and place into a buttered service dish (keep hot). Reboil cooking liquor and add prepared butter mixture to thicken sauce. Adjust seasoning and pass through a coarse chinois on to lobster meat. Decorate with head and tail-fan of lobster shell, sprinkle with chopped parsley and serve accompanied with rice pilaff.

N.B.   Rice and lobster are usually served separately in timbales.

132
LOBSTER NEWBURG (using live lobster)   Homard Newburg à Cru

Yield: 4 portions
Cooking time: 20 min

Unit	Ingredient	Metric	Imperial
	2 Hen lobsters (live)		
1	Fish stock	250 ml	½ pt
1	Cream (double)	250 ml	½ pt
⅕	Marsala	50 ml	2 fl oz
⅕	Butter	50 g	2 oz
⅒	Brandy	25 ml	1 fl oz
⅒	Oil	25 ml	1 fl oz
	Salt and pepper to taste		

Preparation of Live Lobster

As for Homard Américaine (*see* recipe 131) including preparation of butter. A little flour may be added to butter mixture to aid thickening.

Cooking of Lobster

Heat oil in cooking vessel add lobster and cook until it turns red. Flame with brandy, add marsala and reduce by a half. Add cream, fish stock and seasoning. Bring to the boil, skim, cover with lid and stew gently for 15 minutes. Remove from heat and separate lobster from cooking liquor. Remove lobster meat from shell and place into a buttered service dish (keep hot). Reboil cooking liquor, add prepared butter mixture to thicken sauce. Adjust seasoning and pass through chinois on to the lobster meat. Decorate with head and tail of lobster shell for service. Serve accompanied with rice pilaff.

N.B.   Hen lobsters are selected for the above dishes because of their coral, which acts to flavour and colour the sauce.

133
STEWED MUSSELS IN WHITE WINE   Moules Marinière

Yield: 4 portions
Cooking time: 10 – 12 min

Unit	Ingredient	Metric	Imperial
1	Mussels (in shell, washed and scraped)	1 kg	2½ lb
⅕	Fish stock	200 ml	8 fl oz
⅒	Dry white wine	100 ml	4 fl oz
¹/₂₀	Onion (brunoise)	50 g	2 oz
	Squeeze of lemon juice		
	Salt and cayenne pepper		
	Chopped parsley		
*	Beurre manié		

* Sufficient beurre manié lightly to lié the sauce.

Method

Place mussels into a sauteuse with onions, wine, stock, lemon juice, and seasoning. Cover with lid and bring to boiling point, stew for a few minutes to cook mussels and open the shells. Remove mussels from cooking liquor, discard the top shells of opened mussels. Loosen mussels from bottom shell remove any beard, replace mussels into shells and arrange in serving dish (keep hot). Decant the cooking liquor into clean sauteuse leaving behind sediment and sand. Bring to boil, lightly lié with beurre manié, add chopped parsley, correct seasoning and pour onto the mussels for service.

Extensions of Moules Marinière: Added Ingredients in Relation to 1 Unit i.e. 1 kg (2½ lb) Mussels

English term	Unit	Ingredient	Metric	Imperial	French term
Mussels in cream sauce	⅒	Fresh cream (double) Finish sauce with cream	100 ml	4 fl oz	Moules à la Crème
Mussels in poulette sauce	⅒	Fresh cream (double)	100 ml	4 fl oz	Moules à la Poulette
	¹/₂₀	Egg yolk	50 g	2 oz	
		Omit beurre manié and thicken cooking liquor with liaison of yolks and cream. *DO NOT REBOIL*			

Vegetable Stews   Légumes Étuvés

A number of vegetables are cooked by the stewing method and are usually served as an accompaniment with a main course item. They are also ideal as a course for vegetarians.

134
STEWED PEAS   Petits Pois Étuvés

Yield: 4 portions
Cooking time: 30 min (for frozen vegetables reduce by half)

Unit	Ingredient	Metric (g)	Imperial (oz)
1	Shelled peas	200	8
1/2	Button onions (prepared)	100	4
1/4	Lettuce (prepared)	50	2
	Beurre manié to lié		
	Pinch of sugar		
	Salt to taste		

Method

Place peas, onions, and lettuce in pan, barely cover with boiling water, season with sugar and salt. Cover with tight-fitting lid and stew gently until the vegetables are cooked. Lightly thicken with beurre manié, correct seasoning and serve.

Extensions Using Above Formula: Added Ingredients in relation to 200 g (8 oz) shelled peas

English term	Unit	Ingredient	Metric (g)	Imperial (oz)	French term
Peas French style		As for Étuvés			Petit Pois à la Française
Peas housewife style	1/2	As above with cooked lardons of bacon	100	4	Petit Pois Bonne Femme
Peas peasant style	1/2	As for Étuvés with paysanne of vegetables	100	4	Petit Pois Paysanne

135
MARROW
PUMPKIN

Courge Provençale
Potiron Provençale

Yield: 4 portions
Cooking time: 30 – 45 min

Unit	Ingredient	Metric	Imperial
1	Marrow/pumpkin (large dice)	400 g	1 lb
½	Tomato concassé	200 g	8 oz
¼	Onion (shredded)	100 g	4 oz
⅛	Oil	50 ml	2 fl oz
	Hint of garlic		
	Pinch of basil		
	Bay leaf		
	Salt and milled pepper		
	Chopped parsley to garnish		

Method

Sweat onion and garlic in oil without colour for a few minutes. Add marrow, continue sweating, and add tomato, herbs and seasoning. Cover with a tight-fitting lid and stew gently until the vegetables are cooked. Correct seasoning, garnish with parsley and serve.

136

Ratatouille

Yield: 4 portions
Cooking time: 45 min
Cooking temperature: (moderate oven) 150°C (300°F)

Unit	Ingredient	Metric	Imperial
1	Courgette ⎱ peeled and sliced	200 g	8 oz
1	Aubergine ⎰	200 g	8 oz
1	Tomatoes (skinned and quartered)	200 g	8 oz
½	Green pepper ⎱ cut into rough julienne	100 g	4 oz
½	Red pepper ⎰	100 g	4 oz
½	Onion dice	100 g	4 oz
¼	Oil	50 ml	2 fl oz
	Hint of garlic		
	Salt and milled pepper		
	Chopped parsley		

N.B.   Skinned and quartered tomatoes may be replaced by tomato concassé.

Method

Sweat onion, peppers and garlic in oil without colour. Add courgettes, aubergines, and seasoning. Cover with a tight-fitting lid and stew gently on stove top or in oven. When half cooked add tomatoes and continue cooking until vegetables are tender. Garnish with chopped parsley and serve.

Stewed Fruits   Compote de Fruits

Stewed fruits, although mainly used in pastry work, are often served for breakfast and utilized in certain savoury preparations, e.g. stewed prunes used to prepare 'Devils on horseback'. The following list comprises fruits in common use:

Prunes	Pruneaux	} Soaked overnight before stewing
Figs	Figues	
Apples	Pommes	Peeled and quartered before stewing
Pears	Poires	Peeled and quartered or left whole, for stewing
Apricots	Abricots	} Left whole and stewed
Plums	Prunes	
Peaches	Pêches	Blanched, skinned and stewed.

137

Yield: 4 portions
400 g (1 lb) prepared fruit
Cooking time: 5 – 20 min (depending on fruit)

Unit	Ingredient		Metric	Imperial
	Selected fruit			
1	Water		500 ml	1 pt
$\frac{1}{5} - \frac{2}{5}$*	Sugar	} stock syrup	100 – 200 g	4 – 8 oz
	Lemon juice (squeeze of)			
	Cinnamon stick			

* Will vary according to the sweetness of fruit.

Method

Boil water, sugar, lemon, and cinnamon stick together with 10 – 15 minutes to form stock syrup. Place prepared fruit into stock syrup and stew gently until fruit is tender. Allow to cool in liquor ready for use.

To Braise   Braiser

The technique of braising may be described as a long, slow, moist process by which various foods are cooked in the oven, under cover in the minimum of liquor. As with stewing the highly-flavoured liquor or sauce becomes an integral part of the complete product. This technique may involve a combination of cooking liquors (stock, wine, sauce or beer), and cooking methods. In most cases oven braising is preceded by one of the following:

(a) *Shallow frying and sweating* – the initial method used to colour and seal in the flavour of the meat prior to its being braised in the oven. Often utilized for small cuts of butcher's meat and offal.

(b) *Flash roasting* (p. 301) – used for large pieces of butcher's meat, poultry, game and offal, for the reasons outlined in (a).

(c) *Blanching and refreshing in boiling water* – the method used to ensure the colour of the vegetables is retained and their structure made pliable for shaping. Certain offal are also blanched and refreshed before braising commences, enabling the scum to be removed and also setting the meat firm to ensure ease of handling. Cured meats selected for braising are usually blanched and boiled for a longer period, in order to remove excess saltiness and soften hardened protein (one of the results of curing). The permutation of cooking methods will depend upon the foods being braised.

The Braising of Butcher's Meat, Poultry, Offal and Game

The braising of meats may be broadly categorized as follows.

Brown Braising

(a) Using small cuts of meat and offal where the food is portioned prior to braising, e.g. braised steaks; or

(b) Where meat and poultry are braised 'in the piece' then carved into portions once cooking is complete, e.g. braised topside.

White braising

The method is as shown above but keeping braised items white in colour (omit red meats).

Ancilliary Larder Preparations of Meats, etc. for Braising

To Lard or Piqué Meat

When the meat for braising is inserted with strips of pork or bacon fat enabling it to remain moist during cooking whilst at the same time reducing excess shrinkage.

Marinating the Meat

The meat is allowed to stand in a marinade (*see* p. 260) prior to cooking. The marinade enhances colour, flavour and is used as an integral part of the cooking liquor during braising.

Brown Braising

Using Small Cuts of Butcher's Meat and Poultry

The following preparations are similar to many brown stews. They are, however, traditionally cooked in the oven (oven stewing) and appear on the menu as braised items, e.g. braised steaks.

138
BROWN BRAISED MEATS/POULTRY (SMALL CUTS)
Viande Braisée/Volaille Braisée à Brun

Yield: 4 portions
Cooking time: $1\frac{1}{2} - 2$ hr
Cooking temperature: 150°C (300°F)

Unit	Ingredient	Metric (g)	Imperial (oz)
1	Braising meat (*see* chart below)	600	20
$\frac{1}{5}$	Mirepoix (medium)	120	4
$\frac{1}{20}$	Flour	30	1
$\frac{1}{20}$	Oil or dripping	30	1
$\frac{1}{40}$	Tomato purée	15	$\frac{1}{2}$
	Bouquet garni		
	Seasoning		
*	Brown stock/liquid		

* Sufficient stock to cover meat during cooking and also form a lightly thickened sauce.
An *approximate guide* is EQUAL QUANTITIES OF STOCK TO MEAT i.e. 1:1. This will vary according to size and shape of cooking vessel.

Method

Lightly season meat with salt and pepper, seal quickly in heated oil/dripping until brown. Remove meat from cooking vessel and place into braising pan. Sweat vegetables in remaining oil until brown. Add the flour and form a brown roux. Add tomato purée, stir in stock, bring to the boil and skim, add bouquet garni and seasoning. Pour sauce over meat and cover with lid. Braise steadily in a moderate oven, check periodically until meat is cooked. Once cooked remove meat into a clean vessel, correct seasoning and consistency of sauce. Reboil and strain sauce through fine chinois on to the meat. Garnish as required and serve.

Examples of Meats Braised using Above Formula

English term	Main ingredient	French term
Braised steaks	Beef steaks (braising)	Biftecks Braisés
Braised lamb chops	Lamb chops (braising)	Chops d'Agneau Braisés
Braised veal chops	Veal cutlets (braising)	Chops de Veau Braisés

English term	Main ingredient	French term
Braised beef or veal olives	Prepared olives: Prepare escalopes of beef or veal and fill with forcemeat stuffing (*see* recipe 164) roll into cylinders, and secure with string. Use as required. Remove string for service	Paupiettes de Boeuf/Veau Braisés
Braised chicken ballotines	Prepared ballotines: Bone out chicken legs leaving skin and flesh intact. Fill with forcemeat stuffing (*see* recipe 164) secure with string and use. Remove string for service	Ballotines de Volaille Braisés

Garnishes for Above Braised Meats: Garnish — in Relation to 1 Unit i.e. 600 g (1¼ lb) Braising Meat

English term	Unit	Ingredient	Metric (g)	Imperial (oz)	French term
Spring vegetables	$\frac{1}{5}$	Glazed turned carrots	120	4	Printanier
	$\frac{1}{5}$	Glazed button onions à brun	120	4	
	$\frac{1}{5}$	Glazed turned turnips	120	4	
Peasant style	$\frac{2}{5}$	Cooked paysanne of vegetables	240	8	Paysanne
Gardener's style	$\frac{2}{5}$	Cooked jardinière of vegetables	240	8	Jardinière
	$\frac{1}{5}$	Glazed turned carrots	120	4	Bourgeoise
	$\frac{1}{5}$	Glazed button onions à brun	120	4	
	$\frac{1}{10}$	Lardons of bacon	60	2	
In red wine		Replace half stock with red wine			au Vin Rouge

139
BEEF BRAISED IN BEER   Carbonnade de Boeuf

Yield: 4 portions
Cooking time: 1½–2 hr
Cooking temperature: 150°C (300°F)

Unit	Ingredient	Metric	Imperial
1	Lean braising beef (cut into small escalopes)	600 g	1 1/4 lb
1/2	Onions (shredded)	300 g	10 oz
1/2	Brown ale	300 ml	10 fl oz
1/20	Flour	30 g	1 oz
1/20	Oil or dripping	30 g	1 oz
	Seasoning		
	Hint of garlic		
	Chopped parsley		
★	Brown stock		

★ Sufficient to cover meat during cooking.

Method

Pass meat through seasoned flour, seal and brown quickly in oil or dripping. Remove meat from pan and put aside. Sweat onions in remaining fat until light brown. Layer onions and meat alternately in a casserole and lightly season each layer. Sprinkle with garlic and pour on the beer, top up just to cover with stock. Cover with lid and braise steadily in a moderate oven until meat is cooked. Once cooked, degrease, adjust seasoning, garnish with chopped parsley, serve.

Cooking 'en Daube'

Cooking 'En Daube' is akin to braising/oven stewing with the selected meat being cooked in a daubière (earthenware cooking vessel) which is covered with a tight-fitting lid. Prior to cooking, the meat is 'larded', lightly seasoned, flavoured with fine herbs and chopped garlic. It is then placed in a marinade for 4 hours before cooking.

140

Daube de Boeuf/Mouton

Yield: 4 portions
Cooking time: 2 1/2 – 3 hr
Cooking temperature: 150°C (300°F)

Unit	Ingredient	Metric	Imperial
1	Meat (beef topside/leg of mutton – large cubes)	600 g	1 1/4 lb
1	Red wine	600 ml	1 pt
1/4	Bacon (cut into large lardons and blanch)	150 g	5 oz
1/4	Mirepoix	150 g	5 oz
1/20	Brandy	30 ml	1 fl oz
1/20	Oil	30 ml	1 fl oz
1/40	Tomato purée	15 g	1/2 oz
	Chopped fine herbs and garlic		
	Bouquet garni		
	Seasoning		
★	Stock (brown)		

★ Stock may be required in addition to wine to ensure meat is covered for cooking.

Method

Lard the cubes of meat with bacon fat, lightly season and roll in chopped garlic and fine herbs. Place in daubière with bouquet garni, lardons, mirepoix, tomato purée, oil, brandy and cover with red wine to marinade. Allow to stand for approximately 4 hours. Add stock just to cover meat (if required), cover with a light-fitting lid and set to cook in hot oven 230°C (450°F) until liquor comes to boiling point. Reduce heat to 150°C (300°F) and continue cooking until meat is tender. Degrease, correct seasoning and serve in cleaned cooking vessel.

Brown Braises of Offal

141
BRAISED OX-TAIL
Queue de Boeuf Braisée

Yield: 4 portions
Cooking time: 3–4 hr
Cooking temperature: 150°C (300°F)

Unit	Ingredient	Metric	Imperial
1	Ox-tail (sectioned)	1 kg	2½ lb
⅕	Mirepoix (medium)	200 g	8 oz
1/40	Flour	25 g	1 oz
1/40	Dripping	25 g	1 oz
1/40	Tomato purée	25 g	1 oz
	Seasoning		
	Bouquet garni		
*	Brown stock		

* Sufficient stock to cover meat during cooking.

Method

Lightly season ox-tail with salt and pepper, seal quickly in dripping until light brown, add mirepoix continue cooking until brown. Add the flour and singe. Cool slightly, add the tomato purée, moisten with stock, bring to boil, skim. Add bouquet garni, seasoning, cover with a lid and braise in the oven until tender. Stir periodically to ensure even cooking. Once cooked remove ox-tail into clean vessel, correct consistency and seasoning of sauce, strain over meat, garnish as required and serve.

Garnishes: Printanier, Jardinière, Paysanne, etc. as for braised cuts of meat (*see* p. 274)

142
BRAISED LAMBS' HEARTS
Coeur d'Agneau Braisé

Yield: 4 portions
4 lambs' hearts
Cooking time: 2–2½ hr
Cooking temperature: 150°C (300°F)

Unit	Ingredient	Metric (g)	Imperial (oz)
	4 Lambs' hearts (trimmed)		
1	Mirepoix (medium)	120	4
1/4	Flour	30	1
1/4	Dripping	30	1
1/8	Tomato purée	15	1/2
	Bouquet garni		
	Seasoning of salt and pepper		
	Chopped parsley		
*	Brown stock		

* Sufficient stock to cover hearts during cooking and form a lightly thickened sauce.

Method

Lightly season hearts with salt and pepper, seal quickly in dripping until light brown. Add mirepoix and continue cooking until brown. Add flour and singe, cool slightly, add tomato purée, moisten with stock, bring to boil and skim. Add bouquet garni, seasoning, cover with lid and braise in the oven until tender. Check periodically to adjust consistency. Once cooked place hearts into clean vessel, correct consistency and seasoning of sauce, strain over meat, garnish with chopped parsley and serve.

Garnishes: Printanier, jardinière, Paysanne, etc. as for braised cuts of meat (*see* p. 274)

N.B. The hearts may be filled with stuffing (*see* p. 298) before braising. E.g. Coeur d'Agneau Braisé Farci.

143
BRAISED LIVER AND ONIONS   Foie de Boeuf Braisé Lyonnaise

Yield: 4 portions
Cooking time: 1½ – 2 hr
Cooking temperature: 150°C (300°F)

Unit	Ingredient	Metric (g)	Imperial (oz)
1	Ox-liver (portioned)	400	16
1/2	Onions (shredded)	200	8
1/8	Dripping	50	2
1/16	Flour	25	1
*	Brown stock	25	1
	Seasoning of salt and pepper		
	Extra seasoned flour		

* Sufficient stock to cover meat during cooking and also form a lightly thickened sauce.

Method

Pass meat through the seasoned flour, seal and brown quickly in dripping. Remove liver and place in braising vessel. Sweat onions in remaining fat until golden brown, add flour to form a roux. Moisten with stock and bring to boil to form sauce. Skim, season and pour over the liver. Cover with a lid and braise in the oven until tender. Stir periodically to ensure even cooking. Once cooked degrease, correct seasoning, consistency and served unstrained.

144
BRAISED LAMBS' TONGUES   Langues d'Agneau Braisées

Yield: 8 lambs' tongues
Cooking time: 2 hr
Cooking temperature: 150°C (300°F)

Unit	Ingredient	Metric	Imperial
	8 Lambs' tongues (blanched and refreshed)		
1	Brown stock	600 ml	1 pt
$1/5$	Mirepoix (medium)	120 g	4 oz
$1/20$	Flour	30 g	1 oz
$1/20$	Dripping	30 g	1 oz
$1/40$	Tomato purée	15 g	$1/2$ oz
	Bouquet garni		
	Salt and pepper		
	Chopped parsley		

Method

Cover blanched tongues with brown stock, bring to boil, skim, cover with lid and stew gently for one hour. Remove tongues and refresh in cold water, skin, trim and drain. Sweat mirepoix in dripping to brown, add flour to form a brown roux. Cool slightly, add tomato purée and moisten with cooking liquor and extra stock to form lightly thickened sauce. Place tongues in braising dish with bouquet garni, cover with sauce, season and braise under cover until meat is tender. Once cooked place tongues in clean vessel, correct consistency and seasoning of sauce, strain over meat and serve garnished with chopped parsley.

Braised Lambs' Tongues Florentine   Langues d'Agneau Braisées Florentine

As above served on a bed of cooked leaf spinach.

145
BRAISED SWEETBREADS (Brown)   Ris Braisés à Brun

Yield: 4 portions
Cooking time: $1 - 1\frac{1}{2}$ hr
Cooking temperature: 150°C (300°F)

Unit	Ingredient	Metric (g)	Imperial (oz)
1	Sweetbreads (pre-soaked in running water to remove blood)	600	20
$\frac{1}{5}$	Mirepoix medium	120	4
$\frac{1}{20}$	Butter/margarine	30	1
	Arrowroot to thicken		
	Bouquet garni – chopped parsley		
	Salt and pepper		
*	Brown stock		

* Sufficient stock barely to cover sweetbreads during cooking.

Method

Blanch and refresh sweetbreads, skin and remove ducts. Sweat mirepoix in butter to light brown, add sweetbreads, season, moisten with stock barely to cover. Bring to boil, skim, add bouquet garni. Cover with a greased cartouche and tight-fitting lid, braise in oven until tender. Once cooked remove sweetbreads and put aside. Reduce cooking liquor, lié with arrowroot, correct seasoning and strain sauce over sweetbreads. Serve garnished with chopped parsley.

(b) Braising in the Piece (Joints of Butcher's Meat, Poultry, and Offal)

As for small braising the meat is cooked in stock, wine or sauce or a combination of these liquors with added flavourings of vegetables and herbs. During braising, the meat is basted with the cooking liquor to effect a glazed appearance. Once cooked the meat is carved into portions and served with the thickened cooking liquor and the garnish.

Cooking times vary according to the type of meat being braised. As previously explained some meats are larded and marinaded in readiness for braising.

146
BROWN BRAISED MEATS (Joints)   Pièce de Viande Braisée à brun

Yield: 4 – 6 portions
Cooking time: 2 – 2½ hr
Cooking temperature: 150°C (300°F)

Unit	Ingredient	Metric	Imperial
1	Braising meat (prepared)	1 kg	2½ lb
$\frac{1}{5}$	Mirepoix (large cut)	200 g	8 oz
$\frac{1}{20}$	Dripping or oil	50 g	2 oz
$\frac{1}{40}$	Tomato purée	25 g	1 oz
	Bouquet garni		
	Arrowroot to thicken		
	Salt and pepper		
	Chopped parsley		
*	Brown stock/wine		

* Sufficient stock/wine to cover two-thirds of the meat during braising.

Method

Heat dripping in braising vessel, add mirepoix and seasoned meat then seal and colour in a very hot oven. Cover with stock two-thirds of the meat bring to boil, skim and degrease. Add tomato purée, bouquet garni, and seasoning. Braise steadily under cover until meat is almost cooked, basting periodically to effect a glaze. At this stage remove meat and lightly thicken liquor to pouring consistency using arrowroot. Correct seasoning. Strain sauce over meat and continue cooking until meat is tender. Serve as required.

Service

1. Allow meat to set for a period and carve into portions. Napper with sauce, garnish and serve.
2. Present meat whole, lightly napper with sauce, garnish and serve with a sauceboat of braising sauce. Carve the meat at the table.

N.B. Alternatively the sauce may be prepared by reducing the braising stock and adding demi-glace/jus lié sauce to thicken.

Examples of Braised Dishes Using Above Formula: Added Ingredients in Relation to 1 Unit i.e. 1 kg (2½ lb) Braising Beef

English term	Unit	Ingredient	Metric (g)	Imperial (oz)	French term
Braised beef		Plain braised beef			Pièce de Boeuf Braisé
Braised beef in red wine		Braised marinaded beef (see p. 260) (use wine, herbs and vegetables from marinade when braising to replace mirepoix and some of the stock)			Pièce de Boeuf Braisé au Vin Rouge
Braised beef Bourgeoise		As for Vin Rouge garnished with:			Pièce de Boeuf Braisé Bourgeoise
	1/10	turned glazed carrots	100	4	
	1/10	glazed button onions à brun	100	4	
	1/20	lardons of bacon (cooked)	50	2	
Braised beef in the fashion	1/5	As for Bourgeoise: add Calf's foot during cooking then dice to garnish	200	8	Pièce de Boeuf Braisé à la Mode
Braised beef burgundy style		As for Vin Rouge garnished with:			Pièce de Boeuf Braisé Bourguignonne
	1/10	glazed button onions à brun	100	4	
	1/10	glazed button mushrooms à brun	100	4	
	1/20	lardons of bacon (cooked) 4 shaped croûtons	50	2	

English term	Unit	Ingredient	Metric (g)	Imperial (oz)	French term
Using veal as main meat					
Braised cushion of veal		Plain braised cushion of veal			Noix de Veau Braisée
Braised cushion of veal bourgeoise	$\frac{1}{10}$ $\frac{1}{10}$ $\frac{1}{20}$	Garnish: glazed turned carrots glazed button onions à brun lardons bacon (cooked)	100 100 50	4 4 2	Noix de Veau Braisée Bourgeoise
Braised cushion of veal with spinach	$\frac{1}{5}$	Garnish: cooked leaf spinach	100	4	Noix de Veau Braisée Florentine
Braised stuffed shoulder of veal		Veal shoulder stuffed with lemon, parsley and thyme stuffing (*see* recipe 162) then plain braised			L'Epaule de Veau Farcie Braisée
Braised stuffed breast of veal		As for above using breast of veal			Poitrine de Veau Farcie Braisée

N.B. Many other garnishes may be used.

Braised Offal (Large pieces)

Braised Ox-Heart

Coeur de Boeuf Braisé

As for recipe 146 using ox-heart.

Braised Ox-tongue

Langue de Boeuf Braisée

Preparation for Braising

Place tongue in cold water and bring to boil, skim and simmer for one hour. Refresh and remove skin and gristle. Proceed as for recipe 146 using tongue as main meat. Garnish as for Braised Cushion of Veal (*see* p. 281).

Braised Poultry

147
BRAISED DUCK WITH ORANGE

Canard Braisé à l'Orange

Yield: 4 portions
Use 1 medium duck
Cooking time: 2 hr
Cooking temperature: 150°C (300°F)

Unit	Ingredient	Metric	Imperial
	1 Medium duck		
1	Demi-glace	600 ml	1 pt
$1/4$	Brown stock	150 ml	5 fl oz
$1/4$	Fresh orange juice	150 ml	5 fl oz
$1/20$	Fresh lemon juice	30 ml	1 fl oz
$1/20$	Butter	30 g	1 oz
	Bouquet garni		
	Seasoning		
	Orange segments and blanched julienne of zest to garnish		

Method

Place seasoned duck in braising pan and brown in a hot oven. Drain off excess grease, add sauce, stock and bouquet garni, braise under cover in a moderate oven basting frequently until tender. Remove duck from sauce, put aside. Degrease the sauce and reduce to coating consistency. Pass through fine chinois, add orange and lemon juice, correct seasoning and consistency. Add zest of orange, remove sauce from heat and whisk in the butter. Napper duck with sauce and garnish with orange segments. This dish is usually carved at the table and is served accompanied with extra sauce.

N.B.   The flavour of this sauce may be enhanced by the addition of a measure of an orange liqueur, e.g. Curaçao.

White Braising

(a)   Using Small Cuts

The item most commonly used for small white braising is sweetbreads. The main purpose throughout cooking is to keep the food white and present the finished product in a white sauce produced from the cooking liquor.

148
BRAISED SWEETBREADS (WHITE)   Ris Braisés à Blanc

Yield: 4 portions
Cooking time: $1 - 1\frac{1}{2}$ hr
Cooking temperature: 150°C (300°F)

Unit	Ingredient	Metric (g)	Imperial (oz)
1	Sweetbreads (pre-soaked in running water to remove blood)	600	20
$1/5$	Mirepoix medium	120	4
$1/20$	Butter	30	1

> Arrowroot to thicken
> Bouquet garni
> Chopped parsley
> Squeeze of lemon juice
> Salt and pepper
> * White stock (veal where
>   possible)

---

* Sufficient stock barely to cover sweetbreads during cooking.

Method

Blanch and refresh sweetbreads, skin and remove ducts. Sweat mirepoix in butter without colour, add sweetbreads, season, moisten with stock barely to cover. Bring to boil, skim, add bouquet garni. Cover with greased cartouche and tight-fitting lid, braise in oven until tender.

   Once cooked remove sweetbreads and put aside. Reduce cooking liquor, lightly lié with arrowroot, correct seasoning, add lemon juice and strain sauce over sweetbreads. Serve garnished with chopped parsley.

White Braising

(b)   Using Large Cuts

The meat most commonly used for large white braises is veal.

149
BRAISED VEAL (WHITE)   Pièce de Veau Braisé à Blanc

Yield: 4 – 6 portions
Cooking time: 1½ – 2 hr
Cooking temperature: 150°C (300°F)

Unit	Ingredient	Metric	Imperial
1	Braising veal (cushion)	1 kg	2½ lb
⅕	Mirepoix (large cut)	200 g	8 oz
⅟₂₀	Butter	50 g	2 oz
	Bouquet garni		
	Arrowroot to thicken		
	Salt and pepper		
	Chopped parsley		
*	White veal stock		
	Squeeze of lemon juice		

* Sufficient stock to cover two-thirds of the meat during braising.

Method

Sweat lightly seasoned veal and mirepoix in butter without colour. Cover two-thirds of the meat with stock, bring to boil, skim, add bouquet and seasoning. Cover with greased cartouche and tight-fitting lid, braise steadily in oven until meat is tender, basting periodically to effect a glaze. Remove veal from liquor and put aside, lightly lié sauce to pouring consistency using arrowroot, correct seasoning and strain.

Service

1. Allow meat to set for a period and carve into portions. Napper with sauce, garnish and serve.
2. Present meat whole, lightly napper with sauce, garnish and serve with a sauceboat of braising sauce.
   Carve the veal at the table.

N.B. Alternatively the sauce may be prepared by reducing the braising liquor and adding veal velouté to thicken.

Garnishes Commonly Used with White Braises: Added Ingredients in Relation to 1 Unit i.e. 1 kg (2½ lb) Braising Veal

Name of garnish	Unit	Ingredient	Metric	Imperial
à la Crème	$1/10$	Finish sauce with cream	100 ml	4 fl oz
à l'Ancienne		As above garnish with:		
	$1/10$	glazed button onions à blanc	100 g	4 oz
	$1/10$	glazed button mushrooms à blanc	100 g	4 oz
		4 heart-shaped croûtons		
aux Champignons	$1/5$	As for à la Crème garnish:\nglazed button mushrooms à blanc	200 g	8 oz
Bonne Maman	$1/5$	Garnish:\nglazed julienne of vegetables à blanc	200 g	8 oz
Demidoff	$1/5$	Garnish\nglazed paysanne of vegetables à blanc\njulienne of truffle	200 g	8 oz

Braised Fish

Poisson Braisé

Braising is generally associated with stuffed whole fish and in some cases the smaller cuts of round and flat fish on the bone. Due to the structure of fish (*see* p. 55) the cooking times are less than for meats. The method of braising fish is as follows.

150

Yield: 4 portions
4 small whole fish
4 cuts on the bone [150 g (6 oz) each)]
Piece of large fish on bone [600 g (1¼ lb)]
Cooking time: dependant on size of fish
Cooking temperature: 150°C (300°F)

Unit	Ingredient	Metric	Imperial
	Selected fish (*see* yield)		
1	Mirepoix (brunoise)	150 g	5 oz
1	Wine (red or dry white)	150 ml	5 fl oz
⅕	Butter	30 g	1 oz
	Bouquet garni		
	Salt and pepper		
	Beurre manié for thickening		
*	Fish stock		

* Sufficient to cover two-thirds of the fish during braising.

Method

Place mirepoix, and fish into buttered braising vessel, add wine and stock to cover two-thirds of the fish. Bring to boil, skim, add bouquet garni, cover with buttered cartouche and braise in oven basting frequently until fish is cooked. Remove fish put aside to drain. Strain cooking liquor reduce and thicken lightly with beurre manié. Napper fish with sauce, sprinkle with chopped parsley and serve.

Service   Whole pieces of fish may be carved at the table.
   N.B.   Various garnishes may be served with braised fish, in which case the dishes would take on the name of the garnish e.g. Poisson Braisé Julienne—garnished with cooked julienne of vegetables; Poisson Braisé Doria—garnished with glazed, turned, cucumber.

The Braising of Vegetables

Prior to cooking in the oven most vegetables selected for braising are blanched in boiling water and refreshed. This initial process helps to retain the colour of the vegetables and make their structure more pliable for shaping.

Once refreshed and shaped the vegetable portions are placed on to a fine mirepoix in a lightly buttered braising vessel. Stock is then added to half cover the vegetables and they are then braised slowly under cover until cooked. The resultant liquor is often served with the vegetables in the form of a strained thickened sauce.

This method of cookery is particularly suited to the more fibrous vegetables i.e. celery, onions, leeks, cabbage, etc.

Selection and Preparation of Vegetables for Braising

Vegetable	Preparation
Celery	Trim root, remove celery tops to leave hearts (tops to be used for soup, stews, etc.), remove any decaying stalks. Cut in half lengthways and wash thoroughly. Blanch for 10 minutes and refresh, drain ready for use
Cabbage	Remove coarse outer leaves and four large green leaves (trim). Quarter cabbage and remove centre stalk, wash well. Blanch the four large green leaves and quarters for 5 minutes approximately, refresh and drain. Season cabbage, wrap quarters in green leaves, shape into firm balls and squeeze in clean cloth to shape and remove excess moisture
Stuffed cabbage	As above but stuff with sausage meat
Endive (Belgium)	Discard damaged outer leaves, wash thoroughly, leave whole for braising, blanch for 10 minutes, refresh and drain. Shape as required.
Leek	Discard damaged outer leaves, trim tops (retain for soups, stews, etc.) Lightly trim root, half split lengthways leaving root intact, wash well, blanch for 5 minutes, refresh and drain
Lettuce	Lightly trim base, discard damaged outer leaves, wash thoroughly keeping whole. Blanch for 5 minutes, refresh and drain. Squeeze well to remove moisture, shape into cigar shape, leave whole or cut in half lengthways. Neatly fold in point of lettuce to form an even shape.
Onions	Lightly trim root and remove onion skins, blanch for 10 minutes refresh and drain for use. N.B. Select medium onions
Stuffed peppers	Wash, cut across top removing stalk. This opens a cavity ready for stuffing. Shake peppers to remove seeds. Stuff with rice pilaff ready for use
Fennel	Trim tops, stems and base, wash well, blanch for 10 minutes and refresh for use

151
BRAISED VEGETABLES

Légumes Braisés

Yield: 4 portions
Cooking times: 1 – 2½ hr
Cooking temperature: 150°C (300°F)

Unit	Ingredient	Metric (g)	Imperial (oz)
1	Four selected vegetable portions (prepared *see* chart)	400	16
¼	Mirepoix (fine cut)	100	4
¹⁄₁₆	Butter or margarine	25	1
	Salt and pepper		
★	White stock		
	Arrowroot, jus lié or demi-glace where thickening is required		

★ Sufficient stock to half cover vegetable during braising.

Method

Sweat mirepoix with butter in braising vessel without colour. Place selected vegetable on to mirepoix, season and half cover with stock. Cover with buttered cartouche and lid. Braise in the oven until tender. Once cooked remove vegetables to drain well. Prepare thickened sauce if required.

Preparation of Sauce When Required

1. Reduce cooking liquor by a half, lié with arrowroot, correct seasoning strain and coat vegetables.
2. Reduce cooking liquor to a glaze add demi-glace or jus lié correct seasoning and strain to coat vegetables.

Examples of Dishes Prepared Using Above Formula

English term	Sauce and garnish	French term
Braised celery in juice	Coat lightly with thickened stock	Céleri Braisé au Jus
Braised celery in cheese sauce	Napper with mornay sauce sprinkle with grated cheese and gratinate	Céleri Braisé Mornay
Braised celery with parmesan cheese	Napper with demi-glace, sprinkle with grated parmesan and gratinate	Céleri Braisé au Parmesan
Braised celery with poached beef marrow	As for 'Céleri Braisé au Jus' then garnished with slices of poached beef marrow and chopped parsley	Céleri Braisé à la Moelle

Braised Belgium endive	⎫	Chicorée Braisée
Braised leeks	⎬ All may be sauced and garnished as for	Poireaux Braisés
Braised onions	celery	Oignons Braisés
Braised fennel	⎭	Fenouil Braisé
Braised cabbage	⎫ Lightly coat with thickened stock	Chou Braisé
Braised stuffed cabbage	⎭	Chou Farci Braisé
Braised lettuce in juice	Lightly coat with thickened stock. When used as a garnish the lettuce is usually placed on to heart-shaped croutons to absorb excess moisture	Laitues Braisées au Jus
Stuffed braised peppers	Garnish with chopped parsley	Piments Farcis Braisés

152
BRAISED CHESTNUTS   Marrons Braisés

Yield: 4 portions
Cooking time: 30 – 45 min
Cooking temperature: 150°C (300°F)

To Shell Chestnuts

1. Slit the shell of chestnut on both sides. Plunge into boiling water and simmer for 5 minutes. Remove shells and inner skins.
2. Slit shells and oven bake until shell splits open. Remove shells and inner skins.

Unit	Ingredient	Metric (g)	Imperial (oz)
1	Shelled chestnuts	400	16
$1/_8$	Celery stalks	50	2
$1/_{16}$	Butter	25	1
	Salt and pepper		
	Chopped parsley		
*	Brown stock (veal or chicken)		

* Sufficient stock to half cover chestnuts during braising.

Method

Sweat chestnuts and celery in butter without colour, lightly season, half cover with stock. Cover with buttered cartouche and a lid. Braise in oven until chestnuts are tender. Once cooked remove chestnuts and put aside to drain. Strain cooking liquor and reduce to a glaze. Toss chestnuts in glaze and serve garnished with chopped parsley.

153
BRAISED RED CABBAGE FLEMISH STYLE   Chou-Rouge Flamande

Yield: 4 portions
Cooking time: 3 hr
Cooking temperature. 150°C (300°F)

Preparation of Cabbage   Discard damaged outer leaves, quarter, remove stalk, wash well.

Unit	Ingredient	Metric	Imperial
1	Red cabbage (prepared and shredded)	400 g	1 lb
$\frac{1}{4}$	Apples (peeled and sliced)	100 ml	4 fl oz
$\frac{1}{8}$	Wine vinegar	50 ml	2 fl oz
$\frac{1}{16}$	Butter or margarine	25 g	1 oz
$\frac{1}{16}$	Sugar	25 g	1 oz
	Salt and pepper		

Method

Butter a braising dish add cabbage, vinegar, sugar and seasoning, cover with buttered cartouche and tight-fitting lid. Braise in oven, stirring periodically until three-quarters cooked. Add apples and continue cooking until tender. Correct seasoning and serve.

   N.B.   Certain cooking vessels are unsuitable for this product because the foods present react with the metal impairing the colour of the cooked cabbage. *See* p. 59.

154
BRAISED SAUERKRAUT (Pickled White Cabbage)   Choucroute Braisée

Yield: 4 portions
Cooking time: 3 hr
Cooking temperature: 150°C (300°F)

Unit	Ingredient	Metric (g)	Imperial (oz)
1	Sauerkraut	400	16
$\frac{1}{4}$	Carrot (left whole)	100	4
$\frac{1}{4}$	Onion clouté	100	4
$\frac{1}{16}$	Butter or margarine	25	1
	Few juniper berries in muslin		
	Bouquet garni		
	Salt and pepper		
*	White stock		

* Sufficient barely to cover sauerkraut during cooking.

Method

Butter braising vessel, add all ingredients, barely cover with stock. Cover with buttered cartouche and a tight-fitting lid. Braise in oven, stirring periodically until sauerkraut is cooked. Remove onion, bouquet garni, juniper berries and carrots. Correct seasoning and serve garnished with sliced carrot.

155
SAUERKRAUT WITH GARNISH   Choucroute Garniture

As above formula plus:

Unit	Ingredient	Metric (g)	Imperial (oz)
$\frac{1}{2}$	Piece of blanched streaky bacon	200	8
$\frac{1}{2}$	Frankfurters (4–8)	200	8

Method

Add bacon piece to sauerkraut at commencement of cooking period. When almost cooked add frankfurters to heat through.

Service   Place sliced bacon, carrot and whole frankfurters on a bed of sauerkraut to garnish.

Potato Dishes Cooked Using the Braising Principle

Although these do not appear on the menu as braised potato dishes the method of cookery adopted is akin to the braising technique. Many of these dishes are cooked and served in a casserole.

POTATOES   Pommes de Terre
156
BERRICHONNE POTATOES   Pommes Berrichonne

Yield: 4 portions
Cooking time: 1 hr
Cooking temperature: 175°C (350°F)

Unit	Ingredient	Metric (g)	Imperial (oz)
1	Potatoes [diced $1\frac{1}{2}$ cm ($\frac{1}{2}$ in) or small turned]	400	16
$\frac{1}{4}$	Streaky bacon (blanched lardons)	100	4
$\frac{1}{4}$	Onion (medium diced)	100	4
	Salt and pepper		
	Hint of garlic		
	Chopped parsley		
	Melted butter		
*	White stock		

* Sufficient stock to half cover potatoes.

Method

Place onions, potatoes and bacon in casserole, add garlic and season lightly. Half cover with hot stock, brush with melted butter and braise in the oven until potatoes are cooked and golden brown. At this stage most of the stock will have been absorbed by the potatoes. Serve, brushed with melted butter and sprinkled with chopped parsley.

POTATOES BRITTANY STYLE   Pommes Bretonne

As for Pommes Berrichonne (diced) but replace bacon with tomato concassé.

HUNGARIAN POTATOES   Pommes Hongroise

As for Pommes Bretonne flavoured with paprika.

POTATOES WITH BACON AND ONIONS   Pommes au Lard

As for Pommes Berrichonne but replace diced onions with button onions.

157
SAVOURY POTATOES   Pommes Boulangère

Yield: 4 portions
Cooking time: 1½ hr
Cooking temperature: 175°C (350°F)

Unit	Ingredient	Metric (g)	Imperial (oz)
1	Potatoes [sliced into 2 mm (⅛ in) rounds]	400	16
½	Onions shredded	200	8
	Salt and pepper		
	Melted butter		
	Chopped parsley		
*	White stock		

* Sufficient stock almost to cover the potatoes.

Method

Mix two-thirds of potatoes with onion, lightly season and place in casserole. Neatly lay remaining potatoes overlapping on top of filled casserole. Add hot stock almost to cover the potatoes and brush surface with melted butter. Braise in the oven until potatoes are cooked to golden brown and the stock absorbed by the potatoes. Serve brushed with melted butter and sprinkled with chopped parsley.

158
POTATOES WITH BACON AND CHEESE   Pommes Savoyarde

As for Pommes Boulangère with the addition of:

Unit	Ingredient	Metric (g)	Imperial (oz)
¼	Streaky bacon (blanched lardons)	100	4
¼	Gruyère cheese (grated)	100	4
	Chopped garlic		

Method

Mix bacon, garlic and cheese with two-thirds potatoes and all the onions. Continue as for Pommes Boulangère. Sprinkle a little cheese on top layer of potatoes before cooking.

159
DAUPHINOISE POTATOES   Pommes Dauphinoise

Yield: 4 portions
Cooking time: 45 min – 1 hr
Cooking temperature: 175°C (350°F)

Unit	Ingredient	Metric (g)	Imperial (oz)
1	Potatoes (thinly sliced, net weight)	400	16
¼	Gruyère cheese (grated)	100	4
	Salt and pepper		
	Hint of chopped garlic		
	Melted butter		
	Chopped parsley		
*	Milk (boiled)		

* Sufficient boiled milk to half cover potatoes.

Method

Mix half of grated cheese with potatoes, garlic and seasoning. Lightly grease casserole with melted butter, fill with potato mixture, sprinkle with remaining cheese and half cover with boiled milk.

Braise in the oven until potatoes are cooked golden brown and the milk has been absorbed by the potatoes. Serve brushed with melted butter and sprinkled with chopped parsley.

160
DELMONICO POTATOES   Pommes Delmonico

Yield: 4 portions
Cooking time: 1 hr
Cooking temperature: 175°C (350°F)

Unit	Ingredient	Metric (g)	Imperial (oz)
1	Potatoes [diced 1½ cm (½ in) net wt]	400	16
⅛	White breadcrumbs	50	2
	Salt and pepper		
	Pinch of nutmeg		
	Melted butter		
*	Milk (boiled)		

* Sufficient boiled milk to almost cover potatoes on cooking.

Method

Season potatoes, place in casserole and sprinkle with nutmeg. Barely cover with boiled milk and braise in oven until potatoes are almost cooked. Sprinkle liberally with breadcrumbs and melted butter, continue cooking in hot oven until potatoes are cooked and gratinated. Serve as required.

161
FONDANT POTATOES
Pommes Fondant

Yield: 4 portions
Cooking time: 45 min – 1 hr
Cooking temperature: 175°C (350°F)

Unit	Ingredient	Metric (g)	Imperial (oz)
1	Potatoes (large turned net wt)	400	16
1/8	Butter (melted)	50	2
	Salt and pepper		
*	White stock		

* Sufficient stock to half cover potatoes on cooking.

Method

Place potatoes in braising vessel, lightly season, half cover with stock and brush with melted butter. Braise in moderate oven until potatoes are cooked to a light brown colour and have absorbed the stock. Brush with melted butter and serve.

CRETAN POTATOES
Pommes Cretan

As for Pommes Fondant but flavour stock with thyme.

CHAMPIGNOL POTATOES
Pommes Champignol

As for Pommes Fondant but sprinkle cooked fondant with grated cheese and gratinate.

14

The Principle and Practice of Roasting

To Roast Rôtir

Modern roasting may be defined as a method of cooking with dry convected heat in an oven cavity. The dryness of the atmosphere within the oven is modified by the presence of steam. The steam is generated by the action of heat upon the moisture content within the food. Traditional roasting is carried out over an open fire on a rotating spit and the moisture is driven off in the open atmosphere. Modern roasting spits powered by electricity and gas are available for domestic and industrial use.

Foods commonly roasted include prime joints of butcher's meats, poultry, game and certain vegetables. Joints of meat chosen for roasting are designated as first or second class roasting joints, the former being the prime cuts of butcher's meat. To ensure a successful roast product the joints should contain a proportion of surface and intra-muscular fats, which act to keep the lean meat moist and prevent undue shrinkage during cooking.

Initially, on roasting meats are subjected to a high temperature, which seals in the juices by coagulating the surface protein (albumen). Once this is achieved the cooking temperature is reduced to allow even steady cooking. Not all the meat juices are retained, and those that escape into the roasting tray are employed in the formulation of accompanying gravies.

Notes for Guidance

Where a traditional kitchen brigade is employed the following members are involved with the preparation for, and the cooking of, roast products:

Chef Garde-Manger — basic preparation of meats for roasting
Chef Entremettier — basic preparation and roasting of vegetables
Chef Rôtisseur — roasting of butcher's meat, poultry and game.

1. Preparation of Meats for Roasting

Seasoning and Flavouring

Prior to cooking, meats are lightly seasoned with salt and pepper and flavoured with herbs if required. Certain items for roasting may also be filled with a selected stuffing. These procedures enhance the flavour of the finished product.

Larding and Barding

These techniques (inserting or covering meat with pork fat) are used when items selected for roasting need extra fat. This acts to provide moisture throughout roasting preventing the meat from drying out and shrinking excessively.

Use of Trivets

A trivet raises the items being roasted out of the fat, which lies in the base of the cooking vessel. As a result any frying of meat surfaces is prevented. Trivets may be formed with raw bones, but are also commercially available in the form of metal racks.

2.　Care in Cooking

Basting

This is a technical term used to denote the action of moistening meat with melted fat and cooking juices during roasting. This process is carried out at regular intervals by *spooning* the melted fat and juices over the meat.

Turning Items During Roasting

When oven-roasting without a spit, large joints of butcher's meat, poultry and game require turning at intervals, to ensure even cooking and colouring.

3.　Testing for Cooking

See chart for roasting times and degrees of cooking (*see* p. 298). As a general guide meat is:

  (a) underdone (rare) when juices run red and bloody;
  (b) rare to medium when juices run pink;
  (c) just done when juices run clear.

In order to exude meat juices, press the surface of the joint firmly.

Butcher's Meat, Poultry, and Game Commonly Selected for Roasting

English term	French term	Basic preparation in brief	First or second class roast
Beef joints			
Sirloin (on bone)	Aloyau de Boeuf	Chine, trim and season	First
Strip loin (off bone)	Contrefilet de Boeuf	Trim and season	First
Ribs ⎫ Wing			First
on　⎬ Fore	Côte de Boeuf	Chine trim and season	First
bone ⎭ Middle			Second
Fillet heart	Coeur de Filet de Boeuf	Trim, lard and season	First

English term	French term	Basic preparation in brief	First or second class roast
Lamb joints			
Leg	Gigot d'Agneau	Trim knuckle and aitchbone secure with string and season. Aitchbone may be removed after cooking	First
Shoulder	Épaule d'Agneau	Trim knuckle and season, or bone out stuff, roll and secure with string	Second
Best-end	Carré d'Agneau	Skin, chine, trim and score. Trim ends of cutlet bone and season	First
Breast	Poitrine d'Agneau	Skin, bone out, stuff roll, season and secure with string	Second
Long saddle	Selle d'Agneau	Skin, trim, score, secure flaps with string and season (kidneys removed).	First
Short saddle	Selle d'Agneau	Remove chump and continue as above	First
Loin	Longe d'Agneau	Bone, roll, season and secure with string (May be stuffed)	First
Crown	Curonne d'Agneau	Prepare best-ends of lamb shape into crown and sew with string to secure	First
Pork joints			
Leg	Cuissot de Porc	Remove aitchbone, and trotter, score rind and rub with salt	First
Loin (may include chine bone)	Longe de Porc	Trim and loosen meat from chine bone, but leave intact. Score rind and rub with salt	First
Shoulder	Épaule de Porc	Bone out shoulder (may be stuffed), score rind, rub with salt and secure with string	Second
Spare rib	Échine de Porc	Trim, score rind, rub with salt and secure with string	Second
Veal joints			
Leg (small)	Cuissot de Veau	Remove aitchbone, trim knuckle, lard, season and secure with string	First
Loin	Longe de Veau	Trim and loosen meat from chine bone but leave intact, season (may be boned, stuffed and rolled)	First
Best-end	Carré de Veau	Chine and trim. Scrape end of cutlet bones and season	First
Breast	Poitrine de Veau	Bone, trim, stuff, roll, season and secure with string	Second
		N.B. All veal joints, due to lack of fat content are best barded or larded to provide moisture during roasting. Otherwise meat will cook dry and shrink excessively	

English term	French term	Basic preparation in brief	First or second class roast

Poultry

English term	French term	Basic preparation in brief	First or second class roast
Chicken (baby)	Poussin	Clean, singe and trim, Remove wish-	First
(small)	Poulet de Grain	bone, stuff if required, season and truss	
(medium)	Poulet Reine	for roasting	
(large)	Poularde		
Capon	Chapon		
Duck	Canard	As for chicken	First
Duckling	Caneton		
Goose	Oie		First
Gosling	Oison		
Turkey	Dinde	As for chicken but remove heavy sinews	First
Turkey (young)	Dindonneau	from legs	

Game

Feathered		Seasons		
Pheasant	Faisan	Oct. – Jan.	Clean, singe, trim and remove wishbone. Season, truss and bard	First
Partridge	Perdreau	Sept. – Jan.	As for pheasant	First
Grouse	Grouse	Aug. – Dec.	As for pheasant	First
Quail	Caille	All year	As for pheasant	First
Guinea fowl	Pintade	All year	As for pheasant	First
Wild duck	Canard Sauvage	Sept. – Feb.	As for pheasant but omit barding	First
Teal	Sarcelle	Sept. – Feb.	As for wild duck	First
Snipe	Bécassine	Aug. – Jan.	Partially draw by removing gall bladder, gizzard and intestines. Trim, season, bard then truss with beak	First
Woodcock	Bécasse	Oct. – Jan.	As for snipe	First
Plover	Pluvier	Sept. – Dec.	As for snipe but trussed with string	First

Furred				
Saddle of hare	Râble de Lièvre	Aug. – March	Trim, remove sinew, lard and season	First
Saddle of venison	Selle de Venaison	June – Jan.	As for saddle of hare	First
Haunch of venison	Hanche de Venaison	June – Jan.	As for saddle of hare	First

A Guide to Roasting Times

Meat	Approximate times	Degree of cooking
Beef	15 min per $\frac{1}{2}$ kg (1 lb) and 15 min over	Underdone
	20 min per $\frac{1}{2}$ kg (1 lb) and 20 min over	Rare to medium
Lamb/mutton	20 min per $\frac{1}{2}$ kg (1 lb) and 20 min over	Just done
Pork	25 min per $\frac{1}{2}$ kg (1 lb) and 25 min over	Well done
Veal	25 min per $\frac{1}{2}$ kg (1 lb) and 25 min over	Just done
Chickens	15 min per $\frac{1}{2}$ kg (1 lb) and 15 min over	Just done
Ducks/Goose	20 min per $\frac{1}{2}$ kg (1 lb) and 20 min over	Well cooked
Goose	20 min per $\frac{1}{2}$ kg (1 lb) and 20 min over	Well cooked
Turkey	20 min per $\frac{1}{2}$ kg (1 lb)	Just done
Pheasant	30 min to 50 min per pheasant	Just done
Partridge	15 min to 25 min per partridge	Just done
Grouse	20 min to 25 min per grouse	Rare to medium
Quail	8 min to 10 min per quail	Just done
Guinea fowl	30 min to 50 min per fowl	Just done
Wild duck	20 min to 25 min per duck	Underdone
Teal	15 min to 20 min per teal	Underdone
Snipe	10 min to 15 min per snipe	Just done
Woodcock	15 min to 20 min per woodcock	Just done
Plover	15 min to 20 min per plover	Just done
Hare Saddle	25 min to 30 min per saddle	Rare to medium
Venison	15 min per $\frac{1}{2}$ kg (1 lb) and 15 min over	Underdone

Preparation of Stuffings and Accompaniments for Roasts

Stuffing   Farce

Prepared stuffings are used in a variety of ways in culinary operations:

(a) to stuff and flavour joints, cuts of butcher's meat, poultry and game prior to cooking, e.g. loins of lamb, boned, stuffed and rolled prior to roasting, beef olives rolled and stuffed prior to cooking;

(b) prepared and cooked separately and served to accompany roast meats and stews, e.g. roast pork with sage and onion stuffing, deep fried forcemeat balls with Jugged Hare;

(c) to act as a stuffing for vegetables, e.g. tomatoes filled with duxelle stuffing.

162
SAGE AND ONION STUFFING   Farce de Sauge et Oignon

Yield: 4 portions
Cooking time: 20 min (when cooked separately in oven)
Cooking temperature: 150°C (300°F)

Unit	Ingredient	Metric (g)	Imperial (oz)
1	White breadcrumbs	100	4
1	Onion (brunoise)	100	4
¹/₂	Dripping or margarine	50	2
	Sage to flavour		
	Pinch chopped parsley		
	Seasoning		
*	Stock or beaten egg		

Methods

Sweat onions in fat without colour, lightly season during cooking. Add breadcrumbs, sage and parsley to form stuffing and adjust seasoning.

Method 1   *When preparing* and cooking the stuffing as a separate item moisten with a little stock, place into greased cooking vessel, cover with cartouche and bake in moderate oven.

Method 2   *When using* to stuff a cut or joint before cooking bind stuffing with beaten egg prior to use. Egg protein coagulates during cooking, sets the stuffing preventing it from breaking up during carving.

163
LEMON, PARSLEY AND THYME STUFFING
Farce de Persil et Thym au Citron

Yield: 4 portions
Cooking time: 20 min (when cooked separately in oven)
Cooking temperature: 150°C (300°F)

Unit	Ingredient	Metric	Imperial
1	Breadcrumbs	100 g	4 oz
¹/₂	Suet (finely chopped)	50 g	2 oz
¹/₄	Lemon juice and grated zest	25 ml	1 fl oz
	Thyme ⎫ to taste		
	Parsley (chopped) ⎬		
	Seasoning		
*	Stock or beaten egg		

Method

Combine breadcrumbs, suet, lemon juice and herbs to form stuffing. Adjust seasoning and proceed as for sage and onion stuffing.

164
SAUSAGEMEAT STUFFING (FORCEMEAT)

Yield: 4 portions

Unit	Ingredient	Metric (g)	Imperial (oz)
1	Sausagemeat (pork)	100	4
1/2	Breadcrumbs	50	2
1/2	Suet (finely chopped)	50	2
1/4	Beaten egg	25	1
	Mixed herbs to taste		
	Seasoning		

Methods

Combine all ingredients thoroughly to form stuffing.

Method 1   Generally used to stuff poultry before roasting and some vegetables for braising.

Method 2   In addition may be rolled into forcemeat balls, panéed an deep fried to accompany certain game stews.

165
CHESTNUT STUFFING   Farce de Marrons
(For roast turkey)

Yield: 4 portions
Cooking time: 45 min (when cooking as a separate item in oven)
Cooking temperature: 150°C (300°F)

Unit	Ingredient	Metric (g)	Imperial (oz)
1	Sausagemeat stuffing	100	4
1/2	Braised chestnuts (recipe 152; coarsely chopped	50	2

Methods

Combine ingredients thoroughly to form stuffing.

Method 1   When cooking separately, place in greased cooking vessel, cover with cartouche and bake, or roll into cylindrical shape, wrap in foil and steam. When cooked slice into portions.

Method 2   Use raw to stuff the crop of turkey before roasting.

166
YORKSHIRE PUDDING

Yield: 4 portions
Cooking time: individual 15 – 20 min, tray 20 – 30 min
Cooking temperature: 205°C (400°F)

Unit	Ingredient	Metric	Imperial
1	Milk or milk and water	250 ml	10 fl oz
$2/5$	Flour	100 g	4 oz
$1/5$	Whole egg	50 g	2 oz
$1/10$	Dripping	25 g	1 oz
	Salt to taste		

Method

Sift flour and salt into mixing bowl and form a well. Lightly beat egg and half of the milk together, then pour into well. Commence formation of batter by beating flour and liquid together. Gradually add remaining liquid, whisking thoroughly to form a smooth batter. Allow to stand and rest before use.

Divide dripping into pudding moulds or tray and heat thoroughly in the oven. Remove from oven, fill with batter mixture and bake until risen and cooked. Serve immediately.

Method

Oven Roasting   Place prepared butcher's meat, poultry or game on to trivet in a roasting tray. Brush with melted fat, place in hot oven to seal exterior of meat [approximately 10 – 15 min at 205°C (400°F)]. Reduce temperature to moderate heat [150°C (300°F)] and continue roasting until cooked to required degree. Throughout roasting baste item frequently in order to keep the meat moist and add flavour. Once cooked remove meat from oven and allow to set for carving approximately 20 – 30 min.
N.B.   When roasting large joints of meat, poultry or game it will be necessary to turn the item from time to time to ensure even cooking.

Flash Roasting   A term used to describe speedy roasting at a high temperature. This method is particularly suitable for roasting small items of game and for certain beef cuts required underdone, e.g. contrefilets and fillets of beef.

Roast Gravy   Jus Rôti

Take roasting tray containing fat and roast meat sediment. Pour off excess fat leaving behind sediment. Heat sediment on stove top to colour brown, then deglaze with selected brown stock to form roast gravy. Season to taste, strain through fine chinois, degrease and serve as required.

Thickened Roast Gravy   Jus Rôti Lié

As for roast gravy but lightly thickened by the addition of moistened arrowroot.

Experimental Roasting

In today's cost-conscious environment, caterers are continually having to evaluate production methods in order to improve their efficiency and profitability. The techniques employed range from the use of modern technology in the form of plant, equipment, and systems, to the more simple cooking aids such as roasting bags, tin foil, and thermo pins, etc. Continual experiments are conducted in order to determine the most efficient ways of roasting meats with regard to savings in time, energy and labour, whilst at the same time improving the quality and yield of the product. Where comparisons have been made with traditional oven roasting it has been ascertained that roasting in foil or bags reduces the cooking time, results in a higher portion yield and eliminates the need for basting (therefore saving labour time).

Traditional Accompaniments with Roast Butcher's Meat, Poultry, and Game

English term	French term	Traditional garnish
Roast beef	Boeuf Rôti à l'Anglaise	Yorkshire pudding, roast gravy, horse-radish sauce, watercress
Roast lamb	Agneau Rôti	Roast gravy, mint sauce, watercress
Roast mutton	Mouton Rôti	White onion sauce, roast gravy, redcurrant jelly, watercress
Roast pork	Porc Rôti	Roast gravy, sage and onion stuffing, apple sauce, watercress
Roast veal	Veau Rôti	Thickened roast gravy, lemon, parsley and thyme stuffing, watercress
Roast chicken (English style)	Poulet Rôti à l'Anglaise	Roast gravy, bread sauce, grilled bacon, game chips, watercress
Roast chicken with stuffing	Poulet Rôti Farci	Roast gravy, parsley and thyme stuffing, watercress
Roast chicken with stuffing (English style)	Poulet Roti Farci à l'Anglaise	Roast gravy, bread sauce, parsley and thyme stuffing, grilled bacon, game chips, watercress
Roast duck/duckling	Canard/Caneton Rôti	Roast gravy, sage and onion stuffing, apple sauce, watercress
Roast gosling/ goose (f)	Oison Rôti/Oie Rôtie	As for duck
Roast turkey (young m)	Dindonneau Rôti ⎫	Roast gravy, bread sauce, chestnut stuffing, grilled chipolatas, grilled bacon, cranberry sauce, watercress
Roast turkey (f)	Dinde Rôtie ⎬	
Roast guinea-fowl	Pintade Rôtie à l'Anglaise	As for Poulet Rôti à l'Anglaise

Roast

Pheasant	Faisan Rôti ⎫	Roast gravy, brown breadcrumbs, game chips,
Partridge	Perdreau Rôti	bread sauce, watercress, grilled bacon
Grouse	Grouse Rôtie	(optional).
Quail	Caille Rôtie ⎬	N.B. The roasted game is presented on a fried
Woodcock	Bécasse Rôtie	croûton of appropriate size spread with game
Snipe	Bécassine Rôtie	farce. Alternatively shallow-fried heart-shaped
Plover	Pluvier Rôti ⎭	croûtes spread with game farce may be offered

Roast

Wild duck	Canard Sauvage Rôti	} Roast gravy, watercress, orange salad
Teal	Sarcelle Rôtie	
Roast saddle of hare	Râble de Lièvre Rôti	Roast gravy, forcemeat balls, redcurrant jelly, watercress
Roast venison	Venaison Rôtie	Roast gravy, redcurrant jelly, watercress. N.B. Sauce Poivrade is often served

N.B. When required, certain items for roasting may be flavoured with selected fresh herbs prior to cooking or served with an accompanying garnish other than the traditional English accompaniment. *See* below.

English term	French term	Garnish and explanation
Roast lamb with rosemary	Agneau Rôti au Romarin	Rub exterior of meat liberally with rosemary before roasting
Roast lamb with garlic and rosemary	Agneau Rôti à l'Ail et Romarin.	Piqué joint with strips of garlic before roasting Rub well with rosemary
Roast chicken with tarragon	Poulet Rôti à l'Estragon	Rub exterior of chicken liberally with tarragon before roasting
Roast lamb with Boulangère potatoes	Agneau Rôti à la Boulangère	Complete roasting by placing joint on top of cooked boulangère potatoes. Serve lamb and potatoes together
Roast fillet of beef with Dubarry garnish	Coeur de Filet de Boeuf Rôti Dubarry	Serve garnished with fleurettes of cauliflower mornay and château potatoes

N.B. All the above are served with roast gravy (unthickened). Other suitable garnishes may be employed in a similar fashion. In many instances roasts are accompanied by side salads e.g. roast beef with green salad.

Carving of Roast Meats, Poultry, and Game

Carving requires a high level of competence and skill to ensure that roasted meats are attractively presented to the customer in correct portions. For the best results roasted meats are allowed to stand and set after cooking to facilitate carving and to gain maximum portion yield.

In general, meats should be carved across the grain to ensure a short-fibred, tender cut of meat. If the meat is carved with the grain these fibres remain long and stringy, which results in the meat being tougher and less palatable. Throughout carving the selected knife needs to be kept sharp to ensure ease of operation. Carving may be carried out in the kitchen or at the customer's table according to the mode of service and the establishment's style.

When carving feathered game or poultry it is usual to serve a combination of leg and breast meat per portion, however, smaller items may be served whole or jointed according to their size. For instance:

(a) small ducklings divided into two;
(b) small chickens portioned into two legs, and two breasts;
(c) baby chickens and quail, served whole;
(d) medium-sized chicken or pheasant jointed into 4 portions as shown in carving diagrams (*see* overleaf).

Lamb/Agneau

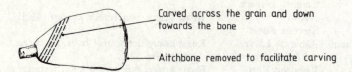

Carved across the grain and down towards the bone

Aitchbone removed to facilitate carving

Leg/Gigot

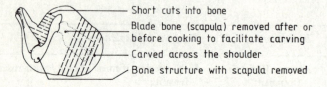

Short cuts into bone

Blade bone (scapula) removed after or before cooking to facilitate carving

Carved across the shoulder

Bone structure with scapula removed

Shoulder/Épaule

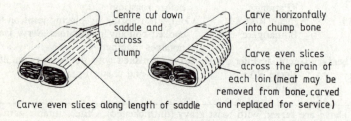

Centre cut down saddle and across chump

Carve horizontally into chump bone

Carve even slices across the grain of each loin (meat may be removed from bone, carved and replaced for service)

Carve even slices along length of saddle

Saddle/Selle

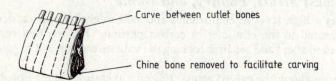

Carve between cutlet bones

Chine bone removed to facilitate carving

Best End/Carré

Pork/Porc

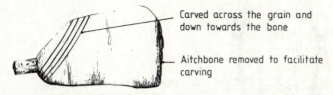

Carved across the grain and down towards the bone

Aitchbone removed to facilitate carving

Leg/Cuissot (also for gammon)

Beef/Boeuf

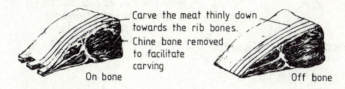

Carve the meat thinly down towards the rib bones.
Chine bone removed to facilitate carving

On bone   Off bone

Rib of Beef/Côte de Boeuf

Poultry/Volaille (also for some feathered game)

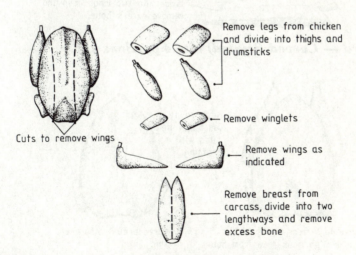

Remove legs from chicken and divide into thighs and drumsticks

Remove winglets

Cuts to remove wings

Remove wings as indicated

Remove breast from carcass, divide into two lengthways and remove excess bone

Chicken/Poulet — Carved (jointed) into 4 portions

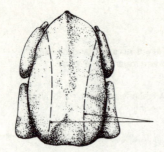

Cuts to remove wings

Remove legs from duck and
divide into two as required. It
is possible to remove all bone
from legs after roasting before
carving each into pieces (two)

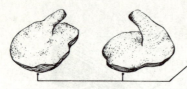

Remove wings as indicated

Remove breast from carcass,
divide into two lengthways and
remove excess bone

Duck/Canard — Carved (jointed) into 4 portions

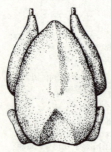

Neck cavity
which may be
filled with a
stuffing

Remove legs from turkey and
carve into portions free from bone

Carve breast into even,
thin slices

Turkey/Dinde

167
ROAST VEGETABLES

Légumes Rôtis

Few vegetables are cooked by this method the most common being potatoes and parsnips.
Yield: 4 portions
Cooking time: *see* chart
Cooking temperature: 205°C (400°F)

Unit	Ingredient	Metric (g)	Imperial (oz)
1	Main item (prepared – *see* chart below)	400	16
1/8	Dripping or oil	50	2
	Seasoning		

Method

Heat dripping or oil in a roasting tray on stove top, add well-drained vegetables, lightly season and agitate roasting tray to coat vegetables with the fat and prevent them from sticking to the cooking vessel.

Place in oven and roast until golden brown and cooked. During roasting baste and turn vegetables to ensure even cooking and to prevent them from adhering to the tray. Once cooked, remove from oven, drain well and serve.

Examples of Roast Vegetables

English term	French term	Preparation	Approximate cooking time (min)
Roast potatoes	Pommes Rôties	Peel potatoes and cut to even size	45
Château potatoes	Pommes Château	Peel potatoes and turn to even shape	45
Roast parsnips	Panais Rôtis	Peel and trim, cut into wedges lengthways. Remove fibrous core from centre if tough	30

15

The Principle and Practice of Pot-Roasting

To Pot-Roast   Poêler

Cooking à la Poêle may be defined as cooking on a bed of aromatic herbs with vegetables in a covered casserole or container, using butter for basting. Only the choice tender joints of butcher's meat, game, and poultry are suitable for this method as little or no moisture is employed during cooking to aid tenderization. Pot-roasting acts to retain the natural juices and flavour of the food being cooked. Upon completion of cooking the juices are utilized in the preparation of an accompanying sauce.

Notes for Guidance

Certain foods, e.g. chicken are poêled and served in a casserole or cocotte dish. In these instances they are designated 'en cocotte' on the menu, e.g. Poulet en Cocotte. Many relevés and entrées (*see* p.385) are cooked by this method.

When a traditional kitchen brigade is employed the following Chefs de Partie are involved with pot-roasted products:

Chef Garde-Manger   —   involved with initial preparation of meats prior to cooking
Chef Saucier   —   relevés and entrées.

Poêle is considered to be a mode of cookery ideally suited for use with premier joints of butcher's meat, poultry, and game. Pot-roasting must not be confused with the domestic-style casserole, which is in essence a type of oven-stew or braise more suited to the tougher cuts of meats. Prior to cooking 'à la Poêle', certain prime joints containing little fat are larded and/or barded with pork fat, which keeps the meat moist and minimizes shrinkage during cooking.

Cooking Vessels

Cooking à la Poêle may be carried out in oven-proof earthenware dishes (cocottes) or in deep metal poêle pots. Cocottes are commonly used with poultry and for some feathered game.

Basting

Throughout cooking the food is enclosed with a tight-fitting lid, which provides a self-basting process, a result of condensation within the vessel. In addition the product is basted in the normal way. When colouring is required the lid is removed near the end of the cooking period.

Service

Whilst the sauce is being prepared the cooked meat is allowed to stand and set to facilitate carving. On service the joint may be presented whole for carving at the table or be carved in the kitchen. For illustrated carving techniques *see* Chapter 14.

Poêled products may be served 'en cocotte' or on a service flat according to requirements.

Examples of Joints Suitable for Poêle

Selected meat	Preparation for Poêle	Portion Yield	Cooking time (approximately)
Poultry and game			
1 Medium chicken ⎫		4	1–1¼ hr
1 Large duck ⎪	Cleaned and trussed.	4	2 hr
2 Small ducklings ⎬		4	1½ hr
2 Small pheasant ⎰	Barded	4	1–1¼ hr
2 Saddles of hare ⎱	Trim away sinew, piqué with pork fat then place in red wine marinade	4	25–30 min
Beef			
Fillet 800 g (2 lb)	Trim away sinew, lard with pork fat	4–6	20–30 min
Strip sirloin 800 g (2 lb)	Trim away sinew and excess fat	4–6	25–30 min
Lamb			
Saddle 3½ kg (7 lb)	Trimmed and secured with string (left on bone)	8–10	2–2½ hr
Loin 800 g (2 lb)	Boned and rolled (may be stuffed before rolling). Secure with string	4	1 hr
Veal			
Cushion 800 g (2 lb)	Trim, lard with pork fat and secure with string	4	1–1½ hr

N.B. Other premier joints may be cooked by the poêle method.

168
POT ROAST

Poêler

Yield: 4 portions (*see* chart above)
Cooking time: *see* chart above for individual cooking times.
Cooking temperature: 175°C (350°F)

Unit	Ingredient	Metric	Imperial
	Selected meat (*see* chart above)		
1	Demi-glace or jus lié	500 ml	1 pt
$^2/_5$	Mirepoix (medium cut to include aromates)	200 g	8 oz
$^1/_{10}$	Butter	50 g	2 oz
	Seasoning		
	Garnish		
	Wine/spirit or other liquid $\left\{\begin{array}{l}\text{See}\\\text{charts}\\\text{below}\end{array}\right.$		

Method

Brush base of cooking vessel lightly with butter, add mirepoix and aromates. Lightly season selected joint and place on to mirepoix. Brush joint liberally with remaining butter, cover with lid and pot roast in pre-heated oven, basting frequently. Once cooked remove joint from cooking vessel and put aside to set in readiness for service.

Deglaze with selected wine/spirit, reduce over heat, add jus-lié or demi-glace and continue to reduce to correct consistency. If cooking has been carried out in earthenware cocotte dish prepare sauce in a sauteuse to avoid damaging the cocotte. Pass sauce through fine chinois, degrease and adjust seasoning.

Service (chicken ducks, and feathered game)   Remove string and cut into portions, place in cocotte, coat with sauce, garnish as required and serve.

Service (ducks, saddle of hare, and butcher's meat)   Remove string from joints, carve into portions, arrange neatly on sauced service flat, surround with garnish, lightly napper with a little sauce. Serve accompanied with extra sauce.

N.B.   Alternatively the above preparations may be left whole and carved at the table.

Extensions of Above Formula Using Chicken: Selected Garnish Wine—Spirit in Relation to 1 Unit—½ l (1 pt) Sauce

French term	Unit	Ingredient	Metric	Imperial
Poulet en Cocotte Bonne Femme	$1/5$ $1/5$ $1/5$	Cocotte potatoes Button onions (glacés à brun) Lardons (cooked) Chopped parsley	100 g 100 g 100 g	4 oz 4 oz 4 oz
Poulet en Cocotte Champeaux	$1/5$ $1/5$ $1/10$	Cocotte potatoes Button onions (glacés à brun) Dry white wine Chopped parsley	100 g 100 g 50 ml	4 oz 4 oz 2 fl oz
Poulet en Cocotte aux Chipolata	$1/5$ $1/5$ $1/5$ $1/10$ $1/10$	Cooked chipolatas Button onions (glacés à brun) Braised chestnuts Lardons (cooked) Dry white wine Chopped parsley	100 g 100 g 100 g 50 g 50 ml	4 oz 4 oz 4 oz 2 oz 2 fl oz
Poulet en Cocotte Fermière	$2/5$	Cooked paysanne of vegetables Chopped parsley	200 g	8 oz
Poulet en Cocotte à la Paysanne	$1/5$ $1/5$ $1/10$ $1/10$	Cooked paysanne of vegetables Cocotte potatoes Lardons (cooked) Dry white wine Chopped parsley	100 g 100 g 50 g 50 g	4 oz 4 oz 2 oz 2 oz
Poulet en Cocotte Grand 'Mère	$1/5$ $1/5$	Fried croûtons (bâton shaped) Quartered mushrooms (sautéed) Chopped parsley	100 g 100 g	4 oz 4 oz

Extensions of Above Formula Using Ducks or Ducklings: Selected Garnish — Wine/Spirit in Relation to 1 Unit — ½ l (1 pt) Sauce

French term	Unit	Ingredient	Metric	Imperial
Canard/Caneton Poêle aux Cerises	$2/5$ $1/10$	Stoned cherries Madeira	200 g 50 ml	8 oz 2 fl oz
Canard/Caneton Poêle à l'Orange	$2/5$ $1/5$ $1/10$ $1/20$	Orange segments Orange juice Lemon juice Orange curacao Blanched julienne of orange zest to garnish	200 g 100 ml 50 ml 25 ml	8 oz 4 fl oz 2 fl oz 1 fl oz

Extensions of Above Formula Using Game: Selected Garnish — Wine/Spirit in Relation to 1 Unit — ½ l (1 pt) Sauce

French term	Unit	Ingredient	Metric	Imperial
Faisan en Cocotte	$1/_5$	Button onions (glacés à brun)	100 g	4 oz
	$1/_5$	Quartered mushrooms (sautéed)	100 g	4 oz
	$1/_{10}$	Madeira	50 g	2 oz
		Chopped parsley		
Râble de Lièvre Poêle Saint-Hubert	$2/_5$	Button mushrooms (sautéed)	200 g	8 oz
	$1/_{10}$	Red wine	50 ml	2 fl oz
	$1/_{20}$	Vinegar	25 ml	1 fl oz
		Few crushed peppercorns		
		Chopped parsley		

Extensions of Above Formula Using Butcher's Meat: Selected Garnish — Wine/Spirit in Relation to 1 Unit — ½ l (1 pt) Sauce

French term	Unit	Ingredient	Metric	Imperial
Filet de Boeuf Richelieu	$1/_{10}$	Madeira	50 ml	2 fl oz
		8 Stuffed mushrooms		
		4 Portions braised lettuce on croûtes		
		4 Stuffed tomatoes		
		8 Small pommes château		
		Chopped parsley		
Contrefilet de Boeuf Niçoise	$2/_5$	Cooked French beans	200 g	8 oz
	$1/_{10}$	Madeira	50 ml	2 fl oz
		8 Small cooked tomatoes		
		8 Small pommes château		
Selle d'Agneau à la Dubarry	$1/_{10}$	Madeira	50 ml	2 fl oz
		8 Cauliflower fleurettes au gratin		
		8 Small pommes château		
Longe d'Agneau Clamart	$1/_{10}$	Madeira	50 ml	2 fl oz
		4 Cooked artichoke bottoms filled with purée of green peas		
		8 Small pommes château		
Noix de Veau Mercédès	$1/_5$	Button mushrooms (glacés à brun)	100 g	4 oz
	$1/_{10}$	Madeira	50 ml	2 fl oz
		4 Cooked tomatoes		
		4 Portions braised lettuce on croûtes		
		8 Small pommes croquettes		

N.B. Many other garnishes may be served with preparations cooked à la poêle.

16

The Principle and Practice of Baking

To Bake   Cuire

Baking may be defined as cooking in the oven with convected dry heat without any significant amount of fat or liquid. During baking the natural moisture within foods is heated and produces an amount of steam, which in turn modifies the dry convected heat.

The action of convected hot air strips away the thin layer of moisture and cool air from the surface of foods being baked. This in turn allows heat to penetrate and cook the food. Modern forced air convection ovens (see p. 36) are fitted with a fan or blower designed to speed up the current of convected air and maintain an even temperature throughout. This results in cold air and moisture being removed from foods more quickly, allowing the heat to penetrate and cook foods more speedily. When using conventional ovens attention must be given to the varying degrees of heat within the oven cavity, a result of a slower convection current. This is illustrated by observing that the top of the oven is usually hotter than the bottom section, e.g. top and bottom heat.

A wide variety of foods may be baked including fish, butcher's meat, poultry, offal, game, vegetables including potatoes.

Points for Consideration

Where a traditional kitchen brigade is employed the following Chefs de Partie will be involved:

Chef Poissonnier   — baked fish products
Chef Saucier   — baked meat, poultry and game products, e.g. entrées and
                       relevés

Chef Entremettier   — vegetable and potato products including vegetable and
                         cheese soufflés
Chef Pâtissier   — dough and pastry bases
Chef Garde-Manger   — basic preparation of meats, fish, poultry and game, etc.

Preparation of Utensils

Care must be taken to ensure baking trays and other cooking vessels are clean and adequately greased to meet cooking requirements: otherwise foods may become soiled and stick to cooking trays or vessels.

Oven Temperatures

Ensure that the oven is pre-heated to the required temperature otherwise cooking times will be increased and the quality of finished products impaired.

Pastry

When covering pies with pastry do not stretch the paste otherwise it will shrink during cooking and slide into the pie dish. When trimming the pastry to fit the dish use a knife at an angle away from the dish to allow for shrinkage during cooking. Before baking pastry products allow resting time so that the pastry can relax, this prevents excessive shrinkage and tough pastry.

Service

Dry baked products or those presented for service in the cooking vessel are served on dish papers or serviettes to facilitate ease of service and to enhance appearance.

N.B.   For 'Pies' and products that involve baking in addition to another method of cookery see chapters concerning 'Combined Methods'.

Baked Butcher's Meat, Poultry, and Game

Although baking is considered to be a dry method of cookery, there are certain products which of necessity are baked with a significant amount of moisture. Baked pies are examples which illustrate this point. The extra moisture, usually in the form of stock, is essential if the filling is to be thoroughly cooked without becoming too dry.

169
BAKED PIES

Steak Pie

Yield: 4 portions
Cooking time: 2 – 2½ hr
Setting temperature: 205°C (400°F)
Cooking temperature: 150°C (300°F)

Unit	Ingredient	Metric (g)	Imperial (oz)
1	Stewing beef (1½ cm (¾ in) dice)	500	20
⅕	Onion brunoise	100	4
	Seasoned flour		
	Pinch of salt and pepper to taste		
	Chopped parsley (optional)		
*	Puff pastry		
†	Brown stock		

* Sufficient for *4 portions* approximately *200 g (8 oz)* at prepared weight.
† Sufficient stock barely to cover meat, approximately ½ unit stock to meat.

Method

Preparation   Lightly season meat and roll through seasoned flour. Mix onions, parsley with the meat, and place filling in the pie dish, add stock to moisten. Roll out puff pastry 3 mm (⅛ in) thick, moisten edge of pie dish and line with strip of pastry. Moisten pastry edge and cover with remaining pastry, taking care not to stretch the pastry otherwise it will shrink and slide into pie dish during baking. Seal well, trim and decorate with pastry trimmings as required. Rest before baking allowing pastry to relax (avoids excess shrinkage during baking). Eggwash for baking.

Baking   Set pie to bake in a hot oven until pastry becomes firm and light brown in colour. At this stage reduce oven temperature to 150°C (300°F) and continue baking until meat is cooked. Once cooked, clean edges of pie dish and surround with pie collar for service.

N.B.   Once pastry is adequately coloured to golden brown, cover with a piece of damp greaseproof paper to prevent overcolouring and excessive cooking of pastry.

Due to the long cooking process it may be necessary to remoisten the paper from time to time.

Extensions of Basic Formula: Added Ingredients to 1 Unit — 500 g (1¼ lb) meat

Name of dish	Unit	Ingredient	Metric (g)	Imperial (oz)
Steak and mushroom pie	⅒	Sliced mushrooms Add to filling	50	2
Steak and kidney pie	⅕	Diced ox-kidney Add to filling	100	4
Steak, kidney and mushroom pie	⅕ ⅒	Diced ox-kidney Sliced mushrooms Add to filling	100 50	4 2

170
POULTRY AND GAME PIES

Yield: 4 portions
= 1 medium chicken cut for sauté
= 1 medium rabbit jointed
= 2 pigeons halved minus carcass
Cooking time: $1\frac{1}{2} - 2$ hr
Setting temperature: 205°C (400°F)
Cooking temperature: 150°C (300°F)

Unit	Ingredient	Metric (g)	Imperial (oz)
	Selected poultry or game (*see* yield above)		
1	Sliced mushrooms	100	4
$\frac{1}{2}$	Onion brunoise	50	2
	8 Slices of streaky bacon		
	Seasoned flour		
	Pinch of salt and pepper		
	Chopped parsley		
*	Puff pastry		
†	White stock		

* Sufficient for *4 portions* approximately 200 g (8 oz).
† Sufficient stock barely to cover meat.

Method

Season selected meat, wrap in bacon and roll through seasoned flour. Lay the portions into pie dish, add onions, mushrooms, parsley and stock to moisten. Roll out puff pastry 3 mm ($\frac{1}{8}$ in) thick, moisten edge of pie dish and line with strips of pastry. Moisten this edge and cover with remaining pastry taking care not to stretch the pastry. Seal well, trim and decorate with pastry trimmings as required. Rest and egg-wash before baking.

Baking   Set pie to bake in a hot oven until pastry becomes firm and light brown in colour, at this stage reduce oven temperature to 150°C (300°F) and continue baking until meat is cooked. Once cooked, clean edge of pie dish and surround with pie collar for service.

Examples of Pies Prepared using Above Formula

Name of dish	Main ingredient
Chicken pie	Medium chicken cut for sauté
Pigeon pie	Pigeons cut in half with carcass removed
Rabbit pie	Medium rabbit jointed

171
HOT VEAL AND HAM PIE

Yield: 4 portions
Cooking time: $1\frac{1}{2} - 2$ hr
Setting temperature: 205°C (400°F)
Cooking temperature: 150°C (300°F)

Unit	Ingredient	Metric (g)	Imperial (oz)
1	Stewing veal [2½ cm (1 in dice)]	400	16
¼	Gammon [2½ cm (1 in dice)]	100	4
¼	Onion brunoise	100	4
⅛	Sliced mushrooms	50	2
	Seasoned flour		
	Pinch of salt/pepper		
	Chopped parsley		
	Squeeze of lemon juice		
*	Puff pastry		
†	White stock		

* Sufficient pastry for 4 portions approximately 200 g (8 oz) prepared weight.
† Sufficient stock barely to cover meat.

Method

Lightly season veal, combine with gammon, roll through seasoned flour and place in pie dish. Sprinkle with mushrooms, onion and parsley, moisten with stock and lemon juice. Cover with pastry and bake as for chicken pie (recipe 170).

172
FILLET OF BEEF IN PUFF PASTRY (en Croûte)   Filet de Boeuf Wellington

Yield: 4 portions
Cooking time: 20 – 30 min
Cooking temperature: 205°C (400°F)

Unit	Ingredient	Metric (g)	Imperial (oz)
1	Beef fillet (cut from centre—left whole)	600	20
⅕	Duxelle	120	4
¹⁄₁₀	Pâté de foie gras	60	2
	Oil		
	Salt and pepper		
	Madeira sauce to accompany		
*	Puff pastry		

* Sufficient pastry to cover fillet approximately 250 g (10 oz), prepared weight.

Method

Lightly season fillet and seal quickly in a film of oil in hot oven or on stove top. Allow to cool. Combine foie gras and duxelle and spread over top of the fillet. Roll out puff pastry into oblong shape 3 mm (⅛ in) thick. Wrap fillet neatly in pastry with the seal underneath the fillet. Decorate with pastry trimmings and allow to rest.

Brush with egg-wash and bake in hot oven until golden brown and cooked. The fillet should be medium rare on carving. Serve accompanied with Madeira sauce and carve at the table.

173
CORNISH PASTIES

Yield: 4 portions
Cooking time. 20 – 30 min
Cooking temperature: 175° (350°F)

Unit	Ingredient	Metric (g)	Imperial (oz)
1*	Short pastry	200	8
¾	Stewing lamb or beef (finely diced)	150	6
½	Potato (finely diced)	100	4
¼	Onion brunoise	50	2
	Salt and pepper		
	Chopped parsley		

* *Weight* indicates amount of flour used to prepare short pastry.

Method

Combine meat, potato, onion, chopped parsley and seasoning to form filling. Roll out pastry 3 mm (⅛ in) thick and cut out into 14 cm (5½ in) rounds. Moisten edges with water and place filling in centre. Draw two opposite edges of pastry together and seal well to enclose filling. Egg-wash and bake until golden brown and cooked. Serve plain or with a suitable sauce, e.g. jus lié.

174
TOAD IN THE HOLE

Yield: 4 portions
Cooking time: 20 – 30 min
Cooking temperature: 205°C (400°F)

Unit	Ingredient	Metric	Imperial
1	Pork/beef sausage	400 g	1 lb
⅝*	Yorkshire pudding batter	250 ml	10 fl oz
⅛	Dripping	50 g	2 oz

* Refers to the amount of liquid used to prepare the batter.

Method

Place dripping and sausage in a tray and set in hot oven for few minutes. Remove from oven and pour the batter on to the sausages. Replace in oven and bake until batter is cooked and golden brown. Serve accompanied with jus lié.

Baked Fish   Poisson (Cuire au Four)

This method of cookery is best suited for use with fillets of fish, small whole round fish, and certain smaller cuts. In some instances the fish is filled with a selected stuffing prior to baking e.g. lemon, parsley, and thyme stuffing *see* p. 299.

Once baked, the product may be served in its own juices or accompanied with a suitable sauce and garnish.

Fish Commonly Used for Baking

English term	French term	Cuts commonly used	Yield for 4 portions
Cod	Cabillaud	Darnes	4 × 150 g (6 oz)
Haddock	Aigrefin	Darnes	4 × 150 g (6 oz)
Hake	Colin	Darnes	4 × 150 g (6 oz)
Herring	Hareng	Whole and stuffed (*see* p. 299)	4 × 200 g (8 oz)
Mackerel	Maquereau	Whole and stuffed (*see* p. 299)	4 × 200 g (8 oz)
Red mullet	Rouget	Whole and stuffed (*see* p. 299)	4 × 200 g (8 oz)
Trout	Truite	Whole and stuffed (*see* p. 299)	4 × 200 g (8 oz)
Pike	Brochet	Small fillets or suprêmes	4 × 150 g (6 oz)

N.B. If baking 'fish in the piece' use 500 g (1¼ lb) fish at prepared weight. For whole fish to be stuffed, backbone is removed prior to stuffing and cooking.

175
BAKED FISH   Poisson au Four

Yield: 4 portions
Cooking time: 10 – 15 min
Cooking temperature: 175° (350°F)

Unit	Ingredient	Metric (g)	Imperial (oz)
1	Selected fish (*see* chart) Melted butter Squeeze of lemon juice Seasoning 4 lemon wedges/sprigs parsley	50	2

Method

Brush base of cooking vessel with butter. Rub fish with lemon juice and lightly season. Place fish into cooking vessel, brush with melted butter, cover with buttered cartouche and bake until cooked. Serve moistened with cooking liquor, garnish with lemon wedges and bouquets of parsley. May be accompanied with a suitable sauce, e.g. baked herrings with mustard sauce. N.B. After cooking, centre bone and outer skin are removed from darnes for service. Where darnes are stuffed, centre bone is removed before cooking and stuffing placed in the cavity.

Examples of Dishes Prepared Using Above Formula

English term	Suggested accompanying sauce for 4 portions	Metric	Imperial	French term
Baked fish steaks	Beurre Fondu	100 g	4 oz	Darne de Poisson au Four
Baked stuffed fish steaks	Sauce Tomate	250 ml	10 fl oz	Darne de Poisson Farcie au Four
Baked stuffed herrings/ mackerel	Sauce Moutarde	250 ml	10 fl oz	Hareng/Maquereau Farci au Four
Baked stuffed red mullet	Sauce Portugaise/ Provençale	250 ml	10 fl oz	Rouget Farci au Four
Baked stuffed trout	Beurre Maître d'Hôtel	50 g	2 oz	Truite Farcie au Four

N.B. Other suitable sauces may be served with baked fish.

Baked Fillet of Pike English Style   Filet/Suprême de Brochet à l'Anglaise

Method

Rub fish with lemon juice and lightly season, pass through seasoned flour, melted butter and white breadcrumbs. Proceed as for baked fish.

Baked Vegetables   Légumes au Four

The vegetables commonly cooked by this method are often filled with a stuffing prior to baking. Few are served plain baked. The main exceptions being tomatoes and potatoes.

Preparation of Vegetables for Baking

English term	French term	Preparation for baking	Yield for 4 portions	Cooking time (min)
Baked stuffed baby marrow	Courgettes Farcies au Four	Top and tail marrow, wash blanch 3–5 min and refresh. Cut in half lengthways, remove seeds, lightly season and fill with duxelle stuffing (*see* recipe 2)	400 g (1 lb)	15–20
Baked stuffed cucumber	Concombre Farci au Four	Peel cucumber, cut into 8 cm (3 in) lengths and proceed as for baby marrow	400 g (1 lb)	5–10
Baked stuffed mushrooms	Champignons Farcis au Four	Select large open flap mushrooms, remove stalks, peel and wash. Lightly season and fill with duxelle stuffing	12 mushrooms	5

English term	French term	Preparation for baking	Yield for 4 portions	Cooking time (min)
Baked tomatoes	Tomates au Four	Skin tomatoes, lightly season	8 medium tomatoes	5
Baked stuffed tomatoes	Tomates Farcies au Gratin	Skin tomatoes, remove top third of tomato, scoop out seeds, lightly season, fill with duxelle and sprinkle with breadcrumbs	8 medium tomatoes	5
Baked stuffed tomatoes Portuguese style	Tomates Farcies Portugaise	As for stuffed tomatoes but filled with pilaff	8 medium tomatoes	5
Tomatoes Provençale style	Tomates Provençale	Skin tomatoes, cut into half, lightly season. Sprinkle with mixture of white breadcrumbs, chopped parsley, garlic and few drops of oil	8 medium tomatoes	5
Stuffed tomatoes Italian style	Tomates Farcies Italienne	As for stuffed tomatoes but filled with risotto	8 medium tomatoes	5

N.B. When using duxelle, pilaff, or rissotto for stuffing vegetables the amounts may vary, but as a guide use 100 g (4 oz) per 4 portions.

Method of Baking Vegetables

Baking temperature: 205°C (400°F)
Place prepared vegetables on lightly oiled baking sheet. Brush with melted butter and bake quickly in hot oven to cook. Serve garnished with bouquet of picked parsley.

176
BAKED POTATOES

Pommes au Four

Yield: 4 portions
take 4 large potatoes
Cooking time: 1½ hr
Cooking temperature: 175°C (350°F)

Method

Scrub potatoes well in cold water. Lay evenly on bed of salt on a baking tray, prick with a fork to prevent splitting (the salt bed acts to absorb moisture from potatoes and to flavour). Bake in the oven until potatoes are cooked. Lift potatoes from salt bed and remove any salt adhering to potato skin. To serve plain baked, criss-cross top of potato with sharp office knife, squeeze the potato open and fill cavity with butter. Garnish with bouquet of parsley and serve.

Extensions of Baked Potatoes: Added Ingredients and Method for 4 Portions Using 4 Large Baked Potatoes

French term	Unit	Ingredient	Metric	Imperial
Pommes Gratinées	1	Grated cheese	100 g	4 oz
	¹/₂	Butter	50 g	2 oz
		Seasoning		
		Cut potatoes in half, scoop out centre, mash with butter and seasoning. Refill potato cases, sprinkle with cheese, re-bake in oven until golden brown		
Pommes Ménagère		As for pommes gratinées with the addition of Cooked ham brunoise	100 g	4 oz
		Combine with mashed potato before refilling potato case		
Pommes Arlie		As for pommes gratinées with addition of	50 ml	2 fl oz
	¹/₂	Cream		
		Chopped chives		
		Combine cream and chives with mashed potato before refilling potato cases		
Pommes Surprise	1	Cream	100 ml	4 fl oz
	¹/₂	Butter	50 g	2 oz
		Seasoning		
		Make a small aperture in the potato skin and remove potato. Pass through potato machine, combine with cream, butter and seasoning. Pipe back in potato skin and place in oven to reheat and seal aperture, serve as required		
Pommes Macaire	1	Butter	50 g	2 oz
		Seasoning		
		Scoop out potato from skins, mash and combine with butter and seasoning. Fill heated, buttered anna mould with the potato mixture and press lightly. Place in hot oven to re-bake to golden brown (approximately 10 – 15 min). Turn out brush with melted butter and serve as required		
Pommes Robert		As for macaire with the addition of		
	1	Egg yolk	50 g	2 oz
		Chopped chives		
		Combine ingredients with mashed potato before re-baking in mould		

Pommes Byron	As for macaire but finished with		
	1	Grated cheese	50 g	2 oz
	1	Cream	50 ml	2 oz

Hollow centre of turned out Pommes
Macaire, fill with cheese and cream then
gratinate in hot oven for service

177
ANNA POTATOES   Pommes Anna

Yield: 4 portions (to fill small mould of 15 cm (6 in) diameter)
Cooking time: 30 – 45 min
Cooking temperature: 205°C (400°F)

Unit	Ingredient	Metric (g)	Imperial (oz)
1*	Potatoes (trimmed to cylindrical shape)	600	20
$\frac{1}{5}$	Butter (melted)	120	4
	Salt and pepper		

* In order to obtain this amount of prepared potatoes trimmed to shape, it is necessary to commence with approximately 800 g (2 lb) at unpeeled weight.

Method

Slice potatoes 1 mm ($\frac{1}{16}$ in) rounds (approximately). Do not store potatoes in water as the starch content is required to enable potatoes to adhere together during cooking. Heat buttered anna mould on stove top, pull to side of stove and overlap potato rounds to form a base at bottom of the mould. Lightly season and brush with melted butter, continue this process until mould is full. Place filled mould over heat until potatoes become loose at base of mould, press lightly, cover with lid and bake in oven until cooked. When cooked ensure potatoes are loose in mould, turn out for service.

N.B.   During cooking it is necessary to press potatoes to ensure they stick together.

Extensions of Anna Potatoes: Added Ingredients with Method in Relation to 1 Unit 600 g (1¼ lb) Potatoes

French term	Unit	Ingredient	Metric (g)	Imperial (oz)
Pommes Voisin/ Ambassadeur	$\frac{1}{5}$	Grated cheese	120	4
		Proceed as for pommes anna but sprinkle grated cheese between potato layers		
Pommes Darphin		Proceed as for pommes anna but cut potatoes into julienne		
Pommes Nana		Proceed as for pommes darphin but cook in copper dariole moulds		

Other Baked Products

Pizzas

In recent years these products along with others have become popularized as a result of the development of speciality restaurants, e.g. Pizza Houses, Bistros, Hamburger restaurants, etc., and the changing tastes of well-travelled customers. Another factor contributing to their popularity is the constant need for caterers to maintain a supply of reasonably priced products and keep within cost limits.

178
PIZZA

Yield: 4 × 20 cm (8 in) pizzas
Bulk fermentation time (B.F.T.): 1 hr
Baking time: 15 – 20 min
Baking temperature: 205°C (400°F)

Pizza Dough

Unit	Ingredient	Metric	Imperial
1	Strong flour	400 g	1 lb
$5/8$	Water [27°C (80°F)]	250 ml	10 fl oz
$1/16$	Lard	25 g	1 oz
$1/16$	Yeast	25 g	1 oz
	Good pinch of salt		

Method

Sift flour and salt together, rub in the fat content and form a well. Combine all yeast with three-quarters of the water and pour into the well. Mix ingredients together to commence formation of dough adding remaining water as required. Knead thoroughly to form smooth elastic well developed dough. Cover with damp cloth and stand in warm place for the required B.F.T. period. Knock back (knead) gently, divide into four pieces and roll out into 4 × 20 cm (8 in) rounds, dock* well. Place on to lightly greased baking sheets, arrange selected pizza filling on top of dough (*see* below) and prove for 10 – 15 minutes until dough begins to rise. Bake in pre-heated oven until cooked. Remove from baking sheet and serve immediately.

* Docking – a technique used to pierce pastry or bread in order to inhibit normal rising.

179
BASIC PIZZA FILLING

Yield: sufficient for 1 × 20 cm (8 in) pizza

Unit	Ingredient	Metric (g)	Imperial (oz)
†1	Tomates concassées (*see* recipe 3)	200	8
½	Selected cheese (thin slices)	100	4
	Pinch of basil – marjoram – oregano		
	Salt and pepper		

† Tinned tomatoes may be used in this preparation.

Method
Spread surface of rolled out raw dough with layer of tomatoes, sprinkle with seasoning and herbs. Arrange cheese slices to cover surface, finish with additional ingredients as required (see chart below), and bake.

Added Ingredients in Relation to Basic Pizza Filling

Name	Unit	Ingredient	Metric (g)	Imperial (oz)
Pizza Napolitana		8 Anchovy fillets		
		8 Black olives (stoned)		
Pizza with Parma ham		4 Slices of Parma ham		
Pizza with mushrooms	1	Mushrooms (sliced and sweated)	200	8
Pizza Mare (pizza with seafood)	1	{ Scampi Mussels (budded) Prawns	200	8
Pizza with spiced sausage	½	Selected sliced continental sausage	100	4

Pizzas often take their name from the region of origin or the main flavouring being used. Other suitable pizzas may be prepared to requirements of customers and culinary flair of the chef.

Savoury Flans   Quiches

The term Quiche denotes an open flan, which is filled and garnished with a savoury filling.

180
BASIC PREPARATION OF QUICHES

Yield: 4 portions
Cooking time: 20 – 30 min
Cooking temperature: 175°C (350°F)

Unit	Ingredient	Metric	Imperial
1	Milk	200 ml	8 fl oz
½	Whole egg	100 g	4 oz
	Salt and pepper		
	Chopped parsley/garlic		
	Selected filling (see chart)		
*	Short pastry		

* Sufficient pastry to line 15 cm (6 in) flan ring, using approximately 150 g (6 oz) of flour.

Method

Roll out pastry to 3 mm (⅛ in) thick and line greased flan ring.
Neatly arrange selected filling in base of flan case, sprinkle with chopped parsley and flavour with garlic. Beat eggs, milk, and seasoning together and pour into flan case, garnish top if required and bake until cooked. Once baked remove flan ring and serve as required. May be served hot or cold.

Savoury Flan Fillings: Added Ingredients in Relation to 1 Unit 200 ml (8 fl oz) Milk

Name	Unit	Ingredient	Metric (g)	Imperial (oz)
Quiche aux Oignons (onion flan)	1	Onions (sliced and sweated)	200	8
Quiche au Fromage avec Oignons (cheese and onion flan)	As for onion flan with addition of: ½	Grated cheese	100	4
Quiche Lorraine (cheese and bacon flan)	½	Lean bacon slices	100	4
	½	Grated cheese	100	4
		Hint of chopped garlic		
Quiche Forestière (Savoury flan)	½	Lean bacon slices	100	4
	¼	Onions (sliced and sweated)	50	2
	¼	Mushrooms (sliced and sweated)	50	2
	¼	Grated cheese	50	2
Quiche Fruits de Mer (Seafood flan)	½	White crab meat	100	4
	¼	Prawns	50	2
	¼	Mussels (budded)	50	2

Other fillings may be used according to taste. These products may be prepared in individual moulds, e.g. barquettes or tartlet moulds.

Baked Soufflés (Savoury)

The making of soufflés is a simple operation, which has been surrounded by unnecessary mystique. If the formula and methods outlined below are followed carefully, little difficulty should be encountered in achieving good results.

Soufflés are prepared to order, and served immediately on completion of cooking. If they are left to stand they gradually fall losing their initial volume and texture. They are usually served as a preliminary or savoury course.

Points for Consideration

Care must be taken to:

(a) prepare a smooth, thick sauce as a base for the soufflé. This is enriched by the addition of the egg yolks;

(b) beat the egg whites until stiff but not dry, this facilitates folding in;

(c) mix approximately a quarter of the beaten whites with the basic mixture (panada) in order to soften the consistency before the remaining whites are folded in. This ensures a more even distribution of the whites resulting in a good lift;

(d) pre-heat the oven to the required temperature before baking. If the oven is too cold the soufflé will not cook or rise sufficiently, if too hot the soufflé will over-bake on the exterior leaving the interior under-cooked.

(e) test whether a soufflé is cooked through by inserting a knife into the centre, which should come out 'clean'.

181
CHEESE SOUFFLÉ   Soufflé au Fromage

Yield: 4 portions
Cooking time: 35 – 45 min
Cooking temperature: 175°C (350°F)

Unit	Ingredient	Metric	Imperial
1	Milk	200 ml	8 fl oz
1	Whole egg (separate yolks from whites)	200 g	8 oz
$1/2$	Grated cheese (Cheddar/Gruyère)	100 g	4 oz
$1/4$	Butter	50 g	2 oz
$1/8$	Flour	25 g	1 oz
	Pinch of salt		
	Pinch of cayenne pepper		

N.B.   When preparing Soufflé au Parmesan reduce cheese content to $1/4$ unit [50 g (2 oz)] due to the strong flavour of this cheese.

Method

Prepare soufflé mould by brushing liberally with melted butter. Form a white roux with the butter and flour and add milk to form a thick white sauce. Add the cheese and stir over heat to blend. Remove from heat and blend in the yolks of egg, season with salt and cayenne pepper. Beat egg whites until stiff and add a quarter of the whites to the basic mixture. Fold in the remaining whites gently until they are evenly distributed through the mixture. Three-quarters fill the prepared soufflé mould, place on to a baking sheet and bake in the pre-heated oven until risen, cooked, and golden-brown. Serve immediately.

N.B.   Cooking may be commenced by placing the soufflé mixture, in its dish, into a stove-top bain marie. Once the souffle has begun to rise it is removed from the water on to a baking sheet in order to complete cooking in the oven.

182
BAKED SAVOURY SOUFFLÉS

Basic Soufflé Mixture (e.g. for ham, chicken, and fish)

Yield: 4 portions
Cooking time: 35 – 45 min
Cooking temperature: 175°C (350°F)

Unit	Ingredient	Metric	Imperial
1	Main cooked flavouring (finely minced)	200 g	8 oz
1	Whole egg (separate yolks from whites)	200 g	8 oz
³/₄	Béchamel	150 ml	6 fl oz
¹/₄	Melted butter	50 g	2 oz
	Seasonings		

Method

Brush soufflé mould liberally with melted butter (enables soufflé to rise without sticking). Moisten main flavouring with béchamel sauce, liquidize or rub through a very fine sieve to form a light purée. Heat this mixture in a saucepan and add the melted butter, seasoning and any additional flavouring (*see* chart). Remove from heat and carefully blend in the egg yolks. Beat egg whites to a stiff snow and blend in a quarter of the whites to the basic mixture. Fold in the remaining whites gently until they are evenly distributed throughout the mixture. Three-quarters fill the prepared soufflé mould, place on to a baking sheet and bake in the pre-heated oven until risen, cooked, and firm to the touch. Serve immediately.

Soufflés Prepared Using the Above Formula

English term	Main and additional flavourings	French term
Chicken soufflé	Cooked chicken, squeeze of lemon juice, pinch of nutmeg, teaspoon of chicken glaze	Soufflé à la Reine
Ham soufflé	Cooked ham	Soufflé de Jambon
Fish soufflé	Cooked fish (poached in white wine), squeeze of lemon juice, teaspoon or fish glaze. Smoked or strong-flavoured fish are also used.	Soufflé de Poisson

N.B. *See* cooking soufflés 'en bain marie' prior to baking in recipe 181.

17

The Principle and Practice of Grilling

To Grill   Griller

Grilling may be defined as a speedy and dry method of cooking by radiant heat. The food is placed near to the source of heat, which acts to cook each item quickly. This method is ideally suited for use with tender cuts of butcher's meat, offal, poultry, fish and vegetables. At the commencement of cooking the surface of food is sealed to assist in retaining the food's juices and flavour. Grilled products remain a common feature on the menu in both traditional and modern catering units.

Traditionally grilling was carried out on bars over an open, ventilated charcoal fire but modern grills also employ the use of gas and electrically heated appliances.

Grilling may therefore be described as:

1. cooking over radiant heat, e.g. over heated charcoal;
2. cooking under radiant heat, e.g. under gas/electric salamanders;
3. cooking between heat, e.g. electrically heated ridged plates.

Broiling is an alternative term used in America to denote grilling.

Points for Consideration

Items for grilling are seasoned with salt and milled pepper just before cooking in order to improve their flavour. In some cases foods are sprinkled with fresh herbs or placed into a marinade to enhance flavour, and in the case of a marinade to aid tenderization. Examples include kebabs in marinade, grilled lamb flavoured with rosemary and garlic.

Prior to grilling certain items are lightly coated in flour, which acts to improve the colour and texture of the cooked product. During cooking the flour browns and crispens, e.g. grilled fish. In all cases foods prepared for grilling are best brushed with oil or melted butter, which keeps them moist and prevents their sticking to grilling bars or trays.

Organization and Preparation

Where a traditional kitchen brigade is employed the following staff are involved with the preparation for and the cooking of grilled products:

Chef Garde-manger   —   basic preparation of meat and fish, etc.
Chef Entremettier   —   basic preparation of vegetables
Chef Grillardin   —   grilling of most products.

Other Chefs de Partie are involved with the preparation of accompanying garnishes and sauces.

In order to ensure speedy and efficient cooking the grilling appliance must be preheated and the grilling bars and trays brushed with a light film of oil to prevent foods sticking during cooking. If a smooth operation is to be achieved advance organization of materials, service and cooking equipment, garnishes and sauces is essential.

Care During Cooking

Most grilling appliances are designed to allow for varying degrees of heat. This is achieved by the use of sloping bars and fuel regulators. As a result food may commence and continue cooking at different degrees of heat, e.g. a steak may be sealed in a hot part of the grill then moved to cook more slowly at a lower temperature.

Grilling tongs are often used to move and turn items during cooking, and are designed to enable the grill chef to turn food safely without having to reach under or over the intense heat. On no account should meat be pierced during grilling as juices escape resulting in less succulent food.

Slices and palette knives are used to turn fish portions or foods that are placed on trays for grilling. Because of the delicate structure of fish, extra care is required to prevent it from flaking and breaking up.

Browning/Gratinating Foods

The salamander is frequently used to colour or glaze foods for service, e.g. fish and vegetable products.

Grilled Butcher's Meat, Offal, Poultry   *Viande Grillée, Abats Grillés, Volaille Grillée*

Grilling is employed in the cooking of a wide variety of butcher's meat, offal and poultry, most of which are prepared into small cuts. Generally speaking only the choice tender cuts are suitable for this method of cookery.

Beef   Boeuf

Sirloin
Fillet
T-bone

Sirloin of Beef on the Bone (Cuts)   Aloyau de Boeuf

English term	French term	Yield for 4 portions	Explanation and illustration
T-Bone steak or Porterhouse steak (U.S.A.)		4 × 400 g (1 lb)	A steak cut across whole sirloin on the bone including the fillet of beef A cut from wing-end of sirloin on the bone excluding the fillet
Club steak (U.S.A.)		4 × 300 g (12 oz)	

Fillet of Beef (Tenderloin – U.S.A.)   Filet de Boeuf

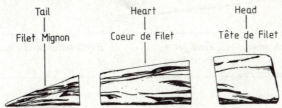

Tail   Heart   Head

Filet Mignon   Coeur de Filet   Tête de Filet

Cuts in Common Use

English term	French term	Yield for 4 portions	Explanation and illustration
	Chateaubriand	2 × 400 g (1 lb) large steaks	A large cut from head of fillet lightly batted to form large steak
Fillet steak	Filet de Boeuf	4 × 200 g (8 oz) steaks	A cut from the head or the heart of the fillet

Tournedos	4 × 150 g (6 oz)	A neat cut from heart of fillet often lightly secured with string to retain round shape

Filet Mignon de Boeuf	7 × 75 g (3 oz) pieces	Small cuts from tail of fillet often used as part of a mixed grill but may be served in their own right

Strip Loin of Beef

Contrefilet de Boeuf
(Boned-out sirloin)

English term	French term	Yield for 4 portions	Explanation and illustration

Double sirloin steak	Entrecôte Double	4 × 300 g (12 oz) steaks	A large cut from boned out sirloin
Sirloin steak	Entrecôte	4 × 200 g (8 oz) steaks	A cut from boned out sirloin
Minute steak	Entrecôte Minute	4 × 150 g (6 oz) steaks	As above but batted out thinly

Rump of Beef   Culotte de Boeuf

- Point of rump
- Rump

Boned-out Rump

English term	French term	Yield for 4 portions	Explanation and illustration
Point steaks	—	4 × 200 g (8 oz)	A steak cut from point of rump 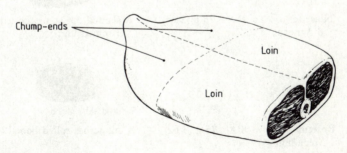
Rump steaks	—	4 × 200 g (8 oz)	A steak from main piece of rump

Lamb   Agneau

Saddle of Lamb (Cuts)   Selle d'Agneau

Chump-ends

Loin

Loin

Saddle on the Bone

English term	French term	Yield for 4 portions	Explanation and illustration
English lamb chop-Barnsley chop	Chop d'Agneau à l'Anglaise	4 × 250 g (10 oz) double chops	A double chop cut across saddle on the bone with kidney skewered in
Lamb chop	Chop d'Agneau	4 × 150 g (6 oz)	A cut across loin of lamb on bone
Chump chop	Chop d'Agneau	4 × 200g (8 oz)	A cut across chump end of lamb on the bone
	Noisette d'Agneau	8 × 75 g (3 oz)	A slanted cut across boned out trimmed loin
	Rosette/ Médaillon d'Agneau	8 × 75 g (3 oz)	A cut across rolled boned out loin
Fillet of lamb	Filet Mignon	4 to 8 lamb fillets fillets according to size	Whole fillets bone out from under saddle of lamb

Best-End of Lamb (Cuts)   Carré d'Agneau

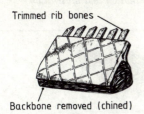

Trimmed rib bones

Backbone removed (chined)

English term	French term	Yield for 4 portions	Explanation and illustration
Lamb cutlet	Côtelette d'Agneau	8 × 75 g (3 oz)	A cut across best-end between rib bones
Double lamb cutlet	Côtelette d'Agneau Double	4 × 150 g (6 oz)	As above to include two rib bones

Pork   Porc

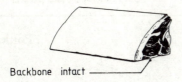

Backbone intact

Pork Loin (Cuts)   Longe de Porc

Rib-bone ends

Back bone removed (chined) and rib-ends trimmed for cutlets (see pork cutlet)

Best-End of Pork (Cuts)   Carré de Porc

English term	French term	Yield for 4 portions	Explanation and illustration
Pork chop	Chop de Porc	4 × 200 g (8 oz)	A cut across the loin of pork on the bone
Pork cutlet	Côtelette de Porc	4 × 200 g (8 oz)	A cut across best-end between rib bones

Offal of Butcher's Meat   Abats de Viande

English term	French term	Yield for 4 portions	Explanation
Lamb ⎫ Calves ⎬liver Pigs' ⎭	Foie d'Agneau Foie de Veau Foie de Porc	400 g (1 lb)	Skin and slice thinly
Lambs' ⎫ Calves' ⎬kidney Pigs' ⎭	Rognon d'Agneau Rognon de Veau Rognon de Porc	8 kidneys 4 kidneys 8 kidneys	Skin, slit open and skewer Skin, slice and skewer Skin, slit open and skewer

Grilled Chicken   Poulet Grillé

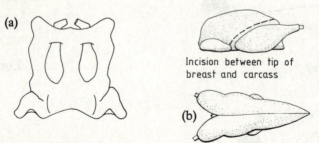

(a)

Incision between tip of breast and carcass

(b)

Chickens are generally prepared in one of two ways in readiness for grilling:

(a) Spatchcock (spread-eagled—English style)
(b) Crapaudine (toad-like—French style).

Smaller chicken cuts may be grilled if required, but it is more common to cook them by shallow or deep frying.

English term	French term	Yield for 4 portions	Explanation and illustration
Chicken Spatchcock (spread-eagled)	Poulet en Spatchcock	2 × 800 g (2 lb) or 4 × 400 (1 lb) chickens	Trim chicken, split down backbone, open and bat. Remove rib cage and backbone. May be skewered to help retain shape when grilling
Chicken cut to toad shape	Poulet en Crapaudine	2 × 800 g (2 lb) or 4 × 400 g (1 lb) chicken	Remove winglets then incise chicken between tip of breast and carcass base to the wing joints. Open out and lightly bat to give toad like appearance

Grilling of Butcher's Meat, Offal and Poultry

Method

Lightly season meat with salt and milled pepper. Brush with oil or melted butter and place on pre-heated grill or trays and commence grilling. Once sealed and brown turn and continue grilling until required degree of cooking is attained. Remove from grill and garnish as required (*see* chart).

N.B. Liver is passed through seasoned flour then lightly oiled prior to grilling.

For service the ends of cutlet bones are dressed with cutlet frills.

Degrees of Cooking

The following usually apply to cuts of beef but on occasion lamb or offal grills may be served slightly underdone according to customer's wishes. Pork/poultry grills should be cooked thoroughly but not allowed to become dry by over-grilling.

Degrees:

Au Bleu	Blue or very rare
Saignant (bleeding)	Rare or underdone
à Point	Medium or just done
Bien Cuit	Well done

The grilling times taken to achieve the required degree of cooking will vary according to:

(a) thickness and quality of the food being grilled
(b) heat of the grilling appliance
(c) customer's requirements.

Due to these factors it is difficult to specify exact grilling times as these are best judged by the grill cook.

Garnishes for Grilled Butcher's Meat and Offal: Garnish and Sauce for 4 Portions

Name	Unit	Ingredient	Metric	Imperial	Examples of uses
à la Maison (in the style of the house	1 1 1	French-fried onions Straw potatoes (cooked) Cooked mushrooms 4 Grilled tomatoes 4 Small bunches of watercress Garnish as required	100 g 100 g 100 g	4 oz 4 oz 4 oz	Grills of beef, lamb pork, chicken
Bouquetière	1	Béarnaise sauce Bouquets of cooked assorted vegetables (*see* p. 185). Garnish as required and serve sauce separately	250 ml	10 fl oz	Chateaubriand
Henri IV	1	Pont-Neuf Potatoes 4 Small bunches of watercress Surround with potatoes and watercress	200 g	8 oz	Grills of beef cuts
Maître d'Hôtel	1 ½	Straw potatoes Parsley butter 4 Small bunches of watercress Decorate with watercress and potatoes Finish with slices of parsley butter	100 g 50 g	4 oz 2 oz	Grills of beef, lamb, pork
Mirabeau	1	Anchovy butter 12 Anchovy fillets (cut into thin strips) 8 Olives 4 Small bunches of watercress Decorate grilled meat with anchovy fillets, surround with watercress and olives. Finish with slices of anchovy butter on service	50 g	2 oz	Grilled entrecôtes

Name	Unit	Ingredient	Metric	Imperial	Examples of uses
au Lard		4 Slices grilled bacon			Grilled liver

Tyrolienne	1 ½	French fried onions
		Tomato concassé
		4 Small bunches of
		  watercress
		Place tomato on grilled meat, surround
		  with onion and watercress
			200 g
			100 g
				8 oz
				4 oz
					Grills of beef and
					lamb

Vert Pré	1	Straw potatoes
		  (cooked)
		4 Small bunches of
		  watercress
		Surround with garnish
			100 g	4 oz	Grills of beef, lamb,
					pork, offal and
					poultry

Garnishes for Grilled Chicken: Garnish and Sauce for 4 Portions

Name	Method of Cutting	Unit	Ingredient	Metric	Imperial
Poulet Grillé Diable (grilled chicken with devilled sauce)	Spatchcock	1 2/5 2/5 2/5	Devilled Sauce Straw potatoes (cooked) Melted butter White breadcrumbs Diluted English mustard 4 Small bunches of watercress	250 ml 100 g 100 g 100 g	10 fl oz 4 oz 4 oz 4 oz

			Half-way through grilling brush
			  chicken with mustard, melted butter
			  and sprinkle with breadcrumbs.
			Continue grilling under salamander
			  until golden brown and cooked.
			Garnish with straw potatoes, water-
			  cress and accompany with devilled
			  sauce		

Poulet Grillé
Américaine
(grilled chicken
American style)
	Spatchcock		As for Poulet Grillé Diable but garnished with the
			addition of:
			  8 Grilled mushrooms
			  4 Grilled tomatoes
			  4 Slices of grilled bacon		

Name	Method of Cutting	Unit	Ingredient	Metric	Imperial
Poulet Grillé à l'Anglaise (chicken spatchcock)	Spatchcock		As for Poulet Grillé Diable but omitting mustard. Garnish with addition of: 8 Fanned gherkins		
Poulet Grillé Crapaudine (grilled chicken in the shape of a toad)	Crapaudine		Cooked and served as for Poulet Grillé Diable but omitting mustard		

Other Grilled Meats in Common Use

Gammon Steaks

Yield: 4 × 200 g (8 oz) steaks

Method

Omit seasoning (gammon has been previously cured with salt), and proceed as for grilled meats.
May be garnished with:

   (a) shallow-fried eggs;
   (b) glazed pineapple rings;
   (c) glazed peaches;
   (d) vert-pré, etc.

Grilled Hamburgers (Recipe 105)

Yield: 4 portions

Method

Cook as for grilled meats. May be garnished and presented in a variety of ways including:

   (a) à la Maison;
   (b) Tyrolienne;
   (c) with fried eggs;
   (d) with sauce charcutière, etc.

In popular catering hamburgers are often grilled and served sandwiched in bread rolls with various salads, sauces, and relishes.

Grilled Bacon/Sausages/Bacon Rolls

Yield: 4 portions 400 g (1 lb) sausages
       4 portions 200 g (8 oz) bacon slices (trimmed)
       4 portions 200 g (8 oz) bacon slices (rolled) may be skewered for grilling.

Method

Place on to lightly greased grilling trays, put to grill under pre-heated salamander and cook on one side. Turn to complete cooking. Use as required.

N.B.   Used as main-course items for breakfasts, lunch and high teas or to complete other preparations.

Mixed Grill

Selection of grilled meat, which may vary according to the establishment's requirements. Yield: 4 portions

4 Grilled lamb cutlets (with frills)
4 Grilled lamb's kidneys
4 Grilled slices of bacon (trimmed)
4 Grilled slices of liver
4 Grilled sausages

Garnish with:

4 Grilled mushrooms
4 Grilled tomatoes
4 Small bunches of watercress
4 Small portions straw potatoes

183
GRILLING ON SKEWERS

En Brochette
Kebab (Turkish)

Yield: 4 portions
Cooking time: 10 – 15 min

Unit	Ingredient	Metric	Imperial
1	Selected meat cut in 2 cm [(³/₄ in cubes)]	600 g	1¹/₄ lb
¹/₅	Onion (large dice)	120 g	4 oz
¹/₅	Oil	120 ml	4 fl oz
¹/₂₀	Lemon juice	30 ml	1 fl oz
	Bay leaves and thyme		
	Salt and milled pepper		

Preparation

Lightly season meat and place in a bowl with remaining ingredients. Mix thoroughly, cover with cartouche and allow to stand for a few hours to marinade before use. Place meat on skewers interspersed with onion and herbs.

Method of Grilling

Proceed as for grilled meats (*see* p. 337) or place on grilling trays and cook under the salamander turning to complete cooking. Serve presented on a bed of braised rice (*see* recipe 59) accompanied with a suitable sauce (*see* chart).

Extensions of Above Formula: Additional Garnish in Relation to 1 unit 600 g (1¼ lb) meat

Name	Main ingredient	Unit	Ingredient	Metric (g)	Imperial (oz)	Suggested Accompanying Sauce
Brochette de foie de Volaille (chicken livers grilled on the skewer)	Chicken livers					Madeira sauce
Brochette de Rognon (kidneys grilled on the skewer)	Lamb ⎫ Veal ⎬ kidneys					Madeira or devilled sauce
Shish kebab or Kebab à la Turque (lamb grilled on a skewer Turkish style)	Fillet of lamb	¹⁄₅	Button mushrooms Marinade with meat and intersperse on skewer for grilling	120	4	Jus lié or Madeira sauce
Brochette à la Maison (skewered grilled meats after the style of the house)	e.g. Pork Kidney Liver Bacon	¹⁄₅ ¹⁄₅	Button mushrooms Peppers (large dice) 4 Small tomatoes (halved) Marinade with meat and intersperse on skewer for grilling	120 120	4 4	Sweet and sour sauce

Grilled Fish   Poisson Grillé

The grilling technique is used in the cooking of a wide variety of fish and shellfish, some of which are prepared into cuts, whilst others are left whole. Those in *common* use are outlined below.

Whole Fish

Gutted and trimmed. Small round fish are also lightly scored (ciseler) in order to aid cooking and prevent the skin from bursting. Burst skin impairs the appearance of the finished product.

English term	French term	Yield for 4 Portions
Herring	Hareng	4 × 200 g (8 oz)
Kippers	Craquelot	4 × 200 g (8 oz)
Mackerel	Maquereau	4 × 200 g (8 oz)
Red mullet	Rouget	4 × 200 g (8 oz)
Sole (Dover)	Sole Douvres	4 × 300 g (12 oz)
Trout	Truite	4 × 200 g (8 oz)
Whiting	Merlan	4 × 200 g (8 oz)
Shellfish		
Lobster	Homard	2 × 500 g (1¼ lb)
Scampi	Langoustine	400 g (1 lb) shelled weight

Fish that are Commonly Prepared as Small Cuts for Grilling

English term	French term	Common cuts for grilling
Cod	Cabillaud	Filet—Suprême—Darne
Dover sole	Sole Douvres	Filet
Haddock	Aigrefin	Filet—Suprême—Darne
Hake	Colin	Filet—Suprême—Darne
Halibut	Flétan	Tronçon
Lemon sole	Sole Limande	Filet
Plaice	Plie	Filet
Salmon	Saumon	Darne
Whiting	Merlan	Filet

Illustrated Fish Cuts used for Grilling

English term	French term	Yield for 4 portions	Explanation and illustration
Fillet	le Filet	4 to 8 fillets according to size, and requirements	A cut of fish free from bone Flat fish yields 4; round fish yields 2
Supreme	le Suprême	4 × 125 g (5 oz) portions	A slanted cut from large fish fillets.

English term	French term	Yield for 4 portions	Explanation and illustration
Steak of round fish	la Darne	4 × 150 g (6 oz) portions	A cut of round fish on the bone
Steak of flat fish	le Tronçon	4 × 150 g (6 oz) portions	A steak of flat fish on the bone

Preparation for Grilling

Fish may be prepared for grilling in one of the following ways:

(a) Dry the fish, lightly season and rub with lemon juice, pass through seasoned flour, oil or melted butter and place on prepared grilling trays. For kippers omit flour and lemon juice.

(b) Dry the fish, lightly season and rub with lemon juice, pass through melted butter and white breadcrumbs, lightly pat to remove excess crumbs. Place on prepared grilling trays. Sprinkle with few drops of melted butter.

(c) When grilling *live lobster* split in half lengthways remove sack from head and waste cord from tail. Crack the claws. Lightly season and brush flesh and claws liberally with melted butter. Place on prepared grilling trays.

Method

Place trays of fish/shellfish under pre-heated salamander and grill until cooked and golden brown. Throughout grilling moisten lightly with melted butter or oil to aid even and moist cooking. When grilling whole fish or thick cuts of fish, e.g. darnes it is necessary to grill fish on both sides. However, with thin cuts, e.g. fillets, the intense heat should be sufficient to cook the fish through and therefore turning may not be required.

Once cooked arrange fish portions neatly on to lightly buttered service dishes, moisten with some cooking liquor and garnish with picked parsley and a wedge of lemon. Serve with accompanying sauce and any additional garnish.

N.B.   Before serving grilled fish steaks remove centre bone, outside skin and trimmings.

Before serving lobster remove the cooked meat from the claw shell and place in carapace (head) cavity.

Name of dish	Method of preparation	Grilling time (min) (approximately)	Additional garnish and accompanying sauce
Poisson Grillé (grilled fish)	1	3 – 10 according to size and thickness of fish	A variety of sauces may be used e.g. sole with parsley butter, herrings with mustard sauce, mackerel with anchovy butter, red mullet with shrimp butter, etc.
Filet/Suprême de Poisson St. Germain	2	3 – 10 according to size and thickness of fish	Noisette potatoes and Sauce Béarnaise
Merlan Entier St. Germain	2	8 – 12	Noisette potatoes and Sauce Béarnaise
Filet de Poisson Caprice	2	3 – 5	Grilled banana halves and Sauce Robert
Langoustine en Brochette (scampi on a skewer)	1 or 2	5	Selected hard butter sauce or Sauce Diable
Langoustine en Brochette au Lard (scampi on a skewer wrapped in bacon)	1	5 – 8	Pilaff of rice and sweet and sour sauce
Homard Grillé (grilled lobster)	3	10	Lobster butter

N.B.   Many other fish may be cooked by this method and served with an appropriate sauce.

Grilled Vegetables   Légumes

Few vegetables are cooked by the grilling method although many are glazed or gratinated under the salamander in readiness for service. The main exceptions are tomatoes and mushrooms.

Grilled Tomatoes   Tomates Grillées

Yield: 4 portions—8 medium tomatoes
Cooking time: 3 – 5 min

Method

Remove eye from tomatoes and lightly score rounded surface in a criss-cross fashion. Place on lightly greased grilling tray, season with salt and pepper, brush with oil and grill steadily under salamander until cooked. Present for service brushed with melted butter and garnished with sprig of parsley.

N.B. Tomatoes may be skinned, left whole or cut into halves prior to grilling.

Grilled Mushrooms   Champignons Grillés

Yield: 4 portions 200 g (8 oz)
Cooking time: 3 – 5 min

Method

Remove stalks and peel if necessary. Place on lightly greased grilling tray and continue as for grilled tomatoes.

18

Combined Methods of Cookery

Extensions Involving a Combination of Cookery Principles as Applied to Meat and Fish Products

The aim of this study is to outline those products, which due to their mode of production, cannot be strictly classified under any one specific principle of cookery. These items are mainly produced by employing a combination of cookery methods. The more common examples are covered in this study and many of these preparations could be classified as rechauffé products.

Poultry

184
CHICKEN PIE (USING COOKED CHICKEN)   Volaille

Yield: 4 portions
Cooking time: 20 – 30 min
Cooking temperature: 205°C (400°F)

Unit	Ingredient	Metric	Imperial
1	Cooked chicken (large dice) (free from bone)	500 g	1¼ lb
³/₅	Chicken velouté	300 ml	12 fl oz
¹/₅	Cream	100 ml	4 fl oz
¹/₁₀	Onion medium dice	50 g	2 oz
¹/₂₀	Butter	25 g	1 oz
	Salt and pepper to taste		
★	Puff pastry		

★ Sufficient puff pastry for 4 portions approximately 200 g (8 oz) prepared weight.

Method

Sweat onions in butter without colour, add chicken, lightly season, moisten with sauce and cream. Bring to the boil, adjust seasoning and consistency then place filling into earthenware pie dish. Roll out puff pastry 3 mm (⅛ in) thick, moisten edge of pie dish and line with a strip of pastry. Moisten pastry edge and cover pie with remaining pastry. Take care not to stretch the pastry otherwise it will shrink and slide into pie dish during baking. Seal well, trim and decorate with pastry trimmings as required. Rest before baking to allow pastry to relax (avoids excess shrinkage during baking). Egg-wash for baking. Bake in oven until cooked and golden brown. Once cooked clean edges of pie dish and surround with pie collar for service.

Extensions of Chicken Pies: Added Ingredients to 1 Unit – 500 g (1¼ lb) of Cooked Chicken

Name of dish	Unit	Ingredient	Metric (g)	Imperial (oz)
Chicken and mushroom pie	⅕	Sliced sweated mushrooms Add to filling	100	4
Chicken and ham pie	⅕	Cooked ham (large dice) Add to filling	100	4
Chicken, ham and mushroom pie	⅕ ⅕	Sliced sweated mushrooms Cooked ham (large dice) Add to filling	100 100	4 4

N.B.   The above pies may also be prepared with cooked turkey.

For service single portions are often prepared in individual earthenware pots.

185
SALPICON OF CHICKEN   Salpicon de Volaille

Yield: 4 portions

Unit	Ingredient	Metric	Imperial
1	Cooked chicken (medium dice) (free from bone)	400 g	1 lb
⅝	Suprême or Madeira sauce (as required)	250 ml	10 fl oz
¹⁄₁₆	Butter	25 g	1 oz
	Salt and pepper to taste		

Method

Toss chicken in melted butter, lightly season and moisten with sauce. Bring to boil, correct seasoning and consistency, use as required.

Chicken Vol-au-Vent   Vol-au-Vent de Volaille

Method

Fill four baked hot vol-au-vent cases with hot chicken salpicon using suprême or Madeira sauce. Garnish as required.

Chicken Vol-au-Vent with Asparagus   Vol-au-Vent de Volaille Princesse

As above using suprême sauce and garnished with hot buttered asparagus tips.

Chicken and Mushroom Vol-au-Vent   Vol-au-Vent de Volaille et Champignon

As for chicken vol-au-vent with the addition of $^1/_5$ unit [(50 g (2 oz)] button mushrooms à blanc.
N.B.   Many other varieties may be prepared, e.g. chicken and ham.

186
CHICKEN PANCAKES   Crêpes de Volaille

Yield: 4 portions
Cooking time: 5 – 8 min
Cooking temperature: 205°C (400°F)

Unit	Ingredient	Metric	Imperial
1	Cooked chicken (medium dice free from bone)	400 g	1 lb
1	Suprême sauce	400 ml	16 fl oz
$^1/_{16}$	Butter	25 g	1 oz
	8 pancakes		
	Salt and pepper to taste		

Method

Sweat chicken quickly in melted butter, lightly season and moisten with half of the sauce to form a hot salpicon. Season to taste.

Stuff pancakes with salpicon, roll to cigar shape and lay in a lightly buttered gratin dish. Brush with melted butter and place in oven to heat thoroughly. Serve accompanied with a sauceboat of sauce suprême.

Chicken Pancakes with Asparagus   Crêpes de Volaille Princesse

As above but garnish pancakes with buttered asparagus tips.

Chicken and Mushroom Pancakes   Crêpes de Volaille et Champignon

As for chicken pancakes with addition of $^1/_5$ unit [50 g (2 oz)] sliced sweated mushrooms added to basic salpicon.

N.B.   Many other varieties of chicken pancakes can be prepared using different sauces and garnishes, e.g. curred chicken pancakes.

187
CHICKEN À LA KING   Émincé de Volaille à la King

Yield: 4 portions
Cooking time: 20 – 30 min

Unit	Ingredient	Metric	Imperial
1	Cooked chicken (cut into large dice on slant, free from bone)	500 g	1¼ lb
1	Sauce suprême (*see* p. 89)	500 ml	1 pt
¹/₅	Button mushroom (white)	100 g	4 oz
¹/₁₀	Pimentoes (diced)	50 g	2 oz
¹/₁₀	Butter	50 g	2 oz
¹/₂₀ 1	Egg yolk	25 g	1 oz
/₂₀	Sherry	25 g	1 oz
	Salt and pepper		
★	Rice pilaff		

★ Sufficient pilaff for 4 portions (*see* recipe 59).

Method

Sweat peppers in butter without colour. Add mushrooms and continue sweating until cooked. Add chicken, lightly season, moisten with sherry and sauce suprême. Bring to the boil, correct seasoning and consistency, simmer to heat the chicken thoroughly, remove from heat and add egg yolk. Present for service with rice pilaff.

Turkey à La King   Émincé de Dinde à la King

As above but replace chicken with cooked white turkey meat.

188
CHICKEN IN CURRY SAUCE (USING COOKED CHICKEN)   Cari de Volaille

Yield: 4 portions
Cooking time: 15 – 20 min

Unit	Ingredient	Metric	Imperial
1	Cooked chicken (large dice on slant, free from bone)	500 g	1¼ lb
1	Curry sauce (*see* recipe 15)	500 ml	1 pt
¹/₁₀	Butter	50 g	2 oz
	Salt to season		
★	Plain boiled rice		

★ Sufficient boiled rice for 4 portions (*see* recipe 57).

Method

Sweat chicken in melted butter without colour. Add sauce, bring to the boil, simmer to heat the chicken thoroughly, adjust seasoning and consistency. Serve accompanied with plain boiled rice and traditional curry accompaniments (*see* p. 256).

Beef   Boeuf

189
BASIC COOKED FILLING FOR STEAK PIES OR PUDDINGS

Yield: 4 portions
Cooking time: $1\frac{1}{2}$ – 2 hr

Unit	Ingredient	Metric (g)	Imperial (oz)
1	Stewing beef ($1\frac{1}{2}$ cm ($\frac{3}{4}$ in) dice)	600	20
$\frac{1}{5}$	Onion (diced)	120	4
$\frac{1}{20}$	Flour	30	1
$\frac{1}{20}$			
	Dripping	30	1
$\frac{1}{40}$	Tomato purée	15	$\frac{1}{2}$
	Salt and pepper to taste		
*	Brown stock		

* Sufficient to cover meat during cooking and form a lightly thickened sauce.

Method

Lightly season the meat and seal quickly in heated dripping, add onions and cook until light brown. Add flour to form a light brown roux, cool slightly and add tomato purée. Moisten with stock to cover meat, bring to boil to form a lightly thickened sauce. Cover with lid and simmer gently on stove top until meat is tender. Correct seasoning and consistency and use as required.

   N.B. During cooking stir periodically to prevent meat sticking to saucepan.
Cooking may be achieved by oven stewing in moderate heat.

Beefsteak Pies (using cooked filling)

Yield: Use 200 g (8 oz) of puff pastry
        or 200 g (8 oz) of flour prepared into short pastry for 4 portions
Baking time: 20 – 30 min
Cooking temperature: 205°C (400°F)

Method

Place filling in earthenware pie dish. Roll out pastry 3 mm ($\frac{1}{8}$ in) thick and proceed as for chicken pies (*see* recipe 184).

Beefsteak Puddings (using cooked filling)

Yield: Use 200 g (8 oz) of flour prepared into suet pastry for 4 portions
Steaming time: 1 hr

Method

Roll out two-thirds of suet pastry and line greased pudding basin. Place filling into lined basin, roll out remaining pastry and form a sealed lid. Cover with greased greaseproof paper and pudding cloth. Set to steam until pastry is cooked. Once cooked clean basin, surround with clean serviette and present for service.

Extensions of Cooked Filling for Steak Pies or Puddings: Added Ingredients to 1 – Unit 600 g (1¼ lb) of meat

Name of dish	Unit	Ingredient	Metric (g)	Imperial (oz)
Steak and mushroom pie/pudding	⅕	Sliced, sweated mushrooms Add to cooked filling	120	4
Steak and kidney pie/pudding	⅕	Diced ox-kidney Seal and cook with beef	120	4
Steak, kidney and mushroom pie/pudding	⅕ ⅕	Diced ox-kidney Sliced, sweated mushrooms Seal and cook kidney with beef and add mushrooms to cooked filling	120 120	4 4

190
BEEFSTEAK AND POTATO PIE

Yield: 4 portions
Stewing time: 1½ – 2 hr
Baking time: 20 – 30 min
Baking temperature: 205° (400°F)

Unit	Ingredient	Metric (g)	Imperial (oz)
1	Stewing beef (medium dice)	400	16
1	Potatoes (medium dice)	400	16
½	Onion (medium dice)	200	8
	Salt and pepper to taste		
★	White beef stock		
†	Short pastry		

★ Sufficient stock to cover meat and potatoes during cooking.

† Sufficient short pastry to cover pie during baking 200 g (8 oz) flour prepared into short pastry.

Method

Place onions and meat in saucepan and lightly season. Cover with stock, bring to boil, skim, cover with tight-fitting lid and stew gently on stove top until threequarters cooked. Add potatoes and continue cooking until meat is cooked and potatoes begin to fall. Correct seasoning and consistency. Place filling into earthenware pie dish, roll out pastry 3 mm (⅛ in) thick and proceed as for chicken pie (*see* recipe 184).

191
COTTAGE PIE

Yield: 4 portions
Baking time: 30 min
Baking temperature: 205°C (400°F)

Unit	Ingredient	Metric (g)	Imperial (oz)
1	Cooked beef (coarsely minced)	400	16
1	Duchess potatoes (prepared)	400	16
¼	Onion (brunoise)	100	4
¹⁄₁₆	Butter	25	1
	Salt and pepper to taste		
*	Jus lié		

* Sufficient jus lié to moisten the meat.

Method

Sweat onion in butter until light brown. Add cooked meat, moisten with jus lié, bring to boil and simmer to heat thoroughly. Adjust seasoning and consistency. Place in pie dish, decorate surface with piped duchess potato and place in oven to bake until thoroughly heated and golden brown. Remove from oven, clean dish and surround with pie collar for service.

192
MIROTON OF BEEF   Miroton de Boeuf

Yield: 4 portions
Cooking time: 20 min
Cooking temperature: 205°C (400°F)

Unit	Ingredient	Metric	Imperial
1	Sliced cooked beef	400	1 lb
⅝	Sauce lyonnaise (*see* p. 95)	250 ml	10 fl oz
¼	Onions (shredded)	100 g	4 oz
⅛	Butter	50 g	2 oz
⅛	White breadcrumbs	50 g	2 oz
	Salt and pepper to taste		
	Chopped parsley		

Method

Sweat onions in butter to golden brown, and lay in gratin dish. Arrange meat in neat overlapping slices on onions, lightly season and cover with heated sauce lyonnaise. Sprinkle with breadcrumbs and place in oven to heat thoroughly and gratinate for service. Once gratinated, present for service garnished with chopped parsley.

193
CORNED BEEF HASH CAKE

Yield: 4 portions
Cooking time: 8 – 10 min

Unit	Ingredient	Metric (g)	Imperial (oz)
1	Corned beef (coarsely chopped)	200	8
1	Dry mashed potatoes	200	8
$1/4$	Onion brunoise (sweated)	50	2
$1/8$	Egg yolk	25	1
	Salt and pepper to season		
	Chopped parsley		

Method

Combine all ingredients together and season to taste. Shape into small cakes and shallow fry in oil on both sides until golden brown.

  N.B.   This dish may also be prepared as a large cake in a frying pan.
When shaping use dusting flour to facilitate handling.

Lamb and Mutton   Agneau et Mouton

Shepherd's Pie

As for Cottage Pie (*see* recipe 191) but replace cooked beef with cooked lamb or mutton.

194
MOUSSAKA

Yield: 4 portions
Baking time: 30 min/1 hr
Cooking temperature: 205°C (400°F)

Unit	Ingredient	Metric	Imperial
	2 Large aubergines (peeled and thinly sliced)		
1	Cooked lamb or mutton (coarsely minced)	500 g	$1\,1/4$ lb
$2/5$	Tomatoes (sliced)	200 g	8 oz

1/5	Sauce jus lié or demi-glace	100 ml	4 fl oz
1/5	Onion brunoise	100 g	4 oz
1/10	Oil	50 ml	2 fl oz
1/10	Butter	50 g	2 oz
1/10	Grated cheese or white breadcrumbs	50 g	2 oz
1/20	Seasoned flour	25 g	1 oz
1/40	Tomato purée	12.5 g	1 oz
	Hint of garlic		
	Salt and pepper to taste		

Method

Preparation of Filling   Sweat onions in butter without colour, add meat, moisten with sauce, add tomato purée and hint of garlic, bring to boil and season to taste. Simmer for a few minutes to re-heat thoroughly.

Preparation of Aubergines   Pass sliced aubergines through seasoned flour and shallow fry quickly in hot oil on both sides then drain well.

Completion of Moussaka   Method 1. Arrange layer of aubergines on base of buttered fireproof dish. Cover with the filling, arrange a neat layer of sliced tomatoes and aubergine to cover the filling. Sprinkle with grated cheese or white breadcrumbs and bake in hot oven to heat thoroughly and gratinate.

N.B.   Alternatively the moussaka may be lightly coated with a layer of thin mornay sauce prior to baking.

Method 2. Arrange alternating layers of aubergine, tomatoes and meat filling in a greased mould, finishing with a layer of aubergine. Bake en bain-marie for approximately 1 hour and turn out of mould for service.

195
EPIGRAMMES OF LAMB'S BREAST   Poitrine d'Agneau en Épigrammes

Yield: 4 portions
Cooking time: 1½ hr
Frying time: 5 – 10 min

Unit	Ingredient	Metric	Imperial
1	Breast of lamb (skinned and trimmed)	600 g	1¼ lb
1/5	Mirepoix (left whole)	120 g	4 oz
1/10	Oil	60 ml	2 fl oz
	Bouquet garni		
	Seasoning		
	Seasoned flour		
	Egg-wash		
	Breadcrumbs for pané		
*	White stock		

* Sufficient stock to cover meat during boiling of lamb.

Method

Place meat and vegetables into cooking vessel and cover with white stock. Bring to boil, skim, add bouquet garni and seasoning. Cover with lid and simmer until lamb is tender approximately 1½ hours. Once cooked remove lamb from stock, bone out and press under light weight until cold and set. Cut into selected shape e.g. squares or diamonds, pané and shallow fry in oil until thoroughly re-heated and golden brown on both sides. Present and serve as for panéed lamb cutlets (p. 227). Traditionally épigrammes are served with lamb cutlets as an integral part of the dish.

Pork   Porc

196
SCOTCH EGGS

Yield: 4 portions
Frying time: 8 – 10 min
Frying temperature: 175 – 190°C (350 – 375°F)

Unit	Ingredient	Metric	Imperial
	4 Hard-boiled eggs (shelled)		
1	Pork sausagemeat	400 g	1 lb
	Seasoned flour		
	Eggwash		
	Breadcrumbs for pané		

Method

Pass eggs through seasoned flour, envelop each egg in sausage meat and seal well. Pané, deep fry until thoroughly cooked and golden brown. Serve hot on flat with dish paper.
  N.B. May be served cold with salad.

197
GRILLED PIG'S TROTTERS WITH DEVILLED SAUCE   Pieds de Porc
                                                 Grillés Diable

Yield: 4 portions
Grilling time: 8 – 10 min

Unit	Ingredient	Metric	Imperial
	4 Pig's trotters (boiled *see* recipe 76)		
1	Sauce diable	250 ml	10 fl oz
⅕	Melted butter	50 g	2 oz
⅒	White breadcrumbs	25 g	1 oz
	Diluted English mustard		
	Salt and pepper to taste		

Method

Lightly season trotters, brush with mustard, melted butter and roll in breadcrumbs. Place on to prepared grilling tray and grill under salamander turning to heat thoroughly and colour golden brown. Arrange on service flat and accompany with devilled sauce.

198
BRAISED HAM (Gammons are often used) WITH MADEIRA

Jambon Braisé au Madère

Applied to whole hams or gammons
Yield: 600 g (1½ lb) raw wt off bone ⎫
            800 g (2 lb) raw wt on bone ⎬ = 4 portions
Boiling time: 20 min per 400 g (1 lb)
Braising time: 45 – 60 min
Oven temperature: 190°C (375°F)

Unit	Ingredient	Metric	Imperial
	Whole ham or gammon (as required)		
1	Madeira	250 ml	10 fl oz
⅕	Soft brown sugar	50 g	2 oz
★	Demi-glace		

★ Allow ¼ l (½ pt) for every four portions.

Method

Boil selected joint until almost cooked. Remove from cooking liquor and trim away skin and excess fat. Score and place into braising vessel, moisten with Madeira and sprinkle surface of joint with sugar. Place in oven to complete cooking. Baste frequently with Madeira to form a glaze with sugar. Once cooked and glazed remove joint from oven and allow to set for carving. To form sauce add demi-glace to cooking liquor, degrease then adjust seasoning and consistency. Pass through fine chinois. For service carve ham into thin slices, place on to service dish and lightly coat with sauce.

Braised Ham with Madeira and Spinach

Jambon Braisé Florentine

As above but place carved ham slices on to a bed of buttered, cooked leaf spinach before coating lightly with sauce.

Baked Ham in Pastry

Jambon en Croûte

Boil selected ham or gammon joint until cooked (*see* recipe 74). Remove from cooking liquor, trim away skin and excess fat and allow surface of joint to cool. Envelop joint in rolled out short or puff pastry and place pastry join/seal down on to a greased baking sheet. Decorate with pastry trimmings, brush liberally with egg wash and cut out small steam vent. Bake until pastry is golden brown and cooked. For service, carve ham and serve accompanied with a piece of pastry and a suitable sauce, e.g. madeira.
N.B.   As a guide use 50 g (2 oz) prepared pastry per portion.

Sugar Baked Hams

Method

Boil selected ham or gammon joint until cooked (*see* recipe 74), remove from cooking liquor, trim away skin and excess fat. Score criss-cross fashion and stud with cloves. Sprinkle with soft brown sugar, place into cooking vessel and bake in hot oven (205°C(400°F) until glazed to rich golden-brown colour. Remove joint from oven and allow to set for carving.

Sugar Baked Ham with Peaches or Pineapple

Serve carved ham with a portion of glazed peach or pineapple and accompany with suitable sauce, e.g. Madeira, hot Cumberland sauce, sweet and sour sauce, etc.

   N.B.   *To glaze fruit* Dust poached peach halves or pineapple rings with icing sugar and glaze under salamander.

Alternative Method of Glazing Hams

Combine soft brown sugar with a little flour, moisten with a few drops of cold water to form a paste. Spread paste over surface of ham before glazing in a hot oven.

Deep-Fried Cooked Meats

199
BASIC COOKED FORCEMEAT

Yield: 4 portions
Cooking time: 4 – 6 min
Frying temperature: 175 – 190°C (350 – 375°F)

Unit	Ingredient	Metric	Imperial
1	Selected cooked meat (coarsley minced or small dice)	250 g	10 oz
$\frac{1}{2}$	Chicken velouté or béchamel (to bind)	125 ml	5 fl oz
$\frac{1}{10}$	Egg yolk	25 g	1 oz
	Chopped parsley		
	Nutmeg (pinch)		
	Salt and pepper		

Method

Place meat in a cooking vessel, bind with velouté, bring to the boil to form a stiff mixture. Remove from heat, add yolks, nutmeg, parsley and season to taste. Spread mixture on to a buttered tray, allow to cool and set. When set, scale off to required weight, mould into required shape, pané then re-shape neatly. Deep fry until thoroughly re-heated and golden brown. Serve garnished with deep fried parsley and accompany with selected sauce (see chart).

Examples of Shapes

(a) *Croquettes* — small cylinders (2 per portion)

(b) *Cutlets – Côtelettes* – mould into cutlet shape, insert blanched macaroni to imitate a cutlet bone. Once fried garnish with 'mock' bone and dress with cutlet frill (1 – 2 per portion).

(c) *Balls* – moulded into neat spheres (2 per portion).

Examples of Dishes Prepared Using Above Formula

English term	Main meat and added ingredients	Example of sauces to accompany	French term
Beef croquettes	Cooked beef	Devilled sauce/Sauce Diable	Croquettes de Boeuf
Chicken cutlets/ Croquettes	Cooked chicken	Piquant sauce/Sauce Piquante	Côtelettes/Croquettes de Volaille
Chicken and ham cutlets/Croquettes	Equal quantities of cooked chicken and ham	Chasseur sauce/Sauce Chasseur	Côtelettes/Croquettes de Volaille et Jambon
Chicken and mushroom cutlets/ Croquettes	Cooked chicken plus $\frac{1}{5}$ unit 50 g (2 oz) sweated chopped mushroom	Madeira sauce/Sauce Madère	Côtelettes/Croquettes de Volaille et Champignon
Game cutlets/ Croquettes	Cooked game	Port wine sauce and redcurrant jelly/ Sauce au Porto	Côtelettes/Croquettes de Gibier

N.B. Drain deep-fried products well and place on dish papers to absorb any excess grease. The above cutlets may be shallow fried.

Kromeskis Russian Style   Cromesquis à la Russe

Prepare basic cooked forcemeat (recipe 199) using a combination of cooked *chicken* and cooked *tongue*, use a quarter the amount of tongue to chicken. Shape into croquettes and wrap each one in a thin slice of *streaky bacon*. Pass through seasoned flour and batter, deep fry until thoroughly heated and golden brown. Garnish with deep-fried parsley and serve accompanied with suitable sauce, e.g. Sauce Smitane, Sauce Tomate.

200
DURHAM CUTLETS

Yield: 4 portions
Cooking time: 4 – 6 min
Frying temperature: 175 – 190°C (350 – 375°F)

Unit	Ingredient	Metric (g)	Imperial (oz)
1	Cooked beef (minced)	200	8
$\frac{1}{2}$	Dry mashed potato	100	4
$\frac{1}{4}$	Onion (brunoise, sweated)	50	2
$\frac{1}{8}$	Egg yolk	25	1
	Chopped parsley		
	Seasoning		

Method

Combine all ingredients thoroughly to form a stable mixture, season to taste. Divide into four portions and shape into cutlets. Pané, reshape, insert blanched macaroni to imitate a cutlet bone. Deep fry until thoroughly heated and golden brown. Serve garnished with deep fried picked parsley. Accompany with a suitable sauce, e.g. jus lié.

N.B. May be shallow fried.

201
RISSOLES

Yield: 4 portions
Cooking time: 5 – 8 min
Frying temperature: 175 – 190°C (350 – 375°F)

Unit	Ingredient	Metric (g)	Imperial (oz)
1*	Cooked meat (coarsely minced)	100	4
$\frac{1}{4}$	Whole egg (beaten)	25	1
$\frac{1}{4}$	Onion brunoise (sweated without colour)	25	1
	Chopped parsley/picked parsley		
	Seasoning		
†	Puff pastry (trimmings may be used)		

* Cooked beef is often used but a variety of cooked meats is acceptable.
† Sufficient pastry for 4 portions, i.e. 200 g (8 oz) at prepared weight.

Method

Combine meat, onion, egg, chopped parsley, and seasoning to form a stable mixture. Divide into four portions. Roll out pastry thinly and cut into four 11 cm (4½ in) squares approximately. Water wash edges, place filling in centre and fold corner to corner to form a triangular shape. Seal edges well. Deep fry until pastry is cooked and golden brown. Drain well and serve garnished with deep fried picked parsley. Accompany with suitable sauce, e.g. jus lié.

202
RUSSIAN FISH PIE   Coulibiac de Saumon à la Russe

Yield: 4 portions
Cooking time: 30 – 40 min
Cooking temperature: 205°C (400°F)

Unit	Ingredient	Metric	Imperial
1	Cooked salmon	300 g	12 oz
¼*	Rice pilaff	75 g	3 oz
¼	Sliced mushrooms (sweated without colour)	75 g	3 oz
¼	Fish velouté	75 ml	3 fl oz
⅛	Vesiga	37.5 g	1½ oz
	1 Chopped hard boiled egg		
	Chopped parsley		
	Seasoning		
†	Puff pastry		

* Indicates amount of raw rice used to prepare pilaff.
† Sufficient for 4 portions, i.e. 250 g (10 oz) approximately, at prepared weight.

Method

Soak vesiga overnight in cold water, boil in lightly salted water for 2 – 3 hours until tender. Refresh and cut into medium dice ready for use. Roll out pastry into a rectangle of approximately 40 cm × 25 cm × 3 mm (15 in × 10 in × ⅛ in). Combine together rice,

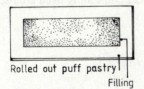
Rolled out puff pastry
Filling

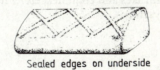
Sealed edges on underside

mushrooms, vesiga, hard boiled egg, chopped parsley, velouté and season to taste. Place half of this mixture along the centre of the rolled out pastry. Follow with the salmon and complete with a layer of the rice mixture. Moisten pastry edges and fold the pastry over to totally enclose the filling. Place on to lightly greased baking sheet with sealed edges underneath. Decorate with pastry trimmings, egg wash and rest before baking. Bake until cooked and golden brown and serve accompanied with a suitable sauce, e.g. beurre fondue, sauce hollandaise.

    N.B.   Classically this product is prepared using brioche pastry.

Russian Chicken Pie

Coulibiac de Volaille à la Russe

Prepared in the same manner as for Russian fish pie (*see* recipe 202) but substitute cooked salmon with diced cooked chicken, and fish velouté with chicken velouté.

Fish

Poisson

203
FISH PIE

Yield: 4 portions
Cooking time: 30 minutes
Cooking temperature: 205°C (400°F)

Unit	Ingredient	Metric	Imperial
1	Cooked flaked fish (free from bone and skin)	400 g	1 lb
1	Duchess potatoes (prepared)	400 g	1 lb
5/8	Béchamel or fish velouté	250 ml	10 fl oz
1/10	Melted butter	25 g	1 oz
	Chopped parsley		
	Salt and pepper to taste		

Method

Lightly butter pie-dish. Boil sauce, correct seasoning and consistency and add chopped parsley to garnish and flavour. Coat base of pie dish with layer of sauce, add flaked fish, lightly season and moisten with remaining sauce. Pipe duchess potatoes over surface to cover the fish. Sprinkle with melted butter and bake in oven until thoroughly heated and golden brown for service.

Salpicon of Fish

Salpicon de Poisson

A term used to define a single or variety of cooked flaked fish cohered with a selected sauce to form a moist fish filling. Such preparations are used when preparing vol-au-vents, savoury pancakes and coquilles, etc. The sauces commonly used are fish based, e.g. fish velouté derivatives.

204

Yield: 4 portions

Unit	Ingredient	Metric	Imperial
1	Selected flaked cooked fish	400 g	1 lb
5/8	Selected sauce (fish velouté based)	250 ml	10 fl oz
	Butter		
	Seasoning		

Method

Re-heat fish in melted butter, season and moisten with sauce, bring to boil, correct seasoning and consistency. Use as required.

Fish Vol-au-Vents

Vol-au-Vent de Poisson

Method

Fill four baked hot vol-au-vent cases with hot salpicon of fish, garnish as required and serve immediately.

Fish Vol-au-Vent with Asparagus

Vol-au-Vent de Poisson Princesse

Method

As above garnished with buttered asparagus tips.

Seafood Vol-au-Vent

Vol-au-Vent de Fruits de Mer

Method

As for Vol-au-Vent de Poisson using a selection of fish and shellfish.

N.B.   Many varieties of Vol-au-Vent may be prepared using selected fish/shellfish and a suitable sauce.

205
FISH IN SCALLOP SHELL
(use four scallop shells)

Coquilles de Poisson

Yield: 4 portions
Cooking time: 8 – 10 min
Cooking temperature: 205°C (400°F)

Unit	Ingredient	Metric	Imperial
1	Selected flaked cooked fish	400 g	1 lb
1	Fish velouté	400 ml	16 fl oz
$^{3}/_{4}$	Duchess potatoes (prepared)	300 g	12 oz
$^{1}/_{8}$	Cream	50 ml	2 fl oz
$^{1}/_{16}$	Egg yolk	25 g	1 oz
	Seasoning		

Method

Pipe border of duchess potatoes around the edge of the scallop shells. Place under salamander to set potatoes and lightly colour. Form a salpicon with fish and half of the sauce, season to taste. Fill shells with salpicon, add yolk and cream to remaining sauce and napper fish. Place in oven to heat thoroughly and glaze brown. Present for service on flat with dish paper.

N.B. Adjust coating sauce to light-coating consistency for use.

Fish in Scallop Shell with Cheese   Coquilles de Poisson Mornay

As above but using fish mornay sauce.

Seafood in Scallop Shell   Coquilles de Fruits de Mer

As for Coquilles de Poisson using a selection of fish and shellfish.
   N.B.   Other varieties of coquilles may be prepared using selected fish/shellfish and a suitable sauce.

206
SAVOURY PANCAKE BATTER   Appareil à Crêpe

Yield: 4 portions (8 pancakes)

Unit	Ingredient	Metric	Imperial
1	Milk	250 ml	10 fl oz
$^2/_5$	Flour	100 g	4 oz
$^1/_5$	Whole egg (beaten)	50 g	2 oz
$^1/_{20}$	Oil	12.5 ml	$^1/_2$ fl oz
	Seasoning		
	Chopped parsley		

Method

Sift flour and seasoning into mixing bowl. Form a well, pour in beaten egg and milk. Whisk ingredients together to form a smooth pancake batter. Add chopped parsley and whisk in the oil.

Cooking of Pancakes   Coat base of pancake pan with film of oil and heat on stove top. Pour off excess oil and add sufficient batter to form a thin pancake. Cook pancake on both sides to golden brown. Turn out ready for use.

207
FISH PANCAKES   Crêpes de Poisson

Yield: 4 portions
Cooking time: 10 min
Cooking temperature: 205°C (400°F)

Unit	Ingredient	Metric	Imperial
1	Fish velouté	500 ml	1 pt
$^4/_5$	Selected, flaked cooked fish	400 g	1 lb
$^1/_{20}$	Egg yolk	25 g	1 oz
$^1/_{20}$	Cream	25 ml	1 fl oz
	8 Pancakes		
	Salt and pepper to taste		

Method

Form hot salpicon with fish and half of the sauce, season to taste. Stuff pancakes, roll cigar shape and lay into lightly buttered gratin dish. Adjust seasoning and consistency of remaining sauce, add egg yolk, cream and mask pancakes. Place in oven to heat thoroughly and glaze brown for service.

Fish Pancakes with Bercy Sauce   Crêpes de Poisson Bercy

As for Crêpes de Poisson using Sauce Bercy.

Crab Pancakes with Thermidor Sauce   Crêpes de Crabe Thermidor

As for Crêpes de Poisson but using a salpicon of crab with Sauce Thermidor. Gratinate with grated parmesan.

N.B. Other varieties of pancakes may be prepared using selected fish/shellfish and suitable sauce.

208
CURRIED PRAWNS   Cari de Crevettes Roses

Yield: 4 portions
Cooking time: 5 min

Unit	Ingredient	Metric	Imperial
1	Peel cooked prawns	300 g	10 oz
1	Curry sauce (*see* recipe 15)	300 ml	10 oz
1	Boiled rice	300 g	10 oz
$1/_{10}$	Butter	30 g	1 oz

Method

Sauté prawns in butter, add curry sauce and simmer for a few minutes to thoroughly heat. Serve accompanied with plain boiled rice.

209
FISH KEDGEREE

Yield: 4 portions
Cooking time: 25 min

Unit	Ingredient	Metric	Imperial
1	Selected flaked cooked fish	400 g	1 lb
1	Curry sauce (heated)	400 ml	16 fl oz
	2 Hard boiled egg (quartered)		
$1/_8$	Butter	50 g	2 oz
	Salt to taste		
*	Rice pilaff		

* Sufficient for 4 portions (*see* recipe 59)

Method

Sauté flaked fish quickly in melted butter, add rice and heat thoroughly. Present in buttered service dish and decorate with egg. Serve accompanied with a sauceboat of heated curry sauce.

210
LOBSTER IN CHEESE SAUCE   Homard Mornay

Yield: 4 portions
Cooking time: 8 – 10 min

Unit	Ingredient	Metric	Imperial
	2 Boiled lobsters (medium sized)		
1	Fish mornay sauce	500 ml	1 pt
$1/_{10}$	Butter	50 g	2 oz
	Salt and cayenne pepper to taste		
	Grated parmesan to gratinate		
	Four sprigs of parsley		

Method

Split lobsters lengthways and remove flesh from tail and claws, slice tail meat leaving claw meat whole. Clean shell and dry for use. Sweat lobster meat in butter without colour, lightly season and cohere with a little mornay sauce, remove from heat. Pour a little sauce into base of lobster shells, add lobster placing claw meat into the head cavity. Napper with remaining sauce, sprinkle with grated parmesan and gratinate until golden brown. Present for service on a dish paper and flat, garnished with picked parsley.

211
LOBSTER NEWBURG   Homard Newburg

Yield: 4 portions
Cooking time: 5 – 8 min

Unit	Ingredient	Metric	Imperial
	2 Boiled lobsters (medium sized)		
1	Cream (double)	250 ml	10 fl oz
$1/_5$	Butter	50 g	2 oz
$1/_5$	Madeira	50 ml	2 fl oz
$1/_{10}$	Brandy	25 ml	1 fl oz
	Salt and pepper to taste		
*	Rice pilaff		
	Salt and pepper to taste		

* Sufficient rice pilaff for 4 portions (recipe 59)

Method

Mix egg yolk with a little of the cream to form a liaison and put aside. Remove lobster meat from tail and claws. Cut tail into thick pieces, leaving claw meat whole. Gently sweat lobster in butter, lightly season, flame with brandy, add Madeira and reduce by a half. Pour on the cream, bring to boil and simmer briskly to coating consistency. Correct seasoning, remove from heat, stir in liaison and do not reboil.

Where possible serve rice and lobster in separate timbales decorating lobster with head and tail shell. N.B. Lobster Newburg may be garnished with slices of truffle flavoured with brandy.

Lobster in Thermidor Sauce   Homard Thermidor

Proceed as for Homard Mornay using thermidor sauce (p. 92), garnish with the addition of 4 truffle slices.

212
LOBSTER CARDINAL   Homard Cardinal

Yield: 4 portions
Cooking time: 8 – 10 min

Unit	Ingredient	Metric	Imperial
	2 Boiled lobsters (medium sized)		
1	Lobster sauce (recipe 21)	250 ml	10 fl oz
$1/5$	Butter	50 g	2 oz
$1/5$	Mushrooms (cooked small dice)	50 g	2 oz
$1/5$	Cream } liaison	50 ml	2 fl oz
$1/5$	Egg yolk }	50 g	2 oz
$1/10$	Brandy	25 ml	1 oz
$1/10$	Parmesan (grated)	25 g	1 oz
	Picked parsley		
	Pinch of salt and pepper		
	4 slices of truffle		

Method

Split lobsters lengthways and remove flesh from tail and claws, slice tail meat and leave claw meat whole. Clean shell and dry for use. Re-heat lobster meat and mushrooms in butter without colour, lightly season, flame with brandy and cohere with a little of the lobster sauce to form a salpicon. Bring remaining lobster sauce to the boil, remove from heat, add liaison of egg yolks/cream and correct seasoning. Moisten base of lobster shells with sauce, fill with salpicon of lobster and mushrooms, placing claw meat into the head cavity. Napper with remaining sauce, sprinkle with grated parmesan and gratinate to golden brown. Present for service on a dish paper and service flat, garnished with truffle and picked parsley.

213
DEEP-FRIED FISH CAKES   Médaillons de Poisson Frits

Yield: 4 portions
Cooking time: 4 – 6 min
Frying temperature: 175 – 190°C (350 – 375°F)

Unit	Ingredient	Metric (g)	Imperial (oz)
1	Cooked white fish (free from bone and skin)	200	8
³/₄	Dry mashed potato (cooked weight)	150	6
¹/₈	Whole egg (beaten)	25	1
	Chopped parsley		
	Anchovy essence		
	Seasoning		

Method

Flake fish and mix with potato. Add parsley, few drops anchovy essence, bind with egg and season to taste. Divide into four equal pieces, shape in médaillons, pané and deep fry until thoroughly reheated and golden brown. Serve accompanied with a suitable sauce, e.g. tomato, tartare or parsley sauce, etc.

Deep-Fried Salmon Fish Cakes   Médaillons de Saumon Frits

As above but substitute white cooked fish with cooked salmon.
  N.B.   Fish cakes may be shallow fried.

Snails   Escargots

Cooked snails are readily available in a canned form. The shells are packed separately and sold with each tin of snails. These commercial snails are ideal for use in the kitchen.

Snails with Garlic Butter   Escargots au Beurre d'Ail

Yield: 6 snails per portion

Method

Place snails into shells and fill with garlic butter (*see* p. 111). Place on to snail dish with shell cavity facing upwards. Quickly heat through in a hot oven [205°C (400°F)] for a few minutes. Present for service.

19

Vegetable Extensions Involving a Combination of Cookery Principles

Introduction

The aim of this study is to outline those vegetable products, which due to their mode of production, cannot be strictly classified under any one specific principle of cookery. These items are produced by employing a combination of cookery methods. The more common examples are covered.

214
DUCHESS POTATO MIXTURE

This is a basic potato mixture, which is used to prepare a wide variety of potato products.
Yield: 4 portions

Unit	Ingredient	Metric	Imperial
1	Snow potatoes (well dried p.186)	400 g	1 lb
$^{1}/_{16}$	Butter	25 g	1 oz
$^{1}/_{16}$	Egg yolk	25 g	1 oz
	Seasoning		
	Pinch of nutmeg		

Method

Combine all ingredients, mix thoroughly, season to taste and use as required.

Extensions of Duchess Potatoes: Preparation and Added Ingredients in Relation to 1 Unit i.e. 400 g (1 lb) Duchess Mixture

Baked varieties into 4 portions

English term	Unit	Ingredient	Metric	Imperial	French term
Duchess potatoes		Fill piping bag and star tube with basic mixture. Pipe 5 cm (2 in) cones on to lightly greased baking sheets. Set in moderately hot oven 205°C (400°F) for a few minutes, egg wash and continue baking until golden brown and thoroughly heated (approximately 5–8 min)			Pommes Duchesse
Rosette potatoes		As for duchess but pipe into small rosettes			Pommes Rosette
Brioche potatoes		Mould basic mixture into spheres and form into small cottage loaf shapes. Proceed as for duchess potatoes			Pommes Brioche
Marquise potatoes	$\frac{1}{4}$	Tomates concassées	100 g	4 oz	Pommes Marquise
		Using a piping bag and star tube, pipe potato nests directly on to a greased baking sheet. Fill centre of nests with tomates concassées and proceed as for duchess potatoes			
Chester potatoes	$\frac{1}{8}$	Grated Cheshire cheese	50 g	2 oz	Pommes Chester
		4 Thin slices Cheshire cheese			
		Combine grated cheese with basic duchess potato mixture and shape into small round potato cakes [1 cm ($\frac{3}{8}$ in) thick]. Place on to lightly greased baking sheet and brush with beaten egg. Lay cheese slices on to potato cakes, bake in moderately hot oven [205°C (400°F)] until golden brown and thoroughly heated (approximately 5–8 min)			

Deep-Fried Varieties

Croquette potatoes		Shape basic duchess mixture into small cylinders, pané and deep fry for service			Pommes Croquettes

Almond potatoes		Divide basic duchess mixture and shape into eight small pears. Pané with a mixture of almonds and breadcrumbs. Decorate top of potato with whole almonds and deep fry for service			Pommes Amandines
Berny potatoes		Combine a garnish of finely chopped truffle with basic duchess mixture. Proceed as for Pommes Amandine but shape mixture into small apricots. Decorate with a piece of parsley stem to represent apricot stalk. Deep fry for service			Pommes Berny
Royal or St. Florentine potatoes	$\frac{1}{4}$	Finely chopped cooked ham	100 g	4 oz	Pommes Royale/St. Florentin
		Combine ham with basic duchesse mixture, shape into small rectangles and pané with a mixture of breadcrumbs and pasta vermicelli. Deep fry for service			
Dauphine potatoes	$\frac{1}{2}$	Choux pastry (net wt)	200 g	8 oz	Pommes Dauphine
		Combine pastry with basic duchess mixture. Mould into small balls or shape oval with oiled tablespoons. Deep fry for service. N.B. May be placed on to strips of oiled greaseproof paper to store prior to frying			
Lorette potatoes	$\frac{1}{2}$	Choux pastry (net wt)	200 g	8 oz	Pommes Lorette
	$\frac{1}{16}$	Grated parmesan	25 g	1 oz	
		Combine choux pastry and cheese with duchess mixture. Mould into cigar shapes and proceed as for pommes dauphine			
Elizabeth potatoes	$\frac{1}{2}$	Choux pastry net wt)	200 g	8 oz	Pommes Elisabeth
	$\frac{1}{8}$	Cooked spinach (dry)	50 g	2 oz	
		Combine pastry with basic duchess mixture and shape into small balls. Depress to form a cavity. Fill with spinach and reshape to seal. Proceed as for dauphine potatoes			

Shallow-Fried Varieties

Galette potatoes	Shape basic duchess mixture into small potato cakes. Shallow fry on both sides and serve	Pommes Galette

Extensions of Boiled/Steamed Potatoes in Jackets: Preparation and Added Ingredients in Relation to 1 Unit i.e. 400 g (1 lb) Boiled Potatoes

215

Yield: 400 g (1 lb) 4 portions
Cooking time: 15–20 min

Method
Boil/steam scrubbed jacket potatoes until almost cooked, drain well, cool and peel for use.

English term	Unit	Ingredient	Metric	Imperial	French term
Shallow-fried potatoes		Cut cooked potatoes into ¹/₂ cm (¹/₈ in) thick slices. Shallow fry in hot fat and toss to brown evenly. Season to taste, then sprinkle with chopped parsley for service			Pommes Sautées
Garlic-flavoured shallow-fried potatoes		As for Pommes Sautées but flavour with chopped garlic during cooking. Brush lightly with garlic butter and sprinkle with chopped parsley for service			Pommes Provençale
Shallow-fried potatoes with onions	¹/₂	Onions (sliced and sautéed)	200 g	8 oz	Pommes Lyonnaise
		Proceed as for Pommes Sautées, when potatoes are almost cooked add sautéed onions and toss to mix. Season to taste, then sprinkle with chopped parsley for service			
		Thinly slice/coarsely grate cooked potatoes. Lightly season and place into a buttered omelet pan to form a loose textured cake. Shallow fry to colour both sides and until thoroughly heated. Serve as required.			Pommes Roesti

Extension of Plain Boiled Potatoes: 1 unit 400 g (1 lb) boiled potatoes

English term	Method of cooking	French term
Shallow-fried turned potatoes	Select the plain boiled turned potatoes and drain well. Shallow fry in hot fat and toss to brown evenly. Season to taste. Sprinkle with chopped parsley for service	Pommes Rissolées
Shallow-fried new potatoes	As above using plain boiled new potatoes	Pommes Nouvelles Rissolées

Vegetables Tossed in Butter   Légumes Sautées au Beurre

Boiled and refreshed vegetables are lightly seasoned then quickly shallow-fried in butter to re-heat for service. In some instances the vegetables take on faint brown tinge as a result of this process.

Vegetables commonly reheated by this method are listed below.

English term	*French term*
Artichoke bottoms (à blanc)	Fonds d'Artichauts Sautés au Beurre
Beans (French)	Haricots Verts Sautés au Beurre
Brussels sprouts	Choux de Bruxelles Sautés au Beurre
Cauliflower	Chou-fleur Sauté au Beurre
Celeriac	Céleri-rave Sauté au Beurre
Oyster plant/salsify	Salsifis Sauté au Beurre
Parsnips	Panais Sautés au Beurre
Spinach (leaf)	Épinard en Branche Sauté au Beurre

During shallow frying the flavour of the vegetables may be enhanced by the addition of other ingredients. These ingredients may also improve the appearance of the finished product. Common examples include the following.

Vegetables Tossed in Butter with Herbs   Légumes Sautés aux Fines Herbes

During cooking sprinkle vegetable with fine herbs.
  Suitable for use with: artichoke bottoms, cauliflower, salsify, parsnips, celeriac, etc.

Vegetables Tossed in Butter with Chestnuts   Légumes Sautés Limousine

During cooking add pieces of cooked chestnuts (recipe 152).
  Suitable for use with: artichoke bottoms and Brussels sprouts.

Vegetables Tossed in Butter Polonesian Style   Légumes Sautés Polonaise

During cooking sprinkle the vegetable with sieved hard-boiled egg, chopped parsley and fried breadcrumbs and finish with beurre noisette.
  Suitable for use with: Brussels sprouts and cauliflower.

Independent Vegetable Preparations Involving Combined Methods

216
STUFFED ARTICHOKE BOTTOMS WITH CHEESE   Fonds d'Artichauts
Farcis au Gratin

Yield: 4 portions
Baking time: 5 – 8 min
Cooking temperature: 175°C (350°F)

Unit	Ingredient	Metric	Imperial
	4 large or 8 small cooked artichoke bottoms (à blanc)		
1	Cheese sauce	250 ml	10 fl oz
$4/_5$	Duxelle	200 g	8 oz
$1/_5$	Grated cheese	50 g	2 oz
	Seasoning		

Method
Season artichoke bottoms and place in buttered gratin dish. Fill with duxelle, coat with cheese sauce and sprinkle with grated cheese. Bake in oven to reheat thoroughly and glaze. Serve as required.

Artichoke Bottoms Stuffed with Spinach   Fonds d'Artichauts Florentine

As above but replace duxelle with dry spinach purée.

217
STUFFED EGG PLANT   Aubergine Farcie au Gratin

Yield: 4 portions
Baking time: 8 – 10 min
Cooking temperature: 175°C (350°F)

Unit	Ingredient	Metric	Imperial
	2 Medium egg plants		
1	Duxelle	200 g	8 oz
$1/_8$	White breadcrumbs	25 g	1 oz
	Seasoning		

Method
Cut aubergines into halves lengthways, score the pulp criss-cross fashion and shallow or deep fry in hot oil until the pulp softens. Remove the pulp leaving the skin intact, chop

pulp and combine with duxelle. Adjust seasoning and fill skins with mixture. Sprinkle with breadcrumbs, place into a buttered gratin dish, bake in oven to thoroughly reheat and gratinate. Serve as required.

218
SHALLOW-FRIED CORN CAKES Galettes de Maïs Sautées

Yield: 4 portions
Cooking time: 3–5 min

Unit	Ingredient	Metric (g)	Imperial (oz)
1	Corn kernels (boiled)	200	8
1/4	Egg	50	2
1/8	Flour	25	1
	Seasoning		

Method

Beat egg, mix with corn and lightly season. Add flour and mix thoroughly to form a cohered mixture.
Drop small portions of mixture into frying pan and lightly press to form corn cakes. Fry on both sides until cooked and golden brown. Serve as required.

N.B. Tinned or frozen corn kernels may be used.

219
BUBBLE AND SQUEAK

Yield: 4 portions
Cooking time: 8–10 min

Unit	Ingredient	Metric	Imperial
1	Cabbage (cooked and chopped)	200 g	8 oz
1	Mash potatoes (dry)	200 g	8 oz
1/4	Melted bacon fat	50 ml	2 fl oz
	Pinch of salt and pepper		

Method

Combine cabbage, potato and season to taste. Shape in small cakes and shallow fry in bacon fat on both sides until golden brown. Often served at breakfast time.
N.B. This product may also be prepared by forming a large cake in a frying pan.

20

Savouries and Hot Hors D'Oeuvres

In English cookery savouries denote a range of products that are served near the end of a meal. These items have never gained the popularity on the continent, which they enjoy on English menus and in the United States of America.

Mainly they are comprised of various preparations (fish, meat, cheese, eggs, etc.), carefully prepared and neatly served on croûtes of toasted bread or in pastry cases. As they are served near the end of the meal they are of a light nature, and in the main highly seasoned, often being prepared with the addition of mustard, cayenne pepper and Worcester sauce, etc.

In addition, these products may be served prior to the main meal as hot hors d'oeuvres or hot canapés (see below). They are also becoming increasingly popular for use in the more modern type of fast-food operation, e.g. snack bar, bistro, motorway operation. In these instances they can be served as a snack 24 hours a day and in many cases are cooked to order.

Where a traditional kitchen brigade is employed the following Chefs de Partie are involved:

Chef Garde-Manger — basic preparation of fish, meats, etc.
Chef Rôtisseur — cooking and service of most savouries.

Savouries are usually cooked to order to ensure freshness. They are widely employed when planning à la carte, luncheon and dinner menus. For service savouries are dressed neatly on flats with dish papers and may be garnished with bunches of picked parsley where appropriate.

The savouries listed in this study are examples of those that are most commonly employed when compiling modern menus. It must be noted, however, that many other such products may be prepared, this being dependent upon local needs as well as the cook's flair and creative ability.

Hot Hors d'Oeuvres and Hot Canapés

These products may be defined as small savoury items prepared from a wide range of foods, which are cooked and presented in a variety of ways.

In addition to the canapés listed in this study, other examples of hot hors d'oeuvres may include the following: deep-fried goujons of fish, pork or chicken fritots, deep-fried savoury croquettes, vegetable fritters, savoury bouchées and choux pastry cases. Such preparations are served for hot finger buffets and also at cocktail and reception parties. They may be accompanied with a selection of hot and cold sauces in the form of 'dips'.

Examples of Savouries in Common Use

The following savouries are served on hot buttered toast which is usually cut into rectangular shapes. The size and shape of these canapés or croûtes will be determined by the preparations being placed upon them for service. Examples of alternative shapes include squares, triangles, diamonds, and circles.

Ingredients and Method for Four Portions:

Name of dish	Unit		Metric	Imperial
Anges à Cheval [Angels on horseback (oysters in bacon on toast]		4 Prepared croûtes 8 Oysters 8 Rashers of streaky bacon Salt and pepper to season		
		Season and wrap the oysters in bacon and secure on skewers . Grill gently until cooked, dress on croûtes for service		
Canapé aux Champignons (mushrooms on toast)	1 ¼	4 prepared croûtes Grilling mushrooms (flat) Melted butter Salt and pepper to season	200 g 50 g	8 oz 2 oz
		Wash and peel mushrooms. Season, brush with melted butter and grill until cooked. Dress on croûtes for service		
Canapé des Gourmets (ham with mustard on toast)	1 1	4 Prepared croûtes Cooked ham (fine dice) Mustard butter (*see* p. 112)	200 g 50 g	8 oz 2 oz
		Mix ham and butter together, spread evenly on to croûtes and place under grill to heat for service		
Canapé Hollandaise (smoked haddock and egg on toast)	1	4 Prepared croûtes Smoked haddock (poached in milk) 2 Hard boiled eggs Salt and cayenne pepper to season	200 g	8 oz
		Flake the poached haddock removing any skin and bone. Place on to croûtes and decorate with sliced or quartered hard boiled eggs. Season the egg, brush with butter and reheat under the grill for service.		

Name of dish	*Unit*		*Metric*	*Imperial*
Canapé Ivanhoë (creamed haddock on toast with mushrooms)		4 Prepared croûtes		
	1	Smoked haddock (poached in milk)	200 g	8 oz
	1/4	Béchamel	50 ml	2 fl oz
	1/8	Cream	25 ml	1 fl oz
		4 Grilled mushrooms		
		Cayenne pepper to season		

Flake the poached haddock removing any skin and bone, combine with the béchamel and cream. Reheat, season with cayenne and place on to croûtes, decorate with grilled mushrooms for service

Canapé Ritchie (creamed haddock on toast with cheese)		4 Prepared croûtes		
	1	Smoked haddock	200 g	8 oz
	1/4	Béchamel	50 ml	2 fl oz
	1/4	Grated cheese	50 g	2 oz
	1/8	Cream	25 ml	1 fl oz
		Cayenne pepper to season		

Proceed as for Canapé Ivanhoë mixing half the cheese with haddock mixture. Place mixture on to croûtes, sprinkle with remaining cheese and brown under the grill for service

Croûte Quo Vadis (soft herring roes and mushrooms on toast)		4 Prepared croûtes		
	1	Soft herring roes	200 g	8 oz
		4 Grilled mushrooms		
		Seasoned flour		
		Melted butter		

Wash the roes, pass through seasoned flour and place on to a buttered grilling tray. Brush with butter and grill until cooked. Place on to croûtes and decorate with grilled mushrooms for service

Croûte Anchois (anchovy fillets on toast)		4 Prepared croûtes		
	1	Anchovy fillets	100 g	4 oz
		Melted butter		
		Squeeze of lemon juice		
		Picked parsley		

Place the anchovy fillets on to croûtes, sprinkle with lemon juice, brush with melted butter and grill to reheat. Serve decorated with picked parsley

| Croûte Baron (mushrooms, bacon and meat marrow on toast) | | 4 Prepared croûtes
8 Grilled mushrooms
8 Slices of poached beef marrow
4 Slices of grilled bacon
Salt and pepper to season | | |

Place the grilled bacon on to croûtes, arrange the grilled mushrooms and poached beef marrow on top. Season and reheat under the grill for service

| Croûte Derby (creamed ham on toast with pickled walnut) | 1
¼
⅛ | 4 Prepared croûtes
Cooked ham (fine dice)
Béchamel
Cream
4 Slices of pickled walnut
Cayenne pepper to season | 200 g
50 ml
25 ml | 8 oz
2 fl oz
1 fl oz |

Mix together the ham, béchamel, cream and boil to reheat, season with cayenne. Spread mixture on to croûtes and garnish with pickled walnut for service

| Croûte/Canapé Diane (chicken livers and bacon on toast) | | 4 Prepared croûtes
4 Trimmed chicken livers
8 Slices of streaky bacon
Salt and cayenne pepper to season | | |

Cut the chicken livers in half, season and wrap in bacon, secure with skewers. Grill on both sides until cooked, arrange on to croûtes for service

| Croûte Windsor (creamed ham on toast with mushrooms) | Proceed as for Croûte Derby, replace the pickled walnuts with four grilled mushrooms |

| Diables à Cheval (devils on horseback prunes in bacon on toast) | 1 | 4 Prepared croûtes
Chutney
8 Rashers of streaky bacon
8 Stewed prunes (*see* p. 271)
Salt and pepper to season | 50 g | 2 oz |

Remove the stones from the prunes and stuff with chutney. Season, wrap in bacon and secure on skewers. Grill gently until cooked and dress on croûtes for service

| Laitances sur Croûtes (soft herring roes on toast) | Proceed as for Croûte Quo Vadis, omit the grilled mushrooms |

Name of dish	Unit		Metric	Imperial
Moelle sur Croûtes (meat marrow on toast)	1	4 Prepared croûtes Poached beef marrow Chopped parsley Salt and pepper to season	200 g	8 oz
		Slice the marrow into $\frac{1}{2}$ cm ($\frac{1}{4}$ in) slices, arrange on to croûtes, season and reheat under the grill. Sprinkle with chopped parsley for service		
Scotch Woodcock (scrambled eggs on toast with anchovies and capers)	1 $\frac{1}{8}$	4 Prepared croûtes Scrambled eggs Capers 8 Anchovy fillets	200 g 25 g	8 oz 1 oz
		Dress scrambled eggs on to croûtes and decorate with strips of anchovy fillet and capers		
Sardines sur Croûtes (sardines on toast)		4 Prepared croûtes 8 Sardines in oil (canned) Melted butter Squeeze of lemon juice Salt and pepper to season		
		Skin the sardines and remove bone if required. Dress on to croûtes, season, sprinkle with lemon juice and brush with melted butter. Heat under the grill for service. N.B. May also be prepared with fresh grilled sardines when available		

Welsh Rarebit (flavoured cheese on toast)	1
	$\frac{4}{5}$
	$\frac{3}{5}$
	$\frac{1}{5}$
		4 Prepared croûtes
		Béchamel
		Grated cheese
		Beer
		Egg yolk
		Seasonings:
		   diluted English mustard
		   Worcester sauce
		   salt and cayenne pepper
			125 ml
			100 g
			75 ml
			25 g
				5 fl oz
				4 oz
				3 fl oz
				1 oz

		Reduce the beer by half, add the béchamel and reboil. Add cheese and simmer until melted. Remove from heat, add egg yolk, seasonings, mix thoroughly, and cool ready for use. Spread on to croûtes and heat under the grill until golden brown and serve.		
Buck Rarebit (flavoured cheese on toast with poached eggs)		Proceed as for Welsh Rarebit and top each portion with a poached egg		

N.B. The above savouries are served on flats dressed with dish papers and may be garnished with bunches of picked parsley where appropriate.

Other Savouries and Savoury Preparations in Common Use

Cheese or Crab Fritters   Beignets de Fromage/Crabe

Choux pastry flavoured with crab or cheese, shaped with spoons and deep fried. See study on deep frying (*see* p. 215).

220
PUFF PASTRY CASES FILLED WITH CURRIED SHRIMPS Bouchées à
l'Indienne

Yield: 4 portions
Cooking time: 5 – 8 min

Unit	Ingredient	Metric	Imperial
	8 Small bouchées (baked)		
1	Shrimps (picked)	200 g	8 oz
1	Curry sauce (*see* recipe 15)	200 ml	8 fl oz
¹/₈	Butter	25 g	1 oz
	Salt and pepper to season		

Method

Melt the butter in a saucepan, add the shrimps, season and sweat without colour. Add the curry sauce and simmer gently for 2 – 3 minutes. Heat the bouchées and fill with the curried shrimps, dress on flats with dish papers for service.

221
CHEESE AND HAM WITH BREAD   Croque-Monsieur
(shallow fried)

Yield: 4 portions
Cooking time: 5 – 6 min

Unit	Ingredient	Metric (g)	Imperial (oz)
	8 Slices (plain bread)		
1	Gruyère cheese (thinly sliced)	100	4
1	Cooked ham (thinly sliced)	100	4
	Clarified butter (for frying)		

Method

Place ham between slices of cheese then sandwich with bread, press firmly together. Cut out with a round cutter or into rectangular shapes as required. Shallow fry gently in clarified butter on both sides until golden brown. Dress on flats with dish papers and serve immediately.

Savoury Flans   Quiches

Open flans garnished with various fillings. They may be prepared in flan rings to serve four people or in small individual pastry cases. *See* Chapter 16.

Cheese Soufflé   Soufflé au Parmesan/au Fromage

Baked savoury soufflés which may be prepared in large or individual soufflé moulds for service (*see* recipe 181).

21

Breakfast Cookery

Meals at breakfast time take a variety of forms, but may be broadly classified as English or Continental. The English breakfast is a substantial meal at which a variety of hot and cold courses is offered. The Continental breakfast, however, is a lighter meal consisting mainly of a selection of bread rolls, croissant, toast, butter, preserves and beverages.

Where the English breakfast is offered a breakfast cook is responsible for preparing and cooking breakfast dishes. In some establishments, however, other members of the kitchen brigade are involved in preparing and cooking items for the breakfast menu, e.g. stewed fruits prepared by the pastry chef.

Examples of breakfast dishes shown on the menus below, along with other suitable items are outlined in the respective studies (*see* index).

Breakfast   Good Morning

Continental – Café Complet

Chilled Juices Orange Grapefruit Tomato

Croissants Brioche Toast Brown and White Rolls with Butter Preserves
Marmalades Honey (clear or cloudy).

Tea Coffee Chocolate Milk

Breakfast   Good Morning

English — Petit Déjeuner

Chilled Grapefruit   Spanish Melon
Oranges   Apples
Chilled Juices: Orange Grapefruit Tomato
Compotes: Figs Plums Pineapple Apples Prunes

Special: Clam Chowder   French Onion Soup

Oatmeal Porridge   Alpen   Rolled Oats
Rice Krispies   Bran Flakes   Shredded Wheat
Puffed Wheat   Special K   Corn Flakes   Sugar Puffs

Kedgeree
Fried Fillet of plaice with Lemon
Grilled Kippers
Poached Haddock Monte Carlo

Eggs: Fried Turned Scrambled Poached Boiled
Omelettes: Plain   Tomato   Cheese   Ham   Prawn

Grilled Lamb's Kidneys   Black Pudding   Grilled Bacon
Lyonnaise Potatoes

To order:

Pork Sausages   Baked Tomatoes   Grilled Gammon

Cold Meat   Green Salad

Spiced Scones

Griddle Cakes with Honey or Maple Syrup

Rolls: White   Energen Breads: Brown, Hovis
Toasts: White Brown Raisin Melba   To Order: French Toast
Muffins   Biscuit Ryvita

Waffles with Demerara Sugar

Croissants   Danish Pastries   Brioches

Preserves   Marmalades   Honey (Clear or Cloudy)

Teas: Ceylon   China   Russian Mint

Coffee: Cona   Nescafé   Sanka

Cocoa   Chocolate

N.B. *French Toast*
Dip slices of selected bread into beaten egg then shallow fry until crisp and golden brown.
If required the beaten egg may be lightly sweetened and flavoured with a pinch of allspice
or nutmeg.

Entrées and Relevés

The nature of entrées and relevés are at first sight difficult to comprehend – similarities and differences exist, concerning these two courses, which require clarification.

Entrées

Generally the word entrée translated means 'enter' and when associated with traditional menu terminology refers to the first main item to appear on the menu. According to the master chef Escoffier, such items could be made up using fish, butcher's meat, poultry, offal or game. On modern menus, however, an entrée indicates a type of culinary product prepared using the above commodities excluding fish – these usually appear as the first main meat items offered on the bill of fare. Technically the term entrée refers to a type of dish that is prepared, cooked and presented in a particular manner. The characteristics of entrées are described below.

Butcher's meat, poultry, offal or game when being prepared for entrées are usually cut into portions prior to cooking. For example topside of beef cut into braising steaks or best-end of lamb into cutlets. Furthermore when producing entrées many methods of cookery are used and the completed item is dispatched from the kitchen sauced and garnished as is required to form the finished dish. The garnish may be simple or complex, the sauce served as an integral part of the dish or as a separate accompanying item.

Luncheon entrées are mainly prepared using the less expensive cuts of meat, e.g. Steak and Kidney Pie, whilst the more expensive cuts are selected for the preparation of dinner entrées e.g. Tournedos Chasseur. When an entrée is not being offered as a main course but as a preliminary course in its own right, it would not normally be accompanied by potato or vegetable dishes. Cold preparations are also served as entrées, e.g. Ham Mousse.

Examples of Entrées

Déjeuner (luncheon)	*Dîner (Dinner)*
Ragoût de Boeuf Jardinière (beef stew with vegetables)	Tournedos Rossini (sautéd fillet steak with Foie Gras, truffle, and Madeira sauce)
Chop d'Agneau Champvallon (a flavoursome lamb stew)	Côtelettes d'Agneau Réforme (shallow-fried breaded lamb cutlets served with Reform sauce)

The list of possible examples is extensive and occasions arise when dinner type entrées would be served at luncheon and vice versa according to requirements.

Relevés

In his book *The Complete Guide to the Art of Modern Cookery* Escoffier suggests that the line of demarcation between entrées and relevés was clearly defined on the old-fashioned French menus. He describes the scene of a typical French dinner at which the selection of soups and entrées would be set out on the dining table before the guests were admitted into the room, and how once the soups were served the relevés would replace the soups on the table thus relieving them. Hence the history of the name relevé. At that time relevés, as with entrées, could be produced using fish, butcher's meat, poultry, offal or game. However, on today's menu the relevé indicates a type of culinary product prepared from prime joints of butcher's meat and offal, along with good class poultry or game. Nowadays the relevé is often served as the main meat item on a dinner, banquet or à la carte menu. As a modern menu term relevé is seldom used because menus are less extensive than in the past. The word 'Viandes' (meats) is now generally used to cover a variety of meat dishes including relevés. Technically a relevé refers to a type of culinary product that is prepared, cooked and presented in a particular way. The characteristics of the relevé are outlined below and it should be noted that the main difference between dinner entrées and relevés is one of size, the latter being of greater volume. When preparing relevés only the choice joints of butcher's meat and offal are selected along with good class poultry or game. Cooking methods employed vary but usually include roasting, braising, and cooking à la poële. The cooked meat is usually presented 'in the piece' with a sauce and garnish. The garnish may be simple or complex with the sauce being served as an integral part of the dish or as an accompaniment. Unlike entrées the meat is not cut into portions prior to cooking and it therefore requires carving for service. Carving may be carried out in the dining room at the customer's table, or alternatively in the kitchen. The relevé may be served with vegetable and potato courses but when a complex vegetable garnish is already involved these extra courses would be omitted. As for entrées, relevés may be prepared cold as well as hot, e.g. Filet de Boeuf Froid. The relevé is sometimes referred to as a 'remove' and perhaps could best be described as a large entrée.

Examples of Relevés

Filet de Boeuf Richelieu
   (poêled fillet of beef garnished with stuffed mushrooms, braised lettuce, stuffed tomatoes and small turned potatoes, served with Madiera sauce)
Selle d'Agneau Bouquetière
   (saddle of lamb roasted, garnished with neat bouquets of various vegetables, served with roast gravy)
Canard Braisé a l'Orange
   (braised duck with orange sauce, garnished with orange segments and blanched zest)
The list of examples is extensive.

N.B.   When a traditional kitchen brigade is employed hot entrées and relevés are the responsibility of the Saucier and cold preparations the Chef Garde-Manger.

Glossary of Culinary Terms

Abats Offal e.g. hearts, liver, kidney, etc. of butcher's meats and giblets of poultry, etc.

à blanc To keep white

à brun To make brown

Aboyeur 'Barker' – the person responsible for shouting out the customer's order to the kitchen departments

Adjunct (vegetable) A vegetable flavouring used when a full mirepoix is unsuitable, e.g. onion flavouring in curry sauce

Aiguillette Small long strips of cooked meat, e.g. aiguillettes of duck

Ail Garlic

Aile Wing of poultry

Aileron Winglet of poultry

Airelles cousinettes Cranberries

à la In the style of . . . e.g. à l'Anglaise (English style)
à la Française (French style)
à la Maison (style of the house, etc.)

à la carte Dishes prepared or cooked to order, which are separately priced

al dente Used to describe Italian pasta cooked 'with a bite'

Aloyau de boeuf Whole sirloin of beef on the bone

Appareil A mixture of different foods for the preparation of a dish

à point Just cooked

Aromates Herbs and spices used for flavouring

Assaisonner To season, or season to taste

au beurre With butter

au bleu Beef steaks cooked 'blue' or very underdone, also a method for cooking live trout (*see* recipe 81).

au four Oven baked

au gratin Foods sprinkled with grated cheese or breadcrumbs and browned under salamander or in a hot oven

au vin blanc With white wine

au vin rouge With red wine

Bain-marie   Mary's bath, an open water bath in which sauces/soups, etc. are stored in bain-marie pans to keep hot

Ballotine   Boned leg of poultry, stuffed and rolled prior to cooking

Barder   To cover pieces of meat, poultry, game, etc. with strips of fat in order to keep them moist, protect from scorching and prevent excess shrinkage

Baron   Double loin of beef or saddle of mutton/lamb with legs attached

Barquettes   Boat-shaped tin moulds used when preparing boat-shaped pastry cases

Baste   The process of moistening foods with the cooking juices and fats throughout cooking, e.g. basting roast meats

Bâtons   Foods cut into small, neat rectangles, e.g. bâton shape or neat sticks of French bread

Baveuse   A term used to describe omelets with a soft texture and moist centre

Beard (to)   Removing the beard from oysters and mussels

Beignets   Deep-fried savoury or sweet fritters

Beurre manié   A mixture of butter and flour manipulated to a smooth paste and used as a thickening agent

Bien cuit   Well cooked

Blanc   A specially prepared cooking medium of water, flour, lemon juice, and seasoning in which certain vegetables are cooked in order to prevent them discolouring

Blanc de volaille   Breast of chicken

Blanch (to)   (a) Blanched meat – meat and bones brought to the boil, then refreshed in
(Blanchir)   cold water to remove scum;

             (b) Blanched vegetables – brought to boil, refreshed in cold water then drained. This process helps to retain colour, softens vegetable fibres to facilitate shaping when braising and aids to retain vitamin C by eliminating destructive enzyme action;

             (c) Deep-fried potatoes, to par-cook certain potato dishes, keep them white in readiness for further cooking;

             (d) Blanched tomatoes, plunging tomatoes into boiling water for a few seconds to facilitate removal of skin.

Blanquette   A type of white stew (*see* p.252)

Bouchées   Small baked puff pastry cases

Bouillabaisse   A French Mediterranean fish stew or soup

Bouillon   A type of stock, e.g. chicken, or broth-type soup

Bouquet garni   A neat bundle of herbs used to flavour culinary products during cooking

Brochet   The French term for the fish 'Pike'

Broche (en)   Spit roasting

Brochette (en)   Cooking on a skewer

Broil   An American term to denote grilling

Brunoise   A cut of very fine dice

Budding   A term used to describe the opening of shellfish (molluscs)

Bulk fermentation time (BFT)   Initial fermentation time for yeast goods prior to moulding

Canapé   Various cooked shapes of bread used as a base for hors d'oeuvre and savoury dishes

Carapace   The body/head shell of lobster

Cartouche   A piece of greased paper to cover foods in cooking or storage

Casserole A type of stewing vessel made of earthenware or metal

Chapelure Brown breadcrumbs

Chateaubriand A large steak cut from the head of the beef fillet

Chauffant A vessel of seasoned boiling water used in the re-heating of vegetables

Chiffonade Finely shredded lettuce or sorrel used to garnish and flavour soups

Chinois fine/coarse (fin/gros) conical strainer

Ciseler To make small incisions e.g. scoring small round fish prior to grilling. Also finely shredding of vegetables

Civet A brown stew of furred game, e.g. Civet de Lièvre (hare), Civet de Venaison (venison)

Clarification A process used to make soup, jellies and butter, etc. of clear appearance

Clouté Studded or to insert nail-shaped pieces of food into various preparations e.g. onion clouté, an onion studded with cloves or ham studded with cloves

Cocotte Large and small fireproof earthenware cooking vessels

Cohere Moistening and light binding of fish meat or vegetables with a sauce

Collops Thin, small, round cuts of meat and fish, etc., e.g. collops of lobster

Compote Stewed fruit

Concassé Roughly chopped

Contrefilet Boned-out sirloin e.g. strip loin

Coquilles Mollusc shells

Court-bouillon A flavoured cooking liquor used in the cooking of fish and some offal, e.g. brains

Cordon Ribbon, indicates a thread or ribbon of sauce used to flavour and garnish culinary products

Correcting A term used to denote the adjusting of colour, flavour, and consistency of culinary preparations

Côte Rib or chop, e.g. rib of beef, pork chop

Côtelette Cutlet, e.g. lamb cutlet

Crapaudine A term denoting a raw chicken prepared for grilling, cut and shaped to represent a 'toad'

Crêpes Pancakes

Croquettes Cooked forcemeats of meat, fish or cooked vegetables, shaped and prepared for frying

Croûtes Various shapes of fried/toasted bread on which various foods are presented

Croûtons Various shapes of fried bread used as a garnish with culinary preparations, e.g. soup croûtons, heart-shaped croûtons

Cru Raw or uncooked

Crustaceans A classification of certain shellfish, e.g. lobster, prawns, crabs, scampi, etc.

Cuisse Leg, e.g. cuisse (of chicken), Cuisse de Nymphes/Grenouilles (frogs legs)

Dariole Small, tin lined copper or aluminium mould

Darne A steak of round fish on the bone, e.g. darne (of salmon)

Daube A type of oven stew cooked in a special vessel (daubière)

Daubière A type of casserole made of earthenware

Déglacer To remove food sediment from a cooking vessel by 'swilling out' with a suitable liquid, e.g. wine or stock. To deglaze

Dégraisser To skim away fat

Déjeuner Luncheon

Devilled   To highly season with a hot flavouring, e.g. cayenne pepper

Dish paper   Plain absorbent paper used on service dishes to absorb excess grease from foods

Doily   A decorative paper base used on service flats to enhance the appearance of pastry goods

Doré   Gilded or golden in colour, e.g. gilded fish (*see* p.240).

Duxelle   A basic preparation of cooked finely chopped mushrooms, flavoured with shallots and seasonings

Écumé   Skimmed

Egg wash   Beaten egg used when breadcrumbing foods or brushing foods to facilitate browning during cooking

Émincer   To cut into thin slices

En papillote   Cooking and serving foods in a paper bag

En-tasse   Served in a cup, e.g. consommé en tasse

Entier   Entire or whole

Entrecôte   Steak cut from boned out sirloin (strip loin)

Escalopes   Thin slices, usually applied to meats, e.g. escalopes of veal

Escargot   Edible snails

Estouffade   A rich brown stock

Faggot   As for bouquet garni

Farce   A stuffing

Fécule   A type of starch thickening

Feuilletage   Puff pastry

Fines herbes   Selected herbs comprised of parsley, chervil, chives, and tarragon

Fleurons   Cooked crescents of puff pastry

Flûtes   Toasted, thin slices of French bread sticks, usually served as an accompaniment with certain soups

Fonds   Foundations, e.g. stocks

Fourrer   To stuff

Fricassée   A type of white stew (*see* recipe 116)

Fruits de Mer   Assortment of sea food

Fumé   Smoked

Fumet   Essence of fish stock

Galette   Small, flat cake of potato, vegetables, etc.

Gastric   A mixture of sugar and vinegar used to sharpen the flavour of tomato sauce or soup

Gibier   Game

Glaze to   To brown products under the salamander

Gourmet   An epicure, a connoisseur of food

Gratinate   To sprinkle foods with grated cheese or breadcrumbs to be browned under the salamander

Gras de Cuisse   Chicken thigh

Grenouilles   Frogs

Hacher   To mince or finely chop

Hâtelette   Elaborately adorned skewer

Haute Cuisine   High class cookery

Indienne (à la)   Indian style, often denotes use of curry flavourings
Italienne (à la)   Italian style

Jardinière   A term used to denote vegetables cut into bâtons
Julienne   A term used to denote foods cut into thin strips
Jus (au)   With juice or gravy
Jus lié   Thickened gravy
Jus rôti   Roast gravy, unthickened
Jus rôti lié   Roast gravy, thickened

Larder   The insertion of strips of bacon or pork fat into meats, poultry and game in order to keep them moist during cooking, and prevent excess shrinkage
Lardons   Bâtons of streaky bacon, blanched and sautéd, used as a garnish
Liasion   Mixture of egg yolks and cream used to thicken and enrich culinary products, e.g. soups and sauces
Macédoine   Various foods cut into neat cubes or dice
Mandolin   A special vegetable slicer
Manié   To manipulate or knead
Mar-For slicer   Manual vegetable slicer
Marinade   A preparation used to flavour and tenderise butcher's meats, poultry, game and fish. Often comprised of oil, wine or lemon juice, vegetables and aromates
Marmite   Stock pot, or earthenware pot in which soups may be cooked and served
Mask   A term used to denote coating foods with a sauce
Matelot   A type of French fish stew
Médaillon   A round shaped portion of meat or fish
Menu   Bill of fare
Mignonette pepper   Milled peppercorns
Mijoter   To simmer
Minute (à la)   Cooked very quickly 'in a minute'
Mirepoix   A vegetable flavouring, roughly cut to various sizes according to requirements
Mise-en-place   Put in place, in culinary jargon refers to advanced preparation
Molluscs   A classification of shellfish, e.g. oysters, mussels, scallops, etc.
Monter au beurre   Mount with butter, adding butter to sauce preparations to enhance flavour, appearance and improve consistency
Mouli (légume)   A manual or mechanical vegetable mill, used to purée vegetables and soups

Napper   To coat items with sauce
Nature (au)   Natural
Navarin   A brown lamb stew
Noisette d'Agneau   A small, trimmed cut of lamb taken from the boned loin

Paillettes au fromage   Cheese straws
Panaché   Mixture
Panada   A term used to describe types of binding agent
Paner   To pass ingredients through seasoned flour, egg wash and breadcrumbs (pané)
Pannequets   Small pancakes
Paw paw   A tropical fruit similar to a small green melon
Paupiette   A stuffed portion of meat/fish rolled into a cylindrical shape
Paysanne (à la)   Peasant style, also indicates the use of particular shapes, i.e. circles, squares, and triangles (*see* p.75)

Petit déjeuner Breakfast
Pilon Drumstick, e.g. pilon de cuisse (chicken drumstick)
Piquant Sharp flavour
Piquer Foods studded with fat, cloves, garlic, truffle etc.
Plat à sauter A shallow frying vessel
Plat du jour Suggested dish of the day
Pré-sale Lamb or mutton, reared and bred on salty meadows
Primevrs Spring vegetables
Printanier Spring vegetables
Proving A second fermentation period for yeast goods following moulding and prior to cooking
Provençale (à la) Regional or provincial style
Pulse Dried or fresh podded vegetables
Purée Pulped foods

Quenelles Various shapes of fine forcemeats produced from veal, chicken, fish, and game
Queue Tail, e.g. ox-tail

Râble (de lièvre) Saddle of hare
Ragoût A stew
Raspings As for chapelure
Ravier A small dish in which hors d'oeuvres are served, manufactured in a variety of materials e.g. glass, plastic, stainless steel, earthenware etc.
Réchauffé Reheated
Refresh To plunge hot foods into cold water in order to halt cooking and cool quickly before draining for use or storage
Rissoler Shallow fry quickly in hot fat/oil to golden brown
Rondeau A large round shallow cooking vessel
Roux A mixture of fat/oil and flour, cooked to varying degrees and used as a thickening agent

Sabayon A mixture of egg yolks and a few drops of water cooked and whisked en bain-marie to ribbon stage. Used to thicken, enrichen, and improve appearance of culinary products
Saignant Rare or underdone (bleeding)
Salamander Overhead grilling appliances
Salmis A brown stew of feathered game
Salpicon A mixture of foods cohered with a sauce and used as a filling
Sauteuse A shallow cooking vessel with sloping sides (*see* p.22)
Sauter To shallow fry or toss over heat in a plat à sauter
Score To incise the surface of foods
Sec Dry, not sweet
Shredded Sliced finely
Singer To colour brown
Sippets Small shallow fried soup croûtons
Soufflé A very light sweet or savoury product
Spatchcock A term denoting a raw chicken split down the back-bone and 'spreadeagled' for grilling (*see* p.336)

Spatula A flat wooden spoon

Suprême Denotes use of delicate cuts taken from breast of poultry or game. Also a cut of fish on the slant, free from bone

Sweat Initial cooking of foods in fat/oil under cover, without significant colour change

Table d'hôte Inclusive menu at a set price

Tammis Very fine sieve

Tammiser To pass sauces through a fine cloth to remove particles and give a fine, smooth sauce

Timbale A drum-shaped serving vessel

Tomatéd Significantly flavoured and coloured with tomato

Tomates concassées Chopped tomato flesh cooked in butter/oil with small amount of onion and garlic

Tomato concassé Chopped tomato flesh

Tourné To turn or trim with a sharp knife to required shape, e.g. vegetables turned barrel-shape, turned (fluted) mushrooms, etc.

Tournedos Small cuts taken from centre of beef fillet

Tranche A slice or cut

Trancher To carve or cut

Tranchelard A French carving knife

Tronçon A cut of flat fish on the bone

Truffle A fungus used in cookery to garnish and flavour

Truss To secure foods with string, e.g. poultry

Vert-pré Indicates use of a green garnish or colour, e.g. watercress to garnish grills

Vesiga Dried spinal marrow of the sturgeon used mainly in the preparation of 'coulibiac' a type of Russian fish pie

Vin Wine

Vol-au-Vent Large puff pastry case

Xérès Sherry

Zest Orange or lemon rind

Index

All dishes are listed under their 'umbrella' ingredient e.g. all vegetables under V (for example for artichokes, *see* under Vegetables), all meat under M (e.g. for beef, *see* under Meats), and all fish under F (e.g. for shellfish, *see* under Fish) etc.

Anchovy, *see* Sauces and savouries
Apple, *see* Sauces
Apricots compote, 271
Aqueous vegetables, 63
Artichokes, *see* Vegetables
Aubergines farcie au gratin, 374
   see also Vegetables
Asparagus, *see* Vegetables

Batters frying, 206–7
   egg, 207
   yeast, 206
Beans, *see* Vegetables
Beef, *see* Meats
Beetroot, *see* Vegetables
Beignets, (fritters), 213, 215
   banana, 215
   choufleur, 213
   crabe, 215
   fromage, 215
   panais, 213
Beurre manié, 82
Binding agents, 66
Bitoks, 237
   see also Meats
Blanc, 179
Blanquettes, 252–5
   see also Meats
Bouchées: *see* Savouries
Bouillabaisse, 265–6
Bouquet garni, 71
Brains poached, 191–2
   see also Meats
Bratt pan, 45–6

Breadcrumbs, 77–8
   browned, 77
   white, 78
Broccoli, *see* Vegetables
Brochet à l'anglaise, 320
Brochettes, 341–2
   see also Meats
Brussel sprouts, *see* Vegetables
Bubble and squeak, 375
Butter clarified, 78
Butter sauces, 111–12
   see also Sauces
Button onions, 76
   à blanc, 76
   à brun, 76

Cabbage, *see* Vegetables
Canard caneton, *see* Meats
Canneloni, 163–4
Carbonnade, 274–5
   see also Meats
Carrots, *see* Vegetables
Cauliflower, *see* Vegetables
Celeriac, *see* Vegetables
Celery, *see* Vegetables
Cheese straws, 114
Chef's knives, 10–13
Chestnuts braised, 288
   see also Vegetables
Chicken à la King, 350
Chicken in curry sauce 350
Chicory, *see* Vegetables
Chili con carne, 257–8

Chop d'agneau Champvallon, 263
Choucroute (sauerkraut) 289−90
    braisé, 289
    garniture, 290
Chou-rouge flamande, 289
Choux pastry, 158
Civets, *see* Meats
Coeur d'agneau braisé, 276−7
Compote de fruits, 271
Connective tissue, 55
Convection ovens, 36−8
Convenience products, 6
Cooking vessels, 18−26
    metals, 18−20
    vessels, 20−6
Coq au vin, 258−9
Coquilles de poisson, 363−4
    see also Fish
Corn, *see* Vegetables
    cakes, 375
Corned beef hash, 354
Cornish pasties, 318
Cottage pie, 353
Coulibiac, 361−2
    chicken, 362
    salmon, 361
Courge provençale, 270
    see also Vegetables
Courgettes, *see* Vegetables
Court-bouillon, 175−6
Crêpes (pancakes), 349, 364−5
    batter, 364
    chicken, 349
    crab, 365
    fish, 364−5
Cromeskis à la russe, 358, 360
Croquettes (cooked forcemeat), 358−9
    see also Meats
Croûtes (bread), 77
Croûtons (bread), 77
Cucumber, *see* Vegetables
Curly kale, *see* Vegetables
Curried meats, 255−6, 350
    see also Meats
Curried prawns, 365
Cutlets (cooked forcemeats), 358−9
    see also Meats

Daube de boeuf, mouton, 275−6
Denaturation, 54, 66

Dextrinization, 62
Dripping, 78
Duck, *see* Meats
Dumplings, 113
Durham cutlets, 360
Duxelle, 73

Eel stew, 264−5
Egg plant, *see* Vegetables
Eggs, *see* also Omelets
    à la coque, 142
    à la française, 147
dur, 141−2
    à la tripe, 142
    aurore, 142
    Chimay, 142
    indienne, 142
    methods of cooking, 141−2
en cocotte, 143−4
    à la crème, 143
    à la reine, 144
    bergère, 143
    bordelaise, 143
    jus lié, 144
    methods of cooking, 143
    perigourdine, 144
    petit-duc, 144
    portugaise, 144
    soubise, 144
fried (shallow), 147
mollet, 142
poached (poché), 139−41
    Argenteuil, 140
    Bénédictine, 140
    florentine, 142
    indienne, 141
    methods of cooking, 139−40
    Mornay, 141
    reine, 141
    Washington, 141
scrambled (brouillés), 147−8
    archiduchesse, 148
    aux croûtons, 148
    champignons, 148
    foie de volaille, 148
    grand' mère, 148
    portugaise, 148
    recipe, 147−8
sizes and weights, 6
sur le plat, 145−6

à la crème, 146
américaine, 145
au lard, 146
aux crevettes, 146
Bercy, 145
chasseur, 146
florentine, 146
Lorraine, 146
method of cooking, 145
Emulsification, 66−9
Emulsions
examples, 68−9
Endive, *see* Vegetables
Entrées and relevés, 385−6
Enzymic browning, 57−8
Epigrammes of lamb, 355−6
Equipment small, 13−17
Escargots, 368
Essences, 81
Estouffade, 80
Experiments, 69−70

Farce, 162−3
à la florentine, 162
italienne, 163
Fennel, *see* Vegetables
Fricassées, 253−5
Fish,
baked, 319−20
extensions, 320
recipe, 319
boiled, 175−7
braised, 285
cakes, 368
coquilles de poisson, 363−4
coquilles de fruits de mer, 364
coquilles Mornay, 364
crab fritters, 215
curried prawns, 365
deep fried, 209−12
à l'anglaise, 211
à la française, 211
à l'orly, 211
Colbert (sole), 211
en colère, 211
fish and cuts, 209−10
fritto misto mare, 212
whitebait, 212
whitebait devilled, 212
eel stew, 264−5

frog's legs (cuisse de grenouilles)
197−8
Bercy, 197−8
florentine, 197−8
Mornay, 197−8
parisienne, 197−8
fumet de poisson, 81
grilled, 342−5
Caprice, 345
fish and cuts, 343−4
lobster, 345
method of cooking, 344
preparation, 344
scampi, 345
St Germain, 345
kedgeree, 365−6
lobster (homard)
américaine, 266−7
boiled, 178
Cardinal, 367
Mornay, 366
Newburg, 366
Newburg à cru, 267
Thermidor, 366
matelote d'anguille, 364−5
moules à la crème, 268
moules à la poulette, 268
moules marinière, 268
oysters (huîtres), 197−8
Bercy, 197−8
florentine, 197−8
Mornay, 197−8
parisienne, 197−8
pancakes (crêpes), 364−5
crab, 364−5
fish, 364−5
pie, 362
pike (brochet) à l'anglaise (baked),
320
poached, 194−7, 198
Bercy, 196
bonne femme, 196
Bréval /d'Antin, 196
Cubat, 197
dieppoise, 195
Dugléré, 195
florentine, 197
Granville, 195
method, service, 194−5
Mornay, 196

Fish, poached (cont.)
    Polignac, 195
    St Valéry, 196
    Suchet, 195
    Véronique, 196
    vin blanc, 195
    Walewska, 197
  quiche de fruits de mer, 326
  salpicon de poisson, 362–3
  scallops (coquilles St. Jacques),
    197–8
    Bercy, 197–8
    florentine, 197–8
    Mornay, 197–8
    parisienne, 197–8
    provençale, 242
  scampi (langoustine), 197–8,
    242–3
    Bercy, 197–8
    florentine, 197–8
    Mornay, 197–8
    Newburg, 242
    parisienne, 197–8
    provençale, 242
    Thermidor, 243
  shallow fried (meunière), 238–41
    amandine, 241
    belle meunière, 241
    bretonne, 241
    Cléopâtra, 241
    cuts, 239–40
    Doria, 241
    extensions, 241
    grenobloise, 241
    method of cooking, 240
    Murat, 241
  shellfish boiled, 178
  skate (raie) au beurre noir, 177
  soufflé, 328
  steamed, 201
  trout (truite) au bleu, 177–8
  vol au vent, 363
    de fruits de mer, 363
    de poisson, 363
    de poisson princesse, 363
Flour, browned, 78
Flûtes, 77
Foams, 66–7
Foie de boeuf lyonnaise, 277–8
Foie de volaille madère, 235

Fonds de cuisine, 78–81
  blanc, 79–80
  brun, 79–80
Fonds d'artichauts, 76
Foods, colour changes, 58–60
French beans (haricots verts), *see*
  Vegetables
French toast, 384
Fritters, 215
  banana, 215
  cheese, 215
  crab, 215
Fruits
  stewed, 271
    apples, 271
    apricots, 271
    figs, 271
    peaches, 271
    pears, 271
    plums, 271
    prunes, 271
Fryers, computerized, 47–8
Frying (deep), 207–8
  à l'anglaise, 211
  à la française, 211
  à l'orly, 211
Fumet de poisson, 81

Game, *see* Meats
Gammon grilled, 340
Garlic pellets, 73
Garnishes, 74–78
  bacon, 78
  bread, 77
  lemon, 77
Gelatinization, 62
Glazes, 81
Glossary, 387–93
Gnocchi, 157–60
  parisienne, 159
  piémontaise, 159–60
  polenta, 160
  romaine, 158–9
Goulash, 256–7
Gumbo (okra), *see* Vegetables

Haddock Monte Carlo, 199
Ham, *see* Meats
Hamburgers grilled, 340
Heat transfer, 49–53

conducted, 50
convected, 50
radiant, 50
Homard, 266−7, 366−7
  see also Fish

Irish stew, 263−4
Italian stuffing, 163

Jerusalem artichokes, *see* Vegetables

Kale (sea), *see* Vegetables
Kitchen organization
  brigade, 27−30
  modified, 30−1
Kebab, 341−2
Kedgeree, 365−6
Kidneys shallow fried, 234−5
  see also Meats
Kohlrabi (chou rave), *see* Vegetables
Kromeskis, 360

Lady fingers (okra), *see* Vegetables
Lamb, *see* Meats
Lamb hearts braised, 276−7
Lambs tongues braised, 278
Lancashire hot pot, 262
Langoustine Newburg, 242
  Thermidor, 243
Langues d'agneau braisées, 278
  florentine, 278
Lardons, 78
Lasagne, 165
Leeks, *see* Vegetables
Légumes tourné, 75
Lentils, *see* Vegetables
Lettuce, *see* Vegetables
Liaisons, 83
Liquidizer, 43
Liver and onions (braised), 277−8
Liver shallow fried, 234
  au lard, 234
  lyonnaise, 234
Lobster américaine, 266−7
  Newburg, 267
  see also Fish

Macaroni, *see* Pasta
Maillard browning, 60
Marinade (red wine), 260
Marrons braisés, 288

Marrow, *see* Vegetables
Marrow provençale, 270
Matelote d'anguille, 264−5
Meat and potato pie, 252−3
Meats, baked
  beef,
    steak pies, 251−2
  game
    pigeon pie, 316
    rabbit pie, 316
  ham
    en croûte, 357
    sugar baked, 357
  lamb
    cornish pasties, 318
  poultry
    chicken pie, 316, 347−8
  veal and ham pie, 317
Meats, boiled
  beef
    à l'anglaise, 171
    à la française, 171
  ham
    à sauce persil, 170−1
  mutton
    sauce aux câpres, 170−1
  offal
    langue de boeuf à l'anglaise,
      170−1
    langue de boeuf à sauce madère,
      170−1
    langue de boeuf florentine,
      170−1
  pig's trotters, 173
  poultry
    à la stanley, 173−4
    argenteuil, 173−4
    aux sauce champignons, 173−4
    hongroise, 173−4
    sauce suprême, 173−4
  tête de veau vinaigrette, 172
Meats, braised, 173
  beef
    carbonnade de boeuf, 274−5
    daube de boeuf, 275−6
  beef joints
    recipe, 279−80
    pièce de boeuf braisé, 280
    pièce de boeuf braisé à la mode,
      280

Meats, braised (cont.)
    pièce de boeuf braisé au vin
      rouge, 280
    pièce de boeuf braisé bourgeoise,
      280
    pièce de boeuf braisé
      bourguignonne, 280
  beef, small cuts
    au vin rouge, 274
    bourgeoise, 274
    jardinière, 274
    paysanne, 274
    printanier, 274
    recipe, 273
  ham
    au madère, 357
    florentine, 357
  lamb small cuts
    chops d'agneau braisés, 273–4
  mutton
    daube de mouton, 275–6
  offal
    coeur d'agneau braisé, 276–7
    coeur de boeuf braisé, 279, 281
    langues d'agneau braisée, 278
    langues d'agneau braisée
      florentine, 278
    langue de boeuf braisée, 281
    liver and onions, 277–8
    queue de boeuf braisée, 276
    ris (sweetbreads)
    ris à l'ancienne, 282–4
    ris à brun, 278–9
    ris à la crème, 282–4
    ris aux champignons, 282–4
    ris bonne maman, 284
    ris Demidoff, 284
  poultry
    ballotines de volaille, 273–4
    caneton braisé à l'orange, 281–2
  veal joints
    l'epaule farcie braisée, 279–81
    noix à la crème, 283–4
    noix à l'ancienne, 283–4
    noix aux champignons, 283–4
    noix bonne maman, 283–4
    noix bourgeoise, 279–81
    noix Demidoff, 283–4
    noix florentine, 279–81

  veal small cuts
    chops de veau braisés, 273–4
    paupiettes de veau braisés, 273–4
Meats, deep fried
  beef
    croquettes de boeuf, 358–9
    Durham cutlets, 360
  game
    côtelettes de gibier, 358–9
    croquettes de gibier, 358–9
  poultry
    chicken southern style, 208
    côtelettes de volaille, 358–9
    croquettes de volaille, 358–9
    fritots de volaille/pork, 208
    pilon de volaille frit, 208
    suprême de volaille cordon bleu,
      208
    suprême de volaille Kiev, 208
  Wiener Schnitzel, 209
Meats, grilled (meat offal poultry),
    330–42
  cuts
    beef, 330–33
    chicken, 336
    lamb, 333–5
    pork, 335–6
  degrees of cooking, 337
  garnishes (meat and offal), 338–9
    à la maison, 338
    au lard, 339
    bouquetière, 338
    Henri IV, 338
    maître d'hôtel, 338
    Mirabeau, 338
    tyrolienne, 339
    vert pré, 339
  garnishes (poultry), 339–40
    à l'anglaise, 340
    américaine, 339
    crapaudine, 340
    diable, 339
  methods of grilling, 337
  miscellaneous
    brochettes à la maison, 341
    brochettes de rognon, 341–2
    brochettes de volaille, 342
    gammon, 340
    hamburgers, 340
    mixed grill, 341

pig's trotters devilled sauce, 356 – 7
Meats, poached
  offal
    cervelles au beurre noir, 191 – 2
    cervelles au beurre noisette, 191 – 2
  poultry
    suprême de volaille aux sauce
        champignons, 191
    suprême de volaille florentine, 190
    suprême de volaille Polignac, 191
    suprême de volaille princesse, 191
Meats, poêle
  agneau (lamb)
    Clamart, 312
    Dubarry, 312
  boeuf (beef) and garnishes
    Clamart, 312
    Dubarry, 312
    Mercédès, 312
    niçoise, 312
    Richelieu, 312
  canard (duck), caneton (duckling)
    à l'orange, 311
    aux cerises, 311
  faisan (pheasant), 312
  hare (râble de lièvre), 312
  poulet (chicken) en cocotte
    aux chipolata, 311
    bonne femme, 311
    Champeaux, 311
    fermière, 311
    grand'mère, 311
    paysanne, 311
  preparation of meats 309
  recipe, 310
  veau (veal)
    noix de veau Mercédès, 312
Meats, sautés
  beef
    bitoks, 237
    cuts of beef, 223
    methods of cooking, 224
    sautés de boeuf
      à l'estragon, 225
      au beurre noisette, 224
      au poivre à la crème, 224
      aux champignons, 224
      bordelaise, 224
      bourguignonne, 245 – 51

      chasseur, 225
      fleuriste, 225
      hongroise, 225
      marchand de vin, 225
      périgourdine, 225
      Rossini, 225
      Strogonoff, 226
  lamb
    cuts of lamb, 226 – 7
    methods of cooking, 227
    sautés of lamb
      à l'anglaise, 228
      chasseur, 228
      Clamart, 228
      fleuriste, 228
      hongroise, 228
      maréchale, 228
      Massena, 228
      niçoise, 228
      Reform, 229
  offal
    foie de volaille à sauce madère, 235
    foie sauté au lard, 234
    foie sauté lyonnaise, 234
  garnishes
    à l'anglaise, 236
    aux champignons, 236
    florentine, 236
    maréchale, 236
    methods of cooking, 235 – 6
    rognons sautés au madère, 234 – 5
    rognons sautés chasseur, 234 – 5
    rognons sautés Turbigo, 234 – 5
    sweetbreads (ris)
  pork, *see* sautés of veal
  poultry
    cuts of chicken, 217 – 8
    methods of cooking, 218 – 221
    poulet sauté
      archiduc, 218
      Bercy, 219
      bonne femme, 219
      bourguignonne, 219
      Champeaux, 220
      chasseur, 220
      Duroc, 220
      hongroise, 220
      portugaise, 220
      provençale, 221

Meats, poultry (cont.)
    pojarski de volaille, 238
  suprême de volaille
    garnishes
      archiduc, 221
      à la crème, 221
      aux champignons, 222
      Doria, 222
      hongroise, 222
      maréchale, 222
      Maryland, 222
      Sandeman, 222
  veal/pork sautés
    bitoks, 237
    cuts of veal, 229 – 30
    garnishes
      à l'anglaise, 230
      à la crème, 231
      au madère, 231
      au marsala, 231
      aux champignon, 231
      cordon bleu, 231
      Holstein, 231
      italienne, 231
      maréchale, 232
      milanaise, 232
      napolitaine, 232
      viennoise, 232
    methods of cooking, 230
    pojarski de veau, 238
Meats, poultry and game roasted,
    294 – 306
  accompaniments, 302 – 303
  carving, 303 – 6
  cooking times, 298
  gravies, 301
  methods of cooking, 301
  preparation, 295 – 7
  stuffings, 298 – 300
Meats steamed, 201
  beef steak pudding, 202 – 3, 351 – 2
Meats, stewed
  beef
    boeuf bourguignonne, 249, 251
    goulache de boeuf, 256 – 7
    hachis de boeuf, 249, 251
    kari de boeuf, 255 – 6
    ragoût de boeuf, 249 – 51
    ragoût recipe and extensions,
      249 – 51

lamb
  blanquette d'agneau, 252, 254 – 5
  chop d'agneau Champvallon, 263
  goulache d'agneau, 256 – 7
  Irish stew, 263 – 4
  kari d'agneau, 255 – 6
  Lancashire hot pot, 262
  navarin d'agneau, 249 – 50
  navarin recipe and extensions,
    249 – 50
game
  blanquette de lapin, 252, 254 – 5
  civet de gibier, 260 – 2
  fricassée de lapin, 253 – 5
  ragoût de lapin, 249 – 251
  salmis de gibier, 259 – 60
mutton
  goulache de mouton, 256 – 7
  kari de mouton, 255 – 6
offal
  ragoût de rognon, 249, 251
  tripe and onions, 264
pork
  blanquette de porc, 252, 254 – 5
  fricassée de porc, 253 – 5
  goulache de porc, 256 – 7
poultry
  coq au vin, 258 – 9
  fricassée de volaille, 253 – 5
veal
  blanquette de veau, 252, 254 – 5
  fricassée de veau, 253 – 5
  goulache de veau, 256 – 7
  kari de veau, 255 – 6
  osso-bucco milanaise, 258
  ragoût de veau, 249, 251
  ragoût de veau au vin blanc, 249,
    251
  ragoût de veau Marengo, 249, 251
Metrication, 2
  weights and measures, 4 – 5
Micro-aire ovens, 34 – 5
Microwave ovens, 32 – 6
Mirepoix, 72 – 3
Miroton of beef, 353 – 4
Mise en place, 71
Mixed grill, 341
Moules marinière, 268
  à la crème, 268
  à la poulette, 268

Moussaka, 354–5
Mushrooms, par cooked, 76
Mutton boiled, 170–1
    aux câpres, 171

Noodles, 165–6
    dough, 161
    see also Pasta

Onions (button)
    bouton glacés à blanc, 76
    bouton glacés à brun, 76
Omelets, 149–52
    extensions, 150–2
        à la turque, 152
        Arnold Bennet, 151
        au fromage, 152
        au jambon, 152
        aux champignons, 152
        aux crevettes, 151
        aux tomates, 151
        espagnole, 150
        fermière, 151
        fines herbes, 152
        limousine, 152
        Lorraine, 152
        paysanne, 151
        parmentier, 151
    methods of cooking, 150
Onion clouté, 72
Osso-buco milanaise, 258
Ox heart braised, 279, 281
Oxtail braised, 276

Paella, 157
Panadas, 83
Pancakes, 349, 364–5
    batter, 364
    crab, 364
    de volaille et champignon, 349
    de volaille princess, 349
    fish, 364–5
Parsley, 77
    bouquets, 77
    chopped, 77
Parsnips, *see* Vegetables
Pasta, 160, 165–6
    boiling, 165
    garnishes, 166

    au beurre, 166
    au gratin, 166
    aux moules, 166
    bolognaise, 166
    italienne, 166
    milanaise, 166
    napolitaine, 166
    niçoise, 166
Pastry, 112–3, 158
    choux, 158
    puff, 113
    suet, 113
Pâte à feuilletage, 113
Pâte à foncer
Peas (petite pois), *see* Vegetables
Peppers, *see* Vegetables
Pies, 347–8, 351–2
    chicken, 347–8
    chicken and ham, 348
    chicken and mushroom, 348
    steak, 351–2
Pig's trotters, 173, 316–7
    boiled, 173
    diable, 356–7
Pizza, 324–5
    fillings, 325
    recipe, 324
Poisson, *see* Fish
Poisson meunière, *see* Fish
Pojarski, 238
    chicken, 238
    veal, 238
Pork, *see* Meats
Potatoes
    baked, 321–3
        Anna, 323
        arlie, 322
        Byron, 323
        Darphin, 323
        gratinées, 322
        Macaire, 322
        ménagère, 322
        method, 321
        Nana, 323
        Robert, 322
        surprise, 322
        voison, 323
    boiled, 185–7
        à la crème, 186
        à la neige, 186

Potatoes, boiled (cont.)
  Biarritz, 187
  en robe de chambre, 186, 187
  maître d'hôtel, 186
  mousseline, 187
  nature, 186
  nouvelle, 187
  nouvelles à la menthe, 187
  nouvelles persillées, 187
  persillées, 186
  purée, 186
  purée à la crème, 186
  purée au gratin, 187
  quelin, 186
braised, 290−3
  au lard, 291
  berrichonne, 290
  bretonne, 291
  boulangère, 291
  champignol, 293
  cretan, 293
  Dauphinoise, 292
  Delmonico, 292−3
  fondant, 293
  hongroise, 290−1
  savoyarde, 291−2
deep fried, 213−4
  alumettes, 214
  bataille, 214
  chips (crisps), 213
  frites (chipped), 214
  gauffrettes, 214
  mignonette, 214
  pailles, 214
  pont neuf, 214
  soufflé, 214
duchesse extensions, 370−1
  amandine, 371
  Berny, 371
  brioche, 370
  Chester, 370
  croquettes, 370
  Dauphine, 371
  Elizabeth, 371
  galette, 371
  Lorrette, 371
  marquise, 370
  noisette, 370
  royale/St Florentin, 371

sautées extensions, 372
  lyonnaise, 372
  provençale, 372
  rissolees, 372
  roesti, 372
shallow fried, 244−5
  à cru, 245
  cocotte, 245
  columbine, 245
  noisette, 245
  parisienne, 245
  parmentier, 245
  sablées, 245
Potiron provençale, 270
Poultry, *see* Meats
Preserved garlic, 73
Protective clothing, 8−9
Puddings, steak, 351−2
Puff pastry, 113
Pumpkin, *see* Vegetables
Pumpkin provençale, 270

Queue de boeuf braisée, 276
Quiches (flans), 325−7
  recipe, 326
    au fromage, 326
    aux oignons, 326
    forestière, 326
    fruits de mer, 326
    Lorraine, 326

Raie au beurre noir, 177
Raspings, 78
Ravioli, 163−4
  paste, 162
Régéthermic oven, 46−7
Relevés, 385−6
Rice, 154−6
  au foie de volaille, 156
  au jambon, 156
  à volaille, 156
  au champignon, 156
  aux crevettes roses, 156
  créole, 156
  fried, 154
  italienne, 156
  milanaise, 156
  nature, 154
  piémontaise, 156
  rissotto/pilaff, 155−6

Ris braisés à brun, 278−9
  agneau, 278−9
  veau, 278−9
Rissoles, 360−1
Roux, 82
Royale, 114

Salmis de gibier, 259−60
Salpicons
  chicken, 348
  fish, 362−3
Salsify, *see* Vegetables
Sauces, 83−112
  basic, 84
  butter, 85
  emulsified, 84
  independent, 85
  non-derivative, 85
Sauce
  Albufera, 90
  allemande, 90
  américaine, 106
  anchovy, 87
  apple, 108
  aurore, 89
  béarnaise, 99
  béchamel, 87
  Bercy, 91, 93
  beurre fondue, 110
  beurre meunière, 110
  beurre noir, 110
  beurre noir aux câpres, 110
  beurre noisette, 110
  bigarade, 105
  bolognaise, 107
  bordelaise, 94
  bourguignonne, 94
  bread, 108
  caper, 90
  champignon, 90, 91, 97
  charcutière, 97
  chasseur, 95
  Chateaubriand, 94
  cheese, 87, 91
  Choron, 100
  cranberry, 109
  crapaudine, 94
  cream, 87
  crevettes, crevettes roses, 91
  Cumberland, 109

curry, 103
demi-glace, 93
devilled, 95
diable, 95
divine, 98
egg, 87
espagnole, 92
estragon, 97
Foyot, 100
Granville, 91
hollandaise, 98
homard, 106
hongroise, 90, 92
indienne, 89
italienne, 95
Ivoire, 90
kari, 103
lobster, 106
lyonnaise, 95
madeira, 96
maltaise, 99
marchand de vin, 96
mayonnaise, 101
melted butter, 110
mint, 109
Mornay, 87, 91
mousseline, 99
moutarde, 88
mushroom, 90, 91, 97
mustard, 88
noisette, 99
oeufs, 88
onion, 95
orange, 105
paprika, 90, 92
parsley, 88
Périgueux, 96
piquant, 96
poivrade, 96
porto, 97
portugaise, 104
poulette, 90
prawn, 91
provençale, 104−5
Reform, 97
rémoulade, 101
Robert, 97
sherry, 97
shrimp, 91

Sauce (cont.)
  smitane, 107
  soubise, 88
  suprême, 89
  sweet and sour, 107
  tartare, 101
  Thermidor, 92
  tomate, 103
  tomatoed demi-glace, 97
  Valoise, 100
  velouté, 88
  vin blanc, 91
  white wine, 91
  xérès, 97
Sauerkraut braised, 289
  garnish, 290
Saumon poché hollandaise,
    175−7
Savouries, 376−82
  canapés
    aux champignon, 377
    gourmets, 377
    hollandaise, 377
    Ivanhoe, 378
    Richie, 378
  croûtes
    anchois, 378
    anges à cheval, 377
    baron, 379
    beignets de crabe, 381
    beignets de fromage, 381
    bouchées à l'indienne, 381
    buck rarebit, 380
    Croque Monsieur, 381
    Derby, 379
    diable à cheval, 379
    Diane, 379
    laitances, 380
    moelle, 380
    Quo Vadis, 378
    sardines, 380
    Scotch woodcock, 380
    Welsh rarebit 380
    Windsor, 379
  quiches, 382
  soufflés, 382
Sea kale, see Vegetables
Scallops provençale, 242
Scampi, 242−3
  Newburg, 242
  provençale, 242
  Thermidor, 243

Scotch eggs, 256
Shellfish, see Fish
Shepherd's pie, 354
Sippets, 77
Skate with black butter, 177
Soufflés, 327−8
  cheese, 327−8
  chicken, 328
  fish, 328
  ham, 328
Soups
  bisques, 124−5
    crabe, 125
    crevettes, 125
    homard, 125
    recipe, 124−5
  bortsch, 134
  broths, 125−7
    beef, 126
    bonne femme, 127
    chicken, 126
    cocky leeky, 127
    game, 126
    minestrone, 127
    mutton, 126
    paysanne, 127
    recipes, 125−7
  chowders (fish broths), 127−8
    clam, 128
    mussel, 128
    oyster, 128
    recipe, 127
    scallop, 128
    seafood, 128
  consommés, 129−30
    alphabétique, 130
    brunoise, 129
    Célestine, 129
    en tasse, 129
    gelée, 130
    julienne, 129
    madrilène, 130
    porto, 130
    recipe, 129
    royale, 130
    tortue, 130
    vermicelle, 130
    xérès, 130
  creams, 119−20
    asperge, 119

argenteuil, 119
carottes, 119
céleri, 119
champignon, 120
cressionnière, 120
crécy, 119
Doria, 119
Dubarry, 119
florentine, 120
Judic, 119
Lamballe, 135−6
légumes, 120
Longchamps, 135−6
oignon, 120
poireaux, 119
portugaise, 132
recipe, 119
Solférino, 132−3
St Cloud, 135−6
St Germain, 135
tomate, 132
Washington, 120
croûte au pot, 138
French onion, 131
gazpacho, 136
Germiny, 135
mulligatawny, 131−2
petite marmite, 137
petite marmite béarnaise, 138
purées (aqueous), 117−8
carottes, 118
céleri, 118
cressionnière, 118
Dubarry, 118
flamande, 118
légumes, 118
navet, 118
oignon, 118
Palestine, 118
parmentier, 118
poireaux, 118
potiron, 118
recipe, 117
rutabaga, 118
purées (pulses), 116−7
condé, 117
conti, 117
égytienne, 117
Esaü, 117
lentilles, 117

recipe, 116−7
soissonnaise, 117
St Germain, 117
soupe de poissons, 133−4
thickened brown, 123−4
game, 123
hare, 124
kidney, 123
mock turtle, 124
oxtail, 123
pheasant, 124
recipe, 123
tomato, 132
veloutés, 120−2
Agnès sorel, 121
asperge, 112
champignons, 122
cressionnière, 122
dieppoise, 121
Doria, 122
huîtres, 121
poisson, 121
recipe, 120−1
volaille, 121
vichyssoise, 137
Spaghetti, *see* Pasta
Spetzli, 167
Spinach, *see* Vegetables
Spinach stuffing, 162
Starches, 61
as thickeners, 62−5
freeze-thaw, 65
pregelatinized, 65
Steak pie, *see* Meats
Steak puddings, *see* Meats
Steamers
pressure type, 38−40
pressureless type, 41−2
Steaming, 201−2
fish, 201
meats, 201
vegetables, 201−2
Steaming pressures, 7
Stocks, 78−81
brown, 79−80
estouffade, 80
fish, 81
white, 79−80
Stuffings, 298−300
chestnut, 300

Stuffings (cont.)
  lemon, parsley and thyme, 299
  sage and onion, 298–9
  sausagemeat, 300
Swede, *see* Vegetables
Sweetbreads, *see* Meats
Sweetcorn, *see* Vegetables
Syneresis, 65

Temperature guide, 6
Tenderizing methods, 55–77
Tête de veau vinaigrette, 172
Toad in the hole, 318–9
Tomatoes
  concasse, 74
  concassées, 74
  skinned, 76
  see also Vegetables
Tripe and onions, 264
Turbot poché hollandaise, 176–7
Turkey, *see* Meats
Turkey à la King, 350
Turgor pressure, 53, 55
Turnip, *see* Vegetables

Veal, *see* Meats
Vegetables
  adjunct, 72–73
Vegetables, baked
  preparation and method, 320–1
    courgettes, 320
    cucumber, 320
    mushrooms, 320
    tomatoes, 321
Vegetables, boiled, 178–87
  artichokes globe (artichauts)
    au beurre fondue, 182, 184
    boiled, 182
    fonds, 76
    fonds farcis au gratin, 374
    fonds florentine, 374
    fonds provençale, 374
    fonds sautés au beurre, 373
    hollandaise, 182, 184
  artichokes Jerusalem (topinambours),
        182, 184–5
    à la crème, 182, 184
    au beurre, 182, 184
    aux fines herbes, 182, 184
    nature, 182, 184
    persillés, 182, 185

  purée, 182, 185
asparagus (asperge), 180, 184–5
  au beurre, 180, 184
  au beurre fondue, 180, 184
  amandine, 180, 184
  hollandaise, 180, 184
  nature, 180, 185
  purée, 180, 185
beans broad (feves), 180
  à la crème, 180, 184
  à sauce persil, 180, 185
  nature, 180, 185
beans butter, 184–5
  à la menthe, 184
  au beurre, 184
  nature, 184–5
beans french (haricots verts fins), 180
  à la crème, 180, 184
  au beurre, 180, 184
  nature, 180, 185
  tourangelle, 180, 185
beans haricots blancs, 184
  au beurre, 184
  bretonne, 184
  nature, 184–5
beans kidney (flageolets), 184
  au beurre, 184
  nature, 184–5
beans kidney red (haricots rouges), 184
  au beurre, 184
  nature, 184–5
beans, panaches, 185
beetroot (betterave), 182, 184–5
  à la crème, 182, 184
  au beurre, 182, 184
  nature, 182, 185
bouquetière, 185
broccoli (brocolis), 180, 184–5
  amandine, 180, 184
  au beurre, 180, 184
  hollandaise, 180, 184
  milanaise, 180, 184
  Mornay, 180, 184
  nature, 180, 185
  polonaise, 180, 185
brussels sprouts (choux de bruxelles),
        180, 184–5
  au beurre, 180, 184
  milanaise, 180, 184
  nature, 180, 185

polonaise, 180, 185
cabbage (chou), 180, 184–5
　au beurre, 180, 184
　nature, 180, 185
cabbage spring (chou de printemps),
　　180, 184–5
　au beurre, 180, 184
　nature, 180, 185
carrots (carottes), 182, 184–5
　à la crème, 180, 184
　au beurre, 180, 184
　glacées, 180, 184
　persillées, 180, 185
　purée, 180, 185
　vichy, 180, 185
cauliflower (choufleur), 180, 184–5
　amandine, 180, 184
　au beurre, 180, 184
　aux fines herbes, 180, 184
　hollandaise, 180, 184
　milanaise, 180, 184
　Mornay, 180, 184
　nature, 180, 185
　polonaise, 180, 185
celeriac (céleri-rave), 182, 184–5
　à la crème, 182, 184
　au beurre, 182, 184
　aux fines herbes, 182, 184
　nature, 182, 185
chicory (endive), 180, 184–5
　à la crème, 180, 184
　au beurre, 180, 184
　Mornay, 180, 184
　nature, 180, 185
　purée, 180, 185
courgette, 181, 184–5
　à la crème, 181, 184
　au beurre, 181, 184
　aux fines herbes, 181, 184
　Mornay, 181, 184
　nature, 181, 185
　persillée, 181, 185
cucumber (concombre), 180, 184–5
　à la crème, 180, 184
　au beurre, 180, 184
　glacé, 180, 184
　milanaise, 180, 184
　nature, 180, 185
　persillé, 180, 185
curly kale (chou frisé), 180, 184–5

au beurre, 180, 184
nature, 180, 185
fennel (fenouil), 183, 184–5
　à la crème, 183, 184
　au beurre, 183, 184
　aux fines herbes, 183, 184
　milanaise, 183, 184
　Mornay, 183, 184
　nature, 183, 185
　persillés, 183, 185
　poulette, 183, 185
gumbo (okra), 180, 184–5
　au beurre, 180, 184
　hollandaise, 180, 184
　nature, 180, 185
jardinière, 185
kale sea (chou de mer), 181, 184–5
　à la crème, 181, 184
　au beurre, 181, 184
　hollandaise, 181, 184
　nature, 181, 185
kohlrabi, 182, 184–5
　à la crème, 182
　au beurre, 182, 184
　nature, 182, 185
　persillés, 182, 185
ladies' fingers (okra), *see* gumbo
leeks (poireaux), 181, 184–5
　à la crème, 181, 184
　au beurre, 181, 184
　Mornay, 181, 184
　nature, 181, 184
lentils (lentilles), 184–5
　purée, 185
　purée à la crème, 184–5
macédoine, 185
marrow (baby), *see* courgette
marrow (courge), 181, 184–5
　à la crème, 181, 184–5
　au beurre, 181, 184
　aux fines herbes, 181, 184
　Mornay, 181, 184
　nature, 181, 185
　persillée, 181, 185
methods, 178–9
onions (oignons), 183, 184–5
　à la crème, 183, 184
　nature, 183, 185
parsnips (panais), 183, 184–5
　à la crème, 183, 184

Vegetables, parsnips (cont.)
    au beurre, 183, 184
    nature, 183, 184
    persillés, 183, 185
    purée, 183, 185
  peas (petits pois), 181, 184−5
    à la menthe, 181, 184
    au beurre, 181, 184
    flamande, 181, 185
    nature, 181, 185
    purée, 181, 185
  peas marrowfat, 184−5
    à la menthe, 184
    au beurre, 184
    nature, 184−5
  primeurs, 185
  pumpkin (potiron), as for boiled
    marrow
  ratatouille, 270−1
  red cabbage, braised, 289
  salsify (salsifi), 183, 184−5
    à la crème, 183, 184
    au beurre, 183, 184
    aux fines herbes, 183, 184
    nature, 183, 185
    persillés, 183, 185
    poulette, 183, 185
    tourangelle, 183, 185
  spinach (épinards en branches), 181,
    184−5
    à la crème, 181, 184
    au beurre, 181, 184
    Mornay, 181, 184
    nature, 181, 185
    purée, 181, 185
  swedes (rutabaga), 183, 184−5
    au beurre, 183, 184−5
    nature, 183, 185
    persillés, 185
    purée, 183, 185
  sweetcorn (maïs) off the cob, 181,
    184−5
    à la crème, 181, 184
    au beurre, 181, 184
    nature, 181, 185
  sweetcorn (maïs) on the cob, 181,
    184−5
    au beurre fondu, 181, 184
    nature, 181, 185

  turnips (navets), 183, 184−5
    au beurre, 183, 184
    nature, 183, 185
    persillés, 183, 185
    purée, 183, 185
Vegetables braised, 285−8
  preparation, 285−6
    cabbage, 288
    celery, 287
    endive, 288
    fennel, 288
    leek, 288
    lettuce, 288
    onion, 288
    peppers, 288
    recipe, 287
Vegetables, cuts, turned, garnishes,
    75−77
Vegetables deep fried, 212−3
  aubergine frite, 212
  beignets de choufleur, 213
  beignets de panais, 213
  champignons frites, 212
  courgettes frites, 212
  oignons frits, 213
Vegetables grilled, 345−6
  mushrooms, 346
  tomatoes, 345−6
Vegetables roasted, 307
  parsnips, 307
Vegetables sautées au beurre, 373
  artichoke bottoms (fonds), 373
    aux fines herbes, 373
    limousine, 373
  beans (haricots verts fins), 373
  brussels sprouts (choux de bruxelles),
    373
    limousine, 373
    polonaise, 373
  cauliflower (choufleur), 373
    aux fines herbes, 373
    polonaise, 373
  celeriac (céleri-rave), 373
    aux fines herbes, 373
  parsnips (panais), 373
    aux fines herbes, 373
  salsify (salsifis), 373
    aux fines herbes, 373
  spinach (épinard en branche), 373

Vegetables shallow fried, 243–4
   aubergines provençale, 243–4
   champignons sautés, 244
   courgettes provençale, 243–4
   oignons boutons sautés, 244
   oignons sautés, 244
Vegetables stewed, 269–71
   courge (marrow) provençale, 270
   petits pois (peas), 269
      à la française, 269
      bonne femme, 269
      paysanne, 269
   potiron (pumpkin) provençale, 270
   ratatouille, 270–71
Venison, *see* Meats
Vertical cutter/mixer, 43–5

Volaille à la King, 350
Vol au vent, 349, 363
   de fruits de mer, 363
   de poisson, 363
   de poisson princesse, 363
   de volaille, 349
   de volaille et champignon, 349
   de volaille princesse, 349

Yorkshire pudding, 301

Watercress bouquets, 77
Whitebait, 212
   devilled, 212
   fried, 212
Wiener Schnitzel, 209

THE NEW WINE COMPANION
David Burroughs and Norman Bezzant
Published on behalf of the Wine and Spirit Education Trust

From vine to palate, here is a complete introduction to wine and the wine trade. The authors have extensively revised, updated, and expanded their earlier *Wine Trade Student's Companion,* adding among much else a section on cider and perry and frequent suggestions for suitable foods to accompany various wines. This version begins with a brief history of the origin and spread of wine-making, followed by profiles of the principal types of wines and spirits, their methods of production, and their use. Sections on sparkling wines, fortified wines, spirits, liqueurs, and beers are included. The book's concluding chapters deal with the trade itself and its products as presented to the consumer. Finally there are seven appendixes — covering everything from pests and diseases to cocktail recipes — and a glossary with pronunciation guide. All chapters are thoroughly illustrated with maps, diagrams, and appropriate decorative drawings. The running question-and-answer footnotes, originally designed as an aid for students will also serve as a valuable checklist for other readers.

434 09867 1- 207 pp

WINE REGIONS OF THE WORLD
David Burroughs and Norman Bezzant
Published on behalf of the Wine and Spirit Education Trust

This book is a comprehensive guide to the main wine and spirit-producing areas of the world (there is also an additional section on cigars).

As well as being a key text for the Wine and Spirit Education Trust Higher Certificate, Wine Regions will be of value for the City and Guilds of London Institute course 707-3 — Food Service, those seeking HCIMA qualifications, and ONC-D or HNC-D in Catering Technology. It is a useful source of background information for the shipping, manufacturing, distribution, restaurant and hotel, and publicity fields.

434 09866 3- 308 pp

MULTIPLE CHOICE QUESTIONS ON COOKERY FOR THE CATERING INDUSTRY
Robert S. Wood

Multiple Choice Questions on Cookery for the Catering Industry covers subjects parallel to those of the City and Guilds of London Institute courses 706-1 and 706-2 and the items progress in depth of subject treatment from the Basic Cookery to Cookery levels. All students of catering will find the book extremely helpful including those on the Ordinary National Diploma courses as well as the Higher National Diploma, HCIMA and TEC courses.

434 92275 7- 142 pp

MULTIPLE CHOICE QUESTIONS ON FOOD SERVICE
Brian K. Julyan

Multiple Choice Questions on Food Service covers subjects parallel to those of the City and
Guilds of London Institute courses 707-1-2-3. The book will also be useful to students
working on the City and Guilds 705 General Catering Course, the OND in Hotel and
Catering 1st and 2nd year, the HND in Hotel and Catering 1st and 2nd year, the HCIMA
Part A course and the Wine and Spirit Education Trust, Wine Certificate course and
Higher Certificate course.

434 90930 0- 140 pp

FOOD COMMODITIES
Bernard Davis
*A complete, up-to-date study of all the major foods used in the Hotel and
Catering Industry*

Designed to provide students and caterers with a basic knowledge of foods as commodities
used in catering, Bernard Davis methodically classifies each food group, their
characteristics, methods of production, varieties available, catering uses, storage requirements and scientific and nutritional aspects so that readers can readily identify those
areas in which they should be conversant.

 The book covers the requirements of students preparing for the following examinations:
City and Guilds of London Institute Examinations in Cookery, Ordinary National
Diploma in Hotel and Catering Operations, Institutional Housekeeping and Catering,
Higher National Diploma in Hotel and Catering Administration-Institutional Manage-
ment, Degree courses in Hotel and Catering Administration-Management.

 It will also be suitable for students following home economics and domestic science
courses or sitting for the Royal Society of Health Examinations in Food Inspection. The
book will be of special interest to practising caterers and hotelkeepers actively engaged in
food purchasing.

 'Bernard Davis is to be congratulated in producing a book of character the use of which
will add substantially to our knowledge of food commodities.' *HCIMA Journal.*

434 90297 7- 346 pp